UNDERSTANDING DIVERSITY

CELEBRATING DIFFERENCE, CHALLENGING INEQUALITY

UNDERSTANDING DIVERSITY

CELEBRATING DIFFERENCE, CHALLENGING INEQUALITY

Claire M. Renzetti
University of Kentucky

Raquel Kennedy Bergen
Saint Joseph's University

Boston   Columbus   Indianapolis   New York   San Francisco   Upper Saddle River
Amsterdam   Cape Town   Dubai   London   Madrid   Milan   Munich   Paris   Montreal   Toronto
Delhi   Mexico City   Sao Paulo   Sydney   Hong Kong   Seoul   Singapore   Taipei   Tokyo

Editor in Chief: Craig Campanella
Acquisitions Editor: Charlyce Jones Owen
Program Manager: Seanna Breen
Editorial Assistant: Maureen Diana
Director of Marketing: Brandy Dawson
Senior Marketing Manager: Maureen Prado Roberts
Marketing Assistant: Karen Tanico
Production Project Manager: Fran Russello
Senior Operations Supervisor: Mary Fischer

Operations Specialist: Diane Pierano
Cover Designer: John Christiana
Manager, Visual Research: Martha Shethar
Text Permission Coordinator: Terenia McHenry
Cover Art: © Vladgrin/Shutterstock
Media Project Manager: Carly Czech
Full-Service Project Management: Aptara
Printer/Binder: Courier Companies, Inc.
Text Font: Palatino LT Std

Library of Congress Cataloging-in-Publication Data on File

10 9 8 7 6 5 4 3 2 1

PEARSON

ISBN 10:   0-205-18277-1
ISBN 13: 978-0-205-18277-0

To our students—past,
present, and future

BRIEF CONTENTS

CONTENTS

PREFACE

This book began several years ago as a collection of excerpts from previously published work on diversity. As we amassed a lengthy list of articles and books that we wished to include, it became clear that we either needed to excerpt very brief pieces of each work, or eliminate many contributions that we deemed essential reading on this topic. Our dilemma was made worse by our desire to not only cover major theoretical works, which can rarely be reduced to a two- or three-page excerpt without losing a great deal of critical content, but also include empirical pieces that demonstrate the application of particular theories—theory-in-action pieces, if you will. In the midst of our struggle over these decisions we were attending conferences at which colleagues were present-ing provocative and insightful research on the very issues in which we were most interested. Ultimately, we decided to revise the book to include original contributions written specifically for this volume, each examining a specific social problem and focus-ing on how different groups experience it, the problem's differential consequences across various groups, the consequences for society as a whole, and potential policy implications or solutions. We identified contributors whose work demonstrates how differences, and inequalities based on differences, are not simply experienced by indi-viduals, but color social relations among groups and reinforce—and are reinforced by—specific institutional arrangements.

Some chapters in this volume are written by well-known sociologists with whose work many readers will already be familiar. But the book also presents newer voices whose cutting-edge work is likely to significantly impact the field. All of the authors are researching topics that are particularly relevant to college students or are likely to be on students' "radar screens"—for example, unemployment, "hooking up," racism on cam-pus, safety issues, internet pornography, homelessness, and environmental destruction. While the authors discuss their own research, contextualizing it in the relevant diversity and inequality literatures, their presentations are accessible even to students never before exposed to sociology. Consequently, in the pages that follow students will learn much about the state of the art in a particular sociological focus area—such as, eco-nomic sociology, criminology and criminal justice, intimate relationships, media, edu-cation, medical sociology, rural sociology—as well as about how the intersecting inequalities of race, gender, social class, sexuality, age, immigration status, and geo-graphic location influence how various problems are socially and politically framed, and how they are differentially experienced.

In short, we gave contributors a rather daunting charge: summarize the extant literature that informs your area of study and show how your research contributes to this knowledge base, while explaining to readers the significance of the interplay of inequalities for understanding and remedying this social problem—and do it all in a highly accessible style and within our specified page limits. We thank our contributors for not laughing at us, or worse, turning away in disbelief, and instead for enthusiasti-cally embracing what we know was a challenging task. Their chapters stand as testi-mony to their passion for social justice and their desire to communicate this commitment to students who will assume responsibility for our social world in the not-too-distant future.

We also wish to take this opportunity to thank Jeff Lasser, formerly our editor at Allyn & Bacon and Karen Hanson, now retired from Allyn & Bacon for their support of our decision to redirect this project from its original course and their encouragement over the years to continue forward with it. Their seasoned knowledge of publishing and the sociological marketplace are hugely helpful to authors and editors, but more valued still are their patience and unwavering friendship. It was truly a pleasure to work with both Jeff and Karen on this project and on many others. It has also been a pleasure working with Charlyce Jones-Owen, our new editor at Pearson. Charlyce deftly picked up where Jeff and Karen left off and guided us through the production process. Charlyce enlisted the assistance of several colleagues, who reviewed an earlier version of the manuscript and offered extensive feedback and many helpful suggestions for revisions: Michael Johnson Jr., Washington State University; Stephanie Williams, Northern Arizona University; Cathy Beighey, Aims Community College; Reid Leamaster, Purdue University; Heather Dalmage, Roosevelt University; Kristy Watkins, University of Massachusetts; Glenn Muschert, Miami University; William Velez, University of Wisconsin-Milwaukee; Barbara Vann, Loyola University, Maryland. We and the contributors are grateful to all the reviewers for generously sharing their time and their knowledge.

A final word of thanks to our students—for inspiring us to be life-long learners, for challenging our taken-for-granted assumptions, and for routinely keeping us on our toes.

ABOUT THE EDITORS

Claire M. Renzetti is the Judi Conway Patton Endowed Chair for Studies of Violence Against Women in the Center for Research on Violence Against Women, and Professor and Chair of the Sociology Department at the University of Kentucky. She is editor of the international, interdisciplinary journal, *Violence Against Women*; coeditor with Jeffrey Edleson of the Interpersonal Violence book series for Oxford University Press; and editor of the Gender and Justice book series for University of California Press. She has authored or edited 16 books as well as numerous book chapters and articles in professional journals. Her current research includes studies of the relationship between religiosity and intimate partner violence, and an evaluation of a horticultural therapy program at a shelter for battered women and their children. Dr. Renzetti has held elected and appointed positions on the governing bodies of several national professional organizations, and is a past president of the Society for the Study of Social Problems (SSSP). She is the recipient of the Saltzman Award for Contributions to Practice, awarded by the Women and Crime Division of the American Society of Criminology, and of the Lee Founders Award, from the SSSP.

Raquel Kennedy Bergen is Professor of Sociology at Saint Joseph's University in Philadelphia, Pennsylvania. She received her BS from Saint Joseph's University in Sociology and her PhD in Sociology from the University of Pennsylvania. She is the author or coauthor of numerous scholarly publications and seven books on violence against women, including *Wife Rape: Understanding the Response of Survivors and Service Providers*; and *Issues in Intimate Violence*. With Claire Renzetti and Jeff Edleson, she edited *Sourcebook on Violence Against Women* and *Violence Against Women: Classic Statements*. She coedited *Violence Against Women: Readings from Social Problems* with Claire Renzetti. She has served as a member of the Pennsylvania State Ethics Commission since 2004 when she was appointed by Governor Edward G. Rendell. She has volunteered as an advocate for battered women and sexual assault survivors for the past 25 years. Her current research continues in the field of violence against women—analyzing how domestic violence and sexual assault programs have implemented changes to the services that they provide to intimate partner sexual assault survivors. She also continues to explore the subject of women's experiences of sexual and physical violence during pregnancy.

1

Understanding Diversity

An Introduction

Raquel Kennedy Bergen and Claire M. Renzetti

This is a book about how diverse groups of people in our society define, experience, and address various social problems. What is *diversity*? Forty years ago, the term *diversity* might have indicated the inclusion of black students at historically white schools, acknowledgement of ethnic divisions within an urban neighborhood, or the presence of women in the corporate boardroom traditionally populated by men. Over the past several decades, our understanding of the term diversity has changed and become more complex in many ways. A sociological understanding of diversity requires that we consider not only race, ethnicity, and gender, but also how other social locating factors such as class, age, religion, sexual orientation, sexuality, and ability shape our experiences and perspectives in society. Growing up in the United States, with a strong focus on individualism, it is easy to assume that we are who we are because of hard work and determination. Indeed, there are examples that support the Horatio Alger myth that anyone can make it to the top, anyone can be successful—just pull yourself up by your bootstraps. A fundamental component of the dominant ideology of the United States is the notion of *meritocracy*—that is, individuals succeed (or fail) on the basis of their own merits, such as their innate talents and how hard they work or apply themselves to a task. However, such an understanding prevents us from exploring why people with certain characteristics are more likely to be successful than others and from asking questions such as why do some people not even have boots to pull up? Why are Native Americans less likely to graduate from high school than their white peers? Why are single women with dependent children the most likely population to live in poverty? What accounts for these differences in experiences and how do the structural arrangements in society shape our experiences and lead to inequality and social problems? What even constitutes a social problem?

PERSONAL TROUBLES AND PUBLIC ISSUES

Answering these questions is not an easy task. To begin to do so, though, it is important to draw on the work of the famous sociologist C. Wright Mills (1959) who, more than 50 years ago, argued that it is critical to distinguish between personal troubles and public issues. Mills characterized *personal troubles* as those private matters that are problematic for us as individuals. A personal trouble may be characterized as something that occurs in our own social realm, which violates or threatens our own individual values. In contrast, *public issues* are problems that transcend the individual; they are problems that stem from the larger social structure and the ways institutions in a society are organized and how they operate. For Mills, the promise of the *sociological imagination* was to cultivate the ability to see the relationship between an individual's own personal troubles and experiences and larger social structural public issues. It is useful to think about unemployment as a way to explore these concepts. One can lose a job and look for personal reasons for this trouble— for example, I was lazy, I was late too often, I did not have the right credentials. Or, one can look at the widespread patterns of unemployment to consider the structural issues—economic downturns, corporate restructuring, racism, homophobia, sexism, and technological advances that have displaced workers. Using the sociological imagination enables us to connect our own personal experience of job loss to larger social factors and the reality that currently in the United States the unemployment rate is 8.1%. However, for certain groups, the rate is even higher, with 10.3% of Hispanics and 13.2% of blacks experiencing unemployment (U.S. Department of Labor, 2013). Understanding how personal troubles are connected to public issues helps us to make sense of our world and to develop social structural solutions to these problems.

There would be little argument that unemployment and poverty are social problems in the United States right now. There is much debate, however, about how social problems should be defined. Some use the *objectivist approach*, which considers social problems as those conditions that harm individuals or society (Best, 2013). For example, Leon-Guerrero (2011) defines social problems as a "social condition or pattern of behavior that has negative consequences for individuals, our social world, or our physical world" (p. 8). This definition, though, begs the questions: harmful to whom, to how many, how much harm, and who decides? There are many examples of issues which are now included in social problems textbooks, such as racism, sexism, homophobia, and violence against women, that would not have been included in textbooks 50, even 30, years ago because although all of these behaviors certainly existed, they were not seen as problematic. A serious concern with the objectivist perspective, then, is that historically, the voices of those who are marginalized in society and who frequently experience the worst effects of social problems have not been heard in the defining process. Often what has been labeled a social problem and how it has been defined as problematic have reflected the interests of those in power. Frankenburg argues that "there is a link between where one stands in society and what one perceives" (Curran & Renzetti, 1993, p. 8). Those who are most marginalized and have the least amount of power to draw attention to how specific problems affect their lives have the greatest difficulty rallying support for social change that will improve their quality of life.

Another way of viewing social problems is from the *subjectivist* or *social constructionist approach*, which defines social problems in terms of how we perceive situations to be, problematic or nonproblematic. Joel Best (2013) argues that "it is not an objective quality of a social condition, but rather the subjective reactions to that condition, that make something a social problem. Therefore, social problems should not be viewed as a type of social condition, but as a process of responding to social conditions" (pp. 9–10). Using this perspective, we explore the social construction of problems, which means that we examine the ways in which meaning (through language) is assigned to issues and how problems are framed. This is considered a social problems *process*. In his classic constructionist paper, Joseph Gusfield (1989) pointed out the value of language and the significance of the framing process. For example, government subsidies to industries that are struggling are not called "aid to dependent factories" as are government subsidies to poor families, which were historically known as "aid to dependent families and children." This language implies personal failure and deficiencies on behalf of these individuals, but this is not the way failing industries are viewed. "Differing language frames mean differing assessments and evaluations" (Gusfield, 1989, p. 435). As Best (2013) indicates, the subjectivist perspective is important because how we conceptualize a problem and the words that we use to describe the condition, those affected by it, and recommendations for change are all social constructions that will have not only different meanings, but more importantly, differential outcomes.

CONCEPTUALIZING DIFFERENCE

We begin with the understanding that the identifiers or categories we use to describe ourselves are also social constructions. Sociologists believe that we live in a society in which these identifiers help determine our access to resources and our place in society. As David Newman (2012) writes, "Our identities dictate our chances for living a comfortable life, our access to valued economic, educational, or political resources; the likelihood of being seen positively or negatively by others; and our susceptibility to victimization, either by crime or by illness" (p. xiv). One's social location in society determines access to resources, opportunities, and power. These identifiers or categories are determined by social, not biological factors. Thus, when someone asks us what race, gender, sexuality, ethnicity, or religion we are, we answer in terms of social categories or social constructs. With regard to race, gender, and sexuality, we have historically expected people to choose one of two binary categories—either white or nonwhite; either male or female, either straight or gay. The U.S. Census Bureau maintained a policy of singularity of racial heritage identification until 2000, when individuals were finally given the option to select more than one racial category. This does not mean that multiracial individuals did not exist prior to 2000, but rather that the federal government did not acknowledge multiracialism until then (Ore, 2006).

We will return to the question of multiple identities shortly, but first it must be emphasized that because all of these categories are social constructions, we create and re-create them through interaction with one another and through culture. As Tracy Ore (2006) writes, "it is the social recognition, definition and the groupings of these factors that make them culturally significant in our daily interactions" (p. 1). Importantly, these classifications and categories are understood as different from each other, but it is not the difference that causes inequality. Each category does not carry inherent value—men are not inherently more valuable than women; being white is not inherently better than being black—but it is the value socially ascribed to these categories, which we learn through our culture, that leads to inequality. From birth, we are socialized by families, peers, the education system, the media and many other institutions to recognize not only differences among people, but also how specific traits or identities are differentially valued and where members of different groups fit into the larger culture (Ore, 2006). We tend to take these values and norms for granted rather than critically analyzing them. Deviation from the normative typically is identified as problematic, rather than the social construction of inequalities and their effects on individuals and groups deemed non-normative. The precise objective of the chapters in this book is to call into question the dominant values and norms that marginalize various groups of people in a host of ways and to show the differential impacts of inequality and marginalization.

It bears repeating that differences do not of themselves produce inequality; instead, the social relations built on differences lead to inequality. Newman (2012) argues that in every society there are power differentials and groupings.

While differences do not have inherent value, the values we attach to the differences have very real consequences in people's everyday lives. Those with the most power and prestige in a culture have the most privilege (i.e., the greatest access to society's resources and rewards). Those in positions of dominance may be unaware of the privilege or power they possess; they experience it as a given without appreciation for the benefits. Often it is not until the question of privilege is raised (e.g., white privilege, male privilege, or heterosexual privilege), usually by a member of a less privileged group, that someone in a position of dominance becomes aware of the differentiation. One of the coeditors of this book experienced such an Aha! moment this year in the classroom when a young, black, male undergraduate student raised the issue in a social problems course. He spoke eloquently and with great passion about his need to continuously and outwardly prove that he was a legitimate member of the campus community by always wearing an ID on a lanyard, carrying a backpack on campus (whether he needed it or not), and trying to walk with white male students as frequently as possible. These aspects of his daily reality were not experienced by any of the other students (none of whom were students of color) or his professor (who is neither young nor a person of color). This student experienced disadvantages on multiple levels because he was young and black and growing up in an urban community where young men of color are often feared. His experience highlights another important point: There are complex intersections of domination, privilege, and identity known as *intersectionality*.

Few of us would identify ourselves as only female or only heterosexual or only Jewish or only white. Instead, we each hold multiple identities simultaneously, and we tend to identify ourselves differently in different contexts throughout our lives. Who we are and our place in society (our access to resources and rewards, including power and privilege) are largely shaped by these multiple identities. Over the last few decades, sociologists have come to understand the complex ways in which the different components of identity may be in conflict with each other in terms of social advantages and disadvantages. Consider a white gay man who is poor. His status as a white man brings him race privilege and status; however, he does not enjoy class privilege or heterosexual privilege (Collins, 1990). Those who are *othered*, who are *marginalized*, have less access to resources. They experience other negative consequences of inequality, and these experiences are more severe for those who are marginalized in multiple ways. Understanding intersectionality is important for providing a richer, more nuanced perspective of difference, but also for acknowledging the diversity of experiences among those who are constructed as members of the same group or category. For example, it is not unusual to see a chapter on racial inequality in a textbook that claims to address the Native American experience or the Asian experience, as if Native Americans and Asians are members of a unified, homogeneous community, allowing us to generalize from the experiences of one Native American ethnic group (e.g., Diné) or one Asian ethnic group (e.g., Chinese) to all Native Americans or all Asians. This ignores the tremendous variation and the disparities in experiences across these groups and can lead to gross inaccuracies (Newman, 2012). Such a homogenous view also prevents us from fully grasping the wide range of inequality and diversity experienced within our culture.

A nuanced understanding of intersectionality demands that we ask who benefits from the existing power structure and inequality, who is disadvantaged by it, and how. Many theorists would argue that those in a position of dominance benefit from their position of power and superiority, which allows them to exploit others. Writers such as bell hooks argue that "oppression based on race, class, gender, and sexuality is part of an interlocking politics of domination which is 'a belief in domination, and a belief in the notions of superior and inferior, which are components of all of those systems'" (Ore, 2006, p. 15). The intent of this book is to provide such a rich and nuanced view of social inequality and diversity.

CELEBRATING DIFFERENCE, CHALLENGING INEQUALITY

The goal of the chapters in this book is to examine diversity and social inequality within major institutions. Specifically, we explore diversity and social inequality within such institutions as the economy, the legal system, the educational system, the media, and health care, and how various groups experience these differences. For example, in Chapter 10, Jennifer Bondy and Anthony Peguero question the popular perception of education as the great equalizer, as providing a level playing field for all children to succeed as their individual talents permit. The authors document the challenges facing different groups of immigrant children as they make their way through the educational system. These challenges include racism, prejudice, xenophobia and hostility, which create serious barriers to their opportunities for upward mobility. Similarly, Susan Clampet-Lundquist, in Chapter 15, explores the issue of upward mobility through her research with low-income male and female teenagers growing up in impoverished urban neighborhoods in Baltimore, Maryland.

The book is organized into four major sections: Work, Health, and Well-being; Crime, Deviance, and Justice; Education, Intimate Relationships, and the Media; and Communities and the Environment. We wish to emphasize that these divisions are purely for organizational purposes; they are not intended to place particular problems or specific groups of people into discrete categories, or what Elliott Currie (1985) so aptly characterizes as "compartmentalizing social problems along bureaucratic lines" (p. 18). The problems discussed in individual chapters overlap with one another and span multiple social institutions at once. For instance, Jennifer Wesely's discussion of violence in the lives of homeless women is in Section I: Work, Health and Well-being, but it could just as easily fit in Section II: Crime, Deviance and Justice, or Section IV: Communities and the Environment. Moreover, we have deliberately avoided organizing the chapters by the social categories of gender, race, class, sexuality, and so on, to again emphasize intersectionality. While it is important to examine social institutions and the social categories of difference, it is not sufficient to simply have a chapter on each type of institution and every type of difference—one on race, one on class, one on sexuality, one on age, and so forth. To fully understand diversity, we must acknowledge the intersectionality of difference and how experiences vary with *layers of marginalization*. Thus, for instance, Leslie Picca, in Chapter 11, discusses how racial inequality is perpetuated on college campuses. She examines the differing views and experiences of racism among white and black college students. In Chapter 12, Kathleen Bogle looks at diversity on college campuses through a very different lens by analyzing the so-called hookup culture and how it is constructed by students.

The contributors to this book also explore the diversity within individuals' experiences of inequality and do not assume that all members of a particular group share the same perspectives and challenges. One important way in which this is done in many of the chapters is by drawing on qualitative research. As Keiko Tanaka, Patrick Mooney, and Brett Wolff write in Chapter 17, "Aggregate data are very good at showing trends among individual categories, but mask variations within them. All people of a given racial group or living situation are not the same and neither is their relationship with food." Drawing on interviews and a case study of a food pantry in Lexington, Kentucky, these authors explore the problem of food insecurity. Similarly, in Chapter 18, Shannon Bell uses qualitative methods to analyze the extreme poverty and environmental injustice among those who are facing marginalization in a variety of ways as they live in rural Appalachia. Other contributors combine qualitative and quantitative data. In Chapter 8, for instance, Holly Foster and Jocelyn Lewis use a mixed-methods approach to explore the diverse experiences of incarcerated women and their children. They address the serious issue of what it means to grow up as a child whose mother is incarcerated, while they simultaneously analyze variations by race and ethnicity with regard to how children are raised. In Chapter 16, Anna Santiago, Amy Restorick, and Eun-Lye Lee answer the question of what home ownership means to three different sets of low-income families. They consider the social benefits of home ownership, such as sense of community, safety, and privacy accrued by some low-income homeowners, and they present the practical implications of new social and economic development policies.

Diverse risks for and experiences of violence, whether interpersonal or environmental, are an important focus of this book. For example, Jennifer Wesely explores these issues in Chapter 4 as she addresses the experiences of violence in the lives of poor women who are homeless and have a history of physical and sexual abuse, while in Chapter 5 Miriam Abelson looks at the risk of violent victimization among transgendered men. The experiences of women who are abused and the significant role that Internet pornography plays in the perpetuation of this violence are the focus of Chapter 14 by Walter DeKeseredy. DeKeseredy offers important suggestions for social change and how we can work to end this problem.

Importantly, many of the chapters in this book address how individuals and groups exercise agency to negotiate and adapt to their life circumstances in order to overcome barriers and constraints in creative ways. For example, in Chapter 7, Nikki Jones and Alexis McCurn examine how poor black young women balance the threat of interpersonal violence with not violating the expectations of feminine behavior of the larger society. These young women do this as they navigate the frequently dangerous public spaces in their urban communities. In Chapter 9, Valerie Jenness, Jennifer Sumner, Lori Sexton, and Nikkas Alamillo-Luchese examine what it means to be transgendered in a total institution—a prison—and they explore how transgendered inmates negotiate life within this system. Drawing on the voice of one of the coauthors, a transgendered prisoner, we come to understand these challenges and develop a richer, more in-depth understanding of the dilemma of difference that transgendered prisoners face daily.

The contributors to this volume challenge many of the most popular stereotypes of U.S. culture. For example, in Chapter 17, Tanaka, Mooney, and Wolfe, by answering the question "Who's hungry?," debunk widely held myths about who is poor and who experiences hunger in this society. Their analysis reveals the complexities of food insecurity in the United States and the reality that many white, educated, older, working Americans require food assistance. In Chapter 6, Ruth Thompson-Miller and Joe Feagin challenge the historical assumption that sexual violence was largely experienced by white women assaulted by black men. Their research documents the power inequities under Jim Crow laws that in effect allowed white men to rape black women and girls with impunity.

While the topics covered and the experiences shared in this book are varied, the common themes that unite all of the chapters are diversity and inequality. Although the focus of the book is differential experiences of social problems, the intent is not to imply that diversity or difference is bad. To the contrary, research indicates that diversity has numerous benefits, from cultural enrichment to economic growth. Educational researchers, for example, report that students who attend colleges and universities with a diverse student body, where socializing across groups occurs on a regular basis, express greater satisfaction with college, have an increased level of cultural awareness, and show a commitment to promoting intergroup understanding (Chang & Astin, 1997). According to economists, diversity increases innovation and stimulates new ideas, which are essential ingredients for economic growth (Legrain, 2007; Ottaviano & Peri, 2006). As one analyst explained, a team of talented individuals with diverse backgrounds is typically more effective at problem solving than a homogenous group of geniuses (Page, 2007). The guiding question is: How do we maximize the advantages diversity offers while minimizing the liabilities? Recall our initial premise that difference is a social construction and, therefore, may be ascribed positive values instead of negative ones. It is from the negative ascription that the liabilities of difference arise. In developing a fuller understanding of difference from a social constructionist standpoint, we will be better equipped to both celebrate our diversity and challenge inequalities.

References

Best, J. (2013). *Social problems* (2nd ed.). New York, NY: W. W. Norton.

Chang, M. J., & Astin, A. W. (1997). Who benefits from racial diversity in higher education? *Diversity Digest.* Retrieved from http://www.diversityweb.org/Digest/W97/research.html

Collins, P. H. (1990). *Black feminist thought.* New York, NY: Routledge.

Curran, D., & Renzetti, C. M. (1996). *Social problems: Society in crisis* (4th ed.). Needham Heights, MA: Allyn & Bacon.

Currie, E. (1985). *Confronting crime: An American challenge.* New York, NY: Pantheon.

Gusfield, J. (1989). Constructing the ownership of social problems: Fun and profit in the welfare state. *Social Problems, 36,* 431–441.

hooks, b. (1989). *Talking back: Thinking feminist, thinking black.* Boston, MA: South End Press.

Legrain, P. (2007). Cosmopolitan masala: Diversity enriches us all. Retrieved from yaleglobal.yale.edu /content/cosmopolitan-masala-diversity-enriches-us-all

Leon-Guerrero, A. (2011). *Social problems: Community, policy and social action* (3rd ed.). Los Angeles, CA: Pine Forge Press.

Mills, C. W. (1959). *The sociological imagination.* New York, NY: Oxford University Press.

Newman, D. (2012). *Identities and inequalities* (2nd ed.). New York, NY: McGraw-Hill.

Ore, T. (2006). *The social construction of difference and inequality: Race, class, gender, and sexuality* (3rd ed.). Boston, MA: McGraw-Hill.

Ottaviano, G. I. P., & Peri, G. (2006). *Rethinking the effects of immigration on wages.* (National Bureau of Economic Research Working Paper No. w12497). Retrieved from http://ssrn.com/abstract=927381

Page. S. E. (2007). *The difference: How the power of diversity creates better groups, firms, schools and societies.* Princeton, NJ: Princeton University Press.

U.S. Department of Labor, Bureau of Labor Statistics. (2013, July 12). Employment status of the civilian noninstitutional population by sex, age, and race. Retrieved from http://www.bls.gov/cps /cpsaat05.pdf and Employment status of the Hispanic or Latino population by sex, age, and detailed ethnic group. Retrieved from http:// www.bls.gov/cps/cpsaat06.pdf

Work, Health, and Well-Being

The *economy* is the social institution responsible for producing, managing and distributing a society's human and material resources. It is through economic activity that the members of a society meet their survival needs. On an individual level, then, the economy of our society shapes our lives in fundamentally significant ways; it determines, for instance, what jobs are available to us, and where and how we live out our daily lives. On a broader, societal level, the economy shapes the stability and operation of every other major social institution, from government to education to health care. It's not surprising, then, that many social scientists consider the economy the most important social institution in any society.

As we have noted, the economy of a society determines the kinds of work the members of the society do. If you live in an agricultural economy, for example, many of the jobs available will be related in some way to farming. In an industrial economy, such as that of the United States from the late 1800s until about the 1970s, most available jobs were related to the manufacture of products. In the 1970s, the U.S. economy began to change dramatically, with a sharp decline in manufacturing jobs and steady growth in service sector jobs, heralding the emergence of what analysts refer to as a *postindustrial economy*—that is, an economy in which the majority of workers provide services, including generating, managing, and distributing information with the use of electronic technology.

Economic change triggers important changes in every aspect of our lives and, in Chapter 2, Carolyn and Robert Perrucci examine both the material and the psychological impacts of recent economic downturns and restructuring on American workers. Through an analysis of economic data as well as interviews with a diverse group of Americans, Perrucci and Perrucci show how job loss, unemployment, and underemployment not only lower Americans' material quality of life, but also demoralize them and shake their confidence in the government's ability to reinvigorate the economy in such a way that future generations will enjoy economic growth and its benefits. This they describe as a loss of hope, trust, and caring.

Perrucci and Perrucci's chapter highlights social class inequalities in the United States. But social class is only one type of *social stratification*—that is, one type or system of *ranking* people in a hierarchy. As Brea Perry, Erin Pullen, and Carrie Oser point out in Chapter 3, economic stratification is exacerbated by racial and gender stratification. Indeed, their analysis shows that these intersecting inequalities are for some groups a matter of life or death. Although many people think that biological factors account for differences in illness or death rates across various groups, Perry and her colleagues show that social inequalities significantly contribute to *health disparities* across groups. Lifestyle, of course, is a contributing factor as well, but economic, racial, and gender inequalities affect one's ability to lead a particular lifestyle, thereby generating a host of health disparities, ranging from a higher rate of premature births to increased stress to lower life expectancy, for members of disadvantaged groups. The findings from their research, Black Women in a Study of Epidemics (B-WISE), illustrate how the phenomenon they identify as *gendered racism*, as well as other cultural factors, impact health and illness, life and death, for members of different social groups.

While Perry and her colleagues discuss what we commonly think of as *health* (i.e., the absence of illness, disability, or dysfunction), the authors of Chapters 3 and 4 focus more broadly on health as a state of physical as well as mental and social well-being. Both Jennifer Wesely and Miriam Abelson are concerned with how issues of safety and the threat of violence differentially affect the lives and well-being of specific social groups.

In Chapter 3, Jennifer Wesely reports on her research with homeless women and demonstrates not only the economic dimensions of homelessness, but also how homelessness is gendered. For example, Wesely discusses how, among women, violence may be a cause and a consequence of homelessness. While men are more likely to become homeless as a result of job loss, women are more likely to become homeless because of relationship loss, including leaving an abusive partner. And although life on the streets is certainly not easy for men, homeless women are more vulnerable to physical and sexual assaults. For women, poverty and sexism combine to make the precariousness of homelessness even more dangerous.

In Chapter 4, Miriam Abelson continues the discussion of gendered vulnerability, but in addition examines sense of safety and fear of violent victimization in terms of race, class, ability, sexuality, and transgender status. Abelson interviewed 35 transgender men (or trans men), who were identified at birth as female and raised as girls, but as adults decided to transition to live as men. She explores how being transgender is related to the men's fears, but also shows that other factors influence the men's feelings of security versus vulnerability, and safety versus danger. Abelson's analysis is important in illustrating how well-being is multifaceted and simultaneously constructed through multiple overlapping dimensions that, in turn, shape individual experience.

Economic Crisis and Its Effect on Hope, Trust, and Caring

Carolyn Cummings Perrucci and Robert Perrucci

"I think we are headed to a Third World type of situation." These are the words of a 70-year-old retiree reflecting on the country's economic and social problems. Is it possible that the United States could be sliding toward becoming a Third World nation? What has happened to the world's most powerful nation, the sole super power? What has happened to the shining city on the hill, the standard and the beacon for all those nations of the world trying to emulate the prosperity and democracy of Americans?

Such claims are disturbing, but they cannot be dismissed as the product of one disillusioned, aging American. Public opinion polls indicate that in 2010 seven of ten Americans believed the country was heading in the wrong direction; barely more than one in ten said they had "a great deal" or "quite a lot" of confidence in Congress; and only 36% said the same about the presidency (*The New York Times*, 2011). Moreover, the lack of trust and confidence in some of our major institutions—political, media, corporations—is not new. In 1979, President Jimmy Carter identified a major threat facing the nation, a threat "even more serious than energy or inflation." That threat was a "crisis of confidence . . . that strikes at the very heart and soul and spirit of our national will."

It is important to note that President Carter issued his warning in 1979, a year we believe was near the beginning of the slow erosion and decline of America's manufacturing economy, and the beginning of 30-plus years of job loss and wage stagnation for tens of millions of American workers. But we are getting ahead of our story. Let's back up.

In this chapter we shall make the following arguments: First, the U.S. economy, beginning in the mid-1970s, experienced over 30 years of slow but persistent loss of good jobs with decent wages and benefits in the goods-producing sector, that were replaced by lower wage jobs with fewer benefits in the service sector. The situation is analogous to a 30-year drought that year after year depletes the soil and produces smaller and smaller yields and economic benefits. The experiences in any one year do not produce great alarm because there is always hope of a turnaround: Next year we will get more rain. However, the cumulative effect of the years of drought is that a land of dried shrubs and trees is a tinderbox, waiting for the right spark to create a conflagration.

Second, we argue that the spark was provided by the 2008 financial crisis, including the subprime mortgage scandal that caused millions of Americans' homes to decline in value and caused their retirement savings to shrink and disappear. Adding to the crisis was the recognition by individuals that the government's response to this crisis was more helpful to Wall Street and to banks than it was to Main Street— the millions of homeowners facing foreclosures. We believe the dramatic and public nature of the financial crisis and the lack of effective government assistance to individuals served to crystallize the anger and despair of middle-class Americans and led them to see a connection between the chronic 30-year decline of jobs and incomes and the current financial crisis. In short, they started to believe there was something fundamentally wrong with the way that the American political and economic systems were working.

Third, we believe the combined effect of the chronic erosion of jobs and wages and the acute failure of the financial system was responsible for stripping average Americans of their traditional can-do spirit and dashing their hopes for renewal. We have chosen to refer to this loss of can-do spirit as a loss of hope, trust, and caring. Hope is having a positive feeling about one's current life situation and a belief that it will either continue or improve in the future. Feelings of hope may extend beyond one's personal situation to an assessment of what the future will bring for children, family members, and friends. Trust may be personal and it may be revealed in feelings about others like coworkers or family members, but it may also be generalized into feelings about major social institutions like government, Congress, or mainstream media. Caring includes the willingness to contribute to the well-being of other Americans, either directly in the form of personal assistance, or indirectly in the form of taxpayer-supported government programs.

Finally, we move beyond research findings and scholarly publications to introduce the voices of Americans from a variety of walks of life who tell us how the declining economy has affected them and how it has influenced their feelings of hope, trust, and caring. The everyday life experiences of average Americans provide a contrast with public discourse in political circles concerning the current economic crisis.

CHRONIC JOB LOSS AND WAGE STAGNATION

For almost two decades after World War II the U.S. economy prospered. Along with it came job and wage growth for American workers. This period is sometimes referred to as the golden years because the United States dominated production in such sectors as automobiles, steel, textiles, and consumer electronics. Between 1950 and 1975, the share of total national income received by different segments of society such as the top 20% of earners and the bottom 20% of earners (quintile groups) was equally shared (Mishel, Bernstein, & Allegretto, 2005, p. 88). As a result, the median annual earnings of full-time workers increased by 25% between 1960 and 1974. During this period, workers were likely to have steady wage growth, pension plans, health insurance, and paid vacations. This period was sometimes described as a labor–management social contract that guaranteed worker wages and benefits in return for high productivity, agreed-upon work rules, and minimal disruption of the workplace in the form of strikes.

By the mid-1970s there was evidence of improvement in the recovering economies of Europe and Asia, resulting in greater global competition in the production of goods and the search for consumer markets. The profit margins of U.S. firms started to decline for the first time in many years. Corporate leaders, politicians, and economic analysts began to search for answers to the decline. Criticism was often directed at organized labor and the cost of the high-wage agreements and union resistance to new innovations in production that might threaten jobs. American workers were also criticized for their lack of work ethic compared to workers in the newly competitive foreign countries—Japanese workers in particular. The search for victims to blame extended to the federal government and the growth of a new arsenal of regulations, including the Occupational Safety and Health Administration (OSHA) and the Environmental Protection Agency (EPA) for imposing excessive costs on corporations and limiting their ability to compete globally.

The response to declining profits by the largest multinational corporations was to seek new ways to improve the bottom line through increased foreign investment, mergers and joint ventures at home and abroad, plant closings, downsizing the workforce, and sending domestic production offshore. By 1981, the United States "was importing 26% of its cars, 25% of its steel, 60% of its televisions, tape recorders, radios, and phonographs, 43% of its calculators, 27% of its metal-forming machine tools, and 53% of its numerically controlled machine tools" (Reich, 1983). One predictable outcome of increased imports was that the United States became a debtor nation, with the value of imported goods exceeding the value of what we exported. In 1970, the value of imported goods from other nations was $3.7 billion; in 1980 it was $30 billion; in 1987 it was $153.4 billion; by 2004 the trade deficit reached $617.7 billion, and in 2011 it was $668 billion (U.S. Department of Commerce, 2011).

By the mid-1980s more than 11 million workers had lost their jobs because of plant shutdowns and relocation of existing production or new production to facilities in other countries. Job loss was greatest for operators in manufacturing, especially among older workers over the age of 55. When displaced workers found new jobs, the jobs were often in a sector with lower wages and no benefits and were often either temporary or part-time employment. During this decade of closing domestic production and shipping production abroad, direct investment abroad by U.S. corporations increased substantially. In 1970, direct investment abroad was $75 billion, which rose to $167 billion in 1978. By the mid-1980s investment abroad was just below $400 billion, and by 1994 it increased to $716 billion. The cumulative result of all this foreign investment was that the largest 100 multinational corporations were reporting anywhere from 30% to 60% of their total revenue from foreign sources (Forbes, 1995, pp. 274–276).

The ability to move production abroad was facilitated by new innovations in production technology and telecommunications, features of what has been called the *new economy* (Perrucci & Perrucci, 2007). The expanded role of computers in production was achieved through Computer Assisted Design and Manufacturing (CAD-CAM), which made it possible to produce products at spatially separated plants and assemble them at a final location for distribution in world markets. CAD-CAM made it possible to build the so-called world car, which was the product of a spatially de-centered production chain. Computerized production was further enabled by the telecommunications revolution that offered the ability to provide centralized control of widely dispersed activities of research, development, design, and production. The technological innovations of the new economy took the iconic mile-long General Motors auto plant located in Michigan and subdivided it into five or more plants located around the world. General Motors reaped the advantages of lower wage workers, more generous tax systems, and less restrictive government regulations for health, safety, and environmental protection. The result of all these innovations was that a Chevy or Ford (each a classic American-made brand) was no longer produced in America by American workers.

In the 1990s, large organizations turned their attention to downsizing their white-collar employees, a practice often described by the terms *downsizing* and *reengineering*. Mid-level managers and supervisors who were engaged in supervision of production workers or in data gathering, compilation, and analysis were rendered obsolete by the oft-repeated long arm of technology. Computer-based surveillance systems could oversee clerical workers and data entry operators, and smart machines were programmed to remind their operators when their work pace fell behind an established standard. Computer-based data systems and searches reduced the need for middle managers who previously had gathered data without the assistance of computers.

In summary, the 1975–1985 decade was one of closing plants in the United States and shifting production and investment abroad, with the greatest toll taken on production workers in manufacturing. In contrast, the 1985–1995 decade was characterized by the concept of becoming lean and mean. Some of the largest household-name corporations like Sears, IBM, Eastman Kodak, and Chase Manhattan Bank undertook efficiencies to eliminate fat and waste—a process taking the greatest toll on well-educated and well-paid employees (Gordon, 1996).

FINANCIAL MELTDOWN 2008

Between 1999 and 2005 housing prices in the United States were on a continuous upward trajectory. According to the Standard and Poor's Case-Shiller housing price index for 20 major metropolitan statistical areas, housing values in the 2001–2006 period in some of the larger cities appreciated by more than 80%, with similar increases in many smaller cities across the country. Home buying became an investment activity rather than simply finding a home for one's family, and the logic of home buying shifted to a focus on short-term appreciation in value that could be leveraged into home equity loans to finance consumption behavior like vehicle purchases or vacations, or flipped (quickly resold) to achieve a significant return on investment. For many people the purpose of buying a home shifted from its residence value as a family home to its exchange value as a property investment.

Many Americans engaged in risky behavior by buying homes that were more expensive than they could realistically afford based on their income. They often did so believing that the ever increasing market value of their homes would protect them against their inability to pay the mortgages. Financial institutions participated in this expanded mortgage market through the creation of new financial instruments based on mortgages that could be sold to investors who also expected the housing market to continue upward.

In 2006, the prices of new and existing homes turned flat and began to decline. By early 2007, the housing bubble started to lose air and home foreclosures rose. The first institutional casualty was New Century Financial (NCF), which was heavily involved in providing subprime mortgages, mortgages extended to buyers whose limited incomes put them in homes that were over their heads financially. As home prices continued downward and subprime mortgage holders defaulted, NCF stock experienced an 84% decline, leading to its eventual bankruptcy in April 2007. Many big banks that held mortgage-backed securities also experienced a sharp decline in earnings and in the value of their shares on the stock exchanges.

During this mortgage crisis a new term was introduced to Americans: *toxic assets.* This referred to the large number of home mortgages that exceeded the market value of the homes. A home that was purchased for $300,000 was now valued at $250,000, resulting in the amount of money owed to a bank exceeding the value of the home. Large financial institutions like American International Group (A.I.G.), which was the main insurer of mortgage-backed securities, were faced with total collapse because they lacked the cash reserves to pay off the banks that had purchased insurance from them (Walsh, 2010). Other institutions like government-sponsored Fannie Mae (Federal National Mortgage Association) and Freddie Mac (Federal Home Loan Mortgage Association), that owned or guaranteed trillions of dollars of mortgage debt, were also in deep trouble.

The financial system faced an acute crisis. The public was told repeatedly by political and economic leaders that the government had no choice but to provide funds for the troubled banks and financial institutions. The public was also warned that a failure to do so could lead to a collapse of our economic system with consequences that would extend to all Americans. Federal bailout money went to the banks, to Wall Street financial institutions, and to the auto industry, and never quite reached the small business owners on Main Street who were also in financial trouble, or the home owners who were facing foreclosures (Wolfson, 2009).

IMPACT ON RACIAL AND ETHNIC GROUPS

It is a long-standing fact that the unemployment rate of minority groups has been consistently higher than the rate for White Americans, often almost twice as much. When such statistics were first collected in 1972, the black unemployment rate was 11% and the rate for whites was 5%. The high differential sometimes declined, as in 2000, when the rate for black Americans was 8% and the rate for white Americans was 5%. Such declines are the exception rather than the rule. The rate in August 2013 was 13.5% for blacks, 6.4% for whites, 9.3% for Hispanics, and 5.1% for Asians.

The national unemployment rate is for the total population, and the level of unemployment increases substantially for teenagers (both black and white), and for people living in large metropolitan areas, especially those with large minority populations (Garofalo, 2009; Lusane, 1999). In addition, what is often ignored when discussing unemployment among black Americans is the impact the high level of incarceration of black men has on estimates of wage rates and unemployment rates. Western and Pettit (2005) examine such effects and conclude that the failure to take into account incarceration rates of blacks and whites leads to underestimating the level of black–white wage inequality and unemployment.

The loss of jobs in the broad manufacturing sector in the 1970s and 1980s had a significant impact on black workers, many of whom had been employed in auto, textile, and consumer electronics manufacture. Although less affected by globalization, there were significant declines in the construction and the retail sector, which also had a negative impact on minority employment.

An additional negative impact on minority employment was that many factories and retail establishments that remained in the United States often left urban centers and moved to the suburbs, leaving urban minority populations with fewer employment opportunities in locations where they lived (Wilson, 1996).

A final effect of the economic crisis on black Americans was associated with the mortgage crisis of 2008 and the declining values of existing homes. There is some evidence indicating that black home owners may have been more involved with subprime loans, leading to higher levels of home foreclosures and bankruptcy rates (Van Loo, 2009). The loss of homes through foreclosure and the involvement in bankruptcy debt also contributed to the existing wealth disparity between blacks and whites, as the wealth engine of most Americans is the capital appreciation associated with home ownership.

GOVERNMENT COMPLICITY IN JOB LOSS AND FINANCIAL MELTDOWN

The actions of corporations to move production abroad or to downsize white-collar employees can be viewed as the normal workings of an unregulated free-market economy. Similarly, the actions of banks or hedge funds to create financial instruments and sell them to customers is part of their normal business. Corporations, banks, and hedge funds will do what is necessary to remain competitive and to deliver value to their shareholders. Problems emerge when the pursuit of self-interest by large financial entities is not balanced by a set of rules to ensure that the aggregate consequences do not negatively impact the economy in ways harmful to all stakeholders, including society at large.

The actions of government officials and the public policies that they created during the long period of job loss and declining wages failed to restrain the actions of corporations and to protect the interests of the public. In fact, government officials' actions often encouraged and facilitated the downward spiral of jobs and wages for most Americans. Tax policies were created that provided incentives for corporations to expand investments abroad, including reduction of taxes on corporations and capital gains, and elimination of taxes on earnings abroad (Browning, 2008). In addition, Congress and the president created trade policies like the North American Free Trade Agreement (NAFTA) that contributed to expanded job loss as U.S. companies moved production to Mexico.

Another contributor to job loss was the expansion of the Internet and the growth of computer-mediated jobs that could be conducted by people from around the globe. This led to outsourcing jobs in two areas: customer service representatives and skilled computer programmers. College-educated, English-speaking women and men from around the globe could be employed for only a fraction of the costs of comparable U.S. workers. One estimate placed the cost of a U.S. programmer at $80,000 a year on average, while a counterpart in India would receive $20,000 (Lohr, 2003). Many of these outsourced jobs enabled foreign workers to remain in their home country yet interact with colleagues in other countries via Internet-linked meetings.

The government also had a large footprint in being complicit in the financial melt-down. Federal regulatory agencies failed to provide oversight of the banks and financial institutions that created the new high-risk investments. The first thing the government did was to change the rules of the game for the banking community. In 1999, under the Clinton administration, Congress repealed the Glass-Steagall Act, which prevented banks from direct involvement in the stock market by separating investment and com-mercial banking activities. With the repeal, large commercial banks could join in the rush to buy mortgage-based derivatives that promised windfall gains but would even-tually become the source of the banks' downfall. Risky behavior by banks was further encouraged in 2004 when the Securities and Exchange Commission allowed banks to increase their debt-to-capital ratio from 12:1 to 30:1, thereby permitting banks to issue mortgages valued at 30 times their total assets. Finally, Congress and the regulatory agencies ignored the role of new investment companies called hedge funds, which pro-vided special opportunities for investments that were available to very wealthy inves-tors. Hedge funds were heavily involved in trading new investments like derivatives but their actions never came under the scrutiny of the federal regulators who lacked oversight authority.

It should come as no surprise that the financial sector in general and hedge funds in particular became very active financial contributors to individual members of Congress and to political party committees. The Center for Responsible Politics (opensecrets.org) tracks political contributions by individuals and groups. It reports that in the 1990–2009 election cycles, contributions to federal candidates from the finan-cial sector totaled $21,838,027 ($12 million to Democrats and $9 million to Republicans). Hedge fund managers also received special treatment in existing tax guidelines that classifies their income as capital gains and not ordinary income. Thus, a hedge fund manager earning $570 million (the average for the top 25 hedge fund managers) pays a 15% capital gains tax of $59,580,000, while the ordinary income tax rate of 35% would be $139,650,000, thus saving $80,070,000 in tax (Dodd, 2007; Thomas, 2007).

Not everyone in the regulatory community turned a blind eye to the growing risky behavior, but their concerns were either ignored or squelched by powerful forces in the investment community and their allies in Congress. Brooksley Born, head of the Commodities Futures Trading Commission (CFTC), expressed concern about over-the-counter derivatives long before the mortgage bubble burst in 2008 (Kirk, 2009). She wrote a proposal calling for greater regulation of derivatives and continued to urge others to support this effort. Her proposal ran into strong opposition from a cluster of free-market economists, including Alan Greenspan, Robert Rubin, Larry Summers, and Timothy Geithner. Born appeared before congressional committees to make the case for regulation of derivatives, but she was consistently opposed by the so-called gang of four who were powerful figures in the Clinton, Bush, and Obama admin-istrations, and key players in shaping the bailout of banks and Wall Street financial institutions. A congressional committee with oversight responsibility for derivatives recommended that Born and her CFTC committee shut down their effort to regu-late derivatives, leading to the resignation of Born. The crisis of the mortgage bubble has vindicated Born's early warnings, and in 2009 she received the John F. Kennedy Profiles in Courage Award in recognition of the "political courage she demonstrated in sounding early warnings about conditions that contributed to the current global financial crisis."

CLASS POLARIZATION AND DECLINING OPPORTUNITY

One of the major unanticipated consequences of the 30- to 40-year transformation of the U.S. economy and its labor force has been the expansion of income and wealth inequality, the creation of a polarized class structure, and a decline in social mobility. Public discussion in mainstream media of social class in America has often been viewed as a taboo topic (Perrucci & Wysong, 1999, 2003, 2008). This indifference to class inequality is perhaps the legacy of the golden years of the 1950s and 1960s, when the image of a middle-class society was prominent and real. Between 1949 and 1970, the distribution of income across segments of society from top to bottom was in roughly equal shares (Mishel et al., 2005, p. 88). This middle-class America would soon change into its current polarized form.

In post-1975 America, the class structure was gradually reshaped into one with extensive income and wealth inequality and increasing rigidity in terms of opportunities for upward mobility by getting better jobs or attaining more education. The disappearance of high-wage jobs in manufacturing in the auto, steel, textiles, and durable goods sectors changed the employment landscape for millions of high school graduates. Chances for upward mobility via educational channels were limited by the increased race- and class-based segregation of primary and secondary schools into those that were resource-rich and those that were resource-poor. Young men and women from low- and middle-income households who sought to pursue higher education faced rising tuition costs that were beyond their families' ability to pay.

Cracks in the window of the American Dream became increasingly visible, and academic research started to focus on issues of job loss and increasing inequality (Kerbo, 2003, Perrucci & Wysong, 1999, 2003, 2008; Wolff, 1996). In addition, the taboo topic even made its way into *The New York Times* on Sunday, May 15, 2005, when the newspaper began a series of articles entitled "Class Matters." The first article on that Sunday presented data on rising inequality and declining opportunities for upward mobility. The slow but steady drip-drip-drip of job losses, declining wages, and shrinking opportunity for younger Americans was making its way into public consciousness. It entered public consciousness in a big way when the 2008 Wall Street crisis hit. Millions of Americans who had been spared the personal experiences of plant closings, outsourcing, and downsizing were now suddenly faced with losses in retirement savings, with mortgages that were under water, and with mountains of consumer debt. It was in the news every day, along with endless reports about how the "fat cats" were doing in terms of annual salaries and bonuses; the salaries of production workers were flat or declining for a decade while the salaries of CEOs had increased tenfold (Wright, 2006). Even President Obama committed a public faux pas when in December 2010, while appearing on *60 Minutes*, he stated, "I did not run for office to be helping out a bunch of fat-cat bankers on Wall Street." Realizing what he had done, a few days later during a press conference, the president was quoted as saying that bankers are "fine guys," and further: "I, like most of the American people, don't begrudge people's success or wealth. That's part of the free-market system."

The New York Times or not, the president or not, the cat was out of the bag, and more Americans than ever became more aware of the magnitude of class differences and the gulf that existed between Wall Street and Main Street. We believe that the combination of the chronic job and income decline, combined with the acute crisis on Wall Street that impacted Americans' savings and home values, set the stage for the erosion of hope, trust, and caring that is at the core of the American psyche today.

EXPLORING THE LINK BETWEEN ECONOMIC CRISIS AND HOPE, TRUST, AND CARING

In the early 1980s when we studied the effects of plant closings on displaced workers and their communities, we interviewed workers who had lost their jobs when a TV production plant closed its doors and moved. The plant employed about 850 production workers, and it was located in a rural county of about 23,000 residents. When the plant closed, we interviewed about 20 displaced workers and also received completed questionnaires from 327 workers (Perrucci, Perrucci, Targ, & Targ, 1988). We asked workers about how the plant closing had affected them. Many of the comments of the displaced workers epitomize the meaning of lost hope, declining trust in government, and the absence of concern for others.

> *26-year-old divorced woman:* I have taken a lot of jobs since I lost my job at RCA. And I have found there is little I can do for the experience and education I have. Waitressing is not my lifelong dream . . . I have no benefits and future and no light at the end of the tunnel. You survive and grow old with nothing to show except varicose veins and a smile from those who say "get me this" and "I thought you went home you took so long." Only four or five tables who want your undivided attention at the same time. And the government that gets 8% of the meager $2.00 per hour I get.

> *45-year-old married man:* We are down to rock bottom and will probably have to sell the house to live or exist until I can find a job somewhere else. I have been everywhere looking . . . The factories have the young. I've been to all the factories.

> *32-year-old married woman:* I personally believe that our country's problems lay with the dishonest persons. From the man drawing a paycheck without service given, to lawyers and Congress holding things up . . . Agencies, like welfare, so big they lost track of people. They play with paper and machines and we are getting ripped off.

> *39-year-old married woman:* I find that working for a company that kicks my backside out the door makes me afraid to trust anyone.

> *41-year-old married man:* The government is trying to cut our wages and put their foot in the working class and poor class face. . . . They also let the illegal aliens take our jobs away, give them welfare, unemployment compensation, college education at our expense. . . . Government of the people, by the people, and for the people—Ha!

These expressions of despair and distrust are understandable given that they come from people who were long-time employees of a company that moved the plant and left them without jobs. Their grievances are specific to them and their situation in 1982 and they may not be indicative of the mood of people today, who have not experienced a plant closing and who may not be unemployed. On the other hand, Americans today are all living with the knowledge of high unemployment and growing inequality, and that can make people feel insecure about their future, mistrustful of their government, and cautious about helping others. We explored these consequences by conducting in-depth interviews with a small number of people from two cities in Indiana in early 2011. Each city has a population of about 75,000, with a state university nearby and a diversified economy based in manufacturing, service, and agriculture. Our respondents included a secretary in a large organization, an unemployed construction worker, a cashier in a restaurant, a retired factory worker, a hairstylist, a factory worker in a union plant, a machine operator in a union plant, a college counselor, and a community agency staff person.

It is important to keep in mind that at the time of these interviews (2011) the level of real unemployment approached that of the Great Depression. There were at least 15 million unemployed and millions more who had part-time jobs but sought full-time work. Job creation in 2011 had occurred primarily in government and health care sectors, helping mainly college graduates. Jobs in manufacturing had declined under the impact of labor-replacing technology and shifting work abroad. The big government stimulus program did not reduce unemployment and at best probably saved the jobs of many public employees around the country; many states used their stimulus funds to help them retain public employees rather than making the hard decision of learning to live with less revenue.

It is also important to keep in mind that at the time of the interviews some prominent examples of major job growth only reinforced the grim outlook for American workers. For example, on April 19, 2011, McDonald's Corporation reported the result of their national campaign to hire new workers. McDonald's reported hiring 62,000 new workers from an applicant pool of 938,000 aspirants. Most of these workers were to receive the industry average of $8.98 an hour, or $20,800 a year (*The New York Times*, 2011).

We began our interviews asking about current employment situations: eight respondents were employed, one unemployed, and one retired. One of the employed persons (the cashier) was planning to retire because her cafeteria was moving to a new location and everyone was told they had to reapply for their job. She had worked at the cafeteria for 13 years but expected to lose her job because "they keep wanting to bring in new people who will get paid less."

> **Question:** I am interested in how the current economic recession has affected you, your family members, or friends.

Five of the ten respondents reported that their employment security was affected directly or indirectly through a family member; for example:

> "My son is unemployed and my friends are very, very scared."

> "I was laid off three years ago when the housing market collapsed, and so did construction and so did my job."

> "My husband was laid off from a job of cleaning carpets."

Others described how their homes had lost value or how rising prices were outpacing their income, which wasn't growing. Two production workers in a union plant didn't feel that their jobs were at risk, but they thought that the company was using the recession to raise the workload and production standards. They both thought their experience of "speed up" was because the company was not hiring new workers but getting more work from current employees. Two respondents did not report a direct or indirect effect, but they nonetheless expressed concerns about the future:

"Not yet, but you never know; my daughter and son who have jobs are prepared for the worst."

"I could be let go anytime because there's another secretary who has more years than me; I've been here for over five years but that don't make me safe."

> **Question:** How hopeful are you that economic conditions will improve in the next year or so?

Seven respondents were unequivocal in their negative views of the near future; for example:

"I can't see any improvement."

"I don't see anything that will turn things around."

"I think we are still on a downward slope and it's not going to get better until it gets worse."

Two respondents expressed uncertainty about improvement in economic conditions:

"I think people want to be optimistic . . . We are up there on a plateau and now we're starting to see an incline, but along comes the war we are now involved in [Libya] and rising food prices, and hope that things might get better takes a hit."

"Hard to say, it's going to take a while before things get better."

The one positive respondent stated:

"I'm hoping they will improve. I expect them to improve. That's what we keep hearing, that everything's getting better."

The next section in the interview focused on trust in major institutions like the media, Congress, and big corporations.

> **Question:** Do you think the mainstream media are telling the American people the facts of the current economic situation?

Eight of the ten respondents expressed little or no trust in mainstream newspapers or TV, often citing specific instances of what they consider to be bias. For example:

"I think they tell us what they're told to tell us. And look at what they do to Sarah Palin; so what if she wrote something on her hand—it's human, lots of people do that. You know the old saying, believe half of what you see and none of what you read."

Several discussed bias as a "normal" part of media, requiring readers or viewers to be more vigilant:

"My view is that there is hardly anyone that just states the facts. Most have a point of view and biased opinions. I watch them all. FOX is biased on the right-wing conservative side and MSNBC is more liberal, with the other channels somewhere in the middle. They all try to influence the masses with their biased opinions.

There's no way they tell the whole story. The news media is biased. Even the newspapers are the same; the editors lean one way or another."

The message in these comments is that "you have to learn to read between the lines because if you take it verbatim, you're not getting the truth."

> **Question:** How much confidence do you have in Congress or the president that they will do the right thing on the economy?

The overriding sentiment expressed by almost all respondents was that Washington is not working, which includes Congress, the president, and both political parties. Lack of confidence in political institutions was revealed in phrases like:

"It's all pettiness and lying."

"I don't have the feeling they are working on these problems."

"I don't see any proposals that will make a difference; the President is up there spinning his wheels."

"Even Obama, he was supposed to save us, but the jobs have been going out at breakneck speed, and there has been no policy."

The closest that any respondents got to expressions of trust focused on specific persons:

"Yeah there are a few who give me a glimpse of something better: the guy from Vermont, the gay senator, there's the Jewish guy and the guy that got killed from Wisconsin—but they're like voices in the wind, nobody is listening."

Two respondents were positive about President Obama, but not because of his achievements:

"I think that Obama has really tried to get jobs for people."

"I think the political system shows that you [Obama] can want to do the right thing but the hands are tied."

The final section of the interview was relatively wide open, asking about what should be done for the elderly, the homeless, and single mothers in society. Respondents could focus on one or all of the groups mentioned. The focus of the interviewer was to learn what kind of help, if anything, the respondent would support.

> **Question:** There are many people in America besides the unemployed who are having a hard time making ends meet. There are older Americans living on social security or in nursing homes. There are millions of homeless Americans who need to get back on their feet. Another group that is hurting are single mothers who need to work full time and need help with their child care. What can we do to help these Americans, and do you think they deserve spending tax dollars to help them?

Three respondents, one retired and two employed individuals, were cognizant of the fact that the need to make budget cuts at the federal level would have a negative impact on social welfare programs, Medicare, and Medicaid. Rather than address how to help the homeless, they emphasized the reasons for being homeless like post-traumatic stress disorder and drug problems.

Five respondents acknowledged that many people need help, but they put the stress on self-help. One older employed woman said:

"It's great to help people, but you can help them too much. Like our kids today; we teach them to go to Mom and Dad when they need help, but they need to learn to do things on their own, figure it out on their own."

An unemployed man responded,

"You have to learn to take care of yourself. I have been doing all sorts of odd jobs to help with the family budget. You can't wait around for someone to help you. I put up water and food for six months; things could really get bad, and we need to be ready."

Regarding providing assistance with child care for single mothers, a young employed mother replied:

"Most definitely, because we've got to get them working. We've got to get them working so that they can help pay for their own child support."

Another employed woman espoused the need for keeping tabs on those receiving help:

"I almost think that the voucher system is the only way. So you'd have your rent paid, your utilities paid, food paid. Any actual cash can't go for stuff like alcohol and drugs."

Thus, while there was support for helping those in need, the help was not always described as a top priority, and it always had strings attached. A frequent theme introduced by four respondents was about the amount of federal aid going abroad, including to fight wars, suggesting that this money is needed at home to help the unemployed and the homeless.

One unemployed man offered a more complex and maybe cynical view of the problem:

"One way or another you are going to pay. If you don't help the homeless, you will have to deal with your house being broken into; you pay one way or another. We need to participate in what FDR did, create jobs like the WPA. Instead, we are spending money in Afghanistan and Iraq; and let's not jump into Libya. We have got to start helping people at home—charity begins at home."

An employed man indicated,

"We help lots of people overseas. I don't disagree with that, but there's people in our own country that need help. We are such a big country and such a rich country that there should be no need for someone to be homeless."

Another employed man replied,

"I know we say people are lazy and don't want to work; they have five, six, seven kids. Maybe if there were jobs, people would work. But Americans are spoiled, and that includes me. People are on welfare but they have cable TV and their cigarettes and beer, and maybe their drugs or whatever."

Conclusion

Unemployment clearly divides people. We believe that policy makers and those who have secure and rewarding jobs fail to understand the full magnitude of how being unemployed affects people who have lost their jobs. Elsewhere we have argued that unemployment should be treated as a public health problem and not simply an economic indicator of the nation's health (Perrucci & Perrucci, 1990). Unemployment, especially when it is long-term, results in income loss and insecurity that is connected to a variety of negative health outcomes for the unemployed, their families, and the larger community.

In this chapter we have argued that the possibility or fear of unemployment during a long-term economic decline can tear apart the social fabric that is held together by hope for a better future, trust in social institutions that can help, and caring about others in need. We documented the chronic (1975–1990) and acute (2008–2011) stages of economic crisis and drew upon a small number of in-depth interviews to make the connection between economic crisis and the essential ingredients for a healthy human being and a healthy society. What we learned from these interviews is that average Americans do not see a light at the end of the tunnel. They do not think things will get better in the near future; they have little or no confidence or trust in major political institutions and the mainstream media; and their support for those in need is not unqualified and does not extend to endorsing government programs for that purpose.

References

Browning, L. (2008, August 13). Study tallies corporations not paying income tax. *The New York Times*.

Class matters. (2005). New York, NY: Times Books.

Dodd, R. (2007, July 24). Tax breaks for millionaires. *Economic Policy Institute* (Memorandun #20).

The Economist. (2011, April 23–29). 102.

Garofalo, Pat (2009, July 13). The disparate impact of job losses on minorities. *Think Progress Economy*, Center for American Progress.

Gordon, D. M. (1996). *Fat and mean: The corporate squeeze of working Americans and the myth of managerial "downsizing."* New York, NY: Free Press.

The hundred largest U.S. multinationals. (1995, July 17). *Forbes*, 274–276.

Kerbo, H. R. (2003). *Social stratification and inequality* (5th ed.). Boston, MA: McGraw-Hill.

Kirk, M. (Producer). (2009, October 20). The warning. [Audiocast]. In *Frontline*. Boston, MA: WGBH Educational Foundation, PBS.org.

Koll, A. (2011, May 8). How the McEconomy bombed the American worker. Retrieved from http://www.tomdispatch.com/post/175389/

Lohr, S. (2003, December 22). Offshore jobs in technology: Opportunity or threat? *The New York Times*.

Lusane, C. (1999, Spring). Persisting disparities: Globalization and the economic status of African Americans. *Howard Law Journal*, 431–450.

Mishel, L., Bernstein, J., & Allegretto, S. (2005). *The state of working America*. Ithaca, NY: Cornell University Press.

Nation's mood at lowest level in two years, poll shows. (2011, April 22). *The New York Times*.

Perrucci, C. C., Perrucci, R., Targ, D. B., & Targ, H. (1988). *Plant closings: International context and social costs*. Hawthorne, NY: Aldine de Gruyter.

Perrucci, R., & Perrucci, C. C. (2007). *The transformation of work in the new economy*. New York, NY: Oxford University Press.

Perrucci, R., & Perrucci, C. C. (2009), *America at risk: The crisis of hope, trust, and caring*. Lanham, MD: Rowman & Littlefield.

Perrucci, R., & Wysong, E. (1999, 2003, 2008, 2013). *The new class society: Goodbye American dream?* Lanham, MD: Rowman & Littlefield.

Reich, R. (1983). *The next American frontier*. New York, NY: Times Books.

Thomas, L., Jr. (2007, January 25). Hedge fund chiefs, with cash, join political fray. *The New York Times*.

U.S. Department of Commerce. (2005). Foreign Trade Division. Washington, DC: U.S. Government Printing Office.

Van Loo, R., (2009). A tale of two debtors: Bankruptcy disparities by race. *Albany Law Review, 72,* 231.

Walsh, M. (2010, January 31). Risky trading wasn't just on the fringe at A.I.G. *The New York Times.*

Western, B., & Pettit, B. (2005). Black-white wage inequality, employment rates, and incarceration. *American Journal of Sociology, 111,* 53–578.

Wilson, W. J. (1996). *When work disappears: The world of the new urban poor.* New York, NY: Alfred A. Knopf.

Wolff, E. N. (1996). *Top heavy: The increasing inequality of wealth in America and what can be done about it.* New York, NY: Twentieth Century Fund.

Wolfson, M. (2009, September/October). Bailout nation: Who gets bailed out and why. *Dollars and Sense,* 14–16.

Wright, D. (2009). *Employment and earnings, 1960–2007.* Wichita, KS: Wichita State University.

3

Inequalities in Health and Well-Being in the United States

Gendered Racism and the Experiences of Black Women*

Brea L. Perry, Erin Pullen, and Carrie B. Oser

INTRODUCTION: AN OVERVIEW OF RACIAL HEALTH DISPARITIES IN THE UNITED STATES

The United States is a country defined by its reputation as a land of opportunity and prosperity. Yet, it is also a nation characterized by substantial economic and racial inequality. This inequality appears in various forms, from differential access to resources like safe housing, to unequal opportunities in employment and education. Since the turn of the last century, sociologists have been examining the ways that these economic and social conditions affect health and well-being, observing that biological differences alone cannot adequately explain patterns of better and worse health in society (Hankin & Wright, 2010). Often, morbidity and mortality (i.e., the incidence of ill health and death in a population, respectively) vary systematically by gender, race, or socioeconomic status such that members of particular groups are more vulnerable than others. These patterns are called *health disparities* or *health inequalities.*

Health disparities have persisted among certain groups of people despite the major overall reductions in morbidity and mortality that have characterized the last few decades. Those living in poverty and certain racial groups tend to live shorter lives and have worse health than those who are wealthier and white (Williams & Sternthal, 2010). For example, blacks have higher mortality rates than whites for the majority of the 15 leading causes of death,

*This research was supported by a grant from the National Institute of Drug Abuse (R01-DA022967, PI Oser). We would like to thank Kathi L. H. Harp, Danelle Stevens-Watkins, and Jennifer Mooney for their contributions to this research.

including cancer, hypertension, heart disease, diabetes, and homicide (Kung, Hoyert, Xu, & Murphy, 2008; Williams & Mohammed, 2009). Women also experience health disparities when compared to men; specifically, despite their longer life spans, women have higher rates of nonfatal acute and chronic conditions, as well as certain types of mental illnesses (Bird & Rieker, 2008). In general, groups with more wealth, prestige, and power in a society tend to enjoy better health. Even though social welfare programs and advances in medicine have seemingly made good health more achievable to the masses, these health disparities remain.

Sociologists have identified a number of social factors that contribute to health disparities among blacks relative to whites. Chief among these are neighborhood effects. Specifically, blacks in the United States are residentially segregated into unhealthy and unsafe neighborhoods with high concentrations of urban poverty (Massey, 2004). These communities are characterized by conditions like pervasive joblessness, material and food deprivation, overcrowding, high crime rates, and social isolation (Massey & Denton, 1993). Living in these segregated neighborhoods increases a person's vulnerability to injuries or illness, and contributes to higher rates of infant mortality and premature birth among racial minorities (Polednak, 1993; Williams & Collins, 1995). For example, segregated black neighborhoods are more likely to contain environmental toxins, increasing exposure to lead, asbestos, or other hazardous materials (Morello-Frosch & Shenassa, 2006; Williams & Mohammed, 2009). Additionally, low-income urban blacks are disproportionately exposed to violence and crime, which can increase stress and contribute to negative physical and mental health outcomes (Dohrenwend et al., 1992; Morenoff, 2003). Also, segregated communities provide limited access to fresh produce and other healthy foods, and there are typically few safe outdoor spaces for physical activity, contributing to poor nutrition and obesity. Through these and other mechanisms, unhealthy environments "get under the skin," influencing health inequalities (Taylor, Repetti, & Seeman, 1997, p. 411).

In the remainder of this chapter, we discuss causes and consequences of gender, racial, and socioeconomic health disparities for Americans in minority groups. First, we introduce the concepts of *intersectionality* and *gendered racism*, discussing how multiple simultaneous status disadvantages (e.g., being a black woman with low socioeconomic status) interact to affect well-being and life chances. Second, we describe the influence of gendered racism on the health of black women in the contemporary United States, focusing on the effects of these experiences in the stress process. Third, we present empirical findings from a project called Black Women in a Study of Epidemics (B-WISE) that illustrate the complex role of gendered racism and other cultural factors in health and illness. Finally, we discuss implications of findings from this study for policies and practices that could help reduce health disparities.

INTERSECTING SOCIAL STATUSES: BLACK WOMEN AND GENDERED RACISM

Racism is a system of "culturally sanctioned beliefs, which, regardless of intentions involved, defend the advantages whites have because of the subordinated position of racial minorities" (Wellman, 1993, p. 10). In other words, there exists in the United States and elsewhere an ideological hierarchy in which some racial groups are thought to be inferior to others. Racism leads to the development of prejudice, or negative attitudes and beliefs, as well as instances of discrimination, or differential and disadvantaged treatment of blacks and other minorities (Williams & Williams-Morris, 2000). For blacks, racism is a structured and pervasive aspect of life in the United States. It sometimes comes in the form of major events, such as being passed up for promotion at work despite superior performance. However, more frequently, racism is reflected in everyday irritations associated with more subtle forms of oppression, such as being mistaken for a waiter at an upscale restaurant (Essed, 1991; Harrell, 2000).

The nature of racist attitudes has changed substantially over the past 50 years, with the majority of Americans now endorsing principles of equality (e.g., racial integration in education; Williams & Williams-Morris, 2000). However, more subtle and covert forms of racism are evident in findings from large, nationally representative studies of public attitudes. For example, there continues to be considerable endorsement of negative stereotypes of blacks, with 29% of whites believing that "most Blacks are unintelligent," 44% agreeing that "most Blacks are lazy," and 51% reporting that "most Blacks are prone to violence" (Williams & Williams-Morris, 2000). In addition, there is substantial opposition to policies that would eliminate institutional inequality, with only 28% of whites stating that they would support government intervention to ensure fair treatment in employment for blacks (Williams & Williams-Morris, 2000). There is evidence that these patterns bear out in everyday experiences, with a majority of blacks reporting instances of prejudice and discrimination by strangers, educators, employers, and institutions (Landrine & Klonoff, 1996; Williams & Mohammed, 2009).

Like racism, sexism is reflected in individual attitudes, collective ideology, and social institutions like the education system. While gender ideology has become increasingly egalitarian over time, a substantial minority of Americans still endorse conservative values regarding gender roles and the institutions of work and family (Bolzendahl & Myers, 2004; Brewster & Padavic, 2000). Along similar lines, there continues to be inequality in the division of household labor, and gender-based complaints to the Equal Employment Opportunity Commission have either remained steady or increased since 1975 (Swim, Aikin, Hall, & Hunter, 1995; Van der Lippe, de Ruijter, de Ruijter, & Raub, 2011). Moreover, research suggests that 97% of women report being the victim of a sexist event (e.g., sexual harassment, name-calling) in the past year (Klonoff & Landrine, 1995).

Existing research on women of color suggests that experiences of racism and sexism are related (King, 2003; Moradi & Subich, 2003; Woods-Giscombe & Lobel, 2008). Black women are disadvantaged by their status both as racial minorities and women, two groups that are devalued in American society relative to whites and men. Consequently, instances of discrimination attributed to simultaneous racism and sexism are commonly reported among black women (King, 2005; Thomas, Witherspoon, & Speight, 2008). In fact, black women are more likely to experience and be distressed by sexism and racism than white women and black men, respectively (Greer, Laseter, & Asiamah, 2009; King, 2003; Klonoff & Landrine, 1995; Landrine, Klonoff, Gibbs, Manning, & Lund, 1995; Moradi & Subich, 2003). This research underscores the inseparable nature of racism and sexism in the lives of black women. As a result, it may be difficult for women of color to distinguish the impact of racism from sexism such that negative experiences of these kinds may be attributed equally to both statuses (Andersen & Collins, 2004; Essed, 1991; King, 2003).

Experiences of racism and sexism combine to affect the educational, occupational, and economic success of black women, creating strong associations among race, gender, and social class. For instance, many ethnic minority women are relegated to the lowest stratum of the employment market, holding feminized jobs in the service industry (e.g., housekeeping) that carry the lowest pay and prestige (Essed, 1991). A disproportionate number of black women also experience low socioeconomic status, adding a third dimension to the particular combination of inequalities that women of color must overcome. Because race and gender embody access to resources like political power, income and wealth, social capital, and higher education that are cornerstones of socioeconomic systems of stratification, the distinct influences of race, gender, and social class are difficult to disentangle (Clark et al., 1999; Williams & Mohammed, 2009).

Kimberlé Crenshaw (1991) first employed the term *intersectionality* to describe the impact of multiple identities and forms of oppression on experiences of inequality. The intersectionality approach was developed in response to the observation that theories of gender and racial inequality had historically focused almost exclusively on the viewpoints and experiences of affluent white women and black men, respectively (e.g., hooks, 1981; Hull, Scott, & Smith, 1982). Focusing on black women's location at the intersection of disadvantaged gender, racial, and class statuses, advocates of this perspective argue that the oppressions associated with each of these disadvantaged statuses combine to produce linked forms of injustice that are not captured in mainstream research (Collins, 2000).

Consistent with this idea of intersecting status disadvantages, scholars argue that black women experience a specific form of oppression called gendered racism that is founded in racist perceptions of gender roles (Jackson, Phillips, Hogue, & Curry-Owens, 2001; Thomas et al., 2008). According to Essed (1991), racism and sexism "narrowly intertwine and combine under certain conditions into one, hybrid phenomenon" such that a specific set of societal stereotypes are applied exclusively to each disadvantaged race and gender subgroup (p. 31). For example, black men are typecast as absent fathers and criminals, while Asian women are stereotyped as being demure, submissive, and exotic.

For black women, gendered racism has historically taken its own unique form characterized by perceptions of strength, sexual promiscuity, deviant bodies, and emasculating behavior (i.e., depriving men of their power and masculinity; Thomas et al., 2008). With the dramatic rise of female-headed black families, being a black woman has also come to be associated with motherhood, poverty, and being on welfare (Essed, 1991). Since the 1970s, women of color have increasingly become the face of poverty, with a disproportionate number of news images of welfare recipients depicting black women (Clawson & Trice, 2000; Gilens, 2000). Likewise, first lady Michelle Obama's body (and especially her backside) has frequently been the subject of derision by politicians and others (e.g., Rush Limbaugh, a talk radio personality, and Representative F. James Sensenbrenner [R-WI]), evoking racialized and objectifying images of black women's bodies that date back to slavery. Because Obama's role as first lady challenges traditional notions of a black woman's place in society, her opponents have sought to emphasize her blackness and nonconformity with white, upper-class, feminine beauty ideals. These kinds of cultural images conflating race, gender, and social class are introduced and reinforced not only in the popular media, but also through literature, the education system, and public and political discourse.

THE ROLE OF GENDERED RACISM IN HEALTH

While little existing research has examined the role of gendered racism in health, ample research suggests that racism alone is a source of chronic strain and psychological distress for blacks, and may contribute to overall physical and mental health disparities between blacks and whites (Brown & Keith, 2003; Landrine & Klonoff, 1996). For instance, perceived racism is significantly associated with subjective well-being, psychological distress, depression, and problem drinking among blacks (Brown et al., 2000; Brown, Keith, Jackson, & Gary, 2003; Jackson et al., 1996; Kessler, Mickelson, & Williams, 1999; Sellers, Caldwell, Schmeelk-Cone, & Zimmerman, 2003). Similarly, experiences of racist events are linked to worse self-reported health and to increased risk for hypertension, common colds, and a range of other physical diseases (Karlsen & Nazroo, 2002; Krieger, 1990; Kwate, Valdimarsdottir, Guevarra, & Bovbjerg, 2003).

As with racial discrimination, chronic and acute stress associated with experiencing sexism are linked to women's mental and physical health outcomes. Recent research indicates that sexism is linked to anxiety, anger, obsessive-compulsivity, somatic symptoms, psychological distress, and depression (Klonoff, Landrine, & Campbell, 2000; Landrine et al., 1995; Moradi & Subich, 2003). Though there is relatively little research on the linkages between sexist experiences and physical health outcomes, a few studies do find that these are related to higher risk for hypertension, premenstrual symptoms, headaches, and nausea (Krieger, 2000; Landrine & Klonoff, 1997; Pavalko, Mossakowski, & Hamilton, 2003).

Stress associated with exposure to gendered racism may adversely affect health through a number of physiological pathways. The sympathetic nervous system and the Hypothalamic Pituitary Adrenal (HPA) axis control the release of epinephrine (adrenaline) and cortisol (Fremont & Bird, 2000). During exposure to stress, the sympathetic nervous system and the HPA axis become overactive, increasing heart rate, muscle tone, and glucose and fatty acid levels. These physiological responses are associated with an elevated risk for many physical and mental health problems, including cardiovascular disease, ulcers, hypertension, depression, and anxiety (Fremont & Bird, 2000; House, Landis, & Umberson, 1988). In addition, social stress can affect immune functioning, increasing or decreasing vulnerability to bacterial and viral infection as well as influencing allergic reaction and healing. Some argue that instances of racial and gender discrimination may provoke a more severe physiological response than generic stressors (e.g., financial troubles or caring for an ill loved one) because they are inherently personal and humiliating (Landrine & Klonoff, 1997).

Gendered racism can also affect the health of black women through psychological and behavioral pathways. For example, experiencing racist and sexist events can reduce self-esteem and feelings of life satisfaction, leading to the internalization of negative stereotypes about one's own race and gender (Utsey, Ponterotto, Reynolds, & Cancelli, 2000). These psychosocial processes can, in turn, increase susceptibility to mental health problems like anxiety and depression. Similarly, gendered racism-related stress can lead to the use of maladaptive, or harmful, coping mechanisms that influence health outcomes, including smoking, overeating, and alcohol consumption (Landrine & Klonoff, 1996).

FINDINGS FROM THE B-WISE PROJECT

To better understand the role of gendered racism and other cultural factors in the health of black women, a research study called Black Women in a Study of Epidemics (B-WISE; R01-DA022967, PI Oser) is being conducted at the University of Kentucky. Longitudinal (i.e., over time) data are being collected from three groups of black women: (1) women about to be released from prison, (2) women on probation, and (3) women in the community with no involvement in the criminal justice system. Data collection will not be completed until the end of 2013, but a number of analyses already have been conducted using the first wave of data measuring health outcomes and predictors for women in the third group, in the community.

Participants in the community sample were recruited using newspaper ads and fliers posted in various parts of the city with a large black population (based on census data). Eligibility criteria included: (1) self-identifying as a black woman; (2) being at least 18 years old; and (3) being currently uninvolved in the criminal justice system. Women who consented to participate in the study were interviewed in person by trained black female interviewers.

After deletion of missing data (two cases dropped), the analysis sample contains 204 black women. These women report an average of about 13 years of education (i.e., one year of college), and are about 36 years old, on average. The mean annual household income among respondents is $20,850, and 13% of the women in the sample were married at the time of the interview. It is important to note that women in the B-WISE sample are not representative of black women nationally. Consequently, the results presented here are based on a sample with a lower socioeconomic status and marriage rate than all black women living in the United States. This may mean that findings cannot be extended to all black women, but can probably be generalized to disadvantaged black women living in racially segregated communities.

HOW COMMON ARE SEXISM AND RACISM AMONG LOW SOCIOECONOMIC STATUS BLACK WOMEN?

The B-WISE data on black women in the community suggest that mistreatment and discrimination on the basis of gender and race are commonplace. Participants were asked whether they had experienced a series of adverse events "because you are a woman" and "because you are Black" (Klonoff & Landrine, 1995; Landrine & Klonoff, 1996). Figure 3-1 and Figure 3-2 depict results from frequency distributions and cross-tabulations on these items. White bars represent the percentage of black women who had experienced an event and attributed it to sexism, while grey bars reflect the same

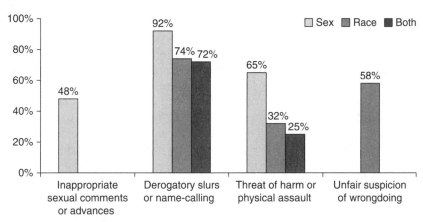

FIGURE 3-1 Adverse experiences attributed to gender, race, and both

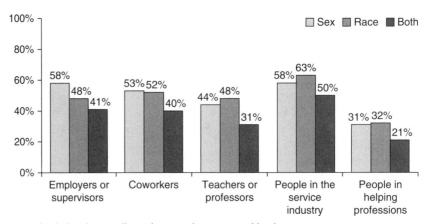

FIGURE 3-2   Discrimination attributed to gender, race, and both

experiences attributed to racism. Finally, black bars signify the percentage of women who reported that each event had occurred because of both race and gender (i.e., gendered racism). For a few events that are particularly likely to occur because of either sexism or racism, women were only asked to report whether it had happened because of gender or race, but not both.

Figure 3-1 shows that nearly half of the black women in the B-WISE sample report that others made inappropriate sexual advances or comments to them because of their gender. Further, 92% had been called a sexist name and nearly three-quarters had been called a racist name, with 72% experiencing derogatory slurs or name-calling because of their gender and their race. In addition, 65% of study participants reported that they had been "made fun of, picked on, pushed, shoved, hit, or threatened with harm" because they are women; 32% said that this occurred because they are black; and 25% had experienced threat of harm or physical assault because of race and gender. Finally, 58% of women reported that they had been unfairly suspected of wrongdoing or criminal behavior because they were black.

Figure 3-2 depicts the percentage of black women who reported experiencing unfair treatment (i.e., discrimination) by various individuals or groups. Over half of study participants had been treated unfairly by employers or supervisors and by coworkers because they were women, about half because they were black, and about 40% because of both their race and their gender. Also, 44% and 48% reported experiencing discrimination at the hands of teachers or professors due to gender or race, respectively, and nearly one third attributed these events to both gender and race. In addition, about 58% of black women had been discriminated against by people in the service industry (e.g., servers, cashiers, flight attendants) due to gender and 63% due to race, while half reported that these events occurred because of both their race and gender. Finally, nearly one third of study participants claimed to have been treated unfairly by people in helping professions (e.g., doctors, nurses, social workers) because of their gender or their race, and 21% attributed this kind of discrimination to both gender and race.

It is important to determine whether the women in the study found these forms of discrimination to be stressful since the stress process is a likely mechanism linking racism and sexism to health. This is sometimes called stress appraisal. After study participants were asked whether the events above had occurred, they were asked to report how stressful these were on a scale of 1–6, with 1 being "not at all stressful" and 6 being "extremely stressful." After averaging responses across the measures, we find that only 18% of women found these experiences to be "not at all" or "a little" stressful. In contrast, nearly half found them to be "very" or "extremely" stressful, with the rest reporting that discrimination events were moderately stressful.

Overall, these findings demonstrate that despite the progress that has been made toward racial and gender equality in the United States, adverse experiences and unfair treatment due to racism and sexism are common among black women with low socioeconomic status. Moreover, a large proportion of those who report discrimination attribute it to both their gender and their race (i.e., gendered racism). Finally, there is evidence that most black women find these experiences to be moderately to extremely stressful, providing a causal mechanism that could link discrimination to health.

HOW DOES GENDERED RACISM AFFECT HEALTH AND WELL-BEING?

Several studies from the B-WISE project have examined the health consequences of gendered racism for black women. These analyses use a statistical method called regression to identify relationships between independent (i.e., predictive or causal) variables and dependent (i.e., outcome) variables. The individual measures asking about racism and sexism experiences are added together to make one scale that represents the overall level of gendered racism that a woman has experienced, with higher values denoting more adverse experiences. For the remainder of the chapter, we highlight findings from this research.

Gendered Racism, Traumatic Life Events, and Health

The first research study to be conducted using the B-WISE data explores the relationship between gendered racism and other traumatic life events that are often predictive of ill health (Perry, Harp, & Oser, 2013). We find that higher levels of lifetime gendered racism are related to higher levels of other stressors occurring in the past year across a range of social roles and contexts. For example, women who report more gendered racism have also experienced more employment and financial problems, social network loss (e.g., divorce or death of a loved one), illness and injury, and victimization (e.g., physical or sexual assault). In short, black women who face high levels of gendered racism also experience increased vulnerability to every other type of stressor measured, with relationships to employment and financial stressors and victimization being the strongest.

In addition, we find evidence that gendered racism has a negative influence on health outcomes. Specifically, black women who experience higher levels of gendered racism report lower levels of well-being and life satisfaction, on average. They are also more likely to report experiencing severe anxiety in the past month and health concerns in the past year. Another type of statistical analysis called mediation suggests that gendered racism shapes these health outcomes both directly and indirectly through other kinds of stressors. For example, gendered racism increases vulnerability to employment and financial stressors (e.g., discrimination in the workforce), which in turn influence well-being. Likewise, higher levels of gendered racism predict instances of personal illness, injury, and social network loss, which then increase vulnerability to self-reported health concerns.

Gendered Racism and Suicidal Ideation and Behavior

The B-WISE data have also been used to examine black women's risk and protective factors for suicidal ideation and behavior (Perry, Pullen, Stevens-Watkins, & Oser, 2012). About 20% of the black women in the sample report having had serious thoughts of suicide or having attempted suicide at some point in their life. However, the most important finding to emerge from this research is that as gendered racism experiences increase, risk for suicidal thoughts and behaviors also increases.

This research also explores different types of coping resources that black women might use to reduce the impact of stress related to gendered racism on suicide outcomes. We find that having an active coping style (i.e., the tendency to react proactively to challenges), high existential well-being (i.e., a sense of purpose and meaning in life), and strong family social support reduce the harmful effects of gendered racism. That is, gendered racism experiences have no adverse influence on the presence of these resources, which may allow black women to manage or neutralize stress that would otherwise lead to despair and suicide (Pearlin, 1999).

Racism, Cultural Protective Factors, and Illicit Drug Use

Other research from the B-WISE study investigates the relationship between racism experiences and illicit drug use (Stevens-Watkins, Perry, Harp, & Oser, 2012). In this study, racism alone is examined because we are interested in identifying protective resources related to ethnic identity and involvement in an ethnic community. Broadly, we find that being exposed to racism is associated with increased risk for using crack, heroin, amphetamines, and other hard drugs. However, the adverse effects of racism on drug use primarily impact younger women in the sample. Generally speaking, young women are more likely to use drugs when compared to older women. In addition, by virtue of being at a more advanced stage of the life course, older black women may have developed healthier strategies over time to neutralize the stress associated with racism, avoiding maladaptive coping mechanisms like substance use.

As with suicide outcomes, results from this study provide evidence that coping resources can reduce the negative influence of racism. For drug use outcomes, culturally specific resources are protective. For example, stronger identification with and participation in black culture protects women from the harmful effects of racism on illicit drug use. It may be that shared experiences and a sense of collective identity with other blacks lead to feelings of belonging and acceptance that counteract the stress associated with experiencing racism. Along these lines, having strong, positive feelings about one's ethnicity might prevent black women from internalizing (i.e., incorporating within one's own attitudes or values) racist slights and humiliations, reducing the likelihood that these events will have a negative impact.

IMPLICATIONS FOR DIVERSITY AND HEALTH

Sociologists argue that health disparities in America are largely attributable to the organization of social life, systems of oppression, and opportunities and resources available to members of different race, gender, and social class groups (Aneshensel, Rutter, & Lachenbruch, 1991). An individual's combination of intersecting statuses results in patterned experiences and identities, which increase or decrease vulnerability to a range of risk and protective factors. For black women, being multiply disadvantaged by their status as racial minorities, women, and often their socioeconomic status constitutes a unique form of gendered racial oppression such that the social stratification effects of racism and sexism are difficult to distinguish (Essed, 1991).

Taken together, findings from the B-WISE project provide evidence that the intersecting statuses of gender and race affect a range of health outcomes in a sample of low socioeconomic status black women, pointing to four potential mechanisms underlying this relationship. First, persistent devaluation on the basis of gender and race may cause women to internalize negative stereotypes, posing a threat to positive self-concept, sense of control, proactive coping, and other social psychological resources (Aneshensel et al., 1991). Second, gendered racism may affect mental health through maladaptive coping strategies (e.g., excessive drug or alcohol consumption) and other behavioral pathways (Martin, Tuch, & Roman, 2003). Third, these experiences may increase vulnerability to a variety of risks and stressors through other social statuses (e.g., social class, marital status) and social contexts (e.g., neighborhood; Williams & Sternthal, 2010). Fourth, as a source of stress, gendered racism can have direct adverse effects on cognitive and emotional functioning through psychobiological pathways, including acute neuroendocrine response and allostatic load (Massey, 2004). Over time, brain structure permanently adapts to severe and chronic stress, making individuals less cognitively resilient and more vulnerable to psychological disorder in response to subsequent stressors (Fremont & Bird, 2000). As a pervasive feature of the social condition of black women, exposure to gendered racism can shape biological processes in ways that critically determine individuals' subsequent health trajectories and well-being.

These findings have important implications for policies and practices that could help reduce racial and ethnic health disparities, only a few of which are discussed here. First, the U.S. government should enact or maintain policies that are likely to reduce prejudice and discrimination, such as increasing racial and ethnic integration in housing and employment. Evidence suggests that having common goals and increasing regular, positive, and meaningful social contact between individuals of different races reduces racist attitudes and behaviors (Pettigrew, 1998).

Second, it is crucial to reduce the extent to which the media introduce and perpetuate gendered racism through inaccurate portrayals of black women. Television shows, news stories, and music videos that debunk myths and stereotypes about black women as welfare mothers on the one hand, or as sexually promiscuous and emasculating on the other, may alter societal perceptions of this group over time. Likewise, public service announcements or educational programming that increase awareness and discussion of gendered racism and related stereotypes may encourage attitude change.

Third, because our findings indicate that coping resources like social support and positive ethnic identity may reduce the harmful effects of gendered racism, one way to combat health disparities may be to strengthen positive ethnic group identification and bonds between women and girls of color. For instance, community organizations and government programs should create opportunities for participation in black cultural activities. Likewise, it is important for teachers, parents, and other role models to openly discuss and discourage racism and sexism; to encourage black girls to have pride in their ethnic identity; and to involve young people of all races and ethnicities in black customs and traditions. These practices may help to build a strong sense of belonging and social integration, enhancing blacks' ability to cope proactively with the stress of concurrent racism, sexism, and often socioeconomic disadvantage.

References

Andersen, M. L., & Hill-Collins, P. (Eds.). (2004). *Race, class, and gender: An anthology* (5th ed.). Belmont, CA: Wadsworth Thompson Learning.

Aneshensel, C. S., Rutter, C. M., & Lachenbruch, P. A. (1991). Social structure, stress, and mental health: Competing conceptual and analytic models. *American Sociological Review, 56,* 166–178.

Bird, C. E., & Rieker, P. P. (2008). *Gender and health: The effects of constrained choices and social policies.* New York, NY: Cambridge University Press.

Bolzendahl, C., & Meyers, D. J. (2004). Feminist attitudes and support for gender equality: Opinion change in women and men, 1974–1998. *Social Forces, 83,* 759–790.

Brewster, K. L., & Padavic, I. (2000). Change in gender-ideology, 1977–1996: The contributions of intracohort change and population turnover. *Journal of Marriage and Family, 62,* 477–487.

Brown, D. R., & Keith, V. M. (2003). *In and out of our right minds.* New York, NY: Columbia University Press.

Brown, D. R., Keith, V. M., Jackson, J. S., & Gary, L. E. (2003). (Dis)respected and (dis)regarded: Experiences of racism and psychological distress. In D. Brown & V. Keith (Eds.), *In and out of our right minds* (pp. 83–98). New York, NY: Columbia University Press.

Brown, T. N., Williams, D. R., Jackson, J. S., Neighbors, H. W., Torres, M., Sellers, S. L., & Brown, K. T. (2000). Being black and feeling blue: The mental health consequences of racial discrimination. *Race and Society, 2,* 117–131.

Clark, R., Anderson, N. B., Clark, V. R., & Williams, D. R. (1999). Racism as a stressor for African Americans: A biopsychosocial model. *American Psychologist, 54,* 805–816.

Clawson, R., & Trice, R. (2000). Poverty as we know it: Media portrayals of the poor. *Public Opinion Quarterly, 64,* 53–64.

Collins, P. H. (2000). *Black feminist thought: Knowledge, consciousness, and the politics of empowerment (Revised tenth anniversary edition)* (2nd ed.). New York, NY: Routledge.

Crenshaw, K. (1991). Mapping the margins: Intersectionality, identity, politics, and violence against women of color. *Stanford Law Review, 43,* 1241–1299.

Dohrenwend, B. P., Levav, I., Shrout, P. E., Schwartz, S., Naveh, G., Link, B. G., Skodol, A. E., & Stueve, A. (1992). Socioeconomic status and psychiatric disorders: The causation-selection issue. *Science, 255,* 946–952.

Essed, P. (1991). *Understanding everyday racism.* Newbury Park, CA: Sage.

Fremont, A. M., & Bird, C. E. (2000). Social and psychological factors, physiological processes, and physical health. In C. Bird, P. Conrad, & A. Fremont (Eds.), *Handbook of medical sociology* (pp. 334–352). Upper Saddle River, NJ: Prentice-Hall.

Gilens, M. (2000). *Why Americans hate welfare: Race, media, and the politics of antipoverty policy.* Chicago, IL: University of Chicago Press.

Greer, T. M., Laseter, A., & Asiamah, D. (2009). Gender as a moderator of the relation between race-related stress and mental health symptoms for African Americans. *Psychology of Women Quarterly, 33,* 295–307.

Hankin, J. R., & Wright, E. R. (2010, S). Reflections on fifty years of medical sociology. *Journal of Health and Social Behavior, 51,* S10–S15.

Harrell, S. P. (2000). A multidimensional conceptualization of racism-related stress: Implications for the well-being of people of color. *American Journal of Orthopsychiatry, 70,* 42–57.

hooks, b. (1981). *Ain't I a woman: Black women and feminism.* Boston, MA: South End Press.

House, J. S., Landis, K. R., & Umberson, D. (1988). Social relationships and health. *Science, 241,* 40–45.

Hull, G., Scott, P. B., & Smith, B. (1982). *All the women are white, all the blacks are men, but some of us are brave: Black women's studies.* New York, NY: Feminist Press.

Jackson, F. M., Phillips, M. T., Hogue, C. J., & Curry-Owens, T. Y. (2001). Examining the burdens of gendered racism: Implications for pregnancy outcomes among college-educated African American women. *Maternal and Child Health Journal, 5,* 95–107.

Jackson, J. S., Brown, T. N., Williams, D. R., Torres, M., Sellers, S. L., & Brown, K. T. (1996). Racism and the physical and mental health status of African Americans: A thirteen year national panel study. *Ethnicity and Disease, 6,* 132–147.

Karlsen, S., & Nazroo, J. Y. (2002). Relation between racial discrimination, social class, and health among ethnic minority groups. *American Journal of Public Health, 92,* 624–631.

Kessler, R. C., Michelson, K. D., & Williams, D. R. (1999). The prevalence, distribution, and mental health correlates of perceived discrimination in the United States. *Journal of Health and Social Behavior, 40,* 208–230.

King, K. R. (2003). Racism or sexism? Attributional ambiguity and simultaneous membership in multiple oppressed groups. *Journal of Applied Social Psychology, 33,* 223–247.

King, K. R. (2005). Why is discrimination stressful? The mediating role of cognitive appraisal. *Cultural Diversity and Ethnic Minority Psychology, 11,* 202–212.

Klonoff, E. A., & Landrine, H. (1995). The schedule of sexist events: A measure of lifetime and recent sexist discrimination in women's lives. *Psychology of Women Quarterly, 19,* 439–472.

Klonoff, E. A., Landrine, H., & Campbell, R. (2000). Sexist discrimination may account for well-known gender differences in psychiatric symptoms. *Psychology of Women Quarterly, 24,* 93–99.

Klonoff, E. A., Landrine, H., & Ullman, J. B. (1999). Racial discrimination and psychiatric symptoms among Blacks. *Cultural Diversity and Ethnic Minority Psychology, 5,* 329–339.

Krieger, N. (1990). Racial and gender discrimination: Risk factors for high blood pressure? *Social Science & Medicine, 30,* 1273–1281.

Krieger, N. (2000). Discrimination and health. In L. Berkman & I. Kawachi (Eds.), *Social epidemiology* (pp. 36–75). Oxford, UK: Oxford University Press.

Kung, H. C., Hoyert, D. L., Xu, J., & Murphy, S. L. (2008). Deaths: Final data for 2005. *National Vital Statistics Reports, 56*(10), 4–26.

Kwate, N. O. A., Valdimarsdottir, H. B., Guevarra, J. S., & Bovbjerg, D. H. (2003). Experiences of racist events are associated with negative health consequences for African American women. *Journal of the National Medical Association, 95,* 450–460.

Landrine, H., & Klonoff, E. A. (1996). The schedule of racist events: A measure of racial discrimination and a study of its negative physical and mental

health consequences. *Journal of Black Psychology, 22,* 144–168.

Landrine, H., & Klonoff, E. A. (1997). *Discrimination against women: Prevalence, consequences, remedies.* Thousand Oaks, CA: Sage.

Landrine, H., Klonoff, E. A., Gibbs, J., Manning, V., & Lund, M. (1995). Physical and psychiatric correlates of gender discrimination: An application of the schedule of sexist events. *Psychology of Women Quarterly, 19,* 473–492.

Martin, J., Tuch, S. A., & Roman, P. M. (2003). Problem drinking patterns among African Americans: The impacts of reports of discrimination, perceptions of prejudice, and "risky" coping strategies. *Journal of Health and Social Behavior, 44,* 408–425.

Massey, D. S. (2004). Segregation and stratification: A biosocial perspective. *Du Bois Review: Social Science Research on Race, 1,* 7–25.

Massey, D. S., & Denton, N. A. (1993). *American apartheid: Segregation and the making of the underclass.* Cambridge, MA: Harvard University Press.

Moradi, B., & Linda Subich, L. M. (2003). A concomitant examination of the relations of perceived racist and sexist events to psychological distress for African American women. *Counseling Psychologist, 31,* 451–469.

Morello-Frosch, R., & Shenassa, E. D. (2006). The environmental "riskscape" and social inequality: Implications for explaining maternal and child health disparities. *Environmental Health Perspectives, 114,* 1150–1153.

Morenoff, J. D. (2003). Neighborhood mechanisms and the spatial dynamics of birth weight. *American Journal of Sociology, 108,* 976–1017.

Pavalko, E. K., Mossakowski, K. N., & Hamilton, V. J. (2003). Does perceived discrimination affect health? Longitudinal relationships between work discrimination and women's physical and emotional health. *Journal of Health and Social Behavior, 44,* 18–33.

Pearlin, L. I. (1999). Stress and mental health: A conceptual overview. In A. Horwitz & T. Scheid (Eds.), *A handbook for the study of mental health: Social contexts, theories, and systems* (pp. 161–175). New York, NY: Cambridge University Press.

Perry, B. L., Harp, K. L. H., & Oser, C. B. (2013). Racial and gender discrimination in the stress process: Implications for African American women's health and well-being. *Sociological Perspectives, 56,* 25–48.

Perry, B. L., Pullen, E. L., & Oser, C. B. (2012). Too much of a good thing? Psychosocial resources, gendered racism, and suicidal ideation among low socioeconomic status African American women. *Social Psychology Quarterly, 75,* 334–359.

Pettigrew, T. (1998). Intergroup contact theory. *Annual Review of Psychology, 49,* 65–85.

Polednak, A. P. (1993). Poverty, residential segregation, and black/white mortality ratios in urban areas. *Journal of Health Care for the Poor and Underserved, 4,* 363–373.

Sellers, R. M., Caldwell, C. H., Schmeelk-Cone, K. H., & Zimmerman, M. A. (2003). Racial identity, racial discrimination, perceived stress, and psychological distress among African American young adults. *Journal of Health and Social Behavior, 44,* 302–317.

Stevens-Watkins, D., Perry, B. L., Harp, K. L. H., & Oser, C. B. (2012). Racism and illicit drug use among Black women: The protective effects of ethnic identity, affirmation, and behavior. *Journal of Black Psychology, 38,* 471–496.

Swim, J. K., Aikin, K. J., Hall, W. S., & Hunter, B. A. (1995). Sexism and racism: Old-fashioned and modern prejudices. *Journal of Personality and Social Psychology, 68,* 199–214.

Taylor, S. E., Repetti, R. L., & Seeman, T. (1997). Health psychology: What is an unhealthy environment and how does it get under the skin? *Annual Review of Psychology, 48,* 411–447.

Thomas, A. J., Witherspoon, K. M., & Speight, S. L. (2008). Gendered racism, psychological distress, and coping styles of African American women. *Cultural Diversity and Ethnic Minority Psychology, 14,* 307–314.

Utsey, S. O., Ponterotto, J. G., Reynolds, A. L., & Cancelli, A. A. (2000). Racial discrimination, coping, life satisfaction, and self-esteem among African Americans. *Journal of Counseling and Development, 78,* 72–80.

Van der Lippe, T., de Ruijter, J., de Ruijter, E., & Raub, W. (2011). Persistent inequalities in time use between men and women: A detailed look at the influence of economic circumstances, policies, and culture. *European Sociological Review, 27,* 164–179.

Wellman, D. T. (1993). *Portraits of white racism.* New York, NY: Cambridge University Press.

Williams, D. R., & Collins, C. (1995). U.S. socioeconomic and racial differences in health: Patterns and explanations. *Annual Review of Sociology, 21,* 349–386.

Williams, D. R., & Mohammed, S. A. (2009). Discrimination and racial disparities in health: Evidence and needed research. *Journal of Behavioral Medicine, 32,* 20–47.

Williams, D. R., & Sternthal, M. (2010). Understanding racial-ethnic disparities in health: Sociological contributions. *Journal of Health and Social Behavior, 51*(1S), S15–S27.

Williams, D. R., & Williams-Morris, R. (2000). Racism and mental health: The African American experience. *Ethnicity and Health, 5,* 243–268.

Woods-Giscombé, C. L. & Lobel, M. (2008). Race and gender matter: A multidimensional approach to conceptualizing and measuring stress in African American women. *Cultural Diversity and Ethnic Minority Psychology, 14,* 173–182.

4

Women's Homelessness and the Role of Violence

Not Just a Personal Problem

Jennifer K. Wesely

Homelessness is a social problem that provokes controversial reactions on the part of the public. Stigma and stereotype tend to fuel dominant perceptions of this group. Typically, these misguided assumptions focus on the individual homeless person, zeroing in on what personal weaknesses or failings could possibly make someone supposedly choose to be homeless. Even the mental picture of a homeless person skews toward an "older man with a scraggly beard pushing a shopping cart" who is mentally ill and has alcohol or drug problems, as Wakin (2011) describes what is conjured up in the minds of her college students (p. 73). These images are media-driven or drawn from what is seen on the streets in major cities. Subsequently, the homeless are often feared as dangerous, a perception furthered by media portrayals of crimes committed by them (Donley, 2008; Snow, Baker, & Anderson, 1989). These stereotypes take on greater significance as they steer political agendas and policy that adversely affect the lives of those trying to survive on the streets. For instance, political and media pressures to get the homeless out of sight influence treatment by police, and recent attempts to criminalize activities associated with homelessness, such as sleeping in public places and panhandling, reflect public attitudes (National Law Center on Homelessness and Poverty and the National Coalition for the Homeless, 2009).

On the academic front, some headway has been made in providing a more complex understanding of homelessness. Yet existing research on homelessness has historically used men's experiences as the standard. When theories began to include female experiences, it was using the "add-women-and-stir approach" (Daly & Chesney-Lind, 1988), plugging girls and women into existing understandings based on men's experiences. Like the image of the "older man with a scraggly beard," this barely scratches the surface of the true face of homelessness. Being attentive to the relevance of gender includes awareness of how "inequalities between the sexes can differentially affect male and female experiences and behaviors" (Belknap, 2007, p. 4) and impact the level of understanding about homelessness.

In this chapter, I draw from in-depth qualitative interviews with women living in a homeless shelter to explore aspects of the social contexts that shape the nature of their homelessness. At the time of the interviews, the ages of the women ranged from 19 to 62 years, with an average age of 40 years. The race and ethnicity of the women was diverse, and they identified themselves as six African Americans, three Hispanics, one African American/American Indian, one Puerto Rican/African American and nine whites. Interviews took place in a private conference room or sitting room on site at the homeless shelter, and were originally conducted as part of a project funded by the National Institute of Justice, resulting in a book called *Hard Lives, Mean Streets: Violence in the Lives of Homeless Women* (Jasinski, Wesely, Wright, & Mustaine, 2010). For this chapter, I will use the interviews to focus on how violence and abuse against the women in their childhood and adult lives severely narrowed their life options and both initiated and maintained their homelessness.

CHILDHOOD EXPERIENCES AND EARLY INDEPENDENCE

In this section, I will discuss the violent childhoods experienced by many of the women I interviewed. I will continue by explaining how the desire to escape these environments led to the women's departure from their homes at a young age, which often resulted in living on the streets or ending up in other situations of high risk to more exploitation and violence. These conditions played a major role in their homelessness.

Childhood Victimization

The early lives of the women I interviewed included a substantial amount of violence. The majority endured some sort of physical or sexual abuse as children, with nearly all identifying experiences of emotional abuse or neglect. These experiences were situated within larger contexts of social exclusion, poverty, and lack of access to resources. For example, Amelia was shuttled between numerous caretakers for most of her childhood and adolescence. She lived with her father until the age of 9, when he died. She then moved in with her brother for a year and a half, and then her grandmother from ages 11 to 15, who then also died. Amelia finally moved in with her mother, only to be kicked out at age 18 by a new stepfather. It took her less than a year to become homeless. Eliza is a similar case. She lived with her mother, father, and siblings until she was age 7. Because of violence and drinking between her parents, she then lived with her uncle for a year. After returning to her parents at age 8, she was removed by the state and sent to a children's home. After a year or two, she was sent back home, where she was molested by her father and physically, verbally, and emotionally abused. She was beaten by her mother when she tried to confide her father's abuse. The parental neglect led her to wander the streets at night looking for food and a little bit of care. The first older man she met at age 13 or 14 who fed her when she was hungry became the father of her first two children. He was both a drug addict and abusive:

> He said, "What's your name?" He was real nice; he had a pocket full of money, wallet full of money. It was a summer night and I got in his car and I felt safe. And we rode over to where we ate. And he actually fed me and I was actually full . . . He would feed me. I would

be hungry. And I would still go home and act like this kid I was. But I'd get hungry. And sometimes there wasn't a pot of beans or some bread in the oven and I'd go find it. And he'd say, "You eat?" And I'd say, "no." And he'd say, "Let's go get something to eat." He fed me . . . But again, it was a nightmare. It was a daydream, waking up from a nightmare, because I thought he was just so nice, and then after I gave up my virginity and the babies started coming, he wasn't so nice anymore. (Eliza)

The childhood lives of many of the other women were similarly chaotic. The husband of Junie's mother "hit on her" when she was age 13, telling her he was "attracted" to her. When she told her mother about this, Junie was sent to live with her grandmother, and when that arrangement ended, she went to live with her biological father, who had begun sexually molesting her at age 7. Junie lived with the father from ages 14 to 16 and was molested by him more or less continually throughout this period. At age 16 or so, she was put in a group home which she eventually "traded in" for a life on the streets.

Childhood Messages and Heightened Risks

When it came to messages about their value as girls and women, participants recalled hearing about how women were only good for one thing, and that one thing did not count for much. Eliza's father told her she should have been a boy, adding, "You're gonna grow up and be a whore and have a belly full of babies. And you're not gonna be any good." Both Ruby and Mo learned that men only wanted women for sex, and that they should use their sexuality to their advantage. Mo remembers seeing her mother with many different men, and reflects on a conversation when her mother told her, "Oh, if you ever want to get a guy's attention, wear this kind of stuff, act this way, do this." These gender-specific attacks were messages absorbed by the girls about what it meant to be a woman. In a different scenario with a similar effect, Ruby learned by both precept and example that selling her body was a technique to get what she wanted.

> She [the mother] used to come to school and beat me at school in front of my classmates. Beat me going down the street, in the grocery store, anywhere. She didn't care . . . She didn't teach me to be—how can I put this—how to grow up. She never taught me how to depend on you and just do for you. She taught me to lay up with the men to get what I want. You know, I thought that's what I was supposed to do. I was supposed to go to bed with all these different men to get what I want.

Having observed her mother acting as a de facto prostitute in the neighborhood, Ruby learned very specifically what she was "supposed to do." This introduced her to a dynamic with men that put her at high risk for exploitation and abuse, and which ultimately came to characterize her adult relationships.

The Bureau of Justice Statistics (Snyder, 2000) determined that 86% of all victims of sexual assault are female: 69% of victims are under 6 years of age, 73% of victims are under 12 years of age, and 82% of victims are under 18 years of age. Many studies find that homeless women have experienced child sexual abuse at a higher rate than homeless men (McCormack, Janus, & Burgess, 1986; Whitbeck & Hoyt, 1999; Whitbeck & Simmons, 1990). For example, the Midwest Longitudinal Study of Homeless Adolescents (MLSHA) shows higher rates of sexual abuse among girls (32.1%) than boys (10%) (Whitbeck & Hoyt, 2002). So does the Seattle Homeless Adolescent Research and Education Project (SHARE), in which females report higher rates (44%) of child sexual abuse compared to males (18%) (Tyler & Cauce, 2002). Although the narratives of the women I interviewed might sound sensationalized or extreme, they are not; far from the most horrific stories, these are, tragically, the relatively common lived experiences of the interviewees. Rena recounted a long history of sexual violence, beginning in third grade when she was raped by a school janitor. During her childhood, her mother attempted to kill her, her father molested and attempted to rape her, and she was gang-raped at age 14. Sara was physically abused by her father, mother, and siblings and molested repeatedly by her best friend's father when she was 8 years old. April was first molested by her step-uncle at age 2, a pattern that continued until she turned 13 years old. Tamara was molested from the ages of 7 to 9 by a female family friend, was raped by her sister's husband when she was 14 years old, and was beaten throughout her childhood by her father. Examples of a similar nature continue, but the experiences of Rena, Sara, April, Tamara, and the others I've already described certainly illustrate the severe abuse that characterized the childhoods of the women.

Lack of Protection and Social Indifference

While they were children, the women's victimizations were frequently ignored, even by close family members, and this lack of intervention was often compounded by blame. Eliza tried to confide in her mother when her biological father began molesting her at age 7 or 8:

> I went into her room one day and I said, "Ma, I have to tell you something." She said, "What?" I said, "Daddy was touching me." She said, "What are you talking about? He wasn't touching you." I said, "Yes, he was, Ma. He was touching me." And she beat me. She beat me because [in her mind] I lied on my father.

Ruby's mother responded similarly when she confided her father's molestation. "But she didn't ever believe me. She said I was a whore. She said I deserved it." Even when the police became involved, the women described situations where the abusers evaded the criminal justice system. Diane's father "terrorized the whole neighborhood," she said. She describes,

> The police were called on him several different times but he always managed to get himself out of it. Once I remember the police came and he faked a heart attack so instead of going to jail, he went to the hospital. He was very manipulative. He was very smart. So he worked the system rather well.

Diane also detailed a particular episode of violence where her father beat her before she left for school. Her black eye and welts on her back drew the attention of school personnel, but when called, her father beat her again, right in front of school officials. In April's case, her abusive step-uncle got a "slap on the wrist" from the court system because there was "insufficient evidence" to sanction him more severely. Dee told her mother about the sexual abuse she experienced at the hands of two teenage male cousins beginning when she was age 5 or 6 and the mother called the police, but that did not end the abuse. "We used to move around a lot," she said, "so that he [one of the cousins] wouldn't know where we were staying. But everywhere we moved, he always knew where we stayed and he always kept his promise" (to return and sexually abuse her). In addition to the feelings of vulnerability and fear generated by institutional indifference, the lack of criminal justice response reinforced the women's distrust in the systems that were supposed to protect them.

Early Independence

The childhood abuse that many women suffered was situated within a grim matrix of social, economic, and interpersonal conditions. Though the women I interviewed self-identified across a range of diverse ethnicities, my findings concerning the intersectionalities of race with gender and poverty are limited. However, it has been found that racism and racial inequality do shape risks for girls and overlap with other oppressions. Scholars like Raphael (2004), Schaffner (2006), and Miller (2008) discuss this in light of the disadvantaged populations of adolescents and young women they study. It has been noted that "sexism and racism combine with class exploitation to produce a three-edged mode of oppression for women of color" (Marable, 2004, p. 163). In my study, the participants recalled being hungry, being on welfare, parental drug and alcohol use, and long periods of neglect when they were alone or poorly supervised at a very young age. Molly describes, "Many times the gas was off, the electricity was off. We ate oatmeal and split pea soup for dinner, breakfast and lunch . . . And the rent wasn't paid, we was all this kind of mess. It was really some bad times." Cammie remembers in her early teenage years that she would leave home for entire weekends without her alcoholic mother even noticing that her daughter was gone. Common throughout the narratives, these lived experiences shook an already fragile sense of self and agency for these women. They also led to the women's transience, displacement, and often a permanent departure from the childhood home while at a young age, known as *early independence*. Sara's childhood is illustrative: she left home at age 15 because she was "tired of being a punching bag." While staying at a hotel she had a severe asthma attack and the Department of Children and Families again became involved, mandating her father to pay for her apartment. During this time, she got pregnant, having her first child at age 15.

In *Neither Angels Nor Demons: Women, Crime and Victimization*, Ferraro (2006) draws on in-depth interviews with 45 criminally offending women and finds that almost all of them married or became "intimately involved with men as a way out of their parents' homes" (p. 131). More specifically, Ferraro noted that "It was often an experience of sexual abuse or assault, at home or by a stranger, that preceded a young woman's pregnancy and decision to leave home" (p. 132). For the women I interviewed, pregnancy or a young marriage sometimes seemed to be a way to escape the childhood environment. Diane, who married at age 18, stated,

> I mean, I ran away from home, I got out and got married and started having kids just to get away from that. And if I wouldn't have been brought up the way I was brought, maybe things would have been different. Maybe I would have gone to school. Maybe I would have waited to have kids and my life would have been more stable and things wouldn't have happened the way they happened.

Diane ultimately ended up homeless after losing her children, losing her home, and leaving her abuser.

Other women I interviewed became homeless early on because it appeared that living on the streets would be the lesser of the evils compared to a violent home. Such situations contributed to the economic instability of the women. Sara, the woman who left home because of severe abuse and had her first child at age 15, says, "But I guess being at the age of 14, 15 years old, you can't fend for yourself, you can't get a job, nothing." The difficulty of supporting themselves at young ages was a major factor in their eventual homelessness, but some still framed this as a choice prefer-able to a violent home. Mo recalled that she became homeless the first time to escape her abusive father, saying, "I just know I kinda left for a little while and [my father] didn't know where I was for about two or three years. I did that on purpose. I didn't contact no one in my family for a long time . . . In my case, sometimes it was a choice because I didn't want to be found. I didn't want nobody to know me so it was easier to be homeless."

Increased Vulnerabilities and Survival Strategies

However, running away and early independence actually create more vulnerability to violent victimization for girls. This is called "risk amplification" (Chen, Tyler, Whitbeck, & Hoyt, 2004, p. 1), and "unlike boys, girls' victimization and their response to that vic-timization is specifically shaped by their status as young women" (Chesney-Lind & Pasko, 2004, p. 27).

> By being a woman—a homeless woman that's on the street, it's dangerous. You have home-less men, and it's co-ed when you're sleeping on the street. It's co-ed and some of them approach women that want women to give them favors sexually. Too, sometimes, they get bold enough, they try to rape the women, and a lot of homeless women do be raped. Raped and murdered. They will murder them in the alleyways and you will find home-less women in the dumpster. Someone slit her throat . . . Always, the homeless women are being approached in the street by homeless men that want to have sex with them, oral sex with them. Some of them offer them money and some of them don't offer them any-thing, or tell them they'll beat them up if they don't. And most of the homeless women are scared, and they'll go ahead and do it . . . Mostly homeless women that don't have checks monthly, how they make their money is tricking to regular men that have families, wives and children. They park on the corners; they meet them at certain times, and these are homeless women. That's how they survive. They do that as we speak. (Tamara)

From Tamara's statement we get the sense that homeless women may be, literally, scared into sex; sex then becomes a strategy for negotiating the streets, if not surviving them. When girls are at a particularly young age the first time they leave home, the likelihood increases that they engage in strategies like survival sex (having sex in exchange for protection, food, or some other essential) (Tyler, Whitbeck, Hoyt, & Cauce, 2004). This is what happened to Marion:

> Well, I remember one time while I was homeless I was walking down the street crying. I was crying—it was late at night and I was tired and I was scared because it was like a weekend and there was a lot of people on the street. And they was looking at me and I was scared and this guy stopped. And he said, "Are you ok?" And I told him no and he said "Why?" because I told him that I stunk so bad that people thought I was a dope addict and I'm not, I was just homeless and he said, "Well, you could come to my house and take a shower" and he said "I won't bother you." And he was a young good-looking guy and I told him ok, you know? So he took me to his place—he said I couldn't spend the night because he had roommates. You know, but he would give me—he said he had some clean clothes and I could take a shower. And he would give me something to eat. So I got—he gave his word . . . He got in the shower. He got in the shower with me. I had sex with him.

When I asked her, "Do you feel like you had sex with him in exchange for these things [i.e., clothes, food, shower]?" Marion seems unsure, replying, "No, he made me feel—I guess he made me feel that I had sex with him because I wanted to have sex with him." Marion does not narrate the event as one of straightforward sexual exchange. She struggles to clarify or explain this event, in which the man capitalized on his position of offering the basic necessities like food, shower, and clothing that Marion desperately needed.

Sex work becomes a viable possibility for young girls trying to survive on the streets. In their study of twenty exotic dancers, Sweet and Tewksbury (2000) discovered that early independence was the most influential factor in choosing an exotic dancing career for the women they interviewed, and Monto and Hotaling (2001) found that a substantial number of prostitutes were minors when they began working. In our book, we found that survival strategies of prostitution and exotic dancing were more than twice as likely to occur among women who left a violent childhood environment (Jasinski et al., 2010). This is consistent with existing literature, which finds large numbers of women in the sex work industry have experienced child victimization, especially sexual abuse. According to Raphael (2004), in the 20 most recent prostitution studies, the lowest percentage of the women sexually abused as children is one third, with 84% being the highest. Within a larger context of gender inequality, limited survival options on the street target young women for sex work, thus putting girls at even greater risk for harm (Chesney-Lind & Irwin, 2008). While trying to survive these environments, "a young woman alone on the streets is often 'fair game' for male violence" (Gilfus, 2006, p. 10). Street prostitution, in particular, is dangerous. One of the women, Tracy, worked as a prostitute for 27 years:

> You don't have feelings when you are messing with a client—a trick. So I don't trip with that. When he gets up on top of me, I just say, ok, what am I going to do with this man's money, now. That's what I do. I've been shot, raped, kidnapped. I was sodomized, the whole nine yards. From tricks. Pulled a gun . . . I can't let my head think about the things that I've been through.

It is deeply tragic that, for the women I interviewed, the desire to escape violence and chaos in childhood was not achieved by leaving. Instead, early independence amplified the women's risks of exposure to violent victimization. Still, they continued to dream of a new family, being loved, and a better life. In Ruby's words:

> I didn't want to live at home no more. I didn't want to—to be honest, when I was growing up I didn't want my own family. I didn't want to be a part of my family. I wanted to be in somebody else's family. To be happy. Because there was no love.

VIOLENCE, ADULT HOMELESSNESS, AND RESISTING THE CYCLE

Many of the women described a strong drive to leave their childhood memories behind and create a new, happy family. They ran away from home or got involved with men as a way to escape. From here, their lives did not follow linear, straightforward paths. Whether or not they became homeless immediately, they still typically experienced episodes of homelessness, moving in and out of temporary living conditions, sometimes alone, sometimes with partners. They experienced violent victimization due to risk amplification on the streets and heightened exposure to danger, and they also experienced it at the hands of boyfriends and husbands. In this section I will discuss how violence and homelessness were intertwined in the women's lives and how this occurred repeatedly and in many different circumstances. Natalie stated:

> I think the violence and abuse probably led to [the homelessness] because when I get down in the dumps, I'm always thinking about all that bad stuff. And then I've been through so much trauma in the last couple of years that I just felt so beat down and just so lost and I'm asking myself, how did I go from self-sufficient, taking care of myself, to I was losing everything?

From within these dismal realities, was it possible for the women to move toward their dreams of love and happiness? Next, I will also address how they struggled within their daily lives to resist repeating their pasts.

Normalized Violence and Family Ideals

Eliza described her mindset growing up:

> I thought it was the way life was. Because in the neighborhood I grew up in, it was nothing to see a woman dragged, knocked down, stomped, and beat. And there was no safe house, there was no shelter that a wife or woman could run to and be protected. So, many women, including my mother—they stood there and they took it. But I saw a lot of women die as a result of being abused. I would tell my mother, he's killing her over there, Ma. And she'd say, leave it alone. So I took on that generational trait. You were just supposed to take it.

Tamara also recalled that male abuse during most of her young life seemed normalized: "I had watched [my father] beat my mother with a belt just like he beat us . . . All my life seeing my father beat my mother with a belt, [and] my sister's abusive husband that raped me and beat me." With these early lives so steeped in violence, the women had strong instincts to avoid this in adulthood. Sara, who I described earlier as leaving home and having her first child at age 15, looked for someone to love her like her family had not. She had six more children by the age of 25, when I interviewed her. For the past eight years (since she was age 17) she had been involved with an extremely abusive man. She says, "I guess I was trying to get affection from anywhere I could, because I wasn't getting it from my father or my parents. So I guess when the other two guys showed me affection, I just kinda clinged to it." The man who became her husband continuously smoked crack cocaine and beat her. When she tried to leave him, he would not allow her to take her children. Sara ended up homeless with her abuser and children. When her children were officially removed from her care and her abuser threatened to kill her one final time, she left him behind and went to a homeless shelter.

When Cammie left home and got married at age 18, she saw her marriage as the start of a new family blueprint:

> Because I was very much in love with the guy that I was marrying and I had it in my head that I was going to be able to show my parents that you could have a marriage and make it work and you know, children, and not have alcohol and drugs in the middle of it and do things right. And I mean, I looked at it in a very positive light . . . My thought was, I'm going to show everybody in my family, especially my parents that you can have a family and you can do it right.

Raphael's (2000) book, *Saving Bernice: Battered Women, Welfare and Poverty*, addresses the efforts that women who grow up in chaotic environments of extreme poverty or sexual violence put toward attaining the ideologically normal, nuclear family. Raphael references the work of Beth Richie (1996), who found battered black women trying to make nuclear families work against all odds. When these relationships became violent, "the physical and emotional abuse so deeply contradicted the women's expectations that they initially deny the seriousness and rationalize the abuse, ultimately finding themselves isolated and in very dangerous situations" (Raphael, 2000, p. 17). Likewise, Cammie (quoted above), endured mental and physical abuse from her husband that went on for years even as she struggled to attain her dream of having a family and "doing it right." "Doing it right" was difficult, if not impossible, from within such a context.

Adult Intimate Partner Relationships and Their Effects

It was rare that the women's adult lives and relationships met their expectations for safety, security, comfort, or love. Over the course of their adulthood, they had different relationships, not all of which had a clear beginning or end. Sometimes the women had partners who would disappear and re-emerge, or they had nonmonogamous or less serious relationships. Different circumstances and experiences in adult relationships sometimes compounded an economic vulnerability that contributed to the women's becoming or remaining homeless. After Cammie left her first abusive husband, whom she had married at age 18, she met her second husband, whom she remained married to for 14 years. She described this as a happy marriage which ended tragically when he was killed in a hit-and-run car accident. At this point, she deteriorated emotionally. "In a four year period of time, my youngest son got killed, my husband got killed, my mother died, my oldest half sister died, and my baby sister died. And I kind of lost my bearings." These losses left her vulnerable, so vulnerable that she was "easy pickings" for the next man in her life, an incredibly violent and financially exploitative man who left her with nothing:

> I did have a little bit of insurance money from when my husband got killed, and between that and what I was making, I was doing ok. Well, then I met this guy and he got into my life and he basically drained me dry. And then I couldn't afford my house payments. My house got into foreclosure and I kept believing what this guy was telling me . . . And I lost my house and so for a year and a half, I was kind of dependent on this guy that I got involved with because we started moving around so much and my car broke down and I didn't have a way to get to work, so I lost my job. Wherever we would stay, if it was a hotel or whatever, I would start trying to get a job. There were days I couldn't even get him to leave me a dollar twenty to get on the bus to go look for a job or when I got a job, to even have the bus fare to get to the job . . . It was a vicious cycle—it didn't matter how much money I made, I couldn't save the money I made, you know? I was forever giving the money over to him or I was trying to pay the rent.

Moe and Bell's (2004) interviews with intimate partner violence victims demonstrate how women struggle to maintain employment amidst abuse. These findings are corroborated by narratives like Cammie's. Further, with her under his control and dependent upon him, this man would be severely violent to Cammie, on different occasions throwing her across the room and tearing the rotator cuff in her shoulder, knocking out her teeth, or head-butting her and breaking her nose. She often called the police for protection and during one call was told that in the last 30 days she had phoned them 15 times. In looking at the progression of Cammie's relationships, it is possible to see how she became so vulnerable to homelessness. In the most recent relationship, the spiral into destitution was facilitated by the boyfriend's violence, exploitation, and control, but Cammie asserts that this relationship never would have occurred if she had not been so grief-stricken by the loss of her loved ones.

Male partners like Cammie's drained the women financially in a range of scenarios, including using family money for drugs, threatening or perpetrating violence, reinforcing economic dependence through limiting or depriving the women of resources, or leaving the woman to be the only breadwinner, trying to support the entire family on meager wages. Diane described a relationship in which her abusive husband had a job with benefits and insurance for her children. Because she did not want to lose this economic support for the kids, she endured beatings that frequently landed her in the hospital. She got multiple restraining orders against the husband, one of which resulted in a domestic violence conviction. Diane also became mired in drug use, numbing herself to get through each day, and the children came to the attention of the state and were removed from the home. Both her and her husband's drug use spiraled out of control and the house went into foreclosure. At that point she escaped and became homeless, alone. In another case, Marion tried to support both herself and her husband while he frittered away money on drugs and threatened her with violence. She said, "He started using more drugs than he could sell, you know . . . And I kept on trying to hold the house together. He stopped giving me money so I had to pay all the bills and stuff . . . I would wake up and he would be holding a chair over my head . . ." It is evident that when intimate partner violence is part of the relationship, the economics of the situation became more convoluted. The partner's power and control tactics generated the women's fear, and their attention narrowed to daily survival and safety for themselves and their children. For many, this left them even more vulnerable to financial exploitation. Sara's husband told her that if she left him he would kill her, and even found her location when she fled to a domestic violence shelter. She said, "I've had knots all throughout my head from him hitting me in the head with his hands and fists. I've had several busted noses, busted mouth, huge bite marks on my arms." As I mentioned above, it was only when she felt she lost everything—her children—that she risked his threats and went to the homeless shelter.

As we can see, hopes for a better life dwindled as burdens of abusive relationships, unstable living conditions and damaging dynamics continued. Eliza says, "I just always knew—there was something in me that knew this way was dysfunctional. This is not the life I want. This is not the life I want for my children. And it's not how I wanted to live." She added, "I only wanted to be a nurse and wife and raise children and live in a normal house, a normal life. And that didn't come." Why was it so hard for the hopes to mesh with reality? One theory is that their abusive childhoods replaced words and dialogue with violence: "The ever-present fear of violence prevents children from developing capabilities for hearing and knowing . . . Because of its unpredictable nature, violence interferes with this necessary sense of an ordered world, essential for the development of healthy children" (Raphael, 2000, p. 19). The abusive childhoods experienced by the women were contexts in which the development of emotional and intellectual skills necessary for successful relationships were absent or disordered. Ferraro (2006) notes that sexual abuse, in particular, challenges the healthy development of boundaries and self-protection for girls and found Herman's (1997) analysis helpful when analyzing the women offenders she interviewed: "The survivor has great difficulty protecting herself in the context of intimate relationships. Her desperate longing for nurturance and care makes it difficult to establish safe and appropriate boundaries with others. Her tendency to denigrate herself and to idealize those to whom she becomes attached further clouds her judgment" (Herman, 1997, pp. 111–112).

Resistance

Despite the mapping of violence across their childhood and adult lives and their ongoing or sporadic homelessness, these women worked hard to resist old patterns. In research about populations who grow up enduring child abuse, there is quite a bit of discussion about the *cycle of violence* theory, which holds as its basic argument that childhood maltreatment is a risk factor for crime and violence in adulthood (Widom, 1989a; 1989b; 1989c; 1992). It is essential to problematize the concept of cyclical violence. What I found among the women I interviewed is they attempted to disrupt the cycle of violence from within it by making decisions to actively resist or avoid victimization or perpetration in adulthood. They did not unthinkingly or passively reproduce experiences from their past.

For instance, Cammie hit a turning point after seeing the effects of her own victimization by her partner on her children. She says:

> Well, what finally made me wake up and realize that I had to leave, that I didn't have a choice is, my oldest son had gotten into school at that point and he had brought a—you know how kids draw little stick pictures of their family? The round faces and stuff? He had drawn one and on the stick figure that was supposed to be me, there were little marks on the face. The teacher asked him what they were and he said, "bruises," and the teacher sent the drawing home with a note requesting a meeting with me. That was when I realized, you know, yeah, I might have been tough enough to put up with it and to take it but it wasn't just me that was getting hurt. I had to get out of there for the kids' sake. That's what made me decide to leave.

It has been found that a catalyst event such as the abuse of a child (Barnett, Miller-Perrin, & Perrin, 2005) may be a turning point for a victim to leave a violent relationship. Eliza stepped in and took a beating for her child to protect him, and she directly identifies her subsequent departure from the relationship as a desire to "stop the cycle."

> He pushed me out of the way and he grabbed my baby and . . . he kicked [the baby]. And when he kicked him, he landed a kick right in his back and that's when I just snapped. And of course I prepared myself for the worst because I had to throw myself on the chopping block because he was—he kicked my baby and was getting ready to beat him to death. And so I took that licking but after he left, I left . . . *That's what made me break that cycle.* It was something in me that snapped that day. And I pressed charges that day and I wouldn't drop them. And he went to jail. And I never went back again. I never went back to him . . . I was glad I broke that cycle in my life, but still I knew I needed to get some healing from my childhood, because my father used to abuse me verbally very bad as well as hit me. And my mother, too. [italics added]

Unfortunately, although effective in the short term, getting out is seldom enough to permanently end cycles of violence. Such patterns are not created or erased by one cataclysmic event, but rather over time. Eliza's solution was effective, but only in that it removed her and her child from immediate danger.

The resources at the homeless shelter where the women were interviewed include individually assigned case managers who tailor services to each client (including mental and physical health and addiction treatment) and group therapy sessions. They also involve transitional housing and job and budgeting skills (including a shelter account where residents deposit money to be used upon their departure). While staying at the shelter, which both removed immediate fears about safety on the streets and provided them with services, the women were less preoccupied with day-to-day survival and more energized to thoughtfully reflect on their experiences. They invoked a cycle of violence concept as part of their growing understanding while in therapy. Sara says, "Well, my father was an alcoholic. And so he was just always in a rage. My mother, I guess she was just raised that way, so she just carried it on. And my father was abusive to her so she just took it out on me." Junie also concludes:

> Yeah, [my mom] used to hit me a lot. I just thought that maybe she didn't love me, you know. And I just thought she didn't love me, because she always on me and I was a really good student, and I did everything she wanted at home, so I couldn't understand why she was always hitting me. But then later on I realized that her mother was the same with her. Her mother would hit her and stuff.

Mo, who was physically abused by her father and spent time on the streets, utilized the shelter's parenting classes in a direct effort to disrupt cycles of violence in her life: "I've caught myself and there was one instance where I didn't catch myself and I did lash out [physically] at [my son] and I felt really crappy for it afterwards. And right now, I'm going to parenting classes [at the shelter] to break the cycle." At the point that I interviewed them, the women were at various stages of engaging and applying the therapeutic insights the shelter counselors provided. I have no way of knowing, however, to what degree the women identified the destructive patterns in their lives prior to these interventions. What is certain is that they will leave the shelter with more tools with which to cope with their patterns. Their narratives demonstrate that turning recognition into resistance against the past is problematic when lack of social supports or intervention leaves them with few strategies for lasting change. Ultimately, they were able successfully to react to events in a way that temporarily disrupted damaging patterns but that lacked longevity or permanence. When social exclusion, lack of resources, and desperate conditions allow people very little, their efforts can only succeed to the extent that it is possible within such limiting conditions.

Conclusion

This chapter began by pointing out the misconception that homelessness is just a personal issue caused by individual flaws or characteristics. It is impossible for a social problem of this magnitude to be explained away by such a myopic view. Even the picture of a homeless person to which the public tends to revert in our minds is stereotyped at best and flat-out wrong at worst. There is much more depth and complexity to the reasons behind homelessness and to the persons who suffer through it. I've focused on the ways that violence and homelessness intersect for girls and women. The solitary struggles of the homeless women I interviewed occur amidst larger oppressive and interlocking inequities which curtail the effectiveness of personal efforts to effect change. Despite these limits, the women clearly actively want or pursue change. Too often, the notions of passivity or acceptance that are implied via political or interest group sound bytes ignore these active desires and efforts. The real tragedy is that decisions the women are able to effectively put into practice as they battled for better lives provided, at most, short-term relief. In essence, the efforts of the women succeed only to the extent that it is possible while receiving little to no support. Their narratives suggest that even a small amount of long-term assistance makes a difference in their abilities to successfully disrupt patterns. If during critical junctures they had received, at minimum, attention via intervention or services, their recognition of patterns early on would have been attached to opportunities for concrete and effective steps toward change.

On a larger level, the ideological focus on the individual, which blames the victim for her victimization, her homelessness, or her choices, must shift to the structures of inequality that create such conditions in the first place. By identifying the social contexts that contribute to violence against women and homelessness, we can activate a social responsibility to lift some of the burden off the most disenfranchised to fix their own marginalization. A responsible society must address violent victimization and homelessness among children and adults—not only by redirecting resources at critical junctures of need, but with challenges to the belief systems that tacitly condone social indifference to populations like homeless women.

References

Barnett, O., Miller-Perrin, C. L., & Perrin, R. D. (2005). *Family violence across the lifespan* (2nd ed.). Thousand Oaks, CA: Sage.

Belknap, J. (2007). *The invisible woman: Gender, crime and justice* (3rd ed.). Belmont, CA: Thomson Wadsworth.

Chen, X., Tyler, K., Whitbeck, L., & Hoyt, D. (2004). Early sexual abuse, street adversity, and drug use among female homeless and runaway adolescents in the midwest. *Journal of Drug Issues, 34,* 1–21.

Chesney-Lind, M., & Irwin, K. (2008). *Beyond bad girls: Gender, violence and hype.* New York, NY: Routledge.

Chesney-Lind, M., & Pasko, L. (2004). *The female offender: Girls, women and crime* (2nd ed.). Thousand Oaks, CA: Sage.

Daly, K., & Chesney-Lind, M. (1988). Feminism and criminology. *Justice Quarterly, 5,* 497–538.

Donley, A. (2008). *The perception of homeless people: Important factors in determining perceptions of the homeless as dangerous.* Unpublished doctoral dissertation, University of Central Florida, Orlando.

Gilfus, M. E. (2006). From victims to survivors to offenders: Women's routes of entry and immersion into street crime. In L. F. Alarid & P. Cromwell (Eds.), *In her own words: Women offenders' views on crime and incarceration* (pp. 5–14). Los Angeles, CA: Roxbury.

Herman, J. (1997). *Trauma and recovery: The aftermath of violence—from domestic abuse to political terror.* New York, NY: Basic Books.

Jasinski, J. L., Wesely, J. K., Wright, J. D., & Mustaine, E. E. (2010). *Hard lives, mean streets: Violence in the lives of homeless women.* Boston, MA: Northeastern University Press.

Marable, M. (2004). Racism and sexism. In P. S. Rothenberg (Ed.), *Race, class and gender in the United States* (6th ed., pp. 160–165). New York, NY: Worth.

Miller, J. (2008). *Getting played: African American girls, urban inequality and gendered violence.* New York: New York University Press.

Moe, A., & Bell, M. (2004). Abject economics: The effects of battering and violence on women's work and employability. *Violence Against Women, 9,* 29–55.

Monto, M., & Hotaling, N. (2001). Predictors of rape myth acceptance among male clients of female street prostitutes. *Violence Against Women, 7,* 275–293.

McCormack, A., Janus, M., & Burgess, A. W. (1986). Runaway youths and sexual victimization: Gender differences in an adolescent runaway population. *Child Abuse & Neglect, 10,* 387–395.

National Law Center on Homelessness and Poverty and the Coalition for the Homeless (2009). *Homes not handcuffs: The criminalization of the homeless in U.S. cities.* Retrieved from http://www.nationalhomeless.org/publications/crimreport/index.html

Raphael, J. (2000). *Saving Bernice: Battered women, welfare and poverty.* Boston, MA: Northeastern University Press.

Raphael, J. (2004). *Listening to Olivia: Violence, poverty and prostitution.* Boston, MA: Northeastern University Press.

Richie, B. E. (1996). *Compelled to crime: The gender entrapment of battered Black women.* New York, NY: Routledge.

Schaffner, L. (2006). *Girls in trouble with the law.* New Brunswick, NJ: Rutgers University Press.

Snow, D. A., Baker, S. G., & Anderson, L. (1989). Criminality and homeless men: An empirical assessment. *Social Problems, 36,* 532–549.

Snyder, Howard N. (2000). *Sexual assault of young children as reported to law enforcement: Victim, incident and offender characteristics.* Washington, DC: U.S. Department of Justice, Bureau of Justice Statistics.

Sweet, N., & Tewksbury, R. (2000). What's a nice girl like you doing in a place like this? Pathways to a career in stripping. *Sociological Spectrum, 20,* 325–343.

Tyler, K. A., & Cauce, A. M. (2002). Perpetrators of early physical and sexual abuse among homeless and runaway adolescents. *Child Abuse & Neglect, 26,* 1261–1274.

Tyler, K. A., Whitbeck, L. B., Hoyt, D. R., & Cauce, A. M. (2004). Risk factors for sexual victimization among male and female homeless runaway youth. *Journal of Interpersonal Violence, 19,* 503–520.

Wakin, M., (2011). Socialization, stereotypes, and homelessness. In K. O. Korgen, J. M. White, & S. K. White (Eds.), *Sociologists in action: Sociology, social change and social justice* (pp. 72–77). Thousand Oaks, CA: Pine Forge Press.

Whitbeck, L. B., & Hoyt, D. R. (1999). *Nowhere to grow: Homeless and runaway adolescents and their families.* New York, NY: Aldine de Gruyter.

Whitbeck, L. B., & Hoyt, D. R. (2002). *Midwest Longitudinal Study of Homeless Adolescents: Baseline summary report for all participating agencies.* Lincoln: Department of Sociology, University of Nebraska-Lincoln.

Whitbeck, L. B., & Simons, R. L. (1990). Life on the streets: The victimization of runaway and homeless adolescents. *Youth & Society, 22,* 108–125.

Widom, C. S. (1989a). The cycle of violence. *Science, 244,* 160–166.

Widom, C. S. (1989b). Child abuse, neglect and adult behavior: Research design and findings on criminality, violence and child abuse. *American Journal of Orthopsychiatry, 59,* 355–367.

Widom, C. S. (1989c). Does violence beget violence? A critical examination of the literature. *Psychological Bulletin, 106,* 3–28.

Widom, C. S. (1992). *The cycle of violence. Research in brief.* Washington, DC: U.S. Department of Justice, National Institute of Justice.

Night and Day

Gendered Violence and Intersectionality in the Everyday Experiences of Transgender Men*

Miriam J. Abelson

Both fears and realities of violence are gendered social phenomena. When we examine individuals' fears and statistics on actual incidents of violence we find quite a bit of difference between men and women. This difference is clear in the stories of people who live part of their lives as women or girls and then transition to live as men. When they transition, their everyday fears of violence from living as women to living as men are as different as night and day.

Yet, because these fears are gendered does not mean they are shaped by gender alone. The most commonly imagined scenario for violent crime in the contemporary United States is a poor black man from the inner city attacking a white middle-class woman. While gender is part of this scenario, race and class shape it as well. Regardless of the actual prevalence of this crime scenario, this and other common ideas about crime influence the fears that structure our everyday lives. Fears of violent crime and the reality of those crimes do not always match, but fears have powerful effects on our everyday behavior, on media coverage, and on police actions. These fears and realities vary depending on gender, race, ability, class, and other categories of difference. This chapter will explore how fears and actual victimization differ, by examining interviews conducted with transgender men, and how the experiences of the interviewees are shaped by their social location.

Women and men have different fears and actual experiences of violence. Women tend to fear sexual assault from strangers (Stanko, 1995) while men mostly say they do not fear violence for themselves but that they fear for the safety of others (Warr, 1992). Men do see some situations as more dangerous than others, but they have a variety of ways of measuring and coping with that danger (May, Rader, & Goodrum, 2010). Conversely, women's fear leads them to avoid public space altogether. Because women are more likely to suffer harassment on the street when fewer women are around, public space becomes

*The author wishes to thank the University of Oregon Center for the Study of Women in Society and Center for Diversity and Community for their support of a portion of this research.

more dangerous for women (Valentine, 1989). The interesting part about this difference in fear is that it does not match men's and women's actual experiences of violence. Men are more likely to experience all kinds of assault, besides rape and other forms of sexual assault, than women (Ferraro, 1995). In fact, women are most likely to experience assault from men they know, spouses or family, at home (Pain, 1997).

Men learn to handle aggressions from other men usually from a young age, through experience with various kinds of violence (Stanko, 1990). They develop a sense of which men or which places might be more dangerous than others (Brownlow, 2005). Men do report fear of violent encounters, but only in situations where the perceived risk of victimization is extreme (Reid & Konrad, 2004). The difference here is that women usually learn to fear all men, or at least strangers, while men learn only to fear men who appear particularly threatening. For example, while women will avoid leaving the house at night altogether, men will venture out but will avoid walking past a particular bar because rowdy drunken men are out front (Brownlow, 2005).

I will show below that while one's sense of safety is affected by whether one is a man or woman, it also is shaped by race, class, sexuality, ability, and transgender status. When men think about their safety, it is not random or on a purely individual basis. Instead, these social categories shape how men perceive their own safety, how others perceive them as dangerous or safe, and how those identities that give them safety are often invisible.

In order to understand how men's sense of safety is related to race, class, and ability, I will use interviews I conducted with transgender men, or *trans men*. In this research trans men are people who were identified, usually by a doctor, as female at birth and raised as girls. They then use medical procedures (e.g., hormone treatment, surgeries) to transition to live as men, although not all transgender people want to or do use medical procedures. Trans men's assigned sex (female) does not match their sense of themselves as men so they undergo procedures that make their body more typically male. These procedures make them comfortable in their bodies and make others see them as men. This experience is not exactly the same for all trans men or transgender people in general; however, it does roughly describe the trans men I interviewed and whose stories appear in this chapter. The experiences of this group of men, who were not raised as boys, will reveal the fears particular to trans men, and will more broadly demonstrate how all men experience safety and fear of violence.

I am often asked how I know that trans men's experiences will be similar to *cisgender* men (people whose assigned sex is consistent with their gender identity). The sociological research on both men's fear in general and the experiences of trans men in particular is quite limited. With a few exceptions, I do not know for sure which fears are true for other men or which are related to these men being transgender. These men all said that strangers see them as men because they almost always call them "he" or "sir," especially after their transition, though often before. People use outward clues such as dress, hairstyle, body shape, and the way a person walks, to determine each other's sex (i.e., whether someone is male or female) in everyday interaction. After all, one doesn't usually inspect the genitals or sex chromosomes of other people walking down the street (West & Zimmerman, 1989). Male is often the default category if there is no evidence to the contrary (Lucal, 1999) and these men are seen as men by others since they have outward signs of maleness such as facial hair, flat chests, and no outward signs of femaleness (Dozier, 2005). Thus, it is likely their experiences in interaction are similar to other men overall, though their history is different. I will discuss at length below that there are distinct fears directly related to being transgender and, although important, these are not the most prominent fears these men experience.

An essentialist understanding of gender suggests that while men and women have different experiences, all men and all women have similar experiences of safety and fear of violence. In contrast, an intersectional approach suggests that other *social locations* (e.g., race, class, sexuality, ability) shape the experiences of men and women (Collins, 2000). In order to understand the complex experiences of men and women, sociologists must take these other locations into account (Bettie, 2003). Intersectionality provides a way to understand how an individual can experience both privilege and oppression (Frankenberg, 1993). For example, an Asian American man may experience privilege because of his gender while simultaneously experiencing oppression as a member of a minoritized racial group in the United States. Because his experience of gender is always influenced by his race and vice versa, this means his experiences cannot simply be understood by combining those of a white man and an Asian American woman.

In order to understand some of the ways in which perceptions of safety differ based on intersectional identities and social locations, I will use the stories of five of the 35 trans men I interviewed in the San Francisco Bay Area and the southeast United States. I will mostly focus on individuals because there were not enough participants in particular racial groups of color or other categories to make blanket generalizations. For example, Leo's story below does not tell us how all black men experience safety or fear of violence, but it suggests how race, gender, and other categories interact to shape individual experience.

LEO'S STORY

Leo, a 36-year-old black man, worked in the office of an industrial company at the time of the interview. His position was not overtly professionalized and he earned a blue-collar income. Because of his middle-class upbringing and level of education, he considered his working-class wages a temporary situation. Leo had transitioned about five years before and said that although he had not thought about it before his transition, he found that being a black man was quite different from his experience of living as a black woman. Like other trans men in this study, he no longer feared sexual assault from men once he transitioned and he found that he was newly perceived by women as a potential assailant. Yet, he said this experience seemed different from white men and other men of color, whether trans or cisgender. He found that other men now feared him as a potential assailant and women seemed even more fearful. As a black man he had a more narrow set of concerns for his safety. I will show in this section that Leo's experiences show how the fear of interpersonal violence and violence by authority figures can be affected by race, class, gender, and age.

After Leo transitioned, his fear of interpersonal violence changed. He told several stories about having a newfound fear of other men. As a woman, any violence he feared from men was in the form of sexual assault or rape, but as a man he felt that he was now vulnerable to other forms of violence from men. For example, he feared physical attack from the poor black youth he encountered on the street or state-sponsored violence from white police officers. The change in Leo's fears was consistent with previous research in that he did not fear all men equally. Rather, he described how his fear varied due to other social locations (Reid & Konrad, 2004; Stanko, 1990). He felt that his experience as a black man was particularly important in shaping his expectations of violence from other men.

In the United States, people perceive black men as the most likely type of person to commit violence (Hollander, 2001). Leo's fear of violence reinforced this image of black men because he thought that as a black man he was more likely to be the victim of violence from other black men in everyday life. His fears were particularly directed toward young or poor black men because in his opinion these men were more likely to react to conflict with the use of violence. Leo's assumption that black men are inherently more prone to violence than other men is problematic and mirrors white stereotypes of black people. In a way, Leo's fear is a more accurate assessment of who is likely to commit a violent crime against him, even though he overestimates his likelihood of being a victim in general. Leo is more likely to experience violence from another black man, not because black men are more violent, but because most violence occurs between members of the same racial group (Peterson & Krivo, 2005). In other words, although black men are the most commonly imagined perpetrators of all kinds of violent crime by all racial groups, this is actually only true for other black men and women. However, Leo misjudged his likelihood of being a victim because, while young men do tend to commit more crimes, they tend to commit them against each other. Since Leo is in his late thirties, he is unlikely to be a victim.

On an individual level, Leo felt that white men were mostly afraid of him as a Black man, owing to an understanding of the common stereotype of black men as violent, however he did express fears of white men related to individual and institutional racist violence. Leo connected his fear of white men not only to individual racism (individual beliefs and actions) but also to institutional racism (policies, laws). Leo said, "I'm definitely on guard. Um, probably more so from Black men than from white men. I don't find white men a threat but in a larger context I'm definitely afraid of white men [laugh!]." To describe his fear of individual racist men he spoke of recent incidents where white men were found carrying guns in venues where newly elected President Obama was speaking. He said:

> It's really disturbing to see white men at rallies with guns strapped to their legs. You know, and these are rallies that the president is supposed to, like, attend. So, as small as a population that's probably doing it, it's probably large enough to be alarming to me. You know, I've, I don't remember how long ago reading in the *Nation* about vigilantes in Louisiana after Katrina. You know, basically scared white people with guns shooting Black people who are trying to get somewhere. You know, white people feeling so threatened that they have to act out. That's my fear.

To Leo, this showed that racism and its potential violent consequences are alive and well in the United States and that President Obama's election did not signal a so-called postracial society.

Leo expressed fear of institutional racism in possible interactions with police and the criminal justice system. He said that he feared meeting a similar fate as Oscar Grant, a Black man who had been shot and killed by local transit police about six months prior to the interview (Bulwa, Buchanan, & Yi, 2009). After learning about Oscar Grant, Leo felt an increased vulnerability to police violence, or, as he worded it, as if he had "a bullseye on his back." Due to police policies of racial profiling, he believed he would be unduly targeted for police attention and violence. He also said that he feared victimization in the criminal justice system. For example, when another man attacked him, he was initially fearful to fight back. He believed if the police were called, then he might be subject to arrest and be subject to unduly harsh treatment in the courts. Leo's belief that his race was most significant in drawing police attention was best illustrated when he said, "I just feel like I get noticed by the police more and it doesn't matter if I'm wearing polos and loafers." Although Leo had not actually been incarcerated, his worries are quite justified by the reality that black men are sent to jail or prison more often than men of other racial groups compared to their rate of committing crimes (Wakefield & Uggen, 2010). Thus, his fear was connected to the effects of racism from politically conservative individuals and institutional racism in the form of interactions with the criminal justice system. While race briefly figured into other men of color's fears of violence, such as Asian men being seen as vulnerable, it appeared most prominently in black trans men's accounts of safety. The prominence of race in black trans men like Leo's understandings of their own safety and how others perceive them is a result of the black–white dichotomy in the common images of victim and perpetrator.

While Leo's fear has been shaped in multiple ways by race and gender, other aspects of social location did not occur to him when he talked about safety. For example, physical ability likely affected his experiences in multiple ways, as it did for Michael, whose story I will explore in the following section. Later, when I discuss Drew's experiences, I will go into more depth about the reasons why Leo did not talk about ability or other social locations.

MICHAEL'S STORY

Michael, a 40-year-old white man, was a student and educational worker, and was about three years into his transition at the time of the interview. He was raised in a working-class family and earned working-class wages, although when he completes his degree, his earning potential may increase. Michael has a disability for which he has to use a wheelchair or walking aids to get around. When Michael spoke about the violence he had experienced both as a man and as a woman, it was his disability that most prominently shaped those experiences, regardless of gender. He experienced a sense of invisibility in relation to gender because he felt that when he used a wheelchair most others only saw him as disabled. Even with this invisibility, the intersection of sexuality, gender, and disability often stood out to Michael as shaping his fears of violence in everyday encounters with other people.

Disability is a complex variable when examining intersectionality because not only does its meaning shift from situation to situation, but the disability itself can also change from day to day as well as over an individual's lifetime. Michael's disability, for example, is expressed differently depending on whether he is using his wheelchair or walking aids. For example, Michael reports that when he uses a wheelchair his gender (in this case others' perception of him as a man or woman or as masculine or feminine) is invisible or irrelevant:

> There's this strange thing when you're in a wheelchair. Where is that everybody sees you. Everyone recognizes you, or think they do—and no one actually looks at your face . . . Part of what was really interesting is that I was seen as such an asexual being. That I started transitioning and its like a lot of people weren't looking close enough to notice. Because they see the wheelchair. They see the chunk of steel under my ass instead of seeing my face.

Michael's differing mobility affects his experiences of gender and sexuality. When he uses walking aids to move around he finds that people notice him and his gender more than when he uses a wheelchair. Thus, the ways in which his gendered experiences of safety intersect with his disability depend on how his physical mobility manifests in a particular situation. In a wheelchair, Michael often loses his sense of safety since people are more likely to invade his personal space, touch him, and touch his chair. In his wheelchair, people feel okay to touch him in a paternalistic way like patting him on the head, but as a man other men "give him props more" and are more likely to pat him on the back instead. When using walking aids, he is seen as less vulnerable and as a potential object of sexual attraction.

While Michael described several instances in which he experienced violence from strangers in public, he said that it largely stopped when he started physically transitioning. He believed that these attacks were usually motivated by homophobia or more generally a nonnormative gender presentation.

> It's a dangerous space to not fit gender norms in this society. A really personally dangerous space I think. <Have you ever felt unsafe?> I have and I feel like I've been privileged that most of my experiences of worrying that I was going to be bashed or being bashed have happened because I was queer or because I was disabled and I feel like I've actually gotten less of that since I've been more male presenting.

When others perceived him as either a masculine woman or a feminine man this led to homophobic violence in some situations. This shows how gender and sexuality can converge to shape the threat of violence. For Michael, this meant that he was vulnerable to homophobia because he was a masculine-appearing woman, and not solely because he was holding hands with or kissing another woman in public.

Sexuality also intersected with disability and gender to shape some additional experiences. For example, when Michael lived as a woman, he was verbally confronted by a woman on public transportation because he was wearing sexually suggestive clothing. When I asked what they said, he explained, "Oh, they were worried about me. Am I really going to go out in public that way? 'Don't you know that it's dangerous for a disabled person to go out in public in a short skirt?'" He believed that people associate his physical disability with a mental disability and more generally with defenselessness. Thus, strangers seemed to have no problem giving him unsolicited advice about how to protect himself. In another situation, after his transition, an attendant wheeled Michael to the men's restroom at the airport in a socially conservative region of the United States. While waiting for the disabled stall, the wheelchair attendant positioned Michael so that he was at eye level with the waists of the men using the urinals. Michael was concerned that the men would think that Michael was looking at their exposed genitals and have a homophobic reaction that would mean physical or verbal violence. This fear was further complicated in terms of Michael's fear because he did identify as bisexual and could have found some of the men physically attractive. Thus, his sense of safety in relation to sexuality changed based on gender and was shaped by his disability. When he was living as a woman, he experienced threats to his safety based on others' perception that his manner of dress was too sexualized, which was heightened by his disability, and as a man he experienced fear based on literally being positioned to be vulnerable to homophobic violence.

It is unclear how being white affected Michael's experience of disability, sexuality, and gender, but, as I will discuss below, it is often difficult for those in the dominant position to recognize that status. It is likely that whiteness shaped Michael's experiences of safety since race is one of the primary organizers of U.S. society. His experiences of disability and sexuality may stand out more because those are areas in which he experiences oppression.

DREW'S STORY

Drew, a 37-year-old white man, worked a blue-collar job at a government agency, and began his transition about two years before the interview. His working-class upbringing and job were central to his sense of himself. Drew's experience of fear and safety revolved mostly around comfort and discomfort with his working-class and sexual identities rather than the threat of physical violence. I will discuss Drew's sense of comfort and discomfort and then focus on why Drew's social location may lead him to have a different relationship than Leo or Michael to the threat of physical violence. Class, sexuality, and his body stood out the most when Drew talked about safety. When thinking about safety, it is important not only to think about what affects a man's physical safety but also what causes someone to experience emotional safety or comfort.

When Drew tried to find support among other trans men, he sometimes had difficulties because he had trouble relating to them in terms of politics and job experiences. First, he found that he had trouble relating to the political correctness he experienced from middle-class men. Second, when he was looking for advice about how to deal with transgender issues at work, he found that their experiences were only with office environments and not relevant to his issues. He explained this difficulty when he looked for advice in online forums,

> Honestly, I couldn't find what I was looking for, I was looking for working-class dudes who didn't go to college and who had working-class jobs who came out at work and who were in their mid-30s and I could never find a topic about that. You know, it was all like office jobs, mostly guys coming out at college and stuff like that.

Through the Internet, he sought, and eventually found, other working-class trans men in various regions to get advice on what issues would arise with being a trans man in a blue-collar workplace.

His transition changed his interactions with other working-class men. When he was a masculine woman, Drew found other working-class men to be standoffish. They would look at him strangely and avoid conversation with him. He noticed that as a man other working-class men would "shake his hand more" and "shoot the shit." Drew liked this feeling of acceptance with other men and over time felt more comfortable joining informal conversations on the street or at work with men he did not know. He also noticed, because he was tall and somewhat muscular, that other men would avoid conflict with him. The short men I interviewed talked about being threatened by other men's size. The combination of his gender and his body made Drew feel like he would not be a victim, although he did mention briefly that his working-class appearance might make others see him as more violent. This is similar to how gender and race intersect in how Leo thought others would perceive him as violent as a black man.

Drew's current and formal sexual identities also affected his sense of safety. Drew had identified as a lesbian in his youth and while he was still mostly attracted to women after his transition, he still identifies as queer. This identity makes sense for Drew because his girlfriend always had thought of herself as queer and they spent most of their time in San Francisco's queer communities, even though if someone were to see him and his girlfriend on the street they would probably see them as a heterosexual couple. Conversely, Drew does not want other working-class men to think that he is gay because he thinks that working-class men are more homophobic than other men and would reject him. It presents a difficult situation for Drew because he has been part of gay and lesbian communities for some time. Some trans men cut off all contact with queer communities after they transition. While Drew had some discomfort, he did not feel he could do the same. He explained,

> I still super feel part of the queer community because I've been part of it for so long. I can't imagine leaving it. It's part of the security blanket like with all my friends. Like, I can't imagine just going off and then not being a part of it.

In order to feel comfortable in multiple situations, Drew has to think about how he presents himself. Other men likely face similar conflicts and feel they have to be more overtly manly in situations they see as less safe.

Class is quite important to Drew's self-perception as a man, but race and ability did not stand out to him in his identity or in his general lack of fear of violence. This may be because people are less likely overall to notice the ways in which our social locations produce privilege. Leo had conducted some interviews with trans men and when I asked him about his findings he said:

> We've noticed as far as like, uh, the white guys that we've interviewed. A lot that they spoke of as far as like their experience with, like, masculinity was gender specific. Where the men of color were really dealing with race issues.

Is it that, for white men, race does not affect their experiences, or that race just does not stand out to them?

Intersectionality not only describes how some groups or individuals experience oppression; it also explores how these categories work in relation to each other and how the hierarchies (which are socially constructed) order categories, create advantage, or create privilege for others. In this light, one can think of the fear of violence related to Leo's experience of race and Michael's experience of disability and start to think about how Drew's race and disability status shape his experience of safety. In other words, how does Drew's relative privilege lessen his fear of violence? The answer is that his whiteness and physical ability most likely allow him to feel less vulnerability to violence, but that this is difficult to measure because he did not talk much about race or ability and violence.

Every trans man of color I interviewed brought up race when talking about his life, but few, if any, white men did. In fact, when I directly asked white men about how being white affected their experience, the conversation often became quite awkward and the men had difficulty talking about race. I believe that this was not because a white man's experiences are less affected by his race than those of a man of color, but because privilege operates by being invisible or unspoken (Frankenberg, 1993). Men experience gender as much as women do, but it is often unmarked, treated as the norm, and invisible. Everyone has a race, a gender, a sexuality, and an ability status, but the experience of them only usually stands out when we think of oppression and not the advantages of privilege. Even though Drew's fear of violence was shaped by his class and sexuality, he likely experienced less fear and more feelings of safety and security than did Michael and Leo. These men are close in age and have some similar experiences with class, but the one thing that they all have in common is gender.

I have discussed gender mostly in terms of man–woman and masculine–feminine, but gender also includes whether someone is transgender or cisgender. Leo, Michael, and Drew have in common that they identify as men and that they are trans men. While race, class, and sexuality shape trans men's experience of gender, ability, and so on, trans men do have some fears that are unique to them as a group. The experiences of a few other men, Bobby and Mark, and Drew again, will illustrate some specific fears of trans men in public and in the workplace.

TRANSPHOBIC VIOLENCE

There is quite a bit of anecdotal evidence that transgender people experience harassment related to being transgender (Lombardi, Wilchins, Priesing, & Malouf, 2001), but there are few large-scale studies that document how prevalent this violence and harassment might be. It can be difficult to survey a large enough group of transgender people to get a sense of patterns of harassment because transgender people can be hard to locate. One reason is that a number of transgender people do not maintain contact with other transgender people or related organizations after they transition. The largest study to date on people who identify as transgender suggests that they experience high levels of various forms of harassment and violence (Grant et al., 2011). The survey of 6,500 transgender and gender nonconforming people showed a pattern of harassment and violence in schools, in employment, housing, and public accommodations. Sixty-three percent of those surveyed reported some kind of discrimination or violence. The high incidence of reported harassment is coupled in the survey results with the finding that 41% of those surveyed reported an attempted suicide, compared to 1.6% in the general population (Grant et al., 2011). Even if this survey overestimates the number of transgender people who have faced discrimination, it is still likely that transphobic discrimination and violence are not rare. In the study, male-to-female transgender people reported a higher incidence of violence in schools and the workplace, whereas female-to-male transgender people reported more harassment in public accommodations.

The trans men in my research did say that they feared physical assault if others were to find out they were transgender, but in everyday interactions this was not the most pressing fear that they faced, likely because they did not think others would find out they were transgender. Again, outwardly most people that these men interacted with recognized them as men. Since many if not most everyday interactions do not involve revealing genitals (or chromosomes), others were unlikely to know that these men were trans men.

There were situations in which some of the interviewees were more afraid of violence and harassment than previously. These were usually when people knew them from before their transition, or through some other means it was discovered that they were transgender. For example, Bobby wished to be closer to his parents and siblings but was afraid to move back to the rural community where he was raised. As a teenager he lived as a masculine-looking woman and he had experienced homophobic violence in the community. He described one incident of violence at a gas station in the "middle of nowhere" where the people knew him:

> I was walking out of the gas station. I had went and bought a coke, and I was fixing to open it, and the last words I remember was, "Fuckin' dyke," [slapping sound] top of my head. I had a two-inch split right back here. And I woke up, people was just walking by—I don't know if I was there for a couple seconds, couple minutes, I don't know. I just got up and went on to my car and . . . What're you gonna do?

Bobby imagined that if he lived in this community again he would encounter people who recognized him from before his transition, that news would spread quickly in the small town, and that he would be vulnerable to transphobic violence. Bobby did not know any transgender people who transitioned and remained in his community.

In some cases a person might reveal to others that a man is transgender. For example, Mark lived in a small rural community and worked for a social services organization. Due to an unrelated disagreement, a family member of Mark's threatened to tell his supervisor that he was a trans man. In order to avoid being blackmailed by his family member, he told his supervisor at work that he was transgender. Although he feared that others at his work would be unaccepting, his supervisor did not see it as a problem and Mark was able to continue in his position with no apparent ill effects. Mark also feared he was vulnerable because the state he lived in did not offer legal protection for transgender people and his company did not have a policy that protected transgender people from discrimination. In fact, a majority of the interviewees mentioned that laws and policies that protect transgender people in many arenas of social life were key to their sense of safety from transgender violence.

In contrast to Mark, Drew's workplace, a government agency, had a policy for how to handle transgender people's transitions. Drew found it fairly easy to tell his supervisor that he was transitioning. Workplace policies related to helping transgender people are important for them to succeed in their jobs; however, policy may not be enough. Drew experienced other problems on the job. A subtle way that others would out him as transgender was to call him "she" in front of others who did not know he was transgender. For example, a friend and coworker of Drew's had difficulty making the transition to calling Drew "he" and would call him "she" in front of unaware coworkers. This made Drew uncomfortable because his friend was disrespecting his gender identity. It also made Drew vulnerable because he could now be subject to transphobic violence. He liked his coworker, but Drew said that he, "gave [the coworker] two more chances and then I just started avoiding him. Unless he's alone but if he's with a group of people I just avoid him altogether." Drew's employer could have further supported him by giving his coworkers training on how to respect transgender people, but the employer, at the time of the interview, had not offered such a program. Perhaps this would have helped Drew's friend in respecting Drew's gender identity and helped them both be better workers.

In relation to transgender violence, it is clear that nondiscrimination policies in employment, housing, and other arenas of life provide the safety and security trans men, and likely trans women, need to survive and flourish. This is why transgender people advocate for these policies at local, state, and national levels. Clearly, these policies are most effective when coupled with education that includes a focus on how transgender people's lives and challenges vary based on the intersection of race, class, ability, and sexuality. Policies and education can be effective, but even transgender people with such protections can experience subtle forms of bias or be fired because they are transgender, but under the guise of other reasons, such as job performance (Schilt, 2010).

Conclusion

Ideas about race, gender, and class play a role in how we envision violence, and they stereotype the perpetrators and the victims of violent crime. There is a great disconnect between commonly held fears about violent crime and actual patterns of experience. Yet, gender, race, class, sexuality, and disability as well as other aspects of social location shape an individual's fears and experiences of violence.

The experiences of the trans men cited above demonstrate that men's fears and their actual encounters with violence differ not only from women, but also among men. Men's experiences of fear and violence vary based on both oppression and privilege in relation to social locations such as race, class, sexuality, and ability. While transgender men may have particular fears about transphobic violence, their most prominent fears are similar to cisgender men in everyday situations. In fact, fearlessness and the freedom that goes with it may be a central privilege for men in dominant social locations. The privilege of fearlessness is not just a psychological benefit, but it allows greater access to public space, freedom to express oneself on the job, or to live where one chooses. Through the lives of five trans men, this chapter showed how fears of violence shape men's everyday lives and how these fears vary along intersecting aspects of social location.

While gendered fears of violence may be as different as night and day, there is variation within the two. Both the quality of light and the activity of people are different in the early morning as opposed to noontime, just as men's and women's experiences are shaped by variants of race, class, sexuality, and ability. Indeed, while night and day often appear to be distinct, the two are hard to distinguish from each other in the in-between times of dawn and sunset. This suggests possible fluidity and overlap in gendered experiences. In this sense, gendered violence and safety are both as distinct and as varied as the night from the day.

References

Bettie, J. (2003). *Women without class: Girls, race, and identity*. Berkeley: University of California Press.

Brownlow, A. (2005). A geography of men's fear. *Geoforum, 36*(5), 581–592.

Bulwa, D., Buchanan, W., & Yi, M. (2009, January 15). Behind murder charge against ex-BART officer. *San Francisco Chronicle*. Retrieved from http://www.sfgate.com.

Collins, P. H. (2000). *Black feminist thought: Knowledge, consciousness, and the politics of empowerment*. New York, NY: Routledge.

Dozier, R. (2005). Beards, breasts, and bodies: Doing sex in a gendered world. *Gender & Society, 19*(3), 297–316.

Ferraro, K. F. (1995). *Fear of crime: Interpreting victimization risk*. Albany: State University of New York Press.

Frankenberg, R. (1993). *White women, race matters: The social construction of whiteness*. Minneapolis: University of Minnesota Press.

Grant, J. M., Mottet, L. A., Tanis, J., Harrison, J., Herman, J. L., & Keisling, M. (2011) *Injustice at every turn: A report of the National Transgender Discrimination Survey*. National Center for Transgender Equality and National Gay and Lesbian Task Force. Retrieved from http://thetaskforce.org/downloads/reports/reports/ntds_full.pdf

Hollander, J. (2001). Vulnerability and dangerousness: The construction of gender through conversation about violence. *Gender & Society, 15*(1), 83–109.

Lombardi, E., Wilchins, R., Priesing, D., & D. Malouf. (2001). Gender violence: Transgender experiences with violence and discrimination. *Journal of Homosexuality, 42*(1), 89–101.

Lucal, B. (1999). What it means to be gendered me: Life on the boundaries of a dichotomous gender system. *Gender & Society, 13*(6), 781–797.

May, D., Rader, N., & Goodrum, S. (2010). A gendered assessment of the "threat of victimization": Examining gender differences in fear of crime, perceived risk, avoidance, and defensive behaviors. *Criminal Justice Review, 35*(2), 159–182.

Pain, R. (1997). Whither women's fear? Perceptions of sexual violence in public and private space. *International Review of Victimology, 4*(4), 297–312.

Peterson, R. D., & Krivo, L. J. (2005). Macrostructural analyses of race, ethnicity, and violent crime: Recent lessons and new directions for research. *Annual Review of Sociology, 31*, 331–356.

Reid, L. W., & Konrad, M. (2004). The gender gap in fear: Assessing the interactive effects of gender and perceived risk on fear of crime. *Sociological Spectrum, 24*(4), 399–425.

Schilt, K. (2010). *Just one of the guys: Transgender men and the persistence of gender inequality.* Chicago, IL: University of Chicago Press.

Stanko, E. (1990). *Everyday violence: How women and men experience sexual and physical danger.* London, UK, and Winchester, MA: Pandora and Unwin Hyman.

Stanko, E. (1995). Women, crime, and fear. *Annals of the American Academy of Political and Social Science, 539*, 46–58.

Valentine, G. (1989). The geography of women's fear. *Area, 21*(4), 385–390.

Wakefield, S., & Uggen, C. (2010). Incarceration and stratification. *Annual Review of Sociology, 36*, 387–406.

Warr, M. (1992). Altruistic fear of victimization in households. *Social Science Quarterly, 73*(4), 723.

West, C., & Zimmerman, D. H. (1987). Doing gender. *Gender & Society, 1*(2), 125–151.

Crime, Deviance, and Justice

When we hear the word *deviance,* we tend to think of someone doing something, usually something bad. But sociologically, deviance is any act, attribute, or belief that violates a cultural norm and elicits from others a negative or even a positive reaction. What this definition tells us, then, is that a person does not have to do anything to be labeled deviant; in fact, people may simply have a certain appearance and others will apply the label deviant to them. The key element of this definition, though, is the emphasis on others' reactions, be they positive or negative. Sociologists point out that nothing is inherently deviant; what is deviant depends not on an act, attribute or belief per se, but rather on how others react to it. Deviance, therefore, is culturally relative; what gets labeled deviant depends on many factors, including historical context, as Ruth Thompson-Miller and Joe Feagin demonstrate in Chapter 6.

One might be inclined to argue that sexual assault is always deviant, but as Thompson-Miller and Feagin show in Chapter 6, the sexual assault of black women and girls during the period of legal segregation known as Jim Crow was not only systematic and routine, but also went unredressed. As the authors point out, these brutal assaults were not the actions of a few bad white men; rather, they were government-sanctioned rapes. Black women and girls were culturally constructed as immoral and promiscuous, and they were not deemed worthy of legal protection from predatory white men. White men could assault them at will, knowing that they would not be held accountable and, even if evidence indicated an assault had occurred, the victim would be blamed. So, while we think of sexual assault as a *crime*—that is, a violation of a norm that our society considers so important that laws have been enacted to enforce compliance—even sanctions against this heinous behavior vary historically and situationally. Under Jim Crow, the rape of a black woman by a white man was not defined as a crime; indeed, it was often ignored by the legal system. The characteristics of the social factors involved—their race, gender, and social class—in addition to the situation and historical period influence whether what they do and say, or how they look, gets labeled deviant or criminal and, in turn, determine what the consequences for the social actors will be. In the case of white men who raped black women and girls under Jim Crow, there were no negative consequences; they assaulted with impunity.

Although legally sanctioned racial segregation began to be dismantled in the 1960s in the United States, young black girls continue to be at greater risk of violent victimization than are white girls. As Nikki Jones and Alexis McCurn show in Chapter 7, black girls in disadvantaged urban neighborhoods face a host of threats to their safety, including street violence, violence perpetrated by people the girls know, and what they call *micro-interactional assaults.* In their chapter, Jones and McCurn not only describe these everyday lived experiences, but also discuss the *situated survival strategies* that the young women use to cope and stay safe as they navigate both public and private spaces. Jones and McCurn show that these strategies are raced, gendered, classed— and necessary. They are survival strategies because the young women cannot count on the police or the legal system to protect them—and not to revictimize them—more than 40 years after the official end of Jim Crow.

Women's survival strategies sometimes lead to their arrest and incarceration. Although men commit far more crimes—both violent and property crimes—than women do and account for the majority of people in jails and prisons in the United States, there has been an increase in the number of women arrested, convicted, and incarcerated on criminal charges in recent years. The majority of these women are young, economically disadvantaged women of color. One significant difference between male and female prison inmates is that more than half of female prisoners lived with their children prior to incarceration, compared with about a third of male prisoners, and were the children's primary caregiver. In Chapter 8, Holly Foster and Jocelyn Lewis examine the effects of imprisonment on incarcerated mothers and their children, and look more specifically at how the children's living arrangements mediate these impacts. Moreover, Foster and Lewis consider cultural influences by investigating differences across families by race and ethnicity.

Valerie Jenness, Jennifer Sumner, Lori Sexton, and Nikkas Alamillo-Luchese continue to explore the differential effects of incarceration in Chapter 9 by examining the experiences of transgender women in men's prisons. Jenness and her colleagues point out at the opening of their chapter that there is considerable diversity among transgender people, making *classification,* especially in a prison setting, difficult at best. But as their chapter vividly demonstrates, the concerns of transgender women in men's prisons—in this case, in California—are far more serious than issues of what to be called or how to be classified. Transgender women in men's prisons face acute problems of health and safety, and Jenness and her colleagues give the prisoners voice in this chapter by inviting coauthor Nikkas Alamillo-Luchese, herself a transgender prisoner, to describe her experiences at their most pressing. Jenness and her colleagues eloquently invite us, as we read the chapter, to engage in *open-hearted listening.* In doing so, we ask readers to carefully reflect on how this chapter, along with the other chapters in this section of the book, challenges popularly constructed notions of what constitutes *justice* in our society.

6

The Hidden Nightmare

Everyday Sexual Assault of Black Women during Legal Segregation

Ruth Thompson-Miller & Joe R. Feagin

In 1865, slavery was abolished in this country after 250 years of existence. Soon after abolishing slavery, whites implemented a system with laws and practices that generally mirrored those of slavery—the system was Jim Crow. Jim Crow (legal segregation—separate but equal) was an unbending, enforced system of social oppression, a near totalitarian mode of control imposed by local and state governments throughout the southern and border states (Packard, 2002; Feagin, 2006). An aspect of slavery that continued during Jim Crow days was the everyday threat of rape or sexual assault of black women and children. The black community coped with the systematic rapes, sexual assaults, and the resulting physical and psychological trauma. In this chapter, we discuss the often-ignored aspects of normalized and institutional violence experienced by survivors of Jim Crow and the impact on future generations. These experiences illustrate an intersectional analysis of racism, sexism, and classism.

Let's be clear here—we aren't talking about individual bad white men—but government-sanctioned rapes. According to Angela Davis (1978), the rapes of black women were institutionalized and systematic: "This pattern of institutionalized sexual abuse was so strongly established that it survived the abolition of slavery. . . . These assaults were ideologically sanctioned by politicians, historians, novelists, and other public figures who systematically represented black women as promiscuous and immoral" (p. 25).

Scholars have noted that historically the recurring rapes of black women in the United States were not considered a crime, but were legitimized by government officials (Spickard, 1989). As such, black women were historically much less likely than white women to report the rape or attempted rape. Wyatt (1990) suggested, "one of the reasons for this [underreporting] during legal segregation could be their lower expectations of receiving support, given the historical roots of a tolerance of sexual exploitation of black women during and after slavery" (p. 27). Angela Davis states that the rape of black women was also "a political weapon of terror" against black men; they were terrorized against trying to protect their sisters, wives, and mothers (Davis, 1990, p. 44). This is a key to understanding this historical and contemporary sexual violence of white men against black women that many social scientists have ignored.

Even today, studies provide the evidence that "Black women often do not report being raped because they fear they will not be believed by those in the criminal justice system" (Hopkins & Koss, 2005, p. 705). Researchers have argued that rape occurrences, especially the rape of black women by white men, are higher than official statistics reveal (Lynn Curtis as cited by Williams, 1986, p. 3). Catherine Clinton (1986) states, "Race continues to inflame the issue and to obscure the fact that Black women are represented in rape statistics in dangerously disproportionate numbers" (p. 206).

In this chapter, we also discuss critically the exploitation and oppression of blacks living in the U.S. south. The everyday social interactions of blacks during Jim Crow duplicate what Erving Goffman (1961) would later refer to as a *total institution*. Goffman (1961) defined a total institution as, "a place of residence and work where a large number of like-situated individuals, cut off from the wider society for an appreciable period of time, together lead an enclosed, formally administered round of life" (p. xiii). Some of the characteristics of a total institution include controlling a person's language, inflicting humiliation and punishment, denying acknowledgment of a person's name (and instead creating demeaning nicknames), fashioning a hierarchy, imposing economic control, devising a loss of personal safety, compelling deference, coercing behavior, inflicting sexual assault, creating an inability to protect loved ones, enforcing constant surveillance, and insisting on suppression of feelings (Goffman, 1961). In our view the institution of slavery in the United States is an example of a total institution (see Goffman, 1961; Elkins, 1968; Knottnerus, Monk, & Jones, 1999; Wacquant, 2001). The total institution of slavery was abolished in 1865; Jim Crow segregation followed in much of the south soon after that abolition, indeed immediately in many areas. Moreover, the pivotal Supreme Court case decided by white men, *Plessy v. Ferguson* (1896), upheld and firmly legalized at the federal level the total institution of Jim Crow that replaced slavery.

During the total institution of Jim Crow the will of the state was enforced by means of racialized coercion, imprisonment, and violence in major institutions of U.S. society, especially in southern and border states. Utilizing Erving Goffman's metaphor of the frontstage and backstage, we demonstrate how complex, frequent, and unpredictable violence or a threat of violence was for blacks, similar to living in a prison without the physical bars typically utilized to entrap individuals. The violence in the frontstage included lynchings, house burnings, and imprisonment; in the backstage, it included sexual coercion, rape, and verbal assault. Erving Goffman's dramaturgical analogy is the study of social interaction in terms of theatrical performance to provide the framework for analysis. We specifically utilize the frontstage and backstage framework to analyze in-depth interviews with elderly black men and women. According to Goffman (1961), the backstage was free safe space where the actor could learn the performance. The participants revealed that in their daily performances during Jim Crow they used their dress, mannerisms, and tone of voice to maneuver their interactions with whites in the frontstage—to ensure their safety. We analyze the frontstage and backstage perceptions, interpretations, and coping strategies.

THE DATA

Historically, the literature on the rape of black women in Jim Crow's total institution is scarce. For this research project, we interviewed nearly 100 elderly blacks in depth about their experiences under legal segregation. We began by contacting key informants, such as ministers and teachers, in two black communities in the south. They provided us with initial names of those who might be willing to participate, and we collected further names by making presentations at organizational meetings and from references by the initial respondents. We interviewed 52 respondents in the southeast (37 women and 15 men). The majority (65%) were over age 70, with the rest between ages 52 and 69. In the southwest, we interviewed 40 respondents (25 women and 15 men). The majority (75%) of the second group were over age 70, with the rest between ages 58 and 69. In both regions, about two thirds held relatively low-paying jobs (such as domestic worker or hospital aide) during their primary work lives under Jim Crow, and most of the rest held modest-paying jobs like school teacher in a segregated school.

From the interviews, we learned that all were strongly committed to education, and a majority managed to secure at least a high school diploma (the requirements for a diploma then often differed from present-day high school diploma requirements), with a quarter having some college. Most interviews took place in the respondents' homes and lasted one to two hours. We used a flexible interview schedule with a series of open-ended questions about their lives under the total institution of Jim Crow.

Some of the questions that we posed to the respondents were:

> Do you remember your first encounter with a white person? Was it a good experience? Can you recall any experience your mother, father, or grandparents shared with you that they had with a white person? Can you recall a memorable story that you had or heard about living under segregation, possibly a story about someone in the community? Did your parents or any family member warn you about anything in reference to being safe in dealing with whites? Can you recall at what age you were when you began to notice as a black person that you were treated differently than white people? How did you and your family cope and survive during legal segregation? Were the coping strategies that you use[d] taught to you by someone? What coping strategies do you use to handle discrimination from whites today?

FRONTSTAGE: RAPE TALK

In the interviews with our respondents, it was difficult to get elderly blacks to share their experiences of rape and sexual coercion in Jim Crow's total institution. However, a few brave women shared stories of family members, neighbors, and friends being raped or having near rape experiences. A respondent in the southeast, while giving a tour of her house and her family photos, showed a picture of her grandfather standing alone. He was an elderly white man with a long white beard. She said, "This is my grandfather. He and my grandmother were married. He married her, they were married." The respondent's continued insistence that her grandparents were married—at a time in the south when interracial marriage was against the law—is an indication of possible shame associated with the dual family arrangements for white men in the total institution of Jim Crow. White men would have a white family and a black family, too. In many of these arrangements, the black woman was not married to the white man. A respondent in the southeast mentioned the dual family arrangement:

> My black grandmother traveled with my white grandfather and their white family to the town in which we now live. . . . My white great-grandfather took care of my great-grandmother, he never married her but he maintained two households. . . . And he [my grandfather] had an advantage. . . . [T]hey came down here with their white family . . . [H]e was a

protected kind of individual . . . He was a mixed blood . . . Just that simple. [He was] connected by blood, the yellow blood. Now he was born here, but could never find out whether his mother came here pregnant or not. . . . He [my grandfather] was born here and he grew up and everything. The house that ended up being their home, they gave that property to him. . . . So he was always kind of in that slightly protected class, so he never really talked about the situation.

In the respondent's narrative there is a tradition of black women in his family having children by white men. So, his great-grandfather and his grandfather were white men. According to the respondent, the white grandfather provided an education and economic resources to the children born to his black so-called companion. Just how consensual such relationships were is something we will never truly know, but again there was no free choice for black women in such a total, and totalitarian, institution. Sadly, with rare exceptions the history of slavery and Jim Crow and the extensive rapes that occurred during these eras have not been documented. Historical literature on the extensive rape of black women and girls is extremely rare.

FRONTSTAGE: RAPE AND SUBSEQUENT INJUSTICES

In much scholarly literature and public discussion of rape, past and the present, the focus is on assaults of white women. However, a much more common problem historically, during the total institution of Jim Crow, was black families regularly facing the raping of their daughters, mothers, and sons by white men, including those with local power and influence (Litwack, 1998; Talty, 2003; Williamson, 1995). Similarly, one of our respondents in the southeast in his late 60s recalls a rape in his community:

> This lady's name was [names a woman] and she was going to the sanctified church around the corner from Mt. Carmel Church and she got kidnapped by a white guy and he took her out in the woods and [he] sodomized her and raped her . . . He never served a day in jail. . . . She wasn't even married or anything at the time.

According to McGuire (2010), "The rape of black women by white men continued, often unpunished, throughout the [total institution] of Jim Crow . . . white men abducted and assaulted black women at an alarming regularity" (p. xviii). It is representative of white male privilege and the total acceptance of the unlawful behavior of white men. In the southwest, a woman in her late 60s responded to a question about rape in her community when she was growing up:

> There were rapes! The white man would rape girls. . . . If a white man see a half-way decent woman, if he wanted her, he went up and just grabbed her and start doing whatever he wanted to do to her. You know, she would fight, and say no, but he would beat her up, slap her, knock her down, and just, just take her. That was the norm back then for the white man to do. If you just happened to be in an area where they [whites] were it could happen to you. We were basically homebound people . . . they always forewarned us to be on the very best behavior, no matter what that white person would say to us. Always "yes sir, no sir, thank you sir" or whatever . . . never show any attitude or any animosity for all that would lead to was either a beating, rape, or killing.

Importantly, this respondent takes it for granted that whites would look for lack of deference as an invitation for violence. This again emphasizes the critical nature of the performance while on the white frontstage. There was also a recognition of institutional support for the hoary white custom that a white man had "paramour rights" (Ellis & Ellis, 2003, p. xv), a euphemistic term that meant the "right" of white men to rape black women and girls with impunity. Unwillingly, family members watched violence targeting spouses, siblings, and parents. Indeed, coercion is an important aspect of a total institution (Goffman, 1961). In fact, rape and violence as a routine part of blacks' daily lives reinforced the reality that they didn't have control over what happened to their bodies. Scholars have documented the long-term consequences of rape on the survivors (McGuire, 2010; Wasco, 2003). A respondent in the southeast in her 80s shared the story of an attempted rape when asked, "Do you remember your first encounter with a white person?"

> I remember one Sunday afternoon . . . a white man came to our house. I must have been about 15. . . . This man knocked on the door. My mom was sleeping. . . . My brother was in the next room sleeping. I answered the door. The man looked like he was spellbound. It frightened me, so I started backing up and he started following me. He went straight through my mom's bedroom and my brother's bedroom. I ran. . . he was following me. My brother sat up in the bed, to see what was happening . . . he came behind him. I can remember . . . my sister saying, "Oh, no, no, Richard. No, no, no." He was going to hurt him . . . I ran up under the house and hid. He walked in the yard looking for me and eventually he went on and got in the car. My dad wanted to know who he was . . . I was never able to tell him who he was. I couldn't remember telling him what he looked like. It frightened me. I was young and it frightened me. I knew that these things happened and I didn't want that to happen to me. . . . It was terrible . . . it was very frightening. My brother wouldn't have been able to do anything about it.

As a teenager, this respondent was aware of the raping of black women, and the stigma that was associated with it. She and her family knew that intervention by male relatives could have terrible consequences; in the extreme case, intervention might lead to their death. The respondent cried continuously as she recalled the incident—a sign of the long-term consequences on her mental health. In the above recounting, the sister's warning shows that she knew that not only would the brother not be able to intervene, but that intervention would bring retribution.

The above narrative demonstrates that children were socialized to understand the power that whites had over blacks even in the blacks' own homes. In the total institution of Jim Crow, if blacks stood up for themselves, one form of punishment that whites used was rape. Rape was used as a weapon of terror to keep blacks in their place. Young black women who wanted to stand up for themselves risked being raped by white men.

FRONTSTAGE: THE VULNERABILITY OF LEARNING THE PERFORMANCE

The socialization process unfolds as parents teach their children the performance in a total institution. In many of the interviews the respondents recalled how they were taught at an early age to, "do what whites tell you to do", that "whites rule this world" . . . and to "say yes sir, no sir." Black parents understood that they had to teach their children the frontstage performance of listening to whites. However, with few economic opportunities, coupled with the socialization to obey whites, young girls were vulnerable to becoming victims of sexual violence and rape at the hands of white perpetrators. Girls at a young age, socialized to obey, and eager to make money to help their families, were easily lured by white men with promises of work.

FRONTSTAGE: LURING LITTLE BLACK GIRLS WITH PROMISES OF MONEY

In the total institution of Jim Crow, the rapes of black girls and women were an ongoing problem. One of the characteristics of a total institution is economic control and a loss of personal safety. Frequently, white men coaxed young vulnerable girls into unsafe spaces with the promise of money—and then raped them. The promise of money, gifts, or work was enticing in the total institution, where young girls didn't have many resources or opportunities (McGuire, 2010). The white perpetrators were aware of the impoverishment in the total institution, coupled with the socialization of blacks, and used it to manipulate young girls, women, and their families.

In a total institution, backstage, black women had to endure listening to their young daughters describe some of the horrific things that happened to them at the hands of white men. Black newspapers often reported the atrocities and injustices that occurred in their communities. The pages also covered the outrage at the raping of black girls and women.

In the total institution, individuals with legitimate authority participated in and committed criminal and heinous acts. The practice of police officers raping black women had a long history. McGuire (2010) reports several incidents where young girls were abducted by uniformed police officers and threatened with imprisonment if they didn't allow police officers to sexually molest them. In the total institution of Jim Crow, the larger social structure and institutions supported and protected whites, including police officers.

A mistrust of the police is one of the long-term consequences of the historical experience (Feagin, 2000). The police are not legitimate in the eyes of the Black community because they are not there to protect blacks and their families from white perpetrators; they are part of the problem.

Throughout the black community, the rapes of black girls and the lack of consequences for white men did sometimes receive attention. On September 8, 1928, the *Baltimore Afro-American* reported, "John C. Carey, a white night watchman, who is alleged to have raped, on August 7, a young colored girl, age 12, was indicted for rape by the Orleans parish grand jury last Thursday" (p. 1). On May 19, 1934, in Petersburg, Virginia, a seven-year-old child who was described as "feeble-minded" was raped by R. C. Smith, a white man in his 50s " (*Baltimore Afro-American*, 1934, p. 3). In many of the rapes, the newspapers published the names, ages, and addresses of both the victims and the perpetrators. The stigma and shame associated with the rape followed the young girls throughout their lives. If the rapes resulted in pregnancy, the families had no recourse; the judicial system handed out minimal if any sentences for the crime of the rape itself. Coupled with subsequent pregnancy, the young girl and her family members were forever changed. According to Fannie Barrier Williams (quoted by McGuire [2010]) "the shameful fact [is] that. . . . Black women [are] engaged in a painful, patient, and silent toil"—an indication of the long-term consequences for the survivors (p. xix).

FRONTSTAGE: TWO TRAUMATIZED LITTLE GIRLS

During Jim Crow, young girls walking with other children (typical safety-in-numbers self-chaperoning) didn't deter a white rapist from kidnapping and rape. Two girls were walking home on a Sunday evening when they were abducted at gunpoint by a white man who raped the 11-year-old while her 17-year-old sister helplessly watched. According to the *Chicago Defender* (1926):

> Charles Merchant forced both sisters to take off their clothes. He raped the younger girl while her older sister sat nude in the street and watched unable to assist her. After the attack, Merchant forced the two, still nude, girls to walk through the streets. The older sister was able to escape and get help. The 11-year-old was later found naked and unconscious. A doctor confirmed that she had been brutally raped. (p. 3)

The paper further reported, "the [11-year-old] is in a sanitarium in a serious condition, due to the assault, and her sister is at home suffering from exposure and severe nervous shock" (p. 3). The trial lasted only a few days. Throughout the trial there were outbursts of tears and sobbing as the older sister explained to the all-white male jury and judge what happened on that Sunday evening. She said, "He ripped off our clothes." The 17-year-old continued, "he made me sit on the ground naked while he—he—attacked Ellie. Then he turned on me" ("Girl testifies," 1926, p. 3). It took the all-white jury less than an hour to find Merchant, "of unsound mind." Charles Merchant was set free.

The trauma of the experience would have forever changed the victims' lives and the lives of their family. These children could clearly suffer from some form of post-traumatic stress disorder. But in the total institution of Jim Crow, blacks didn't have access to mental health care and facilities. The trauma for the younger girl, first the attack, then the resulting trial, and then the verdict added to the stress that the family felt when they didn't get justice for their young child. In addition, the double standard of justice that allowed white men to receive mercy from all-white male juries, while black men would be sentenced to death if found guilty of the same crimes contributed to the collective pain, anger, and frustration of the black community.

FRONTSTAGE: DANGEROUS WORK—BLACK WOMEN WORKING IN WHITE HOMES

In this poignant excerpt, a custodian's use of the term *dipping* signals how common rape was during legal segregation. Hesitantly, he expresses how he realizes black women had no choice:

> My mamma was a maid. She used to work with a lot of white folks. . . . My mama had gray eyes and red hair . . . So, when he [my brother] come out, with blonde head, they ain't no good will where he come from. . . . He come from a [white] man who'd . . . been dipping into my family a long time ago . . . white folk, they love the [black] women especially. . . . Bring them in and [the white men's] wives couldn't say nothing. . . . And so you know about these kids, coming up with the light skin, you know. They know where they come from.

In a total institution, institutionalized men are denied the opportunity to respond to assaults against their family member, thus undermining their masculinity. The respondent mentioned that he had two brothers with blond hair. (His dark-skinned father left his mother when the respondent was young.) The respondents did not realize what occurred until they were older and considered the different colors in their family. The long-term consequences of dipping were the dismantling of a family, the loss of economic support from the father, and the shame associated with the mother having children by a man other than her husband. The research and respondents suggest that black women often had no choice and were coerced into sexual relations with influential white men (Gwaltney, 1993; Talty, 2003; Williamson, 1995).

FRONTSTAGE: WRECKLESS EYEBALLING EQUALS LOOK RAPE

One of our respondents in the southeast recalled reading in the newspaper that several black men were arrested and put on trial for *wreckless eyeballing*. In Jim Crow wreckless eyeballing was defined as when a black man made eye contact with a white, especially a white woman. Prolonged eye contact with whites by blacks was considered a crime of wreckless eyeballing and was considered a form of rape—*look rape*. The respondent states:

> I remember when [named a person] got six years in prison for looking in the direction of a white woman who was 75 feet away from him. He was charged with reckless eyeballing and he spent 6 years in prison. . . . If you look at whites too long white women you could be put in jail. That man went to jail for years and he was standing a long ways from the white women. [She began shaking her head back and forth in disgust].

Indeed, it was reported by the *Philadelphia Tribune* (1952) that a father of nine children was arrested for wreckless eyeballing. According to the *Tribune*:

> Black Man Looks and Goes to Trial for Wreckless Eyeballing. The defendant, a father of nine, "was not within 75 feet of the white girl but was arrested, tried, and convicted of look rape." (p. 1)

This father of nine lost his job and his means of income. These cases carried with them a stigma of guilt instead of innocent-until-proven-guilty. In addition, wreckless eyeballing wasn't considered a crime for white men. In a total institution, the rules and laws were applied differently based upon race and gender. In all of these rape cases the pain and voices of the families were invisible. When a person was accused of rape or was raped it involved the family, the extended family, and the entire community. It was rare in white newspapers to hear the voice of a mother whose son was falsely accused of rape and killed for a crime he didn't commit.

In some instances, the rapes of women and children occurred in their own homes. The homes of blacks in a total institution were usually considered a safe space for them in the backstage to practice their lines and prepare for their performance in the frontstage with whites. However, it was not uncommon for white rapists to enter their homes and commit rape. Black women did resist the rapes (McGuire, 2010).

The body of social science and medical scholarship now accumulated about rape and its consequences (van der Kolk, McFarlane, & Weisaeth, 2006; Wasco, 2003) clearly states that the trauma of rape almost certainly leads to a lifetime of psychological problems. Blacks who were raped suffered additionally from *segregation stress syndrome* (Thompson-Miller & Feagin, 2007)—similar to post-traumatic stress disorder but with specific elements relating to the black experience under the total institution of Jim Crow—including the stigma associated with rape.

FRONTSTAGE: SHAME

Throughout the interviews our respondents frequently mentioned that black women were ladies, that is, morally upright individuals. A respondent in the southeast recalls:

> And to be honest with you and truly, back in those days, women were not promiscuous at all . . . if a young girl messed around and got pregnant, she was ostracized. The child wasn't. But that was a black eye to the family. That was a black eye to the girl. Shame. For

the child and the family, because it was a reflection on the family, I didn't do a good job, and that was the standard back then.

The respondent's testimony challenges the historical narrative that black women were promiscuous in the total institution of Jim Crow. The respondent states, "There was a whole value system." There was a "black eye to the family . . . the girl . . . shame" if a young girl got pregnant. However, in the total institution of Jim Crow young girls were getting raped on a regular basis and unfortunately the black community, in some instances, didn't differentiate between the pregnancies that resulted from rape, and those that resulted from consensual sex.

In the black community, the pregnancies that were the result of the rapes were not viewed favorably. In fact, one of the respondent's interviewed recalled how she was ostracized:

> I was ostracized by the Black community. They [the Black community] chased my mother out of town. . . . My mother was ostracized because she was raped by a white man. I only met my white father once, he gave me a coat. I never saw him again. My mother left town and I was raised by my grandmother. Throughout my life I was treated differently for being mixed. I was just a little girl. It wasn't my fault. I lost my mother and my father. I had to fight to get respect from Blacks.

The respondent didn't have the benefit of being raised by her mother. She expressed the pain she felt at being stigmatized throughout her life because her mother was raped. She was not alone; the evidence of how common the stigmatization was in the black community is the term *kitchen babies.* In the black community, kitchen babies was a term used to identify the children of white salesmen (selling ice, insurance, kitchen appliances, and other items) who were able to gain entry into the homes of black women and coerce them into sex.

BACKSTAGE: KITCHEN BABIES

Another one of our respondents in the southwest in her late seventies responds to the same question, "Can you recall any experiences your mother, father, or grandparents shared with you that they had with a white person?" The respondent recalls a story of rape:

> I remember this little boy [sighs] across the street named Charlie, he was one of my friends, we was the same age, and he was white, but his mother was lighter than I am, his mother looked white but she was black and she married a black man and they had a daughter who was about my complexion. Then Charlie came here with blonde hair and snow white just really, really, white. The daddy said, "I'm outta here" he left and said, "That's not my baby." Charlie went to school with us through about the first or second grade and his mother got such flack, you know in the neighborhood they said, "He was the ice man's baby." They used to deliver ice to the house and come in and put it in your icebox wrapped in those burlap bags . . . you didn't have refrigerators then, it was iceboxes, and they said, "That Charlie's daddy was the ice man." His mother finally after about a year or two she just packed him up and moved to [names place]. [She] reared him as a white boy and then when he got grown he moved back to [names place] and left him. . . . He never accepted the fact that he ever had any black in him, but his mother reared him that way, and when his mother died that's the only time he ever came back to [names place], his sister was living there and the mother was there. He came for the funeral, his sister said, "He got there just in time for the funeral, went to the funeral, and when it was over he told her goodbye

and that was it.". . . She never heard from him anymore. He was a little boy and it wasn't his fault, but the kids teased him and everything.

White salesmen gained entry into black people's homes and raped women. We see the long-term consequences associated with the stigma of rape on the mother and the innocent child. Goffman (1961) defines the stigma of race, "the tribal stigma of race, nation, and religion, these being stigma that can be transmitted through lineages and equally contaminate all members of a family" (p. 4). Black girls and women who survived rape faced the stigma of race, gender, and rape. The children of these rapes bore a lifetime of stigma, shame, and a spoiled identity. Bearing children born of rape forced this mother and child to leave their family, community, and social networks. In a total institution, acts of racial violence left the survivors and their families with an array of emotions including humiliation, self-blame, anger, rage, helplessness, and fear (Bryant-Davis & Ocampo, 2005, p. 492). Such sexual violence was at the heart of the total institution of slavery and Jim Crow. Its often concealed psychological and physical injuries have lasted for generations.

Conclusion

In this chapter, we have documented case after case that shows the systematic rape of black women and young girls. In the chapter, we demonstrate the intersection of race, class, and gender in the accounts from the respondents. The long-term consequences for the survivors include possible mental health consequences, intergenerational transmission of trauma, loss of social support, and a lack of access to wealth associated with inheritance. We have documented the voice of the victim and trauma that they suffered. In addition, with the assistance of newspaper articles, we've provided the regularity in which these rapes occurred in the black communities in the total institution of Jim Crow. Lastly, this chapter clearly provides proof that black men received swift and harsh punishment when they were accused of rape in the total institution of Jim Crow. However, throughout the narratives of the respondents and the newspaper articles we see evidence that white men received little to no punishment for the raping of black women and young girls.

According to van der Kolk et al. (2006), "most victims who are conscious of the effects of trauma on their lives preserve their self-protective instincts and are highly ambivalent about having people find out what has happened to them" (p. 31). In addition, the judicial system's dismissal of the rapes of black women and girls reinforced the silence about the systematic rapes during Jim Crow. This chapter shows the long history of rape and sexual coercion in the black community and the unresolved psychological consequences for the survivors.

References

Black man looks and goes to trial for wreckless eyeballing. (1952, March) *Philadelphia Tribune* (1912–2001). Retrieved from ProQuest Historical Newspapers, http://www.proquest.com/assets/literature/products/databases/phillytrib.pdf

Bryant-Davis, T. & Ocampo, C. (2005). Racist incident-based trauma. *Counseling Psychologist, 33*(4), 479–500.

Clinton, C. (1984). *The plantation mistress: Woman's world in the old south.* New York, NY: Pantheon.

Davis, A. (1990). *Women, culture, and politics*. New York, NY: Vintage Books.

Ellis, A. E., & Ellis, L. C. (2003). *The trial of Ruby McCollum*. Bloomington, IN: First Books Library.

Feagin, J. (2000). *Racist America*. New York, NY: Routledge.

Girl testifies at trial. (1926, May) *Chicago Defender* (1910–1975). Retrieved from ProQuest Historical Newspapers, http://www.proquest.com/assets/literature/products/databases/ChicagoDefend.pdf

Girls reveal story of brutal crime. (1926, April) *Chicago Defender* (1910–1975). Retrieved from ProQuest Historical Newspapers, http://www.proquest.com/assets/literature/products/databases/ChicagoDefend.pdf

Goffman, E. (1961). *The presentation of self in everyday life*. New York, NY: Anchor Books.

Gwaltney, J. L. (1993). *Drylongso: A self-portrait of Black America*. New York, NY: New Press.

Hopkins, C. Q., & Koss, M. P. (2005). Incorporating feminist theory insights into a restorative justice response to sex offenses. *Violence Against Women*, 11(5), 693–723.

Indict white rapist, (1928, September). *Baltimore Afro-American* (1893–1988). Retrieved from ProQuest Historical Newspapers, http://www.proquest.com/assets/literature/products/databases/baltafroamer.pdf

Knottnerus, J. D., Monk, D. L., & Jones, E. (1999). The slave plantation system from a total institution perspective. In T. J. Durant & J. D. Knottnerus (Eds.), *Plantation society and race relations: The origins of inequality* (pp. 17–29). Westpoint, CT: Praeger.

Litwack, L. F. (1998). *Trouble in mind*. New York, NY: Random House.

McGuire, D. (2010). *At the dark end of the street: Black women, rape, and resistance—A new history of the civil rights movement from Rosa Parks to the rise of Black power*. New York, NY: Alfred A. Knopf.

Packard, J. (2002). *American nightmare: The history of Jim Crow*. New York, NY: St. Martin's Press.

Spickard, P. (1989). *Mixed blood: Intermarriage and ethnic identity in twentieth century America*. Madison, WI: University of Wisconsin Press.

Talty, S. (2003). *Mulatto America*. New York, NY: HarperCollins.

Thompson-Miller, R., & Feagin, J. (2007). The reality and impact of legal segregation in the United States. In V. Hernan & J. Feagin (Eds.), *Handbook of the sociology of racial and ethnic relations* (pp. 455–464). New York, NY: Springer.

van der Kolk, B., McFarlane, A., & Weisaeth, L. (2006). *Traumatic stress: The effects of overwhelming experience on mind, body, and society*. New York, NY: Guilford Press.

Virginia white man rapes seven-year-old girl. (1934, May) *Baltimore Afro-American* (1893-1988). Retrieved from ProQuest Historical Newspapers, http://www.proquest.com/assets/literature/products/databases/baltafroamer.pdf

Wacquant, L. (2001). Deadly symbiosis: When ghetto and prison meet and mesh. In D. Garland (Ed.), *Mass imprisonment: Social causes and consequences* (pp. 82–120). London, UK: Sage.

Wasco, S. (2003). Conceptualizing the harm done by rape: Applications of trauma theory to experiences of sexual assault. *Trauma, Violence, & Abuse* 4(4), 309–322.

Williams, L. M. (1986). *Race and rape: The Black woman as legitimate victim*. Unpublished Paper. Durham: University of New Hampshire.

Williamson, J. (1995). *New people: Miscegenation and mulattoes in the United States*. Baton Rouge: Louisiana State University Press.

Wyatt, G. E. (1990). Sexual abuse of ethnic minority children: Identifying dimensions of victimization." *Professional Psychology: Research and Practice*, 21, 338–343.

Black Girls, Gender, and Violence

Nikki Jones & Alexis McCurn

In contrast to the lives of many middle-class, suburban adolescents, black inner-city girls and their parents, grandparents, or caretakers must make hard choices (Richie, 1999) about how to manage the various challenges associated with coming of age in today's inner city, including threats of interpersonal violence and exposure to gender-specific forms of violence. Typically, inner-city girls' experiences with violence are overshadowed in public consideration either by the moral panic surrounding so-called mean girls in the suburbs or the crisis of the young black male in urban settings. Yet, field research among young black women and girls in neighborhoods marked by concentrated poverty and its associated social ills reveal that both boys and girls who come of age in distressed urban neighborhoods develop a preoccupation with safety and survival. In this chapter, we draw on field research conducted in Philadelphia, PA (2001–2003), San Francisco, CA (2005–2010), and Oakland, CA (2008–2010), to describe the common types of violence black inner-city girls encounter in distressed urban areas and the strategies they develop to navigate this often precarious urban terrain. The chapter reveals that black inner-city girls must contend with a range of threats to their personal security and well-being, including neighborhood violence, interpersonal violence, dating violence, and a form of violence we describe as *microinteractional assaults*. Micro-interactional assaults include a range of aggressive interactional exchanges that black women and girls are often drawn into as they navigate urban public space. Young women adapt to these difficult circumstances by developing a set of *situated survival strategies* (Jones, 2009); we describe benefits and limitations of these strategies and their gendered consequences.

RACE, GENDER, AND INNER-CITY VIOLENCE

"It's about survival!"

—Tracey, Philadelphia

"It's about being a survivor, and we have to survive."

—Kiara, San Francisco

Tracey and Kiara are black women in their early 20s.[1] Despite living on opposite coasts of the country, the two young women expressed a common concern with survival that is informed by the settings in which inner-city girls come of age. Tracey, who worked as a violence intervention counselor in Philadelphia when I first interviewed her in 2001,[2] grew up in a predominantly black neighborhood in the southern part of the city. A large, postindustrial, northeastern city, Philadelphia has experienced many of the same structural and economic changes that have impacted cities across the United States over the last 30 years, including deindustrialization, the concentration of poverty, and hypersegregation of its inner-city areas (Anderson, 1999; Massey & Denton 1999; Wilson, 1980, 1987, 1996). In some respects, Philadelphia's central city population has been hit harder by these changes than residents in comparable metropolitan areas. Philadelphia's poverty rate in 2000, the year before I began my field research, was 22.9%—almost double the national rate of 12.4%. Rates of concentrated poverty increased in Philadelphia during the 1990s even as rates leveled or declined in other metropolitan areas across the United States. In some neighborhoods near where Tracey lived, between 30% and 40% of the resident population lived in poverty (Brookings Institution Center on Urban and Metropolitan Policy [BICUMP], 2003; Pettit & Kingsley, 2003). It is now well known that this combination of poverty and segregation tends to concentrate crime, violence, and other social ills in poor communities of color (Anderson, 1999; Lauritsen & Sampson, 1998; Massey & Denton, 1999; Peterson & Krivo, 2005; Sampson & Wilson, 1995; Wilson, 1980, 1987, 1996).

Kiara grew up in a similarly distressed neighborhood in San Francisco. In the mid-1900s, the Fillmore neighborhood of San Francisco where Kiara was "born and raised," as she says, was home to a vibrant black community. During this time, locals often referred to the neighborhood as the Harlem of the west. After World War II, as the shipping industry and many of its black workers moved away, city government officials declared the area a slum. Large portions of the neighborhood were razed and replaced by housing projects. As inner-city conditions worsened across the country, the predominantly black Fillmore neighborhood also experienced the various consequences of the increased concentration of poverty, including increased crime, rapidly deteriorating schools, and an increase in drug trafficking and the violence associated with the drug trade (Anderson, 1999; Massey & Denton, 1993; Wilson, 1980, 1987, 1996).

For many who are familiar with the city, including the residents of the nearby and gentrifying Lower Pacific Heights, Alamo Square neighborhoods, and smaller Japantown neighborhoods, the Fillmore (as it is known locally) is largely considered a bad neighborhood marked by crime and violence. Newspaper reports of shootings and gang activity often reinforce such assumptions (Martin, 2006; Van Derbeken, 2005; Van Derbeken & Lagos, 2006).

Much of the violence that takes place in neighborhoods like the ones Tracey and Kiara grew up in is governed by a hypermasculine eye-for-an-eye ethic that urban ethnographer Elijah Anderson (1999) terms the *code of the street*: a system of

---

[1]The women shared these strikingly similar remarks with the first author during the course of field research in Philadelphia (2001–2003) and San Francisco (2005–2010). (See also, Jones, 2009; and 2010b, p. 203).

[2]The city hospital-based violence reduction project targeted youth aged 12 to 24 who entered the emergency department as the result of an intentional violent incident and lived in one of several zip codes in South and West Philadelphia.

accountability that governs formal and informal interactions in distressed urban areas, especially interpersonal violence. At the heart of the code, Anderson writes, is a battle for respect and manhood. In *Black Sexual Politics* (2004), Patricia Hill Collins writes that as black men embrace the code, they embrace a hegemonic masculinity that is based on the coupling of strength with dominance—white men with wealth and power are able to demonstrate such masculinity through economic or military dominance (in addition to physical dominance), while poor black men in distressed urban areas must rely primarily on physical domination, which makes them and others in their community more vulnerable to violent victimization.[3]

Through instruction, observation, and experience, inner-city girls, no less than boys, learn how reputation, respect, and retaliation—the fundamental elements of the code of the street—organize their social world. These statements from Danielle and Robert, two young people who are adept at avoiding conflicts, illustrate teen-age girls' and boys' shared understanding of the importance of demonstrating that one is willing to fight as a way to deter ongoing challenges to one's well-being.

> DANIELLE: 'Cause sometimes you got to fight, not fight, but get into that type of battle to let them know that I'm not scared of you and you can't keep harassing me thinking that it's okay.
>
> ROBERT: You know, if someone keep picking on you like that, you gonna have to do something to prove a point to them: that you not going to be scared of them. . . . So, sometimes you do got to, you do got to fight. 'Cause you just got to tell them that you not scared of them.

While neither Danielle nor Robert identify as fighters, both are convinced that sometimes you "got to fight." Like adolescent inner-city boys, inner-city girls have stories to tell about peers who get "rolled on" or "jumped," or were involved in a "fair one" gone bad. Like their male counterparts, inner-city girls can often name someone who has been shot, robbed, or stabbed. Inner-city girls understand at early ages that stray bullets do not discriminate between young and old, guilt and innocence, or boys and girls. They know that the settings of inner-city life, whether school buildings or row houses, neighborhood street corners or porch stoops, do not come with a special girls-only pass to live beyond the reach of violence. The need to avoid or overcome dangers throughout their adolescence presents a uniquely gendered challenge for girls who grow up in these neighborhoods.

BETWEEN GOOD AND GHETTO: BLACK GIRLS, GENDER, AND VIOLENCE

As a system of accountability, gender reflects widely held beliefs, or normative expectations, about the "attitudes and activities appropriate for one's sex category" (West & Zimmerman, 1987, p. 127). During interactions and encounters with others, children and adults evaluate themselves and others in light of these normative

---

[3]Anderson's and Collins' analyses are consistent with other masculinity studies that describe how the lack of access to economic resources encourage poor men of color to become men through displays of physical strength and violence.

gender expectations in ways that reinforce or challenge beliefs about the natural qualities of boys and girls, and especially the essential differences between the two (West & Fenstermaker, 1995). Generally, women and girls who are able to mirror normative expectations of femininity during their interactions with others—for example, by assuming a passive demeanor and presenting an appearance that does not significantly deviate from the standards of mainstream culture or local preferences—are evaluated by adults (e.g., family members, teachers, and counselors) and by peers as appropriately feminine girls or *good* girls. Meanwhile, girls or women who seem to violate perceived gender boundaries by embracing stereotypically masculine behaviors (e.g., strength, independence, and an outwardly aggressive demeanor) often are disparagingly categorized as "unnaturally strong" (Collins, 2004, pp. 193–199).

The intersection of gender, race, and class—also understood as *intersectionality*—further complicates the degree to which girls measure up to gender expectations. Black inner-city girls in the United States are evaluated not only in light of mainstream gender expectations but also in light of the expectations of black respectability: the set of expectations governing how black women and girls ought to behave. These expectations are reflected in images of the black lady—think Clair Huxtable from the popular 1980s sitcom *The Cosby Show*—the middle-class black woman who reflects many of the expectations of white middle-class femininity (Collins, 2004, pp. 139–140). Black ladies distance themselves from behavioral displays of physical aggression or overt sexuality that are commonly associated with poor or working-class black women. Black women and adolescent girls whose shade of skin color, body size, attitude, or demeanor deviate even slightly from mainstream expectations of femininity or black female respectability are especially vulnerable to the formal and informal sanctions that accompany such gender violations (Cole & Guy-Sheftal, 2003; Collins, 2004; Richie, 1996).

Inner-city girls who live in distressed urban neighborhoods face a *gendered dilemma*: they must learn how to effectively manage potential threats of interpersonal violence—in most cases this means that they must work the code of the street as boys and men do—at the risk of violating mainstream and local expectations regarding appropriate feminine behavior. This is an especially difficult dilemma for girls, since the gendered expectations surrounding girls' and women's use or control of violence are especially constraining. Conventional wisdom suggests that girls and women, whether prompted by nature, socialization, or a combination of the two, generally avoid physically aggressive or violent behavior: girls are expected to use relational aggression and fight with words and tears, not fists or knives. Inner-city girls, like most American girls, feel pressure to be good, decent, and respectable. Yet, like some inner-city boys, they may also feel pressure to "go for bad" (Katz, 1988) or to establish a tough front (Anderson, 1999; Dance, 2002) in order to deter potential challengers on the street or in the school setting. They too may believe that "sometimes you do got to fight"—and sometimes they do fight. In doing so, these girls, and especially those girls who become deeply invested in crafting a public persona as a tough or violent girl, risk evaluation by peers, adults, and outsiders as *street* or *ghetto*.

Among urban and suburban adolescents, ghetto is a popular slang term that is commonly used to categorize a person or behavior as ignorant, stupid, or otherwise morally deficient. Inner-city residents use the term to describe the same kinds of actions and attitudes Elijah Anderson (1999) termed *street orientation*. Analytically, the pairs "ghetto" and "good," and "street" and "decent," are used to represent "two poles of value orientation, two contrasting conceptual categories" that structure the moral order of inner-city life (Anderson,1999, p. 35). In inner-city neighborhoods, the decent/street or good/ghetto distinctions are powerful. Community members use these distinctions as a basis for understanding, interpreting, and predicting their own and others' actions, attitudes, and behaviors, especially when it comes to interpersonal violence (Anderson, 1999). There is also a gendered dimension to these evaluative categories: good or decent girls are "young ladies" while "ghetto chicks" are adolescent girls whose "behaviors, dress, communication, and interaction styles" contrast with both mainstream and black middle-class expectations of appropriate and respectable femininity (Thompson & Keith, 2004, p. 58).

The branding of adolescent girls as ghetto is self-perpetuating, alienating the institutional forces that protect good girls and forcing adolescent girls who work the code of the street to become increasingly independent. Girls who are categorized by adults or peers as ghetto, as opposed to those categorized as good, ultimately may have the code as their only protection in the too often violent inner-city world in which they live. Their efforts to protect themselves put them at risk of losing access to formal institutional settings like schools or the church, where girls who mirror normative gender expectations—girls who are perceived by others as good—can take some refuge. Yet, even for those good girls, this institutional protection is inadequate—they are aware that they may become targets in school or on the street and they too feel pressure to develop strategies that will help them successfully navigate their neighborhoods. Thus, inner-city girls find themselves caught in what amounts to a perpetual gendered dilemma, forced by violent circumstances to choose between two options, neither of which offers the level of security that is generally taken for granted in areas outside of urban poverty.

Working the Code

A comment shared by Kiara helps to illustrate how inner-city girls work the code. During an interview, Kiara explained that as a child in the Fillmore she garnered a level of respect because of the street reputation of her father. People would "cater" to her because, she says, her father "used to sell a lot of drugs" in the neighborhood. Kiara sums up her appreciation of the importance of being able to move between good and ghetto, depending on the situation. "I had the street element," she says, "and I was aggressive for the streets, pretty for the pictures." As Kiara's comment suggests, real people—and perhaps especially adolescents—do not fit neatly into only one of two conceptual categories. Instead, girls astutely work the code in between the equal and opposing pressures of good and ghetto. From this social location, girls are able to challenge and manipulate the constraining social and cultural expectations embedded in gender and the code, depending on the situation. Elijah Anderson (1999) defines the activity of adapting one's behavior to the set of rules that govern a situation—decent or street, good or ghetto—as *code switching*. Inner-city families and youth, most of whom strive for decency, put a "special premium" on the ability to "switch codes and play by the rules of the street," when necessary (Anderson, 1999, pp. 36, 98–106). Of course, this act is complicated for girls because working the code is likely to challenge expectations regarding appropriate feminine behavior. Inner-city girls work the code with the understanding that they are always accountable to these gendered expectations and that gender violations are likely to open them up to a series of public or private sanctions. Girls' lives seem to be defined by this everyday struggle to balance the need to protect themselves with the pressure to meet normative expectations associated with their gender, race, and class positions. Girls' accounts of how they manage these expectations, including how they work the code, defy any simple categorizations or stereotypical evaluations of girls as either good or ghetto. Instead, girls' accounts of violent incidents reveal that they embrace, challenge, reinforce, reflect, and contradict normative expectations of femininity and black respectability as they work the code. Girls' accounts of navigating inner-city adolescence are characterized by this fluidity.

"IT HAPPENS ALL THE TIME": GHETTO GIRLS AND MICRO-INTERACTIONAL ASSAULTS

In inner-city neighborhoods that are governed by the code of the street, boys and girls come to appreciate the lesson that "sometimes you do got to fight," as Danielle (quoted above) says. Yet, in addition to making sense of neighborhood violence and negotiating potential threats of interpersonal violence, black inner-city girls frequently confront a set of gender-specific threats in their neighborhoods that are often overlooked. These threats include the threat of sexual assault and a range of other assaults and injuries that young women and girls encounter in neighborhood institutions, like corner stores, or while walking from place to place in the neighborhood. Even when they are not physically injurious, these encounters can be humiliating and painful for adolescent girls (see also Miller, 2008; Renzetti & Maier, 2002; Websdale, 2001). These routine interactions also communicate messages about a young black woman's place in the neighborhood, specifically that black women and girls are not deserving of the same sort of public courtesies as others, and especially men (Gardner, 1995). These routine troubled encounters are best described as micro-interactional assaults.

Micro-interactional assaults (MIAs) include a set of aggressive interactional exchanges that Black women and girls are often drawn into as they navigate urban public space. These interactions may involve a range of actors, from store clerks to men on the street. These interactions are characterized by the public degradation of black women and girls (Garfinkel, 1956). The verbal and nonverbal exchanges that are embedded in micro-interactional assaults often reflect biased attitudes and beliefs about marginalized groups in general and black women in particular. During these interactional exchanges, participants routinely engage in behaviors that are typically described as *microaggressions,* especially name-calling or insults that have the effect of intimidating, threatening, or instilling feelings of inferiority in the participant who holds the least amount of power in the interaction (Sue, 2010). These microaggressions often have the consequence of making the targeted person feel unwanted and unsafe (Sue, 2010).

The young women described in this chapter are not only exposed to disapproving looks and disparaging asides from outsiders. They are regularly drawn into aggressive interactional exchanges during routine encounters with others in their neighborhood. Young women cannot always easily avoid these encounters. Checks need to be cashed. Groceries need to be purchased. The necessity of performing these routine tasks in the settings described in this chapter—distressed urban neighborhoods—is what exposes young women and girls to repeated verbal and nonverbal social injuries. For these young women and girls, micro-interactional assaults are best understood not as occasional occurrences but rather as what Erving Goffman (1963) describes as regular occasions, a subcategory of social occasions. Regular occasions are "instances that form part of a series of like occasions, the series being seen as a unit and developing as such as a daily, weekly, or annual cycle" (Goffman, 1963, p. 19). The aggressive interactions described in this chapter are not one-off occasions. As Shante explained, young women are drawn into such encounters "all the time."

The Routine Nature of Micro-Interactional Assaults

In inner-city neighborhoods, young black women often experience micro-interactional assaults in settings where they carry out much of their daily routine. For example, young women and girls report encountering MIAs when they cash checks at the local check-cashing establishment, ride the city bus, or buy groceries. In local businesses like the corner store, store clerks greet neighborhood youth, including young black women, with some suspicion. Young women often complain that they receive poor customer service from store employees. The following field-note excerpt illustrates how these sorts of MIAs unfold. The excerpt also illustrates how understandings of poor black women and girls are revealed during the course of routine encounters like going to the store. The encounter in this excerpt involves a black woman in her early 20s who is negotiating a purchase with her EBT (Electronic Benefit Transfer) card at a local grocery store. In California, residents who receive public assistance can use their EBT card to pay for food (field note recorded by Alexis McCurn on November 28, 2009).

> I wait in the checkout line of the neighborhood grocery store. A young Black woman in her early 20s tells a middle-aged white female store clerk who is ringing up her items that she wants to buy some milk along with her other groceries lying on the conveyor belt. She does so in a calm tone. The young woman explains to the checker that the gallon-size 2% milk that she wants has an expiration date of tomorrow printed on the outside of the container. The checker proceeds to tell the young woman that if she doesn't want to get that particular container of milk then she should get another kind with an expiration date that she prefers. The customer then asks the store clerk if she can have someone go in the back of the store to see if there are any more gallons milk with a later expiration date because all of the containers she sees on the shelf have the same date as the one in front of her. She really needs to buy the milk today, she says. The checker replies in a voice loud enough for others to hear while waiting in line several steps away: "No. You have to get what is on the shelf or come back another day." The customer replies in a calm voice "I just don't want to waste my money on a gallon of milk that is going to spoil in one or two days." The checker replies, "You're not paying with your money, you're paying with that," as she points to the EBT card the woman holds in her hands.

This encounter is troubled in many ways. The level of verbal hostility expressed by the clerk would no doubt upset many middle-class shoppers. Such an exchange might encourage a middle-class shopper to call for a manager. Yet, the clerk seems comfortable and confident in her treatment of this particular customer. The clerk denies this customer's request to check on a product, which is a common request in many other settings. Instead, she directs the customer to make a choice that the customer has already deemed unsatisfactory: go get another gallon of milk from the gallons on the shelf, all of which, by the customer's account, are near expiration. Dismissing a customer's request in this way challenges norms of civility that go along with the expectations that many of us have when we enter a store. The troubled encounter is punctuated by a micro-interactional assault that reveals something about how the clerk sees this particular customer.

Throughout this encounter, the store clerk, instead of displaying deference to the customer in front of her, assumes a position of authority. Her interactions suggest that it is she who demands deference from the customer—a divergence from the common belief that "the customer is always right." During the course of this interaction, the intersecting aspects of the young woman's identity appear to trigger a set of interactions that, in the end, lead to a pubic degradation of the young woman's status position: she is not a valued customer who is paying for food with her own money, instead, she is a poor, black woman who is paying with "that"—she is, put simply, ghetto. The store clerk's behavior suggests that because she uses an EBT card, the young woman does not deserve the same sort of civility that is extended to others with more power and more status. This sort of dismissive comment is a micro-interactional assault that degrades the status of the young black woman—the clerk orients her interactions with this young woman around her understanding of this degraded status (Goffman, 1967).

Many of us would simply shrug off this sort of encounter. It would be more difficult to do so, however, if we encountered these hostilities on a daily basis, as many young women and girls who live in neighborhoods in East Oakland, San Francisco, and Philadelphia do. As Feagin and Sikes write, "Black shoppers at all income levels report being ignored when in need of service" (Feagin & Sikes, 1994, p. 48). Indeed, blacks are subject to hostile encounters and hypersurveillance regardless of their social class status. Other forms of anti-black discrimination, such as exclusion, rejection, and forms of attack are also commonplace experiences for blacks in many public settings (Feagin & Sikes, 1994). However, while all black people are susceptible to episodic racial injuries, poverty and segregation turn such experiences into regular occasions for poor black women and girls who live in distressed urban neighborhoods.

The frustration, humiliation, and pain that emerge in the wake of these encounters do not simply fade away at the close of an interaction, either. These negative feelings can be long lasting; single incidents of hostility and discrimination can produce lifelong memories that inform the worldviews and perspectives of those who are the frequent targets of micro-interactional assaults. For example, research studies using the Rotter Introversion–Extroversion Scale, a scale that measures whether or not an individual feels in control over his or her life, have found that blacks and whites often score differently on measures of control. Black people are more likely than whites to feel as if their lives are controlled by outside forces, which can make it more difficult to maintain a sense of personal well-being. Regular encounters with MIAs can exacerbate feelings of powerlessness (Feagin & Sikes, 1994). Such experiences can also reopen wounds from historical trauma that includes the generational inheritance of injuries from racism and discrimination. For every assault that occurs today, every past wound, even those experienced by prior generations, is deepened.

BLACK GIRLS ON GHETTO STREETS

The sorts of encounters described in the previous section occur alongside other stressful events that many of us encounter on a daily basis. Together, these encounters can result in profound stress for any person to endure (Sue, 2010). For black inner-city girls, these harmful experiences are compounded by a set of MIAs they are exposed to on the street: Inner-city girls are frequent targets of sexual invitations or insults from men. For young women and girls, it is not uncommon for a walk down the street to be accompanied by a sexualized comment or action from a young man around their age group (late adolescence) or sexual harassment by older adult males. These sorts of MIAs follow a typical pattern. A young man launches an invitation at a young woman like "How you doin'" or "Can I talk to you?" The person who initiated the encounter often perceives silence as a rejection of his invitation, which typically leads to an escalation of the troubled encounter. In these cases the person who initiated the interaction, much like the clerk in the excerpt above, will likely launch an insult that degrades the status of the target of the encounter. For example, a young woman who rejects an invitation to an encounter from a young man may be called a "black bitch" or dismissed as a girl who foolishly "thinks she all that" (see also Duneier & Molotch, 1999). In some cases, the escalation of the encounter will move from public degradation to threats of personal injury, including sexual assault (see also Cobbina, Miller, & Brunson, 2008; Miller, 2008).

The following accounts illustrate the typical ways in which these types of encounters unfold. Shante is a young woman in her early 20s. In the following excerpt, she describes how men approach her when she walks through her East Oakland neighborhood:

> Typically when I am walking down the street around here guys act like dogs. They yell "Hey girl" to get me to turn around, but if I ignore them they start calling me all out of my name. It happens all the time. It's like they're always saying something foul; if it's at least two of them out on the corner then you know they probably got something to say to you. It don't matter what you're doing or if you're just going about your business. They either hollering about how they want to "get with you" (sexual invitation) or if you reject them they talk all kinds of shit about you and why you are just a bitch just 'cause you don't want them.

Shante's account reveals the basic elements of the micro-interactional assaults that girls encounter on the streets. The encounter typically occurs when walking by a place where men are in a group, like a local street corner or other such *staging area* (Anderson, 1999). Then, an invitation: "Hey, girl!" If a young woman ignores the invitation, she is open to being "called out her name"—a phrase used to describe the experience of being called a derogatory term, like "bitch" or "ho." This sort of rejection often leads to an escalation of the conflict. In Shante's account, rejection leads to an onslaught of gender-specific insults: "if you reject them they talk all kinds of shit about you and why you are just a bitch just 'cause you don't want them."

Another young woman, Tiffany, describes a similar interaction she had after leaving a neighborhood store. Tiffany left the store carrying a package of baby formula. When she reached the edge of the sidewalk, readying herself to cross the street, a shiny blue sedan came to a screeching halt in front of her. The car blocked her way. She describes how she greeted the driver with an angry stare. The driver had a big smile on his face, she says. He then got out of the car and approached her on the sidewalk as she tried to walk away. Tiffany describes what happened after he approached her:

> I just tried to ignore him, the way he was looking at me was like I was naked or something. He kept saying, "You with the big booty. I want to talk to you," but I just kept on walking. Then he called me a ho with a fucked up attitude and I got really hot (angry), but then I was just like forget it, it ain't even worth it. I was so mad 'cause he doesn't even know me and he thinks it's okay to talk about my ass to my face like that. The twisted thing is he thinks it's a compliment but then if I don't act like I like it I got to be a "ho with a fucked up attitude."

Tiffany's comments are typical of how a standard micro-interactional assault on the street unfolds. "You with the big booty. I want to talk to you," is launched by the driver of the blue sedan as an invitation to engage in an encounter. His invitation is rejected when Tiffany walks away. This leads to an escalation in the form of gender-specific insults directed at Tiffany: "Then he called me a ho with a fucked up attitude." Tiffany and Shante's interactions are shaped by underlying assumptions of the availability of Black women, especially poor Black women who are often seen as more sexually available than other women. Each woman describes how quickly an escalation of a man's invitation leads to the launching of gender-specific verbal assaults.

In some situations, these encounters also end with threats of physical or sexual assault. For example, 19-year-old Kira provides an account of how a micro-interactional assault on the street ended with a threat to her personal security:

> Every day for the past few weeks I see these same guys on the corner. It's usually three, sometimes four of them at a time. At first when I would walk past them on my way to the bus stop one of them would be like "Hi, how you doing," "You look good," or "When you gonna give me your [telephone] number?" and I wouldn't say anything, just keep on walking. Then after like two weeks of passing them every day one of the guys seemed to get all angry and one day was like, "You think you too good to talk to me? You ugly anyway." So I still didn't say anything, I just kept walking and ignoring them. Then one day the same guy saw me walking toward them and started talking crazy and was getting loud so I could hear him. He said "Here come that little stuck up ho, don't nobody want your ho ass anyway" and then they all started laughing. So then I couldn't take it no more, so I started yelling and screaming and cussing him out. He just kept saying, "Girl, get out my face. Don't make me hit you."

Here again we see the routine pattern of invitation-rejection-escalation that characterized Shante and Tiffany's accounts. The trajectory of Kira's account is slightly different, however, because she not only rejects the young men with her silence, but then also offers her own retaliatory attack by "yelling and screaming and cussing him out." This rejection coupled with a challenge leads to a warning and a threat from the young man: "Girl, get out my face. Don't make me hit you." The nature of this man's remark underscores normalization of gender-specific violence in this setting. The young woman's efforts to defend herself are met with the threat of physical violence. According to Kira's account, this threat did not meet with any noticeable sanction from the other young men on the block. These types of encounters place young black women and girls in a lose–lose situation as they try to navigate urban public space. If they try to ignore the harassment it gets worse, and if they call attention to the harasser's behavior by staging a turnabout and deferring the attention back to him, their personal safety is put in jeopardy. In some cases, young women do not even have time to mount a defense. This lose–lose-lose dilemma is illustrated in a final account from Nicole, a 21-year-old mother of a 2-year-old daughter. In this excerpt, Nicole describes her encounter with a middle-aged black man at a bus stop in her East Oakland neighborhood:

> It was early one morning in the winter. The weather was cold and raining and it was still dark outside. I was holding my daughter as we stood in this doorway trying to stay dry. This man who looked old enough to be my father was walking by and slowed down to say, "You are too pretty to be out here by yourself this time of morning. A man like me could take you in that alley and tear you up [sexually assault you]." He shook his head and smiled as he walked away.

Nicole described this encounter as "scary." She explains, "The worst part about it is that I felt trapped. I was holding my daughter who was asleep, it was raining and dark and it wasn't like I could scream and someone would do something, because there was no one around." Nicole explained that she chose to respond to the man's threat with silence because she feared making the situation worse. As she stood in silence she thought of ways to escape from the man, if she had to, while also keeping her daughter safe. Nicole says she "sort of froze" after the man walked away at the thought of what could have happened to her and her child.

SITUATED SURVIVAL STRATEGIES

Interactional assaults like the ones described here make negotiating already troubled circumstances in this space even more challenging for black women and girls. How do young women adapt to these difficult circumstances? Our field research suggests that as urban, adolescent girls navigate a difficult and often unpredictable urban terrain, they learn to develop a set of situated survival strategies (Jones, 2009): patterned forms of interpersonal interaction, and routine or ritualized activities oriented around a concern for securing their personal well-being. The knowledge of threats to their safety shapes the daily lives of women and girls who live in distressed inner-city neighborhoods. Urban adolescent girls craft their situated survival strategies within the context of inner-city life, and between the extreme and oftentimes unrealistic physical and behavioral expectations of the good black girl, who will grow up to be a respectable black lady, and the behavioral expectations of the code, which encourages the adoption of aggressive postures or behaviors that are typically expected of boys and men, yet are essential to managing threats in this context.

Two common strategies teenaged girls use to reduce the likelihood of encountering serious threats to their well-being on the streets or in school settings are *situational avoidance* and *relational isolation.* The concept of situational avoidance captures all of the work teenaged girls do to avoid social settings that pose threats to their well-being and situations in which potential conflicts might arise, like the street corners described above. In contrast to girls who feel confident spending time on the street and in places where others hang out (what Anderson [1999] terms staging areas), situational avoiders confine themselves to the home, spending the majority of their time reading books, doing schoolwork, watching television, or daydreaming about being somewhere—anywhere—other than in their homes or neighborhoods. When they are outside, the same girls will rely on their own mental maps of areas and people to avoid. They restrict their movement in public spaces; they are reluctant to explore new areas of the city or to alter their daily routines outside their home in any significant way.

Situational avoidance is a useful strategy for avoiding a range of potentially troublesome encounters on the street. In contrast, young women and girls who are concerned with reducing the likelihood of being drawn into interpersonal conflicts like fights among girls are likely to use relational isolation. The concept of relational isolation illuminates the work girls do to isolate themselves from close friendships, especially those with other adolescent girls. The ties of loyalty and affection that accompany friendships increase the likelihood that girls will come to the defense of one another, if the need arises. By avoiding close friendships, girls can reduce the likelihood of their involvement in a physical conflict. A common strategy used by girls is to divide relationships with female peers into two categories: friends and associates. It is not uncommon, for example, to hear a girl say, "I don't have friends. I got associates."

In settings governed by the culture of the code, friends and associates connote two distinct status positions, which in turn reflect one person's degree of loyalty to another. Friend indicates a strong loyalty link; associate indicates a weaker link. Generally, it is expected that you will fight for a friend, but there is no equivalent requirement to fight for an associate. Designating other members of one's peer group or social network as associates instead of friends thus limits the likelihood of becoming involved in interpersonal conflicts on the grounds of loyalty. This strategy of insulating themselves from potential conflicts by limiting the strength of their social relationships may have serious long-term consequences for inner-city girls. Some girls are deliberately stunting the growth of their relational networks at a stage in adolescent development typically associated with the creation of healthy, trusting, and loving relationships. The way the culture of the code of the street alters patterns of adolescent development may be particularly significant for young girls, who are generally believed to be more relational-based than young men. The strategies that girls develop to successfully navigate their troubled public school hallways or neighborhood streets may prove to be useful when negotiating threats of interpersonal violence, however, accounts from inner-city girls reveal the limits of these strategies in the face of gender-specific violence like micro-interactional assaults and sexual violence (see Jones, 2010a, pp. 52–60).

Conclusion

There are a number of lessons to be learned from the experiences of the young women featured in this chapter. In many ways, these young women and girls are ghetto survivors: inner-city girls who develop innovative and effective strategies to ensure a basic need— survival—that many of their middle-class counterparts take for granted. These adolescent girls learn at early ages how to navigate the troubled terrain of distressed inner-city neighborhoods. In doing so, these girls reflect what Kiara once described as the more positive aspects of being ghetto. "I think that there are good elements to ghetto," Kiara told me during our interview, "like improvising for what you don't have." While their counterparts who come of age in more stable urban or suburban settings may take survival for granted, inner-city girls like Tracey and Kiara improvise for what they don't have: a reasonable level of personal security in neighborhood and school settings. Yet, these attempts at innovation and resistance come along with consequences.

In many of these neighborhoods the culture of the code of the street (Anderson, 1999) organizes much of social life. In these settings, adolescent inner-city girls must reconcile the gendered dilemmas that emerge as they work the code between the equal and opposing expectations of good and ghetto. As Kiara states so succinctly, black girls who live in distressed urban neighborhoods feel social pressure to be not only "pretty for the pictures" but also "aggressive for the streets." Yet, as protective as the various situated survival strategies that inner-city girls employ in response to real or imagined threats of interpersonal violence may be, such strategies do little to decrease girls' vulnerability to threats of gender-specific violence, including micro-interactional assaults in neighborhood stores or on the streets, the latter of which are often characterized by a threat of physical injury or sexual assault.

Girls living in distressed urban neighborhoods spend a significant amount of their time encountering and challenging micro-interactional assaults. Their efforts at resistance are motivated, in part, by an effort to reclaim or maintain some sense of dignity. Routine patterns of degradation that are directed at girls living in distressed communities send a message about who these girls are and how they can be treated. The routine nature of aggressive micro-interactional assaults sends a false signal that this behavior is appropriate and even warranted when interacting with girls in urban neighborhoods. In the minds of many, these young women are not respectable black ladies. Instead, they are seen as ghetto girls who do not deserve the courtesies of public civility, and they are treated as such. Black inner-city girls rely on a range of strategies to successfully navigate troubled public school hallways or neighborhood streets. The success of these strategies is situational. Some strategies, like relational avoidance, may be useful in avoiding fights among girls. However, accounts from inner-city girls reveal the limits of these strategies, especially when it comes to managing potential threats of gender-specific violence in their day-to-day lives.

References

Anderson, E. (1999). *Code of the street: Decency, violence, and the moral life of the inner city.* New York, NY: W. W. Norton.

Brookings Institution Center on Urban and Metropolitan Policy. (2003). *Philadelphia in focus: A profile from Census 2000.* Living Cities: National Community Development Initiative. Washington, DC: Brookings Institution.

Chesney-Lind, M., & Eliason, M. (2006). From invisible to incorrigible: The demonization of marginalized women and girls. *Crime, Media, Culture, 2*(1), 29.

Cobbina, J. E., Miller, J., & Brunson, R. K. (2008). Gender, neighborhood danger, and risk-avoidance strategies among urban African-American youths. *Criminology, 46*(3), 673–710.

Cole, J. B., & Guy-Sheftall, B. (2003). *Gender talk: The struggle for women's equality in African American communities.* New York, NY: One World/Ballantine Books.

Collins, P. H. (2004). *Black sexual politics: African Americans, gender, and the new racism.* New York, NY, and London, UK: Routledge.

Dance, L. J. (2002). *Tough fronts: The impact of street culture on schooling.* New York, NY, and London, UK: Routledge.

DeKeseredy, W. S., Alvi, S., & Tomaszewski, E. A. (2003). Perceived collective efficacy and women's victimization in public housing. *Criminology and Criminal Justice, 3*(1), 5–27.

Duneier, M., & Molotch, H. (1999). Talking city trouble: Interactional vandalism, social inequality, and the "urban interaction problem." *American Journal of Sociology, 104*(5), 1263–1275.

Feagin, J. R., & Sikes, M. P. (1994). *Living with racism: The black middle-class experience.* Boston, MA: Beacon Press.

Fine, M., Freudenberg, N., Payne, Y., Perkins, T., Smith, K., & Wanzer, K. (2003). Anything can happen with police around: Urban youth evaluate strategies of surveillance in public places. *Journal of Social Issues, 59*(1), 141–158.

Gardner, C. B. (1995). *Passing by: Gender and public harassment.* Berkeley: University of California Press.

Garfinkel, H. (1956). Conditions of a successful degradation ceremony. *American Journal of Sociology, 61*(5), 420–424.

Goffman, E. (1963). *Behavior in public places: Notes on the social organization of gatherings.* New York, NY: Free Press of Glencoe.

Goffman, E. (1967). *Interaction ritual: Essays on face-to-face behavior.* New York, NY: Doubleday.

Jones, N. (2004). "It's not where you live, it's how you live": How young women negotiate conflict and violence in the inner city. In E. Anderson, S. N. Brooks, R. Gunn, & N. Jones (Eds.), *Annals of the American Academy of Political and Social Science* (Vol. 595). Thousand Oaks, CA: Sage.

Jones, N. (2008). Working "the code": Girls, gender, and inner city violence. *Australia and New Zealand Journal of Criminology, 41*(1), 63–83.

Jones, N. (2009). "I was aggressive for the streets, pretty for the pictures": Gender, difference, and the inner city girl. *Gender & Society, 23*(1), 89–93.

Jones, N. (2010a). *Between good and ghetto: African American girls and inner city violence.* New Brunswick, NJ: Rutgers University Press.

Jones, N. (2010b). "It's about being a survivor . . .": African American girls, gender, and the context of inner-city violence. In M. Chesney-Lind & N. Jones (Eds.), *Fighting for girls: New perspectives on gender and violence.* Albany: State University of New York Press.

Katz, J. (1988). *Seductions of crime: Moral and sensual attractions in doing evil.* New York, NY: Basic Books.

Lauritsen, J. L., & Sampson, R. J. (1998). Minorities, crime, and criminal justice. In M. Tonry (Ed.), *The handbook of crime and punishment* (pp. 58–84). New York, NY: Oxford University Press.

Martin, A. (2006, April 29–30). Slain community center worker had criminal record. *San Francisco Examiner,* Weekend Edition.

Massey, D., & Denton, N. (1993). *American apartheid: Segregation and the making of the underclass.* Cambridge, MA: Harvard University Press.

Miller, J. (2008). *Getting played: African American girls, urban inequality, and gendered violence.* New York: New York University Press.

Peterson, R. D., & Krivo, L. J. (2005). Macrostructural analyses of race, ethnicity, and violent crime: Recent lessons and new directions for research. *Annual Review of Sociology, 31,* 331–356.

Pettit, K. L. S., & Kingsley, G. T. (2003). *Concentrated poverty: A change in course.* Washington, DC: Urban Institute.

Renzetti, C., & Maier, S. (2002). "Private" crime in public housing: Violent victimization, fear of crime and social isolation among women public housing residents. *Women's Health and Urban Life, 1*(2), 46–65.

Richie, B. (1996). *Compelled to crime: The gender entrapment of battered black women.* New York, NY, and London, UK: Routledge.

Sampson, R. J., & Wilson, W. J. (1995). Toward a theory of race, crime, and urban inequality. *Crime and Inequality,* 37–54.

Sue, D. W. (2010). *Microaggressions in everyday life: Race, gender, and sexual orientation.* Hoboken, NJ: John Wiley & Sons.

Sue, D. W., & Capodilupo, C. M. (2008). Racial, gender, and sexual orientation microaggressions: Implications for counseling and psychotherapy. In D. W. Sue & D. Sue (Eds.), *Counseling the culturally diverse: Theory and practice.* Hoboken, NJ: John Wiley & Sons.

Thompson, M., & Keith, V. (2004). Copper brown and blue black: Colorism and self-evaluation. In C. Herring, V. Keith, & H. D. Horton (Eds.), *Skin deep: How race and complexion matter in the "color blind" era.* Champaign: University of Illinois Press.

Van Derbeken, J. (2005, December 21). More delays, more killings. *San Francisco Chronicle.*

Van Derbeken, J., & Lagos, M. (2006, April 29). Gym shooting victim was on probation: Hired to work with kids, he had a felony assault conviction. *San Francisco Chronicle.*

Websdale, N. (2001). *Policing the poor: From slave plantation to public housing.* Boston, MA: Northeastern University Press.

West, C., & Fenstermaker, S. (1995). Doing difference. *Gender & Society, 9,* 8–37.

West, C., & Zimmerman, D. H. (1987). Doing gender. *Gender & Society, 1,* 125–151.

Wilson, W. J. (1980). *The declining significance of race: Blacks and changing American institutions.* Chicago, IL: University of Chicago Press.

Wilson, W. J. (1987). *The truly disadvantaged: The inner city, the underclass, and public policy.* Chicago, IL: University of Chicago Press.

Wilson, W. J. (1996). *When work disappears: The world of the new urban poor.* New York, NY: Vintage Books.

Race, Ethnicity and Living Arrangements of Children of Incarcerated Mothers

Comparative Patterns and Maternal Experience*

Holly Foster and Jocelyn Lewis

MASS IMPRISONMENT

Rapid increases in incarceration rates in the United States since the 1970s have ushered in the contemporary context of "mass imprisonment" (Garland, 2001, p. 1). Historically, in the 20th century, the U.S. imprisonment rate held steady at around 110/100,000 of population until the 1990s, when that rate increased to 680/100,000 (including prison and jail inmates) (Garland, 2001). The incarceration rate in 2011 was 716/100,000 U.S. residents (Porter, 2013). Imprisonment rates declined in recent years due to decreases in jail populations and state prisoners; however, there were increases in federal prison populations over this time period (Glaze, 2010; West & Sabol, 2010).

In addition to historical trends, the contemporary United States' rate of imprisonment is also notably high compared to other western industrialized nations. In 2001 the imprisonment rate in the United States was 686/100,000 of population compared to the United Kingdom at 126/100,000, Germany at 96/100,000, and France at 77/100,000. More similar estimates to the U.S. rates

*We gratefully acknowledge support for this research in grants awarded to the first author provided by the Division of Research and Graduate Studies and the Race and Ethnic Studies Institute at Texas A&M University. We also appreciate the support of the women involved in this project for their participation as well as the institution and individuals that facilitated access to the research site. We have benefitted from the comments of the reviewers and editors in the preparation of this chapter.

are found in Russia (628/100,000) and South Africa (400/100,000) (Western, 2006; see also International Centre for Prison Studies, 2011).

Policy changes rather than an increase in crime levels were largely responsible for the increases in American imprisonment (Garland, 2001; Mauer, 2001). There was a shift in American sentencing policy in the 1970s. Previously, sentencing was based on an indeterminate structure accompanied by rehabilitation as a major objective. In an indeterminate sentencing structure, judges had discretion to decide who went to prison and the maximum and sometimes minimum prison terms (Tonry, 1996). Thus, an indeterminate sentence is one that is not fixed but involves a range of years (Stohr & Walsh, 2012). However, this approach came under attack in the 1960s from both the political left and right. The shift in the 1970s was toward the use of determinate sentencing policy with more fixed sentencing structures that decreased judicial discretion (Mauer, 2001). With a determinate sentencing structure, the maximum prison time for a given crime is set by the state legislature in state statutes. Determinate sentences involved a fixed number of years rather than a range (Stohr & Walsh, 2012). In the 1980s the so-called war on drugs also ramped up, increasing drug arrests and mandatory sentencing penalties associated with drug crimes throughout the country (Mauer, 2001). For example, New York's Rockefeller Drug Laws called for a 15-year prison term for persons convicted of possessing 4 ounces of narcotics or selling 2 ounces, regardless of the offender's criminal history (Mauer, 2001). A combination of determinate sentencing structures along with other policies (e.g., truth in sentencing) in America led to a tough on crime context that increased imprisonment levels (Garland, 2001). Analyses have shown that approximately 88% of the increase in the prison population is explained by increases in sanctions, while just 12% is due to changes in offending (Blumstein & Beck, 1999).

RACE, ETHNICITY AND GENDER

A defining feature of mass imprisonment is that it is socially concentrated among groups in the population, particularly young black males in large urban centers (Garland, 2001). Among men aged 20–40 in 2000, 11.5% of black men experienced imprisonment, compared to 4.6% of Hispanic men and 1.6% of white men (Western, 2006). Race and class disparities in imprisonment among young men (ages 20–34) are striking in the work by Pettit and Western (2004). They found that the risk of imprisonment in 1999 among young men with less than high school education was 58.9% among blacks and 11.2% among whites. Percentages were much lower among those with some college education: 4.9% of black men and 0.7% of white men. Pettit and Western (2004) found that the risk of imprisonment was higher among black men (22.4%) than was the likelihood of receiving a Bachelor's degree (17.4%). They concluded that imprisonment is now among the major social institutions affecting social inequality in society.

Although the majority of incarcerated persons are men, women comprise 7% to 8.8% of the state and federal prison population (International Center for Prison Studies, 2011; Kruttschnitt, 2010). Rates of imprisonment in 2009 were 949/100,000 males and 67/100,000 females (West & Sabol, 2010). As Kruttschnitt (2010) indicated, between 1980 and 2008 women's imprisonment rates increased more than sixfold, and men's rates increased threefold. Thus, imprisonment has been increasing faster for women than for men. Racial disparities in imprisonment rates are apparent among women as they are for men. The imprisonment rate for state and federal prisoners per 100,000 residents are 142/100,000 black women, 74/100,000 Hispanic women, and 50/100,000 white women (West & Sabol, 2010). Among men these rates are 3,119/100,000 black men, 1,193 /100,000 Hispanic men, and 487/100,000 white men (West & Sabol, 2010).

Further, although the rates for women are lower than men, there is a paradox of women's imprisonment: fewer women than men are incarcerated but the impact of incarcerating females may be even greater for families and communities (Kruttschnitt, 2010). This is particularly so in the majority of cases where mothers lived with their minor children at the time of admission (Mumola, 2000). During the early life course, mothers on average spend more time with children than fathers (Murnane, Maynard, & Ohls, 1981). Children of incarcerated mothers are also exposed over time to more risks in the home environment than are children of incarcerated fathers (Johnson & Waldfogel, 2004). Children living with mothers who face incarceration also experience a range of incarceration events, including being present at sentencing, compared to children who have incarcerated fathers (Dallaire & Wilson, 2010). The incarceration of women who are mothers is likely to be particularly consequential for children for a number of reasons, including disruptions in living arrangements, associated adversities, and changes in caregiving activities.

Again, changes in sentencing policy are important in understanding how mass imprisonment has affected mothers. Under indeterminate sentencing, judges could consider a range of factors including family responsibilities in sentencing options, including custodial and noncustodial options (Kruttschnitt, 2010). With determinate sentencing judicial discretion was limited; mandatory sentences were instituted that did not take into account gender-linked family responsibilities. Further, the rise in imprisonment among women has been attributed most often to the war on drugs (Pollock, 2002). In the 1980s, most women who were imprisoned were convicted of violent crimes or property offenses but newer estimates reveal a major proportion were drug offenders (Kruttschnitt, 2010; Pollock, 2002). The result of the war on drugs is especially clear in the federal prison system, where the majority of female offenders are incarcerated for drug crimes (Pollock, 2002). Thus, mass imprisonment has been particularly consequential for women and their children. The consequences of imprisonment intergenerationally is the topic of emerging research.

WOMEN AND PRISON

Women in prison are increasingly members of minority groups and are educationally disadvantaged (Greenfeld & Snell, 1999; Pollock, 2002). Economic marginalization plays a central role in women's commission of crimes; disadvantaged women have less power in society and this is associated with a struggle for survival outside of mainstream institutions (Owen, 2009). Many women in state prisons have low levels of education: The percentage with only some level of high school education (37%) is nearly equal to the percentage of high school graduates or those who have their GEDs (39%). A much smaller percentage have some college education (17%) (Greenfeld & Snell, 1999). Unlike women in state prisons, women in federal prisons tend to show more college attendance (29%) (Greenfeld & Snell, 1999). More women than men in prison are likely to report drug problems (Pollock, 2002). Women are also most likely to be sent to prison for nonviolent property and drug offenses (Owen, 2009). Further, many women in prison have histories of having been sexually and physically abused (Mullings, Pollock, & Crouch 2002). Finally, the majority of women in prison are mothers (Mumola, 2000; Pollock, 2002). Almost 62% of women in state prisons are mothers of minor children and 55.9% of women in federal prisons are mothers of minor children (Glaze & Maruschak, 2008).

PARENTS

In the United States in 2007, 1,706,600 minor children had a parent in prison (Glaze & Maruschak, 2008). Again, there were racial and ethnic disparities in parental imprisonment. Among minor black children, 6.7% had a parent in prison, compared with 2.4% of Hispanic children and 0.9% of white children having this experience. Further, the number of children with a mother in prison more than doubled from 1991 to 2007 (up 131%) and the number of children with a father in prison also increased (up 77%). The greater rate of increase of children with a mother in prison reflects the faster growth in the number of mothers imprisoned (Glaze & Maruschak, 2008). Wildeman's (2009) research also highlights how social class intersects with race and ethnicity in understanding patterns of maternal imprisonment. Among black children aged 14 whose mothers were high school dropouts, the cumulative risk of maternal imprisonment was 5%. The risk among similarly situated white children was 1.0%. The risk of maternal imprisonment decreases as maternal education increases, but still shows racial disparities: 2.6% of black 14-year-olds with mothers with some college education were at risk for maternal imprisonment compared to 0.3% of similarly situated white children the same age (Wildeman, 2009). Thus, disadvantaged minority children are particularly at risk of experiencing maternal imprisonment and its associated consequences.

INTERGENERATIONAL EFFECTS OF PARENTAL INCARCERATION

Although in some cases, parental imprisonment may be beneficial for children, research has also found negative sequelae (Hagan & Dinovitzer, 1999). For example, parental incarceration is associated with internalizing (e.g., depressive symptoms) and externalizing behavior problems (e.g., aggression) as well as with educational problems (Foster & Hagan, 2007; Murray & Farrington, 2008; Trice & Brewster, 2004; Wakefield & Uggen, 2010; Wakefield & Wildeman, 2011; Wildeman, 2010). These negative consequences may be the result of strain, socialization, and stigma processes (Hagan & Dinovitzer, 1999). Strain theorists posit that parental incarceration may deplete economic resources, contributing to social stress in families. Socialization perspectives assume that the removal of a parent due to incarceration may decrease resources associated with child-rearing and socialization of children. Socialization factors associated with the absence of a parent may include parental role models, supervision, and support. Finally, stigma perspectives hypothesize that parental incarceration may serve as a negative credential or marker (Pager, 2003) that affects individuals as well as entire families.

However, a competing hypothesis is that children of incarcerated parents fare worse than other children due to selection factors (Hagan & Dinovitzer, 1999).

The selection hypothesis holds that children of incarcerated parents already differ from other children prior to the imprisonment of the parent. Recent research supports social causation processes rather than social selection interpretations (Foster & Hagan, 2009; Wakefield & Wildeman, 2011; Wildeman, 2009), although research on parental incarceration influences must continue to take into account other competing factors affecting children's behavior.

LIVING ARRANGEMENTS

Children's living arrangements are also affected by parental imprisonment, although this varies by parental gender. Using national data on state and federal prisoners, research shows that when fathers are incarcerated, children tend to live with their other parent (88.4%) during his imprisonment, whereas only 37% of children of incarcerated mothers continue to live in this care arrangement (Glaze & Maruschak, 2008; Johnson & Waldfogel, 2004). Further, more women than men tend to be living with their minor children at the time of their arrest (Glaze & Maruschak, 2008). Thus, children are likely to encounter a greater disruption in their care arrangements when their mothers rather than their fathers are incarcerated (Koban, 1983).

These patterns further vary by race and ethnicity. Among women, black and Hispanic women are more likely to have been living with their children at the time of arrest than were white women (Baunach, 1985; Bresler & Lewis, 1986; Enos, 2001; Foster & Hagan, 2009; Ruiz, 2002; Snell, 1994). Thus it is likely that maternal incarceration generates more disruption in the lives of minority children.

There are also differences in living arrangements during parental incarceration by gender and race or ethnicity. When fathers are incarcerated, there are similarities by race and ethnicity in which children are uniformly more likely to live with their other parent (Foster, 2011a; Johnson & Waldfogel, 2004; Ruiz, 2002). Yet there are racial and ethnic differences in living arrangements among children when their mothers are incarcerated. Enos (2001) reviews several early studies finding that children of white mothers are more likely than black or Hispanic children to live with their fathers or in foster care when they are incarcerated (see also Ruiz, 2002; Snell, 1994). Children of black and Hispanic mothers were more likely to live with their grandparents than were white children studied (Enos, 2001; Johnson & Waldfogel, 2004). Enos' (2001) subsequent qualitative research found black incarcerated women were more likely to rely on families for child living arrangements, whites were more likely to rely on husbands, and Hispanic women were likely to employ a combination of both forms of resources.

Detailed research on children of incarcerated mothers' living arrangements by race and ethnicity has been conducted primarily with state data (Enos, 2001; Foster, 2011a; Foster & Hagan, 2009). Research has yet to look systematically at living arrangements of children of mothers in prison in the federal system by race and ethnicity. Further, the number of Hispanic women in Enos' (2001) in-depth study was limited (16%) as was the case in other research with a state sample in Texas (15%) (Foster, 2011a). Since Hispanic groups now comprise a growing proportion of federal prisoners (Lopez & Light, 2009), racial and ethnic patterns should be further examined with contemporary data. That is the focus of the remainder of this chapter.

DATA

This study uses data on a subsample of mothers with minor children from a larger survey study of a voluntary sample of incarcerated women at a federal prison camp for women involving several hundred women (sample size of 201) (Foster, 2012). A federal prison camp is a minimum security prison facility. Respondent data not used in this chapter available in the larger study involves information on those with older children and women without children. All respondents were recruited through posters at the facility as well as announcements. All participants signed informed consent forms prior to the completion of the survey. These questionnaires took between 30–45 minutes to complete and were administered in classrooms with the researchers present at the facility. The subsample used in this chapter involves inmate mothers at the federal prison camp for women with minor children from black, Hispanic, and white racial and ethnic groups reporting on their eldest child under age 18 (with a sample size of 123 mothers of minor children) (Foster, 2012). The racial and ethnic distribution of the mothers in the subsample was 45% Hispanic, 12% black, and 42% white. The broader racial and ethnic composition of inmates at this facility was 40% Hispanic, 18% black, 40% white, and 2% other race or ethnicity. The racial and ethnic composition of this study is therefore similar to the institution statistics.

The vast majority in the subsample were incarcerated for drug crimes (76%). In the broader prison composition, 69% of women were incarcerated for drug crimes. Therefore, women incarcerated for drug crimes were slightly overrepresented in this sample.

Drug offenses also constitute the majority of offenses prisoners are incarcerated for in the federal system (Bureau of Prisons, 2011). The mean age of inmate mothers with minor children was 34 years of age and the average level of education was between 11th and 12th grade levels. Broader institution statistics reported an average age of 36. The sample was therefore similar in a number of ways to the broader inmate population at this facility.

METHODS

This research uses quantitative data analysis of items from surveys gathered from female inmates as well as narrative information from surveys provided from women's written responses to open-ended questions. This approach of gathering and analyzing qualitative and quantitative data in one study is consistent with a *mixed methods approach* (Hesse-Biber & Leavy, 2011). Mixed methods research allows for both the description of general patterns in the data as well as in-depth insight into women's thoughts and experiences regarding the placement of their children while they are incarcerated. The qualitative data therefore expand upon the quantitative patterns revealed in the research study to create a synergistic broader understanding of child living conditions during maternal incarceration.

Quantitative data from the surveys were analyzed with Stata 11 Software (StataCorp, 2009) and narrative responses to open-ended questions were analyzed for common themes using the Atlas 6.2 software (Atlas.ti, 2011). We have preserved quotations from women's written responses verbatim to accurately reflect their experiences, with the exception of removal of identifying dates or names. We have also situated the quotation in terms of the respondent's race or ethnicity and age (Sandelowski, 1994).

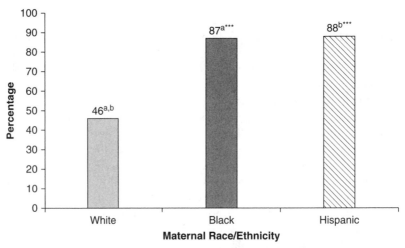

FIGURE 8-1 Percentage of Children Living with Mothers Prior to Maternal Incarceration

Note: Bars with superscripts statistically significantly differ from each other *** $p < .001$, * $p < .05$, † $p < .10$

FINDINGS

The findings reveal both racial and ethnic similarities and differences in the living arrangements of children of incarcerated mothers. As indicated in Figure 8-1, 46% of white children were living with their mothers prior to arrest. Children of black mothers (87%) and Hispanic mothers (88%) are significantly more likely than white children to have been living with their mothers prior to her arrest. The percentage of coresident children of black mothers is similar to the percentage of children of Hispanic mothers living with them at the time of arrest. As found in state data (Foster, 2011a), children of Hispanic mothers and black mothers share similar living arrangements. This finding further builds on the black and white differences observed by Enos (2001). Thus, minority children are at a particular risk for disruption in living arrangements and daily routines given the change in caregiving arrangements necessitated by maternal imprisonment.

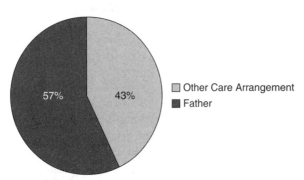

The largest group of children not living with their mothers prior to imprisonment is white children. Among these white children, 57% lived with their fathers at the time of maternal arrest, whereas 43% of the children were living in other care arrangements, as shown in Figure 8-2. This finding builds on prior studies that did not contain questions on where these children were living beyond the information that the children were not living with their mothers at the time of arrest (Johnson & Waldfogel, 2004).

The results in Figure 8-3 refer to the percentage of children living with their fathers

FIGURE 8-2 Percentage of White Children Living in Nonmaternal Other Care Prior to Maternal Incarceration

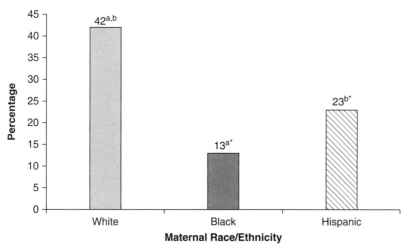

FIGURE 8-3 Percentage of Children Living with Father During Maternal Incarceration

Note: Bars with superscripts statistically significantly differ from each other *** $p < .001$, * $p < .05$, † $p < .10$

during maternal incarceration. Forty-two percent of white children live with their father during maternal incarceration. In contrast, 13% of black children and 23% of Hispanic children live with their fathers during maternal imprisonment. Between group comparisons reveal the differences between white and minority children are significant. Black children and Hispanic children are similar in terms of this living arrangement during maternal incarceration.

As shown in Figure 8-4, a majority of children from all three racial and ethnic groups live with other relatives during maternal imprisonment. However, whites are significantly less likely to be living with other relatives (56%) than are black children (80%) or Hispanic children (73%). Again, the percentage of black children living with other relatives during maternal incarceration is similar to the percentage of Hispanic children in this caregiving arrangement. Social policies and services should be sensitive to these patterns of living arrangements by race and ethnicity to best support children living in various family caregiving arrangements during maternal incarceration.

Although there are both racial and ethnic differences and similarities in living arrangements of children prior to and during maternal incarceration, the vast majority of all women similarly expect to live with their eldest child under age 18 at the time of their release from prison. As indicated in Figure 8-5, 93% of black women, 88% of Hispanic women, and 73% of white women expect to live with their children on release. Between group tests indicate more black women have this expectation than do white women. The difference between Hispanic women and white women shows a trend toward a group difference.

Qualitative Findings

Incarcerated mothers who participated in the survey study at the federal prison camp were also asked open-ended questions to which they could write their

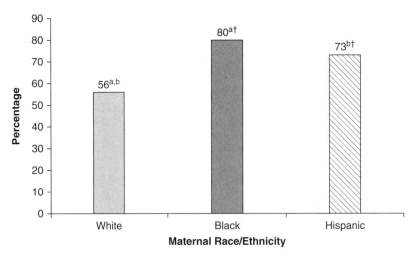

FIGURE 8-4 Percentage of Children of Incarcerated Mothers Living with Relative During Imprisonment

Note: Bars with superscripts statistically significantly differ from each other *** $p < .001$, * $p < .05$, † $p < .10$

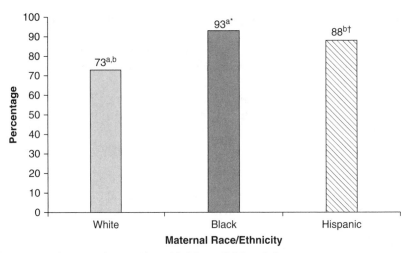

FIGURE 8-5 Maternal Expectations to Live with Minor Child on Release

Note: Bars with superscripts statistically significantly differ from each other *** $p < .001$, * $p < .05$, † $p < .10$

responses in their own words. After being asked about their expectancies to live with their minor child after release from prison as discussed in reference to Figure 8-5, the women were then asked "If applicable: How do you feel about resuming responsibility over this child after release?" The most common response across women was an indication of positive effect regarding living with their children on release, including being excited about it and looking forward to it. Women's written responses were entered into a qualitative software coding package (Atlas 6.2) and analyzed for common themes. This code of positive effect was found in 77 of the women's responses to this question. Looking at co-occurring themes in the data to see if patterns were similar or different by race or ethnicity, it was found that 67% of black women expressed excitement or positive effect in response to this question. Similarly, 62% of Hispanic women expressed positive effect as did 70% of white women. Thus, there were similarities across women by race and ethnicity where the majority expressed positive effect around assuming responsibilities for children upon release from prison.

The anticipation of living with their children after release has positive associations for women in prison. For example, illustrative quotes among incarcerated mothers include:

1. Hispanic mother (age 37): "I feel wonderful and excited about resuming the daily care for my children."
2. Hispanic mother (age 26): "I am anxious and excited to resume responsibility of my child when I go home. I miss him so much. I never wanted to leave him, but I made a mistake in [year], that I have to pay for, so I had to go away."
3. Hispanic mother (age 30): "Excited. I miss her and love her so much. I never meant to hurt her when I left so I will do everything in my power to make it up to her."
4. Hispanic mother (age 26): "I'm excited because I have missed a lot and I want her to have me like I have my mother."
5. Black mother (age 32): "I am excited, my heart longs to just hold them and let them lay in bed with me."
6. Black mother (age 33): "I feel that it shouldn't be any other way and I can't wait to get my children back."
7. Black mother (age 22): "I feel good and am glad I can keep that position as a good mother to my son."
8. Black mother (age 32): "I have a good feeling about resuming responsibility over my child."
9. White mother (age 42): "I'm excited! I am missing many things in his life and look forward to being part of his daily life."
10. White mother (age 28): "I feel comfortable. I have learned a lot and I was caring for them before but now I will interact with them more and show them more care when I get home."
11. White mother (age 32): "I can't wait I am so excited to be with my children."
12. White mother (age 41): "I feel excited, happy, and a little nervous. It will be a challenge to get back on my feet, but I welcome it."

These quotations suggest relationships with children serve as an important source of mothers' future expectations while imprisoned. They also serve as a source of hope and are relationships they value and look forward to reestablishing on release. The women's responses also reveal some of the anguish mothers feel at being separated from their children due to incarceration. As one mother comments, she hopes to make up for her absence to her children. Other mothers discuss taking on active roles in child-rearing on release.

The qualitative data also revealed that among the minority of women not expecting to live with their children on release, they still expected to be part of their children's lives. Thus research on incarcerated mothers should also attend to the concerns of nonresident mothers and their relationships with children. For example, a white mother (age 40) wrote, "I will always be a part of his life. I'm his mom. But he deserves to stay with his father and in the school he's attending with his friends." Nonresident mothers should also be supported in their efforts to maintain relationships with children on release.

WOMEN'S FEELINGS ABOUT CHILDREN'S LIVING ARRANGEMENTS

Mothers of minor children were also asked: "What were your concerns, if any, about the placement of your children while you were incarcerated?" In their written comments to this open-ended survey question, the majority of mothers across race and ethnicity were relieved and grateful regarding their children's living arrangements and felt that their children were being well taken care of during their incarceration. A number had concerns, however, about the level of disruption involved. One Hispanic mother (age 33) was concerned for: "them being treated and cared for like I would and never being separated from them all they new [sic] was me no one else." Her concerns stem from having been her children's sole caregiver prior to her imprisonment. Another Hispanic mother (age 36) echoed this concern: "They were not use to anyone else caring for them besides me. It would be a difficult transition for all." Similarly, another Hispanic mother (age 39) commented regarding her concerns: "My daughter and my 17-year-old son need me emotionally and morally and economically I have been their only provider their entire lives." Others with family caregivers felt their children would be well taken care of, although it was not the same as living with their mother. As one black mother (age 30) commented, "I know that he is well taken care of, however it's not the same as if he was with his mother." Similarly, a Hispanic mother (age 38) reflected: "I know she is in a good place with her family. But I know that she needs me too." In contrast, one Hispanic mother (age 26) had concerns about her child's living situation. Similar to the others, she was concerned about the loss of his mother from his life: "I was concerned that he would not be properly taken care of. No one can take care of a child, better than his mother, most of the time. I was concerned that he would be so sad and depressed because his mommy wasn't going to be there anymore, for the next 5 yrs." Finally, some mothers were concerned they would lose contact with their children. As one white mother (age 34) wrote: "My concerns were my relationship with him. His dad stopped family contact. We just recently started communication back up." This gatekeeping role has been reported by incarcerated fathers regarding mothers' control over their children's association with them (Edin, Nelson, & Paranel, 2004; Nurse, 2004). The gatekeeping role also extends in some families to fathers regarding contact with incarcerated mothers. Another white mother (age 40) noted the role of different living arrangements for her children in her response: "My son is in a great home with his father. My youngest daughter I've had a hard time with. She was placed in a foster home that I feel was abusive. After she'd been there over 1 year she was finally moved in with her aunt and now is with her daddy." Therefore, care arrangements can be complex and involve multiple transitions. Foster care was uniquely cited as a source of concern for this mother.

Conclusion

These findings add to research outlined by Kruttschnitt (2010) on the paradox of women's imprisonment: Maternal incarceration is anticipated to have stronger effects on children than is paternal imprisonment, although fewer women are incarcerated. However, as we highlight in this chapter, there are further contingencies in children of incarcerated mothers' experiences that are likely affected by race and ethnicity. As we have shown, more minority children are living with their mothers at the time of her arrest and thus more disruption may be experienced by ethnic minorities than by white children in terms of subsequent living arrangements. Further, children of black and Hispanic mothers are more likely to live with relatives than are children of white mothers during maternal imprisonment. Children of incarcerated white mothers are more likely to live with their fathers during maternal imprisonment. These variations in living arrangements of children of incarcerated mothers suggest policies to support family caregivers should be sensitive to racial and ethnic variations in care arrangements and children's needs during this period. Support may be required for a range of caregivers including grandparents (Ruiz, 2002) as well as husbands.

Theoretical explanations for differences in living arrangements of children include cultural and economic explanations. Enos (2001) highlights that there are cultural and structural differences in family support by race and ethnicity. Her qualitative research found that black and Hispanic women were more likely to rely on families for caretaking for children. White women tended more often to be estranged from their families and thus to rely on foster care and husbands instead. Foster (2011a) further found that household income explained racial and ethnic differences in child living arrangements during arrest. Black and Hispanic mothers had lower income levels than white mothers at the time of their arrest. Hispanic women tended to be less likely than whites to have children living with their other parent during maternal imprisonment. However, taking income levels into account, differences among women were statistically explained.

This chapter adds to emerging research on the implications of maternal incarceration by race and ethnicity by an in-depth examination of patterns with a sample of prisoners from a federal facility. The sample also provides information from a larger group of Hispanic prisoners than represented in prior work, consistent with trends in federal data of growing Hispanic populations (Lopez & Light, 2009). The patterns found with the federal data are in support of those found with state samples. Findings tended to show similarities in the living situations of children in black and Hispanic families and differences between Hispanic and black families and white families. This project also yielded new data on where children were living if not with their mother at the time of arrest among whites, the largest group with children in these care situations. The majority of children not living with their mothers at the time of arrest were living with their fathers. As research with male samples has found, mothers act as gatekeepers in determining incarcerated men's relationships with children (Edin, Nelson, & Paranel, 2004; Nurse, 2004). Attention must also be given to the role of fathers in facilitating mothers' relationships with children in some situations. More work with larger samples would yield comparisons by race and ethnicity in living arrangements at the time of maternal imprisonment.

Another finding from this project is that while the majority of women expect to live with their children on release, more black and Hispanic women have this expectation than do white women. These expectations may be particularly important for women's mental health during imprisonment (Foster, 2011b).

These expectations should be supported by policies and programs where possible. Further, since some women do not expect to live with their children on release, it would be useful to set up mental health initiatives that attend to the needs of women who do not have resident mother expectations but do expect to have relationships with their children.

This chapter includes qualitative data in addition to the quantitative information on children's living arrangements. Similarities were revealed by race and ethnicity where the majority of all women had positive expectations regarding their role in children's lives following release from prison. Maternal role occupancy expectations are associated with fewer depressive symptoms while incarcerated compared to those without these expectations (Foster, 2011b). Prison efforts to support mothers' relationships with children were revealed in the qualitative component of this study as particularly valued by the women. As well, family ties represent social bonds that may decrease recidivism among prisoners (Holt & Miller, 1972).

Mothers also reported in the qualitative data that they were generally relieved by their children's caregiving arrangements while the mothers were incarcerated. Some expressed concerns, though, regarding the level of disruption involved. Some children had known their mother as their sole source of support. These situations presented mothers with concerns that their children wouldn't be taken care of similarly to how they, the mothers, would have done. Variability in children's care situations should be acknowledged in addressing the needs of incarcerated mothers and their families.

Further research is needed on how children fare during maternal imprisonment, with more attention to race and ethnicity. This research would look at children's functioning during maternal imprisonment. Wakefield and Wildeman (2011) recently note that the detrimental influence of paternal incarceration on children's internalizing and externalizing behavior problems contributes to racial and ethnic gaps in problem behaviors. More work along these lines, attending to effects of maternal imprisonment, may illuminate how imprisonment contributes to social inequalities across generations. Research on resources in children's lives that offset the effects of parental imprisonment would also be informative for social policies and prison programs. Ultimately, in light of findings on the detrimental effects of parental imprisonment, reducing the scope of this experience in children's lives, and its disproportionate experience by race and ethnicity, may also be particularly important for children's well-being in the contemporary U.S. societal context. Finally, researchers who study children's living arrangements should investigate the number of transitions experienced by children of incarcerated mothers, given that some situations involve multiple moves.

References

Baunach, P. J. (1985). *Mothers in prison*. New Brunswick, NJ: Transaction.

Blumstein, A., & Beck, A. J. (1999). Population growth in U.S. prisons, 1980–1996. *Crime & Justice, 26,* 17–61.

Bureau of Prisons. (2011). *Quick facts about the Bureau of Prisons*. Retrieved from http://www.bop.gov/news/quick.jsp

Bresler, L., & Lewis, D. K. (1986). Black and White women prisoners: Differences in family ties and their programmatic implications. *Prison Journal, 63,* 116–122.

Dallaire, D. H., & Wilson, L. C. (2010). The relation of exposure to parental criminal activity, arrest, and sentencing to children's maladjustment. *Journal of Child and Family Studies, 19,* 404–418.

Edin, K., Nelson, T. J., & Paranal, R. (2004). Fatherhood and incarceration as potential turning points in the criminal careers of unskilled men. In M. Patillo, D. Weiman, & B. Western (Eds.), *Imprisoning America: The social effects of mass incarceration* (pp. 46–75). New York, NY: Russell Sage Foundation.

Enos, S. (2001). *Mothering from the inside: Parenting in a women's prison*. Albany: State University of New York Press.

Foster, H. (2011a). The influence of incarceration on children at the intersection of parental gender and race/ethnicity: A focus on child living arrangements. *Journal of Ethnicity in Criminal Justice, 9*, 1–21.

Foster, H. (2011b). Incarcerated parents and health: Investigating role in occupancy strains by gender. *Women & Criminal Justice, 21*, 225–249.

Foster, H. (2012). The strains of maternal imprisonment: Importation and deprivation stressors for women and children. *Journal of Criminal Justice, 40*, 221–229.

Foster, H., & Hagan, J. (2007). Incarceration and intergenerational social exclusion. *Social Problems, 54*, 399–433.

Foster, H., & Hagan, J. (2009). The mass incarceration of parents in America: Issues of race/ethnicity, collateral damage to children and prisoner reentry. *Annals of the American Academy of Political and Social Science, 623*, 179–194.

Garland, D. (2001). Introduction: The meaning of mass imprisonment. In D. Garland (Ed.), *Mass imprisonment: Social causes and consequences* (pp. 1–3). London, UK: Sage.

Glaze, L. E. (2010). *Correctional populations in the United States, 2009* (NCJ 231681). Washington, DC: U.S. Department of Justice, Bureau of Justice Statistics.

Glaze, L. E., & Maruschak, L. M. (2008). *Parents in prison and their minor children* (NCJ 222984). Washington, DC: U.S. Department of Justice, Bureau of Justice Statistics.

Greenfeld, L. A., & Snell, T. L. (1999). *Women offenders* (NCJ 175688). Washington, DC: U.S. Department of Justice, Bureau of Justice Statistics Special Report.

Hagan, J., & Dinovitzer, R. (1999). Collateral consequences for children, communities and prisoners. *Crime & Justice, 26*, 121–162.

Hesse-Biber, S., & Leavy, P. (2011). *The practice of qualitative research* (2nd ed.). Thousand Oaks, CA: Sage.

Holt, N., & Miller, D. (1972). *Explorations in inmate-family relationships*. Research report no. 46, Research Division, Department of Correction, State of California, Sacramento.

International Centre for Prison Studies. (2011). *Entire world: Prison population rates per 100,000 of the national population*. University of Essex, London, UK. Retrieved from http://www.prisonstudies.org/

Johnson, E. I., & Waldfogel, J. (2004). Children of incarcerated parents: Multiple risks and children's living arrangements. In M. Patillo, D. Weiman, & B. Western (Eds.), *Imprisoning America: The social effects of mass incarceration* (pp. 97–131). New York, NY: Russell Sage Foundation.

Koban, L. A. (1983). Parents in prison: A comparative analysis of the effects of incarceration on the families of men and women. *Research in Law, Deviance, and Social Control, 5*, 171–183.

Kruttschnitt, C. (2010). The paradox of women's imprisonment. *Daedalus*, 32–42.

Lopez, M. H., & Light, M. T. (2009). *A rising share: Hispanics and federal crime*. Washington, DC: Pew Hispanic Center.

Mauer, M. (2001). The causes and consequences of prison growth in the United States. In D. Garland (Ed.), *Mass imprisonment: Social causes and consequences* (pp. 4–14). London, UK: Sage.

Mullings, J. L., Pollock, J., & Crouch, B. M. (2002). Drugs and criminality. *Women & Criminal Justice, 13*, 69–96.

Mumola, C. J. (2000). *Incarcerated parents and their children* (NCJ 182335). Washington, DC: U.S. Department of Justice, Bureau of Justice Statistics.

Murnane, R. T., Maynard, R. A., & Ohls, J. C. (1981). Home resources and children's achievement. *Review of Economics and Statistics, 63*, 369–377.

Murray, J., & Farrington, D. P. (2008). The effects of parental imprisonment on children. *Crime & Justice, 37*, 133–206.

Nurse, A. M. (2004). Returning to strangers: Newly paroled young fathers and their children. In M. Patillo, D. Weiman, & B. Western (Eds.), *Imprisoning America: The social effects of mass incarceration* (pp. 76–96). New York, NY: Russell Sage Foundation.

Owen, B. (2009). Perspectives on women in prison. In C. M. Renzetti & L. Goodstein (Eds.), *Women, crime and criminal justice: Original feminist readings* (pp. 243–254). New York, NY: Oxford University Press.

Pager, D. (2003). The mark of a criminal record. *American Journal of Sociology, 108*, 937–975.

Pettit, B., & Western, B. (2004). Mass imprisonment and the life course: Race and class inequality in U.S. incarceration. *American Sociological Review, 69*, 151–169.

Pollock, J. M. (2002). *Women, prison, & crime* (2nd ed.). Belmont, CA: Wadsworth.

Porter, N. D. (2013, January). The state of sentencing 2012: Developments in policy and practice. Sentencing Project. Retrieved from http://sentencingproject.

org/doc/publications/sen_State%20of%20 Sentencing%202012.pdf

Ruiz, D. S. (2002). The increase in incarceration among women and its impact on the grandmother caregiver: Some racial considerations. *Journal of Sociology and Social Welfare, 29,* 179–197.

Sandelowski, M. (1994). Focus on qualitative methods: The use of quotes in qualitative research. *Research in Nursing & Health, 17,* 479–482.

Snell, T. L. (1994). *Women in prison* (NCJ 145321). Washington, DC: U.S. Department of Justice, Bureau of Justice Statistics.

Stohr, M. K., & Walsh, A. (2012). *Corrections: The essentials.* Los Angeles, CA: Sage.

Tonry, M. (1996). *Sentencing matters.* New York, NY: Oxford University Press.

Trice, A. D., & Brewster, J. (2004). The effects of maternal incarceration on adolescent children. *Journal of Police and Criminal Psychology, 19,* 27–35.

Wakefield, S., & Uggen, C. (2010). Incarceration and stratification. *Annual Review of Sociology, 36,* 387–406.

Wakefield, S., & Wildeman, C. (2011). Mass imprisonment and racial disparities in childhood behavioral problems. *Criminology & Public Policy, 10,* 793–817.

West, H. C., & Sabol, W. J. (2010). *Prisoners in 2009* (NCJ 231675). Washington, DC: U.S. Department of Justice, Bureau of Justice Statistics.

Western, B. (2006). *Punishment and inequality in America.* New York, NY: Russell Sage Foundation.

Wildeman, C. (2009). Parental imprisonment, the prison boom, and the concentration of childhood disadvantage. *Demography, 46,* 265–280.

Wildeman, C. (2010). Paternal incarceration and children's physically aggressive behaviors: Evidence from the Fragile Families and Child Wellbeing Study. *Social Forces, 89,* 285–309.

9

Cinderella, Wilma Flintstone, and Xena the Warrior Princess

Capturing Diversity among Transgender Women in Men's Prisons*

Valerie Jenness, Jennifer Sumner, Lori Sexton, and Nikkas Alamillo-Luchese

In 2007 *Newsweek Magazine* introduced transgender America to the masses when it ran a cover story, "The Mystery of Gender: Aside from the Obvious, What Makes Us Male or Female? The New Visibility of Transgender America is Shedding Light on the Ancient Riddle of Identity" (Rosenberg, 2007). This story covered considerable territory and estimated that there are between 750,000 and 3 million transgender Americans (fewer than 1%), including "soccer moms, ministers, teachers, politicians, even young children" (Rosenberg, 2007, n.p.). Tellingly, however, the article did not mention that transgender America also includes convicted offenders and prisoners.

Because there is no consensus on how best to define transgender, there is also no consensus on how best to delineate transgender prisoners. With regard to the former, Girshick (2008) commented in her book, *Transgender Voices: Beyond Women and Men*: "Writing this book, I was immediately constrained by the limitations of the English language, which does not capture the wide diversity of sex and gender characteristics of the people I interviewed." At one end of a range of definitions, transgender is used as an umbrella term to refer to gender variant individuals, with gender variance referring to gender expressions and

*We would like to thank the California Department of Corrections and Rehabilitation for providing financial support for the larger project from which this chapter derives and for providing us with access to transgender prisoners in California prisons for men. Also, we want to express appreciation to the hundreds of transgender inmates in California prisons who agreed to be interviewed and share their experiences with us. Finally, this chapter has benefitted from helpful comments and attendant insights provided by Kitty Calavita, Sarah Fenstermaker, Dr. Lori Kohler, Alexander Lee, Kristy Matsuda, Cheryl Maxson, Jodi O'Brien, and Dr. Denise Taylor.

behaviors that do not match the expectations associated with a binary understanding of sex or gender (i.e., there are males and there are females, but nothing else) (Girshick, 2008). This understanding includes all nonnormative sexual and gender identities and lifestyles. At the other end of a range of definitions, transgender is used as a proxy for transsexuals or transvestites in the narrowest sense of the term (Jenness & Geis, 2010).

Complicating matters further, there is also no agreement on what transgender means in the context of a men's prison and by what criteria an inmate could be—and should be—classified as transgender. In one of the most illuminating articles on the topic, Donaldson (1993) vividly describes distinctions between a jocker, a punk, a queen, a booty-bandit, a Daddy, and a Man. Although he is careful to explain that "the prison subculture fuses sexual and social roles and assigns all prisoners accordingly" (Donaldson, 1993, p. 5), he does not delineate the social status and behavioral repertoire of transgender inmates *sine qua non*. Likewise, prison officials do not have an agreed upon definition of transgender that is used to identify and classify inmates. Officials often include transgender in the category of "homosexual" prisoners (Jenness, 2010; Jenness, Sexton, & Sumner, 2011).

Nonetheless, transgender inmates in prisons for men—often easily recognized as biologically male by the California Department of Corrections and Rehabilitation (CDCR), but who identify or present as female in prison—are increasingly visible in major newspaper stories, quite often as a result of lawsuits brought by transgender prisoners contesting conditions of their confinement in county jails and state prisons for men. For example, in 2011, the *Los Angeles Times* ran a front page story titled "Inmate Sues State for Sex Change," with a subtitle that read: "She Says She Needs Surgery for Safety. The Case Shows Challenges Faced by Transgender Prisoners" (Dolan, 2011, p. 1). A few months later, the Associated Press reported on another lawsuit (Potter, 2011):

> Crouched in her cell, Ophelia De'lonta hoped three green disposable razors from the prison commissary would give her what the Virginia Department of Corrections will not—a sex change. [I]t had been several years since she had felt the urges, but she had been fighting them for weeks. But like numerous other times, she failed to get rid of what she calls "that thing" between her legs, the last evidence she was born a male. [M]onths after the October castration attempt, De'lonta filed a federal lawsuit Friday claiming the state has failed its duty to provide adequate medical care because it won't give her the operation. She says the surgery is needed to treat her gender identity disorder, a mental illness in which people believe they were born the wrong gender. [I]f she wins, De'lonta would be the nation's first inmate to receive a state-funded sex change operation. Similar lawsuits have failed in a handful of other states, and lawmakers in some states are trying to ban the use of taxpayer money for the operations. [I]f she loses, she says she will continue to try self-surgery—acknowledging another attempt could kill her.

AP Photo/Steve Helber.

Ophelia De'lonta speaks during an interview at the Buckingham Correctional Center in Dillwyn, VA, in this March 9, 2011 photo.

These dramatic and sometimes salacious stories raise a plethora of serious questions about how transgender prisoners manage prison life, correctional policy and practice, and the workings of gender in prisons. Fortunately, there is a growing body of literature that speaks to the many challenges transgender prisoners face in prisons (Baus, Hunt, & Williams, 2006; Brown & McDuffie, 2009; Emmer, Lowe, & Marshall, 2011; Jenness et al., 2011; O'Day-Senior, 2008), the ways in which correctional officials can and cannot proceed when meeting their responsibility to incarcerate transgender people in safe and constitutionally defensible ways (Arkles, 2008–2009; Brown & McDuffie, 2009; Browning & Cagney, 2002; A. Lee, 2008; A. L. Lee, 2003; Mann, 2006; Petersen, Stephens, Dickey, & Lewis, 1996; Rosenblum, 1999–2000; Sumner & Jenness, 2014; Tewksbury & Potter, 2005), and the complicated nature of the social organization of gender and sexuality in prison (Britton, 1997, 2003; Coggeshall, 1988; Donaldson, 1993; Fleisher & Krienert, 2006; Hensley, Wright, Tewksbury, & Castle, 2003).

Unfortunately, however, very little is known about diversity among transgender prisoners as a population that is unique by virtue of being both transgender and incarcerated. From a social science research point of view, they are what Tewksbury and Potter (2005) dubbed a "forgotten group" of prisoners and what Sexton, Jenness, and Sumner (2010) more recently identified as a "special population" that raises "the dilemma of difference" (Minow, 1990). For these and many other reasons, there is considerable need for empirical answers to basic sociological questions about transgender prisoners. Demographically speaking, who are they? How do transgender prisoners fare in terms of social capital as well as health and welfare? How do they think about themselves as people with gendered identities, sexual orientations, sexual identities, and attractions as well as contextually sensitive masculinities and femininities? Finally, how do they think of themselves as transgender people, prisoners, and both?

Drawing on recently collected original data on California transgender prisoners (Jenness, 2010, 2011; Sexton et al., 2010; Sumner, 2009), we address these questions in this chapter. We do so with an eye toward showing how prisons, quite literally, capture diversity; as a result, diversity is imprisoned. We also do so to set the stage for the incorporation of the voice of a single transgender prisoner (i.e., one of the coauthors of this chapter) into the social science portrayal put forth by researchers who are not transgender and who are not imprisoned. The extended voice and attendant portrayal of a single transgender prisoner provides depth, even as it may or may not be representative of the population at large. As such, it can be read as both a rejoinder and as a supplement to the social science data and the analysis advanced by social scientists. Our hope is that this atypical approach to a chapter in an edited volume on diversity effectively invites readers to engage in what Anzaldúa (1987) refers to as "open-hearted listening" by all parties—the researchers, the transgender prisoner, and the other readers (transgender prisoners or not!).

DATA ON TRANSGENDER PRISONERS IN CALIFORNIA

It is very difficult to collect data on currently incarcerated transgender prisoners, in large part because doing in-prison research is difficult (Arriola, 2006; Jenness, 2010; Jenness, Maxson, Sumner, & Matsuda, 2010) and because identifying transgender prisoners within larger prison populations is difficult (Jenness, 2010; Jenness et al., 2011; Sumner, 2009). Fortunately, we were able to overcome these challenges, as well as many others, to successfully conduct the first systematic social science study of transgender prisoners in California prisons (Jenness, 2010; Jenness et al., 2011; Sexton et al., 2010;

Sumner, 2009). The project from which the data for this chapter derive was funded by the CDCR and required us to work both collaboratively with, and independently from, the CDCR to identify and access transgender prisoners in men's prisons in California in a way that meets the requirements of the University of California's Institutional Review Board, the CDCR's Research Office, and the State of California's Committee on the Protection of Human Subjects (Jenness, 2010; Jenness et al., 2011).

More specifically, we collected valuable original interview data and official data on 315 transgender prisoners incarcerated in 27 of the CDCR's 30 prisons for men.[1] To collect these data, we utilized an innovative interview schedule that was specifically designed to be sensitive to transgender inmates and to capture a wealth of information on their lives both inside and outside prison. With regard to collecting original self-report data on life in prison, this project broke new ground by empirically examining the housing environments in which transgender inmates live, the social networks in which they are embedded, their personal relationships in prison, and their identities and conduct as transgender inmates. With their informed consent, we conducted face-to-face interviews with transgender prisoners in a way that successfully allowed them to provide valid and reliable self-report information along these lines, knowing that they would not be paid for doing so and that doing so would not have any consequences for their programming or release date. Our response rate was 95%, which leads us to conclude that the findings reported below are not biased by refusals to participate in the study.

Because California is home to one of the largest correctional systems in the western world, surpassed only by the U.S. federal system, it is an ideal site for this research. Browne and McDuffie (2009) recently estimated that there are approximately 750 transgender prisoners in the United States; if accurate, this number suggests that California is home to nearly half of all transgender prisoners in the United States. Therefore, they are a valuable state level population of transgender prisoners. As is clear from the analysis presented below, this population of transgender prisoners certainly reveals considerable diversity.

CAPTURING DIVERSITY OF TRANSGENDER PRISONERS IN MEN'S PRISONS: DEMOGRAPHY, HEALTH AND WELFARE, AND SELF AND IDENTITIES

Volumes of research literature on prisoners and an increasingly growing body of knowledge on transgender people have yet to produce a systematic profile of transgender inmates.[2] Thus, the analysis that follows fills a gap in the sociology, criminology, and corrections literature by providing the first empirically driven profile of transgender

---

[1] The length of the interviews depended upon the volume of victimization reported, the loquaciousness of the inmate, and the pace of the interviewer. The shortest interview was less than a half hour (19 minutes), while the longest extended to just under three hours (two hours and 55 minutes). The mean duration for interviews was slightly less than one hour (56 minutes), with individual interviews ranging from a mean duration of 40 minutes to one hour and 12 minutes. The total amount of live interview time approached 300 hours (294 hours and six minutes).

[2] A report by the Sylvia Rivera Law Project (2007) is a welcome exception.

prisoners in prisons for men. The presentation is organized around three sets of concerns: demographic and criminological distinctions, health and well-being, and self and identity.

Demographic and Criminological Distinctions

Drawing on the data described above and official data on the prison population in men's prisons in California, we first consider eight demographic and criminological variables for purposes of comparison: age, race or ethnicity, offense category, custody level, type of life sentence (or not), registered sex offender (or not), verified gang affiliation (or not), and mental health status. Table 9-1 reveals that transgender inmates are distinguishable from the larger population of inmates in prisons for adult men in terms of age, with transgender inmates more represented in the middle ages (36–45);[3] race or ethnicity, with transgender inmates disproportionately white and black; commitment offense, with transgender inmates disproportionately admitted to prison for crimes against property; custody level, with transgender inmates disproportionately classified as Level 3 and Level 4 inmates; sex offender status, with transgender inmates more frequently classified as sex offenders; gang status, with transgender inmates less frequently identified as gang members; and mental health status, with transgender inmates more often classified as CCCMS (Correctional Clinical Case Management System) and EOP (Enhanced Out Patient).[4] Transgender inmates and the larger population of inmates in prisons for men are roughly equivalent on only one dimension reported in Table 9-1. Namely, 15.7% of transgender inmates and 16.9% of inmates in prisons for adult men are serving life sentences (for more along these lines, see Sexton et al., 2010).

Health and Welfare

Moving beyond these standard demographic and criminological variables reported in Table 9-1, transgender prisoners are situated at the nexus of intersecting marginalities. Specifically, when examined along the lines of employment, marital status, mental health, substance abuse, HIV status, homelessness, sex work, and victimization, transgender inmates are more perilously situated than nonincarcerated and/or nontransgender populations (Sexton et al., 2010). With regard to victimization in the form of sexual assault in particular, for example, transgender prisoners are

---

[3] This finding is no doubt related to the age at which transgender people "come out" (i.e., a process whereby gay men, lesbians, bisexuals, and transgender people inform others of their nonnormative identity). A recent study based on a survey of 3,474 transgender people from across the U.S. revealed the following: although the vast majority of trans women "felt different" and reported feeling "uncertain about their gender identity" very early in life (age 12 and under), only 1% disclosed their gender identity to others when they were age "12 and under." According to this study, 6% of trans women disclosed their gender identity to others between the ages of 13 and 19, 16% disclosed their gender identity in their 20s, 17% disclosed their gender identity in their 30s, and 38% disclosed their gender identity when they were age 40 or older. In other words, trans women most often come out as such later in life (*Understanding Transgender Lives*, by Brett Genny Beemyn and Sue Rankin [In press]); see a related power point presentation at: http://www.umass.edu/stonewall/translives/, last retrieved March 17, 2013). For a more complicated view of coming out as transgender, see Gagne, Tewksbury, and McGaughey (1997).

[4] To arrive at these findings, we concatenated existing official data retrieved from the CDCR's database on inmates—the Offender Based Information System (OBIS)—to self-report data described (for more along these lines, see Jenness et al., 2011; Sexton et al., 2010).

Table 9-1	A Comparison of Select Characteristics of the Transgender Inmate Population in California Prisons for Men and the Total Population in CDCR Prisons for Men			
	Total adult transgender population in CDCR prisons for men		Total adult population in CDCR prisons for men[*]	
	n	%	N	%
Total	332	100	146,360	100
Age				
Mean		38.05		37.39
Median		38.50		36.00
Std. Dev.		9.61		11.18
Range		19, 63		18, 92
18–25	33	9.9	22,968	15.7
26–35	90	27.1	46,738	31.9
36–45	135	40.7	40,884	27.9
46+	74	22.3	35,770	24.4
Race/ethnicity				
Hispanic	94	28.3	56,880	38.9
White	93	28.0	37,954	25.9
Black	115	34.6	43,451	29.7
Asian/Pacific Islander	3	.9	1,337	.9
Other	27	8.1	6,738	4.6
Offense				
Crimes against persons	162	49.8	80,202	54.8
Property	98	30.2	26,892	18.4
Drug	53	16.3	26,418	18.1
Other	12	3.7	12,841	8.8

	Total adult transgender population in CDCR prisons for men		Total adult population in CDCR prisons for men[*]	
	n	%	N	%
Custody Level				
1	39	13.3	25,226	19.6
2	75	25.6	43,288	33.6
3	85	29.0	31,037	24.1
4	94	32.1	29,405	22.8
Life sentence				
Life	44	13.3	21,271	14.5
Life without parole	8	2.4	3,524	2.4
Sex offender registration				
Yes	68	20.5	21,381	14.6
Gang (verified)				
Yes	17	5.1	22,070	15.1
Mental health (official)				
CCCMS[**]	180	54.2	25,148	17.2
EOP[***]	33	9.9	4,458	3.0

*The total adult male prison population figures include the study population and exclude those residing in camps.
**Correctional Clinical Case Management System.
***Enhanced outpatient.

more likely than others in the prison population to be sexually assaulted in prison—by a factor of 13 (Jenness, Maxson, Matsuda, & Sumner, 2007; Jenness et al., 2011). By this and many other measures, transgender prisoners in men's prisons constitute a vulnerable population.

Educational attainment is the notable exception to this pattern of accumulated disadvantage. Transgender inmates' levels of education fall short of the nonincarcerated population, but exceed those of the U.S. and California prison populations (Sexton et al., 2010). Tellingly, education does not translate into other types of accumulated advantage, most notably employment and health (Emmer et al., 2011; Sexton et al., 2010). Despite this single—albeit promising—factor in their favor, transgender inmates are located at the intersection of a daunting array of marginalities. As we concluded in another article, transgender prisoners are drastically disproportionately marginalized at multiple turns, and these sources of marginality are manifested both inside and outside of prison (Sexton et al., 2010).

Self and Identities

Transgender inmates are a diverse prison population in terms of important dimensions of self and identity. Here we focus on just a few, including: continuity in terms of presenting as female, essentialized and constructed views of self, and self-referencing labels (i.e., gender identity, sexual orientation, sexual attraction[s], and femininities). Taken individually and collectively, these features of self, as expressed by over 300 transgender prisoners in California, reveal considerable diversity.

CONTINUITY AND DISCONTINUITY IN GENDER PRESENTATION. Reported in Table 9-2, over three fourths (76.7%) of transgender inmates presented as female outside prison and anticipate presenting as female if or when they are released from prison. These transgender inmates display consistency between their gender presentation and their status as transgender both inside and outside prison. For them, prison life does not disrupt this particular dimension of how they situate socially and in terms of what Erving Goffman (1963) calls presentation of self. This calls into question the commonly held notion that transgender prisoners turn to femininity as an adaptation to being in a sex-segregated environment organized around masculinity and its many displays.

In contrast, a little less than a quarter of transgender inmates in prison report discontinuity along these lines. Specifically, 13.6% did not present as female prior to their most recent incarceration, but plan to present as female if or when they leave prison; 5.2% presented as female prior to their most recent incarceration, but do not plan to present as female if or when they leave prison; and a little less than 5% did not present as female before their most recent incarceration and do not plan to present as female if or when they leave prison. For most transgender inmates, then, being transgender is imported into prison. For others, becoming transgender—at least in terms of presenting as female—is a life event that occurs for the first time in prison.

ESSENTIALIZED AND CONSTRUCTED VIEWS. Transgender inmates expressed contrasting views on the degree to which being transgender is an ascribed dimension of the self

Table 9-2	Distribution of Transgender Inmates in California Prisons for Men Presenting as Female Before and After Incarceration*						
		Expected female presentation upon release from prison					
		Yes		No		Total	
Female presentation prior to most recent incarceration		N	%	N	%	N	%
	Yes	237	76.7%	16	5.2%	253	81.9%
	No	42	13.6%	14	4.5%	56	18.1%
	TOTAL	279	90.3%	30	9.7%	309	100%

*Statistically significant at $p < .001$

versus a feature of the self that is socially–environmentally dependent. In the vernacular of social science, this is often framed as the realism versus constructionism debate, which, to quote Abbott (2004), boils down to a question about "whether the things and qualities we encounter in reality are enduring phenomena or simply produced (and reproduced) in social interaction as need be" (p. 46).

Some transgender prisoners expressed an essentialized, immutable view of self. For example, a middle-aged white inmate serving a multi-decade sentence expressed the following in a letter to the lead researcher after being interviewed for the current study:

> Although there is no test, I believe a true t/g could describe certain feelings or/and mutilation/prosthesis that one has had during their mind-boggling "oh my god! I'm not in the right body." Being tg is something that one doesn't just wake up and become. This is something that we have been born with.

Sharing this view, a 26-year-old Hispanic transgender inmate who did not present as female prior to being incarcerated, but began presenting as female while incarcerated, said: "I was holding it secret for a long time. I found a friend who was comfortable with it who told me: 'just come out and be yourself' and I got more respect and feel much better about myself."

In sharp contrast to this essentialized view of being transgender, other transgender inmates see being transgender as time and place dependent. For example, a self-identified homosexual inmate expressed a transition to "becoming" transgender as an adaptation to prison life:

> When you come into prison being homosexual, you're automatically a girl. It's your place to play the female role. If you're open with your homosexuality. . . . But if you're a guy and you're fucking around with me, they're the man and I'm the girl. I don't understand it because you're doing the same things I am doing. . . . When I first got here I had a bald head and was more tough. One transgender told me, "you have to gay it up!" And then the guys were really receptive. Real life is so different than prison life. Here, you're gay so there's pressure right away to grow your hair out. . . . If you're a manly gay boy you don't fit in with the guys or the homosexuals. You have to adapt or be a total loner. I came in more manly and now am more feminine so people are more receptive. It's an adaptation but I wouldn't take hormones for it. That's too far.

As a final example of the malleable nature of being a transgender inmate, consider the trajectory of an inmate who has lived for decades as a transgender inmate in a California prison, but no longer defines himself as transgender. At the beginning of an interview, this middle-aged black inmate who has been in prison for over two decades reported that he is no longer on hormones and does not participate in groups with transgender inmates. He then politely and simply declared: "I'm not transgender anymore." As he described his life, he began taking hormones in the late 1960s, used to be transgender for many years (including on the streets in the city in which he grew up and in which he lived prior to coming to prison in the mid-1980s on his current term), and quit taking hormones in prison in the mid-2000s after testing HIV positive, receiving news his mother died, and finding god. He reported:

> I always wanted to be a little girl. Since 1968, I took hormones early on. I was living as a woman and looking good. I had the clothes, the jewelry. I had it all going on. Girl, you should have seen me. . . . [But] transgenders have a very big problem in the prison

system. When I came in, they were automatically ostracized. They were not treated well by anyone—not the inmates, not the guards, not the people who were supposed to help them. . . . I'm a people person. I like everybody, but everybody does not like me [as a transgender person].

When asked why he "quit" being transgender, he said:

I learned I wasn't happy as transgender, but I came to prison as transgender. I was the person everyone wanted to be around. I followed a guy to [name of another prison], but he never went there. I sure loved him. I came here [name of prison] to settle down. Lord, I've been doing this for 40 some years and I'm not happy. I came to [name of prison] to settle down, it was just too much of a lifestyle. I just wanted to be happy. So I gave it up. I quit being transgender and a woman.

When asked if being transgender is "something you can just choose to quit," he said: "Yes, I still see guys and get that tingly feeling, but I resist. I just don't act on it—and some of the young ones are sooooooo cute. They really are, but I just look the other way." Granted, this view could be an exception to the rule, but it is telling nonetheless when considering the malleability of being a transgender inmate.

SELF-REFERENCING LABELS.   Transgender inmates report a range of labels to describe themselves. The vast majority (76.1%) identify as female when asked about their gender identity, with considerably fewer identifying as "male and female" (14%), "other" or "it depends" (3.5%), "neither female nor male" (3.2%), and "male" (3.2%). In one case, an inmate identified as hermaphrodite and emphasized that federal papers affirmed her identity with legal standing. Respondents used other self-referencing labels throughout the interviews as well, revealing diverse perceptions of self and femininity. For instance, they drew connections between themselves and widely divergent iconic female figures, such as Cinderella, Wilma Flintstone, and Xena the Warrior Princess.[5]

Transgender inmates also self-identify with a range of sexual orientations. About a third (33.3%) of transgender inmates in California prisons identify as "homosexual," while 19.4% identify their sexual orientation as "transgender;" 18.1% identify as heterosexual, 11.3% identify as bisexual, and the remaining 17.8% identify as something else. "Something else" includes a range of self-signifiers, such as: "a girl transsexual," "a queen that likes men," "androgynous," "both transgender and heterosexual," "heterosexual in a transgender world," "homosexual and transgender," "I'm my mother's daughter," "just sexual," "just normal," "just myself," "just a person," "just natural," "just me," and "human."

There is less variation in sexual attractions for transgender inmates in California prisons. The majority of transgender inmates are sexually attracted to men (81.9%), but a considerable minority indicated being attracted to both men and women (15.6%). Only 1.3% of transgender inmates reported being sexually attracted to women only. The remaining respondents reported being sexually attracted to "neither" men nor women or some combination of "transgender" or "transsexual" persons and women.

---

[5] Cinderella, Wilma Flintstone, and Xena the Warrior Princess are a fairy tale heroine, television cartoon comedy character, and television action heroine, respectively.

This pattern is not specific to the prison environment. The vast majority of transgender inmates (75.8%) reported being attracted to men both outside of prison and inside prison, effectively dispelling the notion that they turn to men as an adaptation to being in a sex segregated environment in which (presumably) biological women are not available.

Clearly, the transgender prisoners in California are a diverse group of prisoners who display a bricolage of characteristics, subjectivities, and sensibilities. With this in mind, in the next section of this chapter we turn to Nikkas Alamillo-Luchese, a transgender prisoner serving time in a California prison for men, to offer a view from the inside.

COMMONALITY AND DIFFERENCE: A TRANSGENDER LIFE IN PRISON

Nikkas grew up in Santa Cruz and Monterey Counties, where she donated time to advocate for local AIDS Projects. She is 49 years old and lives with disabilities and as a survivor of sexual assault and a recovered alcoholic. She is serving a life sentence. As a coauthor of this chapter, she speaks from the point of view of someone who lives the life of a transgender prisoner, is embedded in a transgender prisoner community, and has thought a lot about what it means to be transgender and imprisoned. To contribute to this chapter, we invited her to write whatever she wished to be shared and prompted her with the following questions: What do you think of how we have portrayed transgender prisoners in California prisons for men? What resonates with your experience and understanding? What doesn't? What should we be discussing? What would you like to tell us—and the readers of this volume—about transgender prisoners in prisons for men? As a result of her life experiences and current institutional location, her answers to these questions are instructive, quite apart from whether they are generalizable to the larger transgender prisoner population. Indeed, in the sections below, she emphasizes the importance of hearing the voices of transgender prisoners in order to understand the diversity that characterizes their lives. She cautions against overcategorizing transgender prisoners and overgeneralizing when it comes to thinking about transgender prisoners.

On Voice[6]

We are the CDCR transgender prisoner community, as shown in Table 9-1, currently living in California men's prisons. It is studies and reports like these[7] that allow you the opportunity to understand who we are and what we have been through. This is important to transgenders. It allows us to express ourselves and provide you—the readers— a proper view into our lives without distorting our characters. You have the unique chance to learn more about us. Whether you do so is entirely up to you. Please remember that each transgender's statement(s) belongs to that specific individual and does not necessarily reflect the transgender community at large in California men's prisons. My

---

[6] The subsection headings that follow were inserted by the academic authors to organize the text and facilitate ease of reading. Likewise, the text that follows, which was written by the transgender prisoner author, has been lightly edited for ease of reading.

[7] "These" is a reference to an earlier draft of the previous sections of this chapter, which was sent to her along with an invitation to contribute to this chapter.

opinion and comments are based upon my lifetime's experience and not influenced by anyone else's. Don't judge us, all of us, based upon one transgender's actions or comments. It's unfair. Understanding is the key. Whether you approve of transgenderism or not, your understanding is crucial. Life pivots on understanding people and events.

On Commonality and Difference

We each deserve the same dignity and respect that you expect, want and deserve, there is no difference in that. It is important that people—including you who are reading about transgenders in men's prisons—keep an open mind and understand that we are all individual people, with the same likes and dislikes and wants as anyone else. Like you. Some transgenders want a life partner and a house with a picket fence, while some prefer other avenues. We may enhance our features but we have always been women. Most of us don't like being referred to as transgenders. How would you like to be categorized under a term that holds no official definition? According to the DSM-IV, we suffer from GID (Gender Identity Disorder), which they claim is a mental condition. The only condition is the one between our legs. That's a physical condition. Our minds know we are female but our bodies do not quite match up. If you really want confusion, conduct a poll and ask transgenders if they would have a SRS (sexual reassignment surgery)—not just plastic surgery but the full SRS. How many would say "yes"; "no"; "other?" Ask why?

Keep an open-mind and view me, Nikkas, as an individual. View each person as an individual. If one of us screws up or becomes true drama, don't judge us all based upon her actions. Don't drag all other transgenders down, too. We are all valued people just like you or anyone else. One of the worst things you can do is to refer to us all as the same, by lumping us into a group. That's ridiculous.

So why do so many hold this negative attitude and opinion against us? That narrow-minded perception is offensive and degrading. Most think of Cher impersonators or queens performing on stage but those are drag queens and performers, not us. We are simply regular individuals. So please do not place us all in the same category or consider lumping us in any set category. Transgender prisoners are a diverse community. Most often we are misunderstood, by people inside and outside of prison walls. We are thought of in a negative light. We are no different than others. The media has the horrific habit of exploiting transgenders in men's prisons to the general population, portraying us as a burdensome, expensive liability. They twist our words to fit their set agendas. Lately the high cost of our HRT (Hormone Replacement Therapy) has been taunted on television and the prisons where transgender prisoners reside has been portrayed as an apparent paradise, as we are surrounded by so many men, trying to push an illusion that we are all man-hungry women. This stigma and stereotypical mentality places us in an awful category. This is what we are up against. We are a culture of transgenders who are victimized, harassed, and treated with prejudiced double standards. We are transgender women in men's prisons.

On Challenges We Face in Prison

Ignorance and fear are both evident in the staff's demeanor and attitude. Prisoners and staff alike fail to try and understand who we even are. We are dumped into a group and held hostage. These are their preconceived ideas and general negative demeanor, displayed towards transgenders in men's prisons. We are a growing culture that is mistreated by the majority of prison officials, staff, and inmates. Unfairly treated. There are laws in place that are supposed to protect us, but they are ignored or forgotten. Unfortunately, we are also forgotten, as transgenders, ignored by the general public and usually exploited by the media to meet their negative needs. We, transgenders, are a very vulnerable, minority population in men's prisons, bullied by various administrations, even though we are the vulnerable ones. They are aware of that and exploit it.

Years ago one particular prison was the transgender prisoners' homeland—our mothership. An open-door rapport was created and established with the then administration who assisted in reducing the victimization of our sisters. We used to meet with the then warden every quarter. We had a small transgender council, were respected, proud of ourselves and we all worked to help others and each other stay safe. Now, it is the opposite, with the current administration preferring to toss us all together, segregated in the same unit and in the same wing. If you happen to be victimized you'll be sent to ad-seg (i.e., administrative segregation or "the hole"), pending a unique investigation with interesting results. You may end up with "unspecified enemies," which is the prison's way of dumping you elsewhere. As a result, transgenders and victims don't want to report their victimization for fear of punishment. Now we have transgenders scattered throughout the entire CDCR system.

If transgender prisoners are sexually assaulted and report it, there are no guarantees or promises that any actual help will come. The final findings or end results may be left undone—with no finalizing documentation and both parties still residing in the same location or still able to. No one deserves to be treated this way. Transgenders in a men's prison who are sexually assaulted, coerced, raped, attacked or touched, should call an outside agency and report it. They shouldn't trust simply the prison's staff. They need treatment and therapy. Staff are accountable for our well-being. An outside agency can help provide support and ensure the investigative findings are factual and not altered but truly based upon the evidence and testimony. In prison, sexual predators, rapists, molesters, and any individuals who attempt to force sexual advances on others are despised and loathed. Men don't want these individuals near their loved ones, children or family members either. Transgenders in California men's prisons, as well as other systems, need outside support and advocacy to ensure our rights are being met. Advocacy helps us remind the administration not to ignore our rights. We need help to stop the double standards we have to battle simply to get feminine products like brassieres.

On Making a Difference

I fully comprehend and have truly experienced the isolation—the feeling(s) of being outside the world's general view of norms. But these stereotypical barriers/walls of our yesteryears are slowly tumbling down. 2011 is an era the older generations never had the chance to experience, in reference to such outspoken freedom as we have today. I never had this freedom. There are LGBTQGV (Lesbian, Gay, Bisexual, Transgender, Queer, Gender-Variant) Centers most places nowadays, on a campus, in cities, towns, and neighborhoods. For me, school was rough in terms of others' acceptance of alternative genders. My mother attended the same high school that I did. Now she is a teacher there and there is a LGBT Center onsite for students and faculty. I could barely believe an LGBT center was on campus. I was awestruck when she told me. I was happy and proud of people I never knew nor would ever meet. To me it's beautiful as there is now a LGBT Center for the younger generation students and others to meet and, more importantly, to meet in a safe environment without all the peer pressures of high school. Even for an hour, they can recharge their batteries and feel good about themselves. I feel that many of these younger generation students and non-students are warriors and heroes for being out and remaining themselves. I understand the name-calling, hateful glares and glances that biased attitude of people just tolerating you because they don't get you. They don't understand. This requires patience and understanding on our part as well. Most lack of understanding is fear, which is near the center of each negative attitude.

There are many LGBTQGVs still hidden, not out of that closet, afraid of doing so, both in the free world and in men's prisons. Perhaps they have good reasons for doing so; nonetheless, they require our support and all our understanding. Our LGBTQGV culture is an enriched one, with different ethnicities, walks of life and a diverse array of beliefs. It is our own melting pot. Our sexual preferences should not be called into question, as it isn't anyone's damn business. How would you feel if people began judging you based upon your sexual orientation and your gender preference? Do they have a right to? Perhaps in their deluded eyes they do, because they are the "norm" but you are not. Some people may belittle you, give you those dagger glares, look at you in disgust or as if you're a freak from a carnival attraction. Is it fair? Now, magnify all those negative vibes, hatreds, bigotries and feelings, and remember you're also in the minority, 20 of 1,600. Welcome to a men's prison.

As transgenders we all face a multitude of misunderstandings. A day usually won't pass by where we do not hear or experience some form of transgender bashing. A sneered look or comments made for us to hear. We are known as "drama" according to prison staff and some inmates. It's true that some transgenders are dramatic, just like anyone else, but not every one of us is. I am in an established, committed, loving, healthy life partnership, with the same man for four years. My mother and my stepfather have been extremely supportive. They are a diversified and non-judgmental couple who lovingly provide me with an additional foundation. My partner and my parents are all a family and a very positive one who have grown as we all continue to encourage each other. Everyone deserves to be happy and content. I think whatever floats your boat, all the power to you, but you have no right to knock someone else off course or rock their boat. Never at the expense of others.

It's important to our culture to have unity and form a community balance. We can make differences for the benefit and betterment of transgenders in men's prisons. We have our own system since their system is biased against transgenders. If you don't stand and unite you really have no grounds for complaints. Our unique transgender culture and community must have that unity to ensure our rights and welfare are provided for. Who else is going to fight for us? Look at the beautiful LGBT community in the world—out there where you are—and how their culture and community band together, uniting for a cause. Transgenders who unite as friends, with fellow LGBTQGVs, are better off and less likely to be solely targeted or harassed. It's not always easy for transgenders to make friends, as some view such LGBTQGV friends as competitive threats in trying to gain male attention. My concerns are in prevention; trying to ensure our transgender community is safe. Safe from being coerced, victimized, threatened, battered/beaten, sexually assaulted, attacked and/or raped. We need to develop and educate our own transgender community, as we construct a positive and healthier self.

Conclusion

Two telling things happened on the way to concluding this chapter. First, the Cook County [IL] jail adopted a policy that establishes guidelines and procedures for matters involving the custody, safety, and security of inmates who self-identify or are otherwise identified as transgender.[8] Prior to adoption of this new policy, transgender inmates in the Cook County jail were treated as members of the gender that aligned with their sex at birth. Since March 21, 2011, however, the new policy specifies that transgender inmates can be housed, dressed, and searched according to their gender identity rather than the sex or gender they were assigned at birth. Accompanying this change in policy, a gender identity committee is charged with considering the case of each inmate who self-identifies as a transgender person or who is clinically verified as being transgender and to recommend appropriate accommodations for the inmate. With this change in policy, both men's and women's facilities are now options for where to house transgender inmates, and according to one report at least one transgender inmate is being housed in the women's division. This committee is also authorized to specify what clothes and toiletries transgender inmates should have as well as how officers can (and can't) search transgender inmates.

This historic shift in policy and the charge of the committee recognizes and publicly reveals diversity within the transgender inmate population. Related, it reveals the problematic nature of treating transgender women as men in facilities designed to detain male inmates; treating all transgender prisoners in men's jails the same; and the perilous consequences of failing to understand the diversity within the transgender population in detention facilities.

Second, as we worked on finalizing the text in the section devoted to Nikkas' perspective on being transgender in a prison for men, we had an Aha! moment that revealed the power of institutions to define diversity away. After Nikkas sent her handwritten text to the lead author, it was lightly edited by the academic authors and then sent back to Nikkas for final review. Nikkas approved of the lightly edited version[9] and offered a handful of small editorial suggestions herself. One of the seemingly small changes she suggested, however, was gigantic because it was substantively illuminating. Namely, Nikkas pointed out that she is not white, as her coauthors had assumed and indicated in a previous version of the biography that introduces her section of this chapter. As she wrote, "Your bio on page 15 was great. Thank you for taking the lead, as I wasn't sure how to do one without seeming self-important. I am considered 'other' (FYI)."

The fact that this correction was presented as an "FYI"—quite literally a parenthetical mention that our assessment of her race did not correspond to the way she is situated in prison—reveals the power of corrections to define away her diversity as a racialized subject. Whether this correction

---

[8] Retrieved from http://www.nbcchicago.com/news/local/cook-county-jail-transgender-inmates-119516094.html

[9] Actually, she did more than approve. She expressed enthusiasm, even going so far as to call the text "perfect."

indicates that she embraces an "other" identity for herself,[10] or simply accepts and conveys the label as ascribed by the CDCR,[11] she affirmed her membership in this category by conveying it to us as something that needed to be correctly portrayed in this chapter.[12] In fact, this was the only substantive clarification she made to the text written by the academic authors.

We conclude this chapter with these two facts—that the Cook County jail has a new policy that complicates the management of transgender prisoners and that Nikkas offered a correction to the academic authors' portrayal of her as a type of person—to emphasize the ways in which institutionally recognized categorical meanings can broaden or delimit our understanding of diversity. In the case of changes in policy at the Cook County jail, diversity is further granulated insofar as not all transgender prisoners are oriented to as equivalent. In the case of California prisons' specifications of race, diversity is eclipsed as only a handful of possibilities for backgrounds, subjectivities, and self-identification are officially recognized.

Likewise, we included a social science portrayal of transgender prisoners and a first-person account of transgender prisoners in this chapter to showcase the diversity among transgender inmates, even as we treat them as an analytically meaningful type of prisoner (i.e., transgender prisoner) within a larger group of inmates (i.e., prisoners). In simple terms, transgender prisoners represent a source of gender diversity and a source of diversity among prisoners. They sit at the intersection of numerous self-identifications and official categorizations—what we call diversity within diversity—such that they are at once recognizable as a unique population and, at the same time, a lesson in the fluid and contingent nature of axes of differentiation that produce diversity and the lives that are impacted by the social organization that structures them. Clearly, transgender prisoners are defined by both their commonality and their difference.

---

[10] Nikkas' racial or ethnic classification tells more about who or what she is *not* than who or what she is. "Other" is a residual category, presumably composed of a multitude of racial and ethnic identities that have been homogenized as simply "not black, white, or Hispanic" (see the next footnote below). Similarly, transgender can be seen as an "other" category, encompassing a range of gender identities and presentations that do not fit into conventional gendered classifications.

[11] Many scholars have noted the tension between the racial classifications used by correctional systems and prisoners' own racial and ethnic identification. Goodman (2008) demonstrated the ways in which the CDCR assigns and ascribes racial categories in very specific and delimited ways through routine institutional processes of intake, classification, and housing. He found that the official racial categories of black, white, and Hispanic (and if not, then "other") belie the true complexity of racial and ethnic identification. More recent work by Calavita and Jenness (2013) complicates this picture further. As they report in their study of inmate grievances:

> Our designations of the race/ethnicity of these prisoners are based on their self-identifications, some of which differ in a number of interesting ways from their official racial classifications. For example, many of those officially classified as "Hispanic" self-identified as "Mexican," regardless of how many generations they and their families had been U.S. residents or citizens. Conversely, the CDCR sometimes classified men as "Mexican" when they told us they were "Hispanic", or in one case "Hispanic/White." Six of the 37 men officially classified as "Black" self-identified as "African American." One man who the CDCR classified as "Black" said he was "Cuban." In the four cases in which people told us they were of mixed backgrounds—"Indonesian/Mexican", "Mexican and Cuban", "African American/Puerto Rican", and "Korean/Black"—the CDCR classified them as "Hispanic", "Mexican", "Black", and "Black", respectively. One person who said he was "Native American/Pima" was classified by the CDCR as "Hispanic." Interestingly, the category that remained most consistent across CDCR classification and self-identity was "White." The only exception to this was an individual who was officially classified as "White" but who referred to himself as "European," followed by the statement, "It doesn't matter—whatever they normally do, 'White,' 'Caucasian,' 'European'—it's just my ancestry"(#117). Beyond the issue of different classification categories, we are sensitive to the fluid and contingent nature of racial identification, and it must be stressed that these self-descriptors may reflect this moment in time and the prison context.

Related, Saperstein and Penner's (2010) recent work reveals that the experience of imprisonment can shift how people self-identify as racialized subjects as well as how others identify them as racialized subjects.

[12] Whether "other" is a mere official classification or an identity label chosen for herself is unknown and, in some ways, beside the point. Either way, her decision to rely on an official category as a corrective to our erroneous assumptions speaks volumes about the power of official categories to define and inscribe race.

References

Abbott, A. (2004). *Methods of discovery: Heuristics for the social sciences*. Chicago, IL: University of Chicago Press.

Anzaldúa, G. (1987). *Borderlands/La frontera: The new Mestiza* (1st ed.). San Francisco, CA: Aunt Lute Books.

Arkles, G. (2008–2009). Safety and solidarity across gender lines: Rethinking Segregation of Transgender People in Detention Symposium—Intersections of transgender lives and the law. *Temple Political & Civil Rights Law Review, 18*, 515–560.

Arriola, K. R. J. (2006). Debunking the myth of the safe haven: Toward a better understanding of intra-prison HIV transmission. *Criminology & Public Policy, 5*(1), 137–147.

Baus, J., Hunt, D., & Williams, R. (2006). *Cruel and unusual* [Motion Picture]. United States: Reid Productions LLC.

Beemyn, G., & Rankin, S. (In press). *The lives of transgender people*. New York, NY: Columbia University Press.

Britton, D. M. (1997). Gendered organizational logic: Policy and practice in men's and women's prisons. *Gender & Society, 11*(6), 796–818.

Britton, D. M. (2003). *At work in the iron cage: The prison as gendered organization*. New York: New York University Press.

Brown, G. R., & McDuffie, E. (2009). Health care policies addressing transgender inmates in prison systems in the United States. *Journal of Correctional Health Care, 15*(4), 280–291.

Browning, C. R., & Cagney, K. A. (2002). Neighborhood structural disadvantage, collective efficacy, and self-rated physical health in an urban setting. *Journal of Health and Social Behavior, 43*(4), 383–399.

Calavita, K., & Jenness, V. (2013). Inside the pyramid of disputes: Naming problems and filing grievances in California prisons. *Social Problems, 60*(1), 50–80.

Coggeshall, J. M. (1988). "Ladies" behind bars: A liminal gender as cultural mirror. *Anthropology Today, 4*(4), 6–8.

Dolan, J. (2011, April 20). Lawsuit asks state to pay for inmate's sex-change operation. *Los Angeles Times*. Retrieved from http://articles.latimes.com/2011/apr/20/local/la-me-prisons-transgender-20110420

Donaldson, S. (1993). A million jockers, punks, and queens. Retrieved from http://www.justdetention.org/en/docs/doc_01_lecture.aspx

Emmer, P., Lowe, A., & Marshall, R. B. (2011). *This is a prison, glitter is not allowed: Experiences of trans and gender variant people in Pennsylvania's prison systems*. Philadelphia, PA: Hearts on a Wire Collective.

Fleisher, M. S., & Krienert, J. L. (2006). *The culture of prison sexual violence*. Washington, DC: U.S. Department of Justice, National Institute of Justice.

Gagne, P., Tewksbury, R., & McGaughey, D. (1997). Coming out and crossing over: Identity formation and proclamation in a transgender community. *Gender & Society, 11*(4), 478–508.

Girshick, L. B. (2008). *Transgender voices: Beyond women and men*. Hanover, NH: University Press of New England.

Goffman, E. (1963). *Stigma: Notes on the management of spoiled identity*. Englewood Cliffs, NJ: Prentice-Hall.

Hensley, C., Wright, J., Tewksbury, R., & Castle, T. (2003). The evolving nature of prison argot and sexual hierarchies. *Prison Journal, 83*(3), 289–300.

Jenness, V. (2010). From policy to prisoners to people: A "soft mixed methods" approach to studying transgender prisoners. *Journal of Contemporary Ethnography, 39*(5), 517–553.

Jenness, V. (2011). Getting to know "the girls" in an "alpha-male community": Notes on fieldwork on transgender inmates in California prisons. In S. Fenstermaker & N. Jones (Eds.), *Sociologists backstage: Answers to 10 questions about what they do* (pp. 139–161). New York, NY: Routledge.

Jenness, V., & Geis, G. L. (2010). Transgender lives and lifestyles. In C. D. Bryant (Ed.), *The handbook of deviant behavior*. New York, NY: Routledge.

Jenness, V., Maxson, C. L., Matsuda, K. N., & Sumner, J. (2007). *Violence in California correctional facilities: An empirical examination of sexual assault*. Report to the California Department of Corrections and Rehabilitation. Irvine, CA: University of California, Irvine.

Jenness, V., Maxson, C. L., Sumner, J. M., & Matsuda, K. N. (2010). Accomplishing the difficult but not impossible: Collecting self-report data on inmate-on-inmate sexual assault in prison. *Criminal Justice Policy Review, 21*(1), 3–30.

Jenness, V., Sexton, L., & Sumner, J. (2011). *Transgender inmates in California prisons: An empirical study of a vulnerable population*. Report to the California Department of Corrections and Rehabilitation. Irvine, CA: University of California, Irvine.

Lee, A. (2008). Trans models in prison: The medicalization of gender identity and the Eighth Amendment right to sex reassignment therapy. (Student article). *Harvard Journal of Law & Gender, 31,* 447–471.

Lee, A. L. (2003). Nowhere to go but out: The collision between transgender and gender-variant prisoners and the gender binary in America's prisons. (Unpublished article.) University of California Berkeley, Boalt Hall School of Law. Available at http://www.justdetention.org/pdf/nowhere-togobutout.pdf

Mann, R. (2006). The treatment of transgender prisoners, not just an American problem: A comparative analysis of American, Australian, and Canadian prison policies concerning the treatment of transgender prisoners and a universal recommendation to improve treatment. *Law & Sexuality, 15,* 91–133.

Minow, M. (1990). *Making all the difference: inclusion, exclusion, and American law.* Ithaca, NY: Cornell University Press.

O'Day-Senior, D. (2008). Forgotten frontier: Healthcare for transgender detainees in immigration and customs enforcement detention. *Hastings Law Journal, 60,* 453–475.

Petersen, M., Stephens, J., Dickey, R., & Lewis, W. (1996). Transsexuals within the prison system: An international survey of correctional services policies. *Behavioral Sciences & the Law, 14*(2), 219–229.

Potter, D. (2011, June 7). Va. inmate sues after gruesome tries at sex change. *Associated Press.*

Rosenberg, D. (2007, May 21). (Rethinking) gender. *Newsweek,* 149.

Rosenblum, D. (1999–2000). Trapped in Sing Sing: Transgendered prisoners caught in the gender binarism. *Michigan Journal of Gender & Law, 6,* 499–571.

Saperstein, A., & Penner, A. M. (2010). The race of a criminal record: How incarceration shapes racial perceptions. *Social Problems, 57*(1), 92–113.

Sexton, L., Jenness, V., & Sumner, J. M. (2010). Where the margins meet: A demographic assessment of transgender inmates in men's prisons. *Justice Quarterly, 27*(6), 32.

Sumner, J. (2009). *Keeping house: Understanding the transgender inmate code of conduct through prison policies, environments, and culture.* Unpublished doctoral dissertation, University of California, Irvine, Irvine, CA.

Sumner, J., & Jenness, V. (2014). Gender integration in sex-segregated prisons: The paradox of transgender correctional policy. In D. Peterson and V. R. Panfil (Eds.), *The handbook of LGBT communities, crime, and justice* (in press). New York, NY: Springer.

Sylvia Rivera Law Project. (2007). *It's war in here: A report on the treatment of transgender and intersex people in New York state men's prisons.* Retrieved from http://srlp.org/files/warinhere.pdf

Tewksbury, R., & Potter, R. H. (2005). Transgender prisoners: A forgotten group. In S. Stojkovic (Ed.), *Managing special populations in jails and prisons.* New York, NY: Civic Research Institute.

III

Education, Intimate Relationships, and the Media

For most Americans, education is considered a vehicle to upward mobility. Although underemployment is a serious concern for many college graduates today, data continue to show a strong correlation between median earnings and level of educational attainment. But as Jennifer Bondy and Anthony Peguero point out in Chapter 10, for the children of immigrants to the United States, the educational system presents both opportunities and challenges. School is where immigrant children not only learn basic skills such as reading and writing, but also where they become Americanized. This may speed assimilation, but it may also speed cultural loss for individual children, their families, and their immigrant communities. In Chapter 10, Bondy and Peguero explore several factors that influence the positive and negative educational experiences of various groups of immigrant children in the United States, and they argue that educators and policy makers need to be cognizant of each of these factors so as to reduce the marginalization of immigrant children in the U.S. educational system. Theirs is not an idle call to action, for as they note, immigrant children are one of the fastest growing segments of the U.S. population.

In Chapter 11, Leslie Picca shows how the promise of equal opportunity for all students, regardless of race or ethnicity, on college and university campuses is undermined by racism that is enacted "backstage"—that is, in informal social situations, where students think it is safe to use racist slurs or promote racist stereotypes. In her research with Joe Feagin, in which they asked more than 1,000 students to keep a diary in which they recorded everyday social interactions, Picca discovered that although students regarded overt, explicit racism as a thing of the past, more subtle or hidden racism is common on most college and university campuses today. The diaries that Picca and Feagin analyzed offered plentiful examples of racist behavior and language on the part of white students. And even though these students typically regard such actions and speech as "harmless," "trivial," or "just a joke," the diaries of the students of color demonstrate far more serious emotional consequences. Picca's chapter reminds us that despite rosy media reports that characterize the United States as a postracial society, our college and university campuses, where one might expect greater equality and openness than in the society at large, are failing to provide all students with a safe learning environment and a positive, enriching educational experience.

For many students, college is their first chance to live away from the watchful eye of their parents, allowing them to engage in dangerous or high-risk behavior. In Chapter 12, Kathleen Bogle discusses one such behavior—"hooking up." But as Bogle notes, while the media portray hooking up (i.e., casual, impersonal sexual encounters) as ubiquitous among college students today, there are significant differences across groups of students with regard to their likelihood of hooking up and their attitudes toward these types of relationships. Bogle's study of the hookup culture on two different university campuses, for example, showed that the practice was much more common among students involved in Greek life and athletics. Level of alcohol consumption, which is related to involvement in fraternities and sororities and athletic teams, is also related to likelihood of hooking up. Like Picca, Bogle cautions us to question media depictions of typical campus life and social relationships.

Chavella Pittman also examines media depictions in Chapter 13, but she is particularly concerned with how the media serve as a *socialization agent*—a means by which cultural norms and values are taught. Given the significant amount of time most people spend each day consuming media images, Pittman was curious as to what specific media content—popular situation comedies on television—may convey to viewers about white people's racial behavior. Although it is exploratory, Pittman's research reveals several common themes across the programs she analyzed. For one thing, Pittman found that while in real life whites may interact with people of color in a variety of social settings, on these programs whites rarely, if ever, interacted with people of color. The programs, then, reinforce and subtly support racial segregation. When cross-racial behavior was depicted on the programs, it tended to further reinforce racial stereotypes with regard to how people of color dress, speak, and behave.

When confronted with findings such as those in Pittman's study, whites often respond that it's just TV, and nobody really believes what they see on television, especially on sitcoms. But after reading the other chapters in this section, it becomes more difficult not to share Pittman's concern about the socializing impact of media constructions of race and cross-racial interaction.

This section concludes with a look at a disturbing media trend, the widespread availability of pornography on the Internet. As Walter DeKeseredy notes in Chapter 14, pornography played a pivotal role in the development of the Internet. The Internet allows us to search for specific content, send and receive video and audio files, and move quickly from one site to another with a simple click of the mouse. And this is all done privately, conveniently, anonymously, and cheaply, making the viewing of pornography—much of which is free on the Internet—easier than ever before. Calls to regulate pornography are promptly met with strong, sometimes strident, objections from those who worry about safeguarding First Amendment rights to free speech as well as those who claim that viewing pornography can be sexually liberating for both women and men. But as DeKeseredy points out, the Internet content he is discussing is not simply people having sex, nor is it what is commonly referred to as "erotica." The images available are often violent, involving intense degradation of women (and sometimes children), and they frequently reinforce racist stereotypes. Given the ease with which any individual with a computer and an Internet connection—including children—can access these images, DeKeseredy's concern about the effects of the proliferation of Internet pornography hardly seem unjustified or alarmist. So far, however, the courts have been reluctant to intervene, except in cases involving the production and distribution of child pornography. In the meantime, the fact that pornography is currently the single most searched-for item on the Internet should at least give us reason to more rigorously investigate its potential effects on social relationships—and social inequality—in our society.

10

Immigration and Education

Complexities and Intersecting Factors with Schooling the Children of Immigrants

Jennifer M. Bondy and Anthony A. Peguero

INTRODUCTION

In this chapter, we discuss the importance of diversity in the relationship to immigration and education. The concept of diversity suggests an understanding that each individual and culture is unique and recognizes that individual and cultural differences are essential for a democratic society. Individual and cultural differences can include various dimensions of immigration, communities, political beliefs, race, ethnicity, nationality, language, family and socioeconomic status, and gender. The exploration of these differences in a safe, positive, and nurturing environment is fundamental to an open, pluralistic, and democratic society like that of the United States. Therefore, as you read this chapter, we encourage and challenge you to pursue an understanding of the intersecting factors related to immigration and education.

School is an important social institution that the children of immigrants first encounter in the United States. Indeed, the waves of immigration to the United States, both historical and current, have resulted in numerous changes in educational policy, school leadership, curriculum, and classroom instruction (Olsen, 2008; Rong & Preissle, 2008). While schools are an institution of education and socialization for all students, they are also an institution of Americanization for the children of immigrants. School is where the children of immigrants learn not only about U.S. values, beliefs, and behaviors but also about immigrants' social and cultural role in American society (Olsen, 2008; Portes & Rumbaut, 2001, 2006; Rong & Preissle, 2008). It is within schools that the children of immigrants are exposed to mainstream American culture and where they learn and form beliefs about what U.S. society and people outside their families expect from them. The role of schools in the socialization of the children of immigrants helps to highlight educators' responsibility to understand and appreciate the unique schooling experiences of one of the fastest grow-ing and diverse segments of the population—the children of immigrants.

The children of immigrants are often considered to be more at risk for maltreatment than other children in school due to the stress and pressure that they and their families experience in the migration process (Portes & Rumbaut, 2001). It is critical to point out that for many children of immigrants, the immigration experience denotes a major life transition that often engenders fear, loss, isolation, confusion, and uncertainty about the present and future. Although there are countless reasons for migration, such as war, famine, religious persecution, and disaster, the process of leaving one's home, country, and culture is not a single event. Rather, educators should be reminded that migration is a lengthy and difficult process that can sometimes involve danger for children and their families. As we will note throughout this chapter, many immigrant families are victimized during the immigration process (Olsen, 2008; Portes & Rumbaut, 2001). Language barriers, racism, discrimination, prejudice, xenophobia, and unfamiliar customs are all part of the diverse social and cultural experiences for the children of immigrants (Stratton et al., 2009).

While there is a wide array of intersecting factors that are associated with immigration and education, we focus on the following seven factors: generation and assimilation; immigrant enclaves; the social, political, and educational climate of immigration; race, ethnicity, and region of origin; English language proficiency; fam-ily and socioeconomic status; and, gender. Research on immigration and education suggests that we need to emphasize these issues in order to better understand and meaningfully address the marginalization of the children of immigrants in U.S. schools (Olsen, 2008; Rong & Preissle, 2008; Suárez-Orozco & Suárez-Orozco, 2001). Immigrant families with children who come to the United States are of special interest because these children are part of the nation's future: its social, educational, political, and eco-nomic leaders; its parents; and its voters. Furthering the understanding of the children of immigrants' schooling experiences is therefore essential for the nation's success, stability, progress, and democracy. Of course, generation and assimilation, immigrant enclaves, the climate of immigration, race, ethnicity, and region of origin, English-language proficiency, family and socioeconomic status, and gender are not mutually exclusive categories of educational barriers and challenges; they are all interacting fac-tors of the children of immigrants' educational experiences. In the following sections, however, we separate these seven aspects to ensure that challenges and barriers of each are addressed directly.

GENERATION AND ASSIMILATION

Currently, one of four children in U.S. schools has at least one immigrant parent. This proportion is expected to rise to one of three within the next 20 years (U.S. Census Bureau, 2009). Contrary to popular media depictions, approximately 94% of children in immigrant families in U.S. schools were born in the United States (Rong & Priessle, 2008). This means that many children of immigrants are, in fact, U.S. citizens. Despite how one may perceive U.S. immigration policies, there is no refuting that the children of immigrants who live in the United States deserve an educational experience that is fair, equitable, and effective. The challenges faced by schools in relation to the chil-dren of immigrants are not new. The United States has been experiencing immigration since its inception and schools have always been charged with the task of integrating newcomers into U.S. society (Apple & Franklin, 2004). A historical and current question that many must continue to answer is how the process of assimilation is being implemented in the educational system. As noted, schools are one of the first institutions that the children of immigrants encounter in the United States; but how are the children of immigrants prospering over generations? The research evidence suggests that the direct link between assimilation and increased opportunities is mixed and debatable. A number of researchers have argued that there are factors that complicate the relationships among generation, assimilation, and education.

It is first important to define what we mean by generation in relation to immigration and education. First-generation children of immigrants are children who were born outside the United States. Second-generation children of immigrants are children who were born in the United States and have at least one foreign-born parent. Third-plus-generation refers to children who were born in the United States whose parents were also born in the United States. Many researchers explore the role that schools play in how the children of immigrants adapt and assimilate to U.S. society and culture; however, these researchers debate how effective the assimilation and educational processes are over generations. As immigrants, their children, and their grandchildren assimilate to the United States, do their chances for social, economic, and educational success increase with each generation?

Conventional assimilation theories have indicated that there is a straightforward perception of assimilation that facilitates upward mobility (Alba & Nee, 2003; Gordon, 1964; Kasinitz, Mollenkopf, & Waters, 2002; Kasinitz, Mollenkopf, Waters, & Holdaway, 2009). In other words, as each subsequent generation assimilates, it is believed that the pathways to higher social and economic status will increase as immigrants, their children, and their grandchildren become more culturally and linguistically similar to the middle class. On the other hand, segmented assimilationists argue that there are a number of intersecting factors (e.g., immigrant enclaves; the climate of immigration; race, ethnicity, and region of origin; English-language proficiency; family; gender) that are significant in the assimilation process. Segmented assimilationists suggest that social institutions such as schools have persistent inequalities that present barriers and hurdles to the children of immigrants in their attempts to advance and succeed in the United States (Gans, 1992; Portes & Rumbaut, 2001, 2006; Rumbaut, 1997; Zhou, 1997). Consequently, the process of assimilation may be divergent or segmented because assimilation may facilitate upward mobility or it may facilitate downward mobility.

Even though there is evidence supporting both conventional and segmented assimilation approaches in relation to educational progress, neither assimilation conceptual framework fully depicts, predicts, or explains the educational trajectories for the children of immigrants. When thinking about the relationship between assimilation and education, there are a number of differences between first-, second-, and third-plus generations. Some find that educational optimism increases from the first to the second generation; however, that educational optimism declines by the third-plus-generation (Kao & Tienda, 1995; Suárez-Orozco & Suárez-Orozco, 2001). Others reveal that as first-generation children of immigrants assimilate, their educational achievement and attainment improves (Kasinitz et al., 2002). On the other hand, many report that rather than following the same path of the first-generation's educational achievement and attainment, third-plus-generation youths have higher dropout rates than their parents (Perreira, Harris, & Lee, 2006; Portes & Rumbaut, 2001, 2006). Further, students' relationship with teachers is an essential building block toward students' progress and success. Yet, some researchers find that while first-generation youths have strong relationships with teachers, that relationship steadily deteriorates across generations and lessens students' chances for success in school (Peguero & Bondy, 2011). Finally, many argue that third-plus-generation youths are more likely to be exposed to school violence, misbehave while at school, and have perceptions of school disorder in comparison to their first- and second-generation counterparts (Ewert, 2009; Peguero, 2009, 2011a; Watkins & Melde, 2009). Clearly, understanding the educational process for the children of immigrants is complicated as well as significant. Thus, the remainder of the chapter describes how seven distinct and closely related factors—the climate of immigration, immigrant enclaves, race, ethnicity, region of origin, English-language proficiency, family, and gender—intersect and differently influence the children of immigrants' education and experiences within U.S. schools.

IMMIGRANT ENCLAVES

When immigrants migrate to the United States, immigrants and their children often settle in communities where family and friends from earlier migrations from their country of origin have settled (Kao & Tienda, 1995; Portes & Rumbaut, 2001, 2006; Suárez-Orozco & Suárez-Orozco, 2001). A community with concentrated levels of immigrants is referred to as an immigrant enclave. There are benefits and hurdles for immigrants who reside in immigrant enclaves. Immigrant enclaves can offer social networks, anchors for identity, and representations of an immigrant's home culture as well as provide information and employment in an immigrant enclave labor market for newly arriving immigrants and their families. On the other hand, immigrant enclaves are often segregated from mainstream society and plagued with poverty, joblessness, lack of social services, and other social problems (Kao & Tienda, 1995; Portes & Rumbaut, 2001, 2006; Suárez-Orozco & Suárez-Orozco, 2001).

Research studies have demonstrated that immigrant enclaves may protect immigrants' cultural identities and their strong bonds to the values and beliefs of their countries of origin (Portes & Rumbaut, 2001, 2006; Suárez-Orozco & Suárez-Orozco, 2001). Strong social bonds among immigrants can make immigrant enclaves feel like mini-homelands, helping to preserve cultural norms and values, and providing ethnic solidarity. Strong social bonds may also provide resources to aid in adaptation to U.S. social life, such as by helping new immigrants to learn the language and pick up local cultural norms (Portes & Rumbaut, 2001, 2006; Suárez-Orozco & Suárez-Orozco, 2001). Strong social bonds may be particularly important to immigrants and their children because of the support, information, and opportunities they can facilitate.

Theoretically, cultural preservation, informal social control, and strong social bonds evident within an immigrant enclave dissuade youth residing there from engaging in violence and strengthen their educational bond. Portes and Rumbaut (2001) describe the "challenges confronting immigrant children in U.S. neighborhoods in a social context promoting dropping out of school, joining youth gangs, or participating in the drug subculture" (p. 59). Although some immigrants reside in poor communities with the presence of disorder, cultural and social values that place importance on community and family responsibility, optimism for and realization of employment success, strong interpersonal social bonds, and commitment to educational progress can facilitate success for the children of immigrants (Portes & Rumbaut, 2001, 2006; Suárez-Orozco & Suárez-Orozco, 2001; Valenzuela, 1999).

THE CLIMATE OF IMMIGRATION

The social and political debate on U.S. immigration policy is heated and controversial. The debate over immigration is a complex issue that is often discussed with biased views as well as conflicting information. Much of this debate is centered on the links between immigration, crime, employment, and education (Portes & Rumbaut, 2001; Suárez-Orozco, Suárez-Orozco, & Todorova, 2008). Even though there is a myth of immigrants being deviant, criminal, and unintelligent, research reveals evidence to the contrary. The children of immigrants are less likely to be involved in crime, substance use, and general deviance (Portes & Rumbaut, 2001, 2006). Immigrant youths educationally outperform their U.S.-native-born counterparts (Portes & Rumbaut, 2001; Rong & Priessle, 2008; Suárez-Orozco et al., 2008). In fact, the children of immigrants have strong beliefs that hard work, progress, and success within school will lead to adult educational and economic success (Portes & Rumbaut, 2001, 2006; Suárez-Orozco et al., 2008). A common reason for family migration is to provide children with educational opportunities that are not available in their countries of origin. Parents' emphasis on education leads children to make pragmatic decisions to enhance their educational success, developing high educational aspirations and building attachments to their schools and classmates (Portes & Rumbaut, 2001, 2006; Suárez-Orozco et al., 2008).

Unfortunately, however, it appears that the climate of immigration and a public discourse that vilifies immigrants and their children is seeping into schools. In early 2011, Alabama legislation mandated schools to verify the citizenship of students and inform police about families who don't have proper identification. As a result, there have been increased reports of the children of immigrants being threatened with deportation by other students and school personnel. The children of immigrants are often subjected to negative treatment such as discrimination, ridicule, bullying, and harassment from other students, teachers, and school administrators (Lee, 2005, 2009; Olsen, 2008; Peguero, 2009; Portes & Rumbaut, 2001, 2006). The children of immigrants are also often placed in classes or academic tracks far below the mainstream classes, which hinders their educational advancement and success (Olsen, 2008; Suárez-Orozco et al., 2008; Valenzuela, 1999). Rejection by peers, fear of safety, and perceptions of low academic ability are all reflective of the children of immigrants' experiences within the U.S. school system (Lee, 2005, 2009; Olsen, 2008; Peguero, 2009; Suárez-Orozco et al., 2008; Valenzuela, 1999). Moreover, it appears that teachers within classrooms can sometimes present barriers toward the children of immigrants' pursuit of educational success.

Some school personnel view the children of immigrants as problems within their schools, feeling burdened by their lacking capabilities. These personnel argue that the children of immigrants diminish the administrator's and teacher's ability to teach all students effectively and efficiently. School personnel often hold negative and unwelcoming attitudes toward the children of immigrants being placed in their classes (Olsen, 2008; Suárez-Orozco et al., 2008). A few rationalizations for holding negative or unwelcoming views include having a chronic lack of time to address the unique needs of the children of immigrants, perceived intensification of teacher workloads when the children of immigrants are enrolled in their classes, and feelings of professional inadequacy to work with immigrant children (Olsen, 2008; Reeves, 2006; Valdés, 2001). Because the perception that the children of immigrants restrict the advancement and educational progress of the entire class is not uncommon within U.S. schools, school personnel can be reluctant to accept, have, keep, and teach the children of immigrants in their schools and classrooms. In August 2007, U.S. Immigration and Customs Enforcement (ICE) conducted a raid at the Koch Foods chicken-packaging factory in Fairfield, Ohio. One hundred-and-sixty workers, with an impact on an estimated 1,000 family members, were arrested. The arrests of fathers and mothers disrupt families and their internal cohesion and functioning as well as the external community. As a result, the children of detained immigrants who missed class to visit their parents and to be the English translators advocating for their parents in the deportation process were designated as truants because school personnel might have seen this event as an opportunity to exclude problem students—the children of immigrants (La Botz, 2007).

RACE, ETHNICITY, AND REGION OF ORIGIN

Unlike the immigrants who arrived in the United States at the turn of the 20th century, immigrants today are mainly non-European. Approximately 85% of immigrants coming to the United States migrate from Latin America, Asia, Africa, the Middle East, or the Caribbean (Rong & Preissle, 2008; U.S. Census Bureau, 2008). It is estimated that within 20 years, racial and ethnic minority youths will comprise more than half of the total student population in U.S. schools (U.S. Census Bureau, 2008). In the midst of this demographic shift, it is important to point out that immigrant youths enter an educational system that has a persistent history of racial and ethnic inequality. As Apple and Franklin (2004) write on the history of curriculum and its relationship to social control in the United States:

> When the public school system became increasingly solidified, schools were seen as institutions that could preserve the cultural hegemony of an embattled "native" population. Education was the way in which the community life, values, norms, and economic advantages of the powerful were to be protected. Schools could be the great engines of moral crusade to make the children of the immigrants and Blacks like "us." (p. 63)

Researchers have historically and consistently reported the racial and ethnic inequalities embedded in many U.S. educational school processes. Racial and ethnic minority students perceive that they are unfavorably viewed in their educational capabilities or potential (Kozol, 1991, 2005; Valenzuela, 1999; Waters, 2001). Racial and ethnic minority students report experiencing low teacher expectations; less access to educational resources; placement in lower educational tracks; and guidance toward seeking low-paying employment (Kozol, 1991, 2005; Valenzuela, 1999; Vélez, 2008; Waters, 2001). The race and ethnicity of the majority of contemporary immigrants clearly sets them apart from the conventional historical trend of white European immigrants. Many of the current wave of immigrants have never previously experienced prejudice associated with a particular skin color, racial and ethnic category, or their country of origin (Portes & Rumbaut, 2001, 2006; Waters, 2001). Moreover, the diversity among the immigrant youth population also emerges in the distinctly unique challenges and barriers they face in their efforts to achieve educational progress and success.

Generally speaking, the children of black immigrants come from two major regions, the Caribbean islands and the African continent. The children of Caribbean black immigrants in the United States mainly migrate from three Caribbean countries: Jamaica, Haiti, and Trinidad. The children of African immigrants in the United States primarily migrate from three countries: Nigeria, Ethiopia, and Somalia. The children of black immigrants are clearly diverse in terms of country of origin, languages spoken, and religion. Despite the diversity among black immigrant youths, they are often placed into one racial and ethnic category that dismisses, invalidates, and erases their different cultural, national, linguistic, and religious heritages (Koch, 2007; Portes & Rumbaut, 2001, 2006; Waters, 2001). Further, the children of black immigrants are confronted with racial and ethnic segregation and discrimination within their schools and communities. Because of the United States' history of slavery, racial segregation, and marginalization, the children of black immigrants often attempt to distance themselves from nonimmigrant blacks. These ethnic distinctions, though, do not protect black immigrant youths from experiencing discriminatory practices that occur within schools (Koch, 2007; Portes & Rumbaut, 2001, 2006; Rong & Preissle, 2008; Waters, 2001). There are often many social tensions between the children of black immigrants and U.S.–native-born black youths (Koch, 2007; Rong & Preissle, 2008; Waters, 2001). As a result, the children of black immigrants are isolated, marginalized, and disenfranchised from other racial and ethnic minority groups.

Although the children of Latino immigrants represent one of the fastest growing populations in the United States, the children of Latino immigrants are at risk for health and educational marginalization. They continue to be overrepresented among those at risk for poor behavioral, physical, and mental well-being (Portes & Rumbaut, 2001, 2006; Valenzuela, 1999; Vélez, 2008). Within the child welfare system, the number of children of Latino immigrants has steadily risen over the past several years (Dettlaff, Earner, & Phillips, 2009; Vélez, 2008). In U.S. schools, the children of Latino immigrants have the lowest rates of college enrollment; the highest rates of high school and college attrition; low and failing test scores, educational attainment, and educational aspirations; and are three times more likely to drop out in comparison to white native-born students (Feliciano, 2001; Vélez, 2008).

The stereotype of the *model immigrant* is often assigned to the children of Asian immigrants; however, that label is detrimental. Although the children of Asian immigrants are stereotypically portrayed as academic and economic overachievers, Asian immigrant families often live in poverty, are underserved by human services, are underpaid, and are subjected to discrimination and harassment (Chou & Feagin, 2008; Lee, 2005, 2009; Segal, 2002). Moreover, due to teacher expectations and the model minority syndrome, teachers often assume that the children of Asian immigrants do not need help or assistance because of their supposed natural or biological ability (Zhao & Qiu, 2008). Additionally, the children of Asian immigrants indicate that they are pushed into particular academic subjects, such as math and science, in order to be accepted by school administrators, faculty, and staff; otherwise, the children of Asian immigrants are harassed, put down, and discriminated against (Chou & Feagin, 2008; Lee, 2005, 2009; Pang, 2006; Tseng, 2006). As a result, the children of Asian immigrants often do not get the assistance, mentoring, guidance, and support they need in pursuit of educational achievement and attainment.

In recent years, the children of Arab immigrants have migrated to the Unites States because of wars such as the Gulf War, Iraq–Iran War, and the U.S. invasion of Iraq and Afghanistan. Although recent political events have drawn attention to the Arab world, greater media coverage and news reports have not translated into increased research and improved understanding of Arab culture, particularly within the United States and its school system (Abu El-Haj, 2005; Haboush, 2007; Rong & Preissle, 2008). There is little consideration extended to the educational experiences of the children of Arab immigrants. Although research indicates that Arab immigrant families tend to be well-educated and to place high value on education (Abu El-Haj, 2005; Haboush, 2007; Rong & Preissle, 2008), the school experiences of the children of Arab immigrants are frequently characterized by marginalization. Without a doubt, the events of September 11, 2001, have significantly exacerbated an already well-established negative stereotype of Arab culture. As a result, the victimization, harassment, and verbal and physical threats that the children of Arab immigrants experience have increased exponentially (Abu El-Haj, 2005; Haboush, 2007; Rong & Preissle, 2008). It is evident that the children of Arab immigrants face a number of social and political barriers and challenges within U.S. schools.

ENGLISH-LANGUAGE PROFICIENCY

Given the numerous regions from which immigrant youths originate, it is perhaps not surprising that there are typically between 20 and 100 different languages spoken by students in U.S. schools (Rong & Preissle, 2008). In the midst of this linguistic diversity, educators are challenged to provide all students with the academic skills they need to be successful in life. Teachers who work to improve the educational opportunities of English language learner (ELL) students can certainly rely on the hard work, support, and high value that immigrant youths and their families place on education and learning English (Olsen, 2008; Rong & Preissle, 2008; Suárez-Orozco et al., 2008). Yet, attention to ELL students such as English-as-a-second-language programs, bilingual education programs, and language immersion programs has not resulted in advanced and consistent academic gains across grade levels and subject areas (Chudowksy & Chudowsky, 2010). Although the children of immigrants vary in their English-language proficiency skills, it is important to help educators continue to understand the unique challenges and barriers that ELL students face. Not only is the number of immigrant youths in U.S. schools increasing, but English-language proficiency is an essential element for academic success in the current English-only, high-stakes testing environment in the United States (Miller & Endo, 2004). It is thus imperative to better understand the role of the English language in the socialization and Americanization of the children of immigrants as they strive for educational achievement.

One theme emerging from the research on ELL students in the United States is that curriculum and pedagogy, especially when it is Eurocentric and English-only, minimizes the language, identity, and culture of immigrant youths. Research demonstrates that when schools adopt policies and practices that attempt to linguistically and culturally assimilate ELL students into dominant U.S. society, lower self-esteem, higher depression rates, and detachment from school often result (Olsen, 2008; Valenzuela, 1999). In addition, while teachers and administrators do not explicitly state that they think ELL students are not as intelligent as their nonimmigrant peers, the behavior toward and treatment of ELL students by teachers and administrators can sometimes suggest otherwise. Schools often use approaches that are not content-based (e.g., work-sheets about holidays, food, and customs), and that do not take into consideration ELL students' ages or previous educational experiences (Miller & Endo, 2004; Olsen, 2008; Valdés, 2001). Perhaps because teachers and administrators do not have the time to explore the current research regarding bilingual and bicultural development, they continue to use curricular and pedagogical practices that lack both academic rigor and appreciation for ELL students' linguistic and cultural diversity.

A second theme emerging from the research on ELL students in U.S. schools is their treatment as a result of their spoken English. Although all people who speak English speak it with an accent, ELL students who speak English with an accent tend to experience negative feedback from their teachers and peers. ELL students report being patronized by and receiving low and failing grades from their teachers because of their English-speaking accents and skills (Olsen, 2008; Valenzuela, 1999). It is possible that teachers' lack of knowledge about second language acquisition and second language literacy development can unintentionally result in lower grades and unique educational barriers and challenges for ELL students. There is also research that describes situations in school where ELL students are verbally and physically harassed by their nonimmigrant peers who claim to not understand their spoken English (Lee, 2005, 2009; Olsen, 2008). Perceptions of ELL students' English-speaking competencies restrict their access to American culture by creating obstacles to fitting in with and talking to nonimmigrant students. Negative feedback from teachers and peers bars ELL students from the kinds of interactions that would help them attain a more advanced level of academic knowledge, acquire a greater level of English proficiency, and develop a sense of themselves as valued citizens of the United States (Lee, 2005, 2009; Olsen, 2008). Lack of English proficiency acts as a barrier for participation in some school-based extracurricular activities such as sports because coaches sometimes believe that ineffective communication between players impedes play and limits team cohesion (Peguero, 2011b). As Creese and Kambere (2003) note, language and accents are not about communication; rather, they are about "power and exclusion, marginalization and 'Othering,' racism and discrimination" (p. 571). Put another way, English-speaking accents and skills can draw a distinction between youths who are and who are not perceived as academically, socially, and culturally competent in U.S. schools and society.

FAMILY AND SOCIOECONOMIC STATUS

Immigrants and their children generally come to the United States with high aspirations and a strong work ethic to pursue the globalized phenomenon of the American Dream (Portes & Rumbaut, 2001, 2006). Ideally, these strengths should help insulate the children of immigrants from various negative influences in U.S. society, but these strengths are not always sufficient to keep children on pathways to educational success over time. Upon arrival, immigrants and their children are confronted with the reality of inequality, discrimination, and stratification in U.S. schools (Olsen, 2008; Portes & Rumbaut, 2001, 2006; Rong & Preissle, 2008). Chaudry and colleagues find that political policy and law enforcement's practice of increasing immigration raids within the United States are resulting in serious detrimental outcomes for the children of immigrants (Chaudry et al., 2010). Chaudry and colleagues investigated the consequences of parental arrest, detention, and deportation on 190 children, most of whom were U.S. citizens, across the United States and found that separations from parents and economic hardships experienced by the children of immigrants contributed to detrimental outcomes such as educational failure, emotional distress, and social withdrawal (Chaudry et al., 2010).

Unfortunately, many immigrant families encounter a significant number of social, economic, and cultural barriers and hurdles that often marginalize them. Immigrant parents are more likely to live in poverty, social isolation, and be emotionally depressed due to the stressful experiences of adjusting to a new culture. Immigrant parents are also less likely to have health insurance or educational degrees that are recognized in the United States (Bankston & Zhou, 2002; Forum on Child and Family Statistics, 2007; Kao, 2004; Rong & Preissle, 2008; Suárez-Orozco, Todorova, & Qin, 2006; Valenzuela, 1999; Xu, Bekteshi, & Tran, 2010). As a result of the obstacles that immigrant parents face, the children of immigrants may impose a significant amount of pressure on themselves to do well in school. The children of immigrants may feel a sense of responsibility to repay their parents for the sacrifices they made to come to the United States, and a desire to obtain well-paying jobs to help support their families in the future (Fuligni & Witkow, 2004; Portes & Rumbaut, 2001, 2006). In other words, from an economic perspective, both immigrant parents and children view education as a long-term investment for future financial returns. If children go on to college, they can have greater access to well-paying jobs, which in turn will allow them to financially assist their entire family.

Even though many children of immigrants are motivated to do well in school, immigrant parents are often restricted from helping their children navigate a new, unfamiliar, and complex school system. Parental involvement is particularly instructive for illuminating how immigrant parents are limited in their ability to participate in their children's school experiences. Although there are a number of ways that parental involvement can facilitate educational progress for children, we highlight two limitations that immigrant parents face in relation to parental involvement. First, parental involvement should ideally provide parents with a means of social control over their child's education. Involved parents get to know other parents, teachers, and administrators who may, in turn, discuss their children's performance with them. However, research reveals that teachers, school administrators, and other parents do not approach immigrant parents because of language barriers, xenophobia, and discrimination (Carreon, Drake, & Barton, 2005; Turney & Kao, 2009). Second, involved parents are privy to information about their children because teachers tell parents when their children are struggling so that parents can intervene. Studies have shown that immigrant parents are often not contacted by school officials, nor do they contact the school because translators are frequently not available or offered (Carreón et al., 2005; Turney & Kao, 2009).

GENDER

Another barrier and challenge that immigrant youths face in U.S. schools is negotiating gender roles. Often times, immigrant youths must bridge the gender expectations of two different cultures—their homeland culture and U.S. culture—in the socialization and Americanization processes. Many immigrant youths find that their racial and ethnic identification in the United States as well as their English-language proficiency mark them for specific academic tracks and future career opportunities. Yet, gender plays a key role in the educational struggles that immigrant girls and boys experience in their adjustment to the United States (Lee, 2005, 2009; Olsen, 2008; Waters, 1996; Williams, Alvarez, & Andrade Hauck, 2002).

Research studies suggest that few immigrant families are able to economically survive in the United States without both the mother and the father working outside of the home (Feliciano & Rumbaut, 2005; Portes & Rumbaut, 2001, 2006). As a result, female children of immigrants often assume traditional caretaker duties that include child-rearing, cooking, and cleaning. These responsibilities make it difficult for them to socialize and seek employment outside their homes. This, in turn, leads many female children of immigrants to rely solely on education to help them realize future professional and economic success in the United States. Though it is a concern that U.S. schools place both female and male children of immigrants in low academic tracks, the effects can be more pronounced for female children of immigrants who do not have multiple paths to achievement open to them (Feliciano & Rumbaut, 2005). In addition, many female children of immigrants report that because they dress or wear their hair differently, they are ostracized by their nonimmigrant peers. Without the proper support from teachers, administrators, and guidance counselors, this social isolation can to lead to low self-esteem, shame, and high depression rates the longer that the female children of immigrants are in the United States (Olsen, 2008). And finally, it is important to point out that religion, culture, and U.S. racial stereotypes influence how female children of immigrants experience and face these challenges. The daughters of black Caribbean, African, Latino, Asian, and Arab immigrants encounter and respond to these educational barriers in unique ways (Lee, 2005; Olsen, 2008; Waters, 1996; Williams et al., 2002).

Gender also influences the educational challenges and barriers that male children of immigrants experience. Boys across generational, racial and ethnic groups are more likely to be disciplined by teachers, administrators, and school security guards; less likely to be academically engaged; and, more likely to report experiencing racism in school than immigrant girls (Lee, 2005, 2009; Olsen, 2008). The detachment from school that male children of immigrants demonstrate, rather than a result of laziness or lack of intellectual capabilities, may be a response to the school's hostile and racist environment. Disengagement might thus be better understood as the attempt by male children of immigrants to deal with largely negative encounters in U.S. schools. Further, because immigrant boys (unlike their female counterparts) frequently work outside of the home, they may envision paths other than school that will lead to future professional and economic success in the United States. Again, it is critical to point out the role that the children of immigrants' regions of origin play in their attempts to realize success in the United States. Although most immigrant boys are aware of the pervasive attitude of animosity in U.S. schools and in U.S. society, male children of immigrants who come from racial and ethnic backgrounds (e.g., Latino and black Caribbean or African) that have historically been negatively stereotyped by U.S. society are especially at risk for academic detachment and failure (Koch, 2007; Valdés, 2001).

Conclusion

The children of immigrants face a myriad of complex issues in U.S. schools. The research we presented suggests that children of immigrants may not struggle in school due to lack of motivation, low intelligence, or inherent deviance. Rather they may struggle because U.S. schooling contexts provide them little support and guidance to do well. The connections between school, home, region of origin, and broader U.S. culture must be taken into consideration when discussing the possibilities for the children of immigrants' educational success.

Although there are no easy solutions to the barriers and challenges that the children of immigrants experience in U.S. schools, there are many steps that policy makers, educators, and community stakeholders can take in order to create more welcoming and healthy learning environments. The following suggestions are not intended to be a one-size-fits-all approach. They are instead points of consideration to help policy makers, educators, and community stakeholders begin thinking about how U.S. schools and classrooms can better respond to the needs and experiences of the children of immigrants.

Raise awareness of the social, political, and educational climate of immigration. Schools should educate their staff members on the U.S. cultural contexts that the children of immigrants encounter. U.S. society does not easily value, accept, or tolerate immigration (Chavez, 2008). The children of immigrants' motivation, academic attainment, and success are certainly influenced by such negative reception. Schools need to embrace the notion that immigration and the children of immigrants are assets to the United States (Rong & Priessle, 2008), and confront the educational procedures, policies, practices, and attitudes that result in unwelcoming environments.

Raise awareness that there is tremendous variation across and within immigrant groups. U.S. racial and ethnic stereotypes are not the same for all immigrant students. Black immigrant youths are often stereotyped as lazy and thugs; Latino immigrant youths are often labeled as illegal and criminal; Asian immigrant youths are often stereotyped as model minorities; and, Arab immigrant youths are often labeled as terrorists (Abu El-Haj, 2006; Chavez, 2008; Lee, 2005, 2009). Further, not all immigrant boys detach from school and not all immigrant girls depend completely on education to help them realize success. Within racial and ethnic immigrant groups that are considered to have more traditional gender expectations (e.g., Latino and Arab), there are instances in which immigrant boys have a higher level of educational attainment and achievement than immigrant girls (Olsen, 2008; Rong & Preissle, 2008; Williams et al., 2002). School programs designed to effectively meet the needs of the children of immigrants will obviously have to account for these differences.

Raise awareness that curriculum and pedagogy are not neutral, and that learning and speaking English are not straightforward tasks. School curriculum, pedagogy, and learning English are at the center of national debates over what it means for the United States to be a multicultural nation and to integrate immigrants from around the world (Olsen, 2008; Rosaldo, 1994; Valenzuela, 1999). This debate plays out in schools where the children of immigrants are learning their roles in U.S. society. Eurocentric curriculum and pedagogy subtract immigrant students' cultural identities (Valenzuela, 1999). By subtract we mean Eurocentric curriculum and pedagogy are assimilationist educational practices that minimize the culture and language of children of immigrants. Teachers and administrators should be attentive to the cultures that are represented in the school curriculum; how these cultures are represented; and the instructional strategies that help immigrant youths positively adjust to U.S. classrooms. In addition, schools need to remember that English is not just a means of communication. Rather, learning and speaking English, especially with non-American accents, are not markers of belonging and intellectual capabilities for the children of immigrants (Creese & Kambere, 2003; Olsen, 2008; Williams et al., 2002). Policy makers, educators, and community stakeholders need to understand and recognize the potential for social and academic isolation that the children of immigrants may experience when they speak English. Schools should provide support if these problems arise. School personnel play a vital role in protecting the children of immigrants from harassment as well as being positioned to disrupt the climate of immigration that vilifies immigrants and their children. The concept of *restorative justice*, which emphasizes repairing the harm that was caused, holding offenders accountable, bringing together the person who was harmed with the person who did the harm and the community, and preventing similar actions in the future is a growing approach that school personnel are

utilizing to address bullying. Thus, if bullying offenders are required to investigate their own family's immigrant history and reinforce the importance of immigration in their own history and in U.S. history, restorative justice may teach bullying offenders to identify with the children of immigrants. Moreover, school administrators must provide a safe space where the children of immigrants can express their concerns and fears to school personnel. They should also implement programs that ameliorate the harassment of the children of immigrants.

For diverse students to learn from each other and become culturally competent citizens and leaders of a diverse democracy within the United States, institutions of education have to go beyond simply acknowledging students of different backgrounds. Educational institutions must practice and implement structural mechanisms that acknowledge and honor the intersecting factors associated with the differences we discussed in this chapter, especially for the rapidly growing number of students in immigrant families. The children of immigrants are a diverse population who bring with them linguistic and cultural proficiencies, knowledge, and ideas that are essential for U.S. democracy and U.S. collaboration with other nations. We believe that policy makers, educators, and community stakeholders should consider the educational barriers and challenges that the children of immigrants face in U.S. schools and society, and the opportunities that are lost when these barriers and challenges are not effectively addressed. Perhaps most important, we must consider the drastic consequences that lack of attention may cause for all youths and the future of the United States and global collaboration.

References

Abu El-Haj, T. R. (2006). Race, politics, and Arab American youth: Shifting frameworks for conceptualizing educational equity. *Educational Policy, 20*(1), 13–34.

Alba, R., & Nee, V. (2003). *Remaking the American mainstream: Assimilation and contemporary immigration.* Cambridge, MA: Harvard University Press.

Apple, M. W., & Franklin, B. (2004). Curricular history and social control. In M. W. Apple (Ed.), *Ideology and curriculum* (3rd ed., pp. 59–76). New York, NY: Routledge Falmer.

Bankston, C. L., III, & Zhou, M. (2002). Being well vs. doing well: Self-esteem and school performance among immigrant and non-immigrant racial and ethnic groups. *International Migration Review, 36,* 389–415.

Carreón, G. P., Drake, C., Barton, A. C. (2005, Fall). The importance of presence: Immigrant parents' school engagement experiences. *American Educational Research Journal, 42*(3), 465–498.

Creese, G., & Kambere, E. N. (2003). What colour is your English? *Canadian Review of Sociology and Anthropology, 40*(5), 565–573.

Chaudry, A., Capps, R., Pedroza, J. M., Castañeda, R. M., Santos, R., & Scott, M. M. (2010). Facing our future children in the aftermath of immigration enforcement. Washington, DC: Urban Institute.

Chavez, L. (2008). *The Latino threat: Constructing immigrants, citizens, and the nation.* Stanford, CA: Stanford University Press.

Chou, R., & Feagin, J. (2008). *The myth of the model minority: Asian Americans facing racism.* Boulder, CO: Paradigm.

Chudowsky, N., & Chudowsky, V. (2010). *State test score trends through 2007-08, part 6: Has progress been made in raising achievement for English language learners?* Washington, DC: Center on Education Policy.

Dettlaff, A. J., Earner, I., & Phillips, S. D. (2009). Latino children of immigrants in the child welfare system: Prevalence, characteristics, and risk. *Children and Youth Services Review, 31*(7), 775–783.

Ewert, S. (2009). Student misbehavior during senior year: A comparison of immigrants and the native-born. *Social Science Research, 38,* 826–839.

Feliciano, C., & Rumbaut, R. (2005). Gendered paths: Educational and occupational expectations and outcomes among adult children of immigrants. *Ethnic and Racial Studies, 28,* 1087–1118.

Forum on Child and Family Statistics. (2007). *America's children in brief: Key national indicators of well-being, 2007.* Washington, DC: Federal Interagency Forum on Child and Family Statistics.

Fuligni, A. J., & Witkow, M. (2004). The postsecondary educational progress of youth from immigrant families. *Journal of Research on Adolescence, 14*(2), 159–183.

Gans, H. J. (1992). Second-generation decline: Scenarios for the economic and ethnic future of the post-1965 American immigrants. *Ethnic and Racial Studies, 15,* 173–192.

Gordon, M. (1964). *Assimilation in American life.* New York, NY: Oxford University Press.

Haboush, K. L. (2007). Working with Arab American families: Culturally competent practice for school psychologists. *Psychology in the Schools, 44*(2), 183–198.

Kao, G. (2004). Parental influences on the educational outcomes of immigrant youth. *International Migration Review, 38,* 427–450.

Kao, G., & Tienda, M. (1995). Optimism and achievement: The educational performance of immigrant youth. *Social Science Quarterly, 76,* 1–19.

Kasinitz, P., Mollenkopf, J. H., & Waters, M. C. (2002). Becoming American/becoming New Yorkers: Immigrant incorporation in a majority minority city. *International Migration Review, 36*(4), 1020–1036.

Kasinitz, P., Mollenkopf, J. H., Waters, M. C., & Holdaway, J. (2009). *Inheriting the city: The children of immigrants come of age.* New York, NY: Russell Sage Foundation.

Koch, J. M. (2007). How schools can best support Somali students and their families. *International Journal of Multicultural Education, 9*(1), 1–15.

Kozol, J. (1991). *Savage inequalities: Children in America's schools.* New York, NY: Crown.

Kozol, J. (2005). *The shame of the nation: The restoration of apartheid schooling in America.* New York, NY: Three Rivers Press.

La Botz, D. 2007. *The emerging Latino immigrant community of Cincinnati, Southwest Ohio, and Northern Kentucky.* Cincinnati, OH: Intercommunity Justice and Peace Center.

Lee, S. J. (2005). *Up against whiteness: Race, school, and immigrant youth.* New York, NY: Teachers College Press.

Lee, S. J. (2009). *Unraveling the model-minority stereotype: Listening to Asian American Youth* (2nd ed.). New York, NY: Teachers College Press.

Miller, P. C., & Endo, H. (2004). Understanding and meeting the needs of ESL students. *Phi Delta Kappan, 85*(10), 786–791.

Olsen, L. (2008). *Made in America: Immigrant students in our public schools.* (10th ed.) New York, NY: New Press.

Pang, V. (2006). Fighting the marginalization of Asian American students with caring schools: Focusing on curricular change. *Race, Ethnicity, and Education, 9*(1), 67–83.

Perreira, K. M., Harris, K. M., & Lee, D. (2006). Making it in America: High school completion by immigrant and native youth. *Demography, 43,* 511–536.

Peguero, A. A. (2009). Victimizing the children of immigrants: Latino and Asian American student victimization. *Youth & Society, 41*(2), 186–208.

Peguero, A. A. (2011a). Immigration, schools, and violence: Assimilation and student misbehavior. *Sociological Spectrum, 31*(6), 695–717.

Peguero, A. A. (2011b). Immigrant youth involvement in school-based extracurricular activities. *Journal of Educational Research, 104,* 19–27.

Peguero, A. A., & Bondy, J. M. (2011). Immigration and students' relationship with teachers. *Education and Urban Society, 43*(2), 165–183.

Portes, A., & Rumbaut, R. (2001). *Legacies: The story of the immigrant second generation.* Berkeley: University of California Press.

Portes, A., & Rumbaut, R. (2006). *Immigrant America: A portrait.* Berkeley: University of California Press.

Reeves, J. (2006). Secondary teachers' attitudes towards English language learners in the classroom. *Journal of Educational Research, 99*(3), 131–142.

Rong, X. L., & Preissle, J. (2008). *Educating immigrant students: What we need to know to meet the challenges.* Thousand Oaks, CA: Sage.

Rosaldo, R. (1994). Cultural citizenship and educational democracy. *Cultural Anthropology, 9*(3), 402–411.

Rumbaut, R. G. (1997). Assimilation and its discontents: Between rhetoric and reality. *International Migration Review, 31,* 923–960.

Segal, U. A. (2002). *A framework for immigration: Asians in the United States.* New York, NY: Columbia University Press.

Stratton, T., Pang, V. O., Madueño, M., Park, C. D., Atlas, M., Page, C., & Oliger, J. (2009). Immigrant students and the obstacles to achievement. *Phi Delta Kappan 91*(3), 44–47.

Suárez-Orozco, C., & Suárez-Orozco, M. (2001). *Children of immigration.* Cambridge, MA: Harvard University Press.

Suárez-Orozco, C., Suárez-Orozco, M., & Todorova, I. (2008). *Learning a new land: Immigrant students in American society.* Cambridge, MA: Harvard University Press.

Suárez-Orozco, C., Todorova, I., & Qin, D. B. (2006). The well-being of immigrant adolescents: A longitudinal perspective on risk and protective factors. In F. A. Villarrue & T. Luster (Eds.), *The crisis in youth mental health: Critical issues and effective programs* (Vol. 2: Disorders in Adolescence, pp. 45–62): Santa Barbara, CA: Praeger.

Tseng, V. (2006). Unpacking immigration in youths' academic and occupational pathways. *Child Development, 77*(5), 1434–1445.

Turney, K., & Kao, G. (2009). Barriers to school involvement: Are immigrant parents disadvantaged? *Journal of Educational Research, 102*(4), 257–271.

U.S. Census Bureau. (2008). *Current population survey.* Washington, DC: U.S. Census Bureau, Population Division.

Valdés, G. (2001). *Learning and not learning English: Latino students in American schools.* New York, NY: Teachers College Press.

Valenzuela, A. (1999). *Subtractive schooling: US-Mexican youth and the politics of caring.* Albany: State University of New York Press.

Vélez, W. (2008). The educational experiences of Latinos in the United States. In H. Rodriguez, R. Sáenz, & C. Menjívar (Eds.), *Latinas/os in the United States: Changing the face of America* (pp. 128–148). New York, NY: Springer.

Waters, M. C. (1996). The intersection of gender, race, and ethnicity in the identity development of Caribbean American teens. In B. J. R. Leadbetter & N. Way (Eds.), *Urban girls: Resisting stereotypes, creating identities* (pp. 65–81). New York: New York University Press.

Waters, M. C. (2001). Growing up West Indian and African American: Gender and class differences in the second generation. In N. Foner (Ed.), *Islands in the City: West Indian migration to New York* (pp. 193–215). Berkeley, CA: University of California Press.

Watkins, A., & Melde, C. (2009). Immigrants, assimilation, and perceived school disorder: An examination of the "other" ethnicities. *Journal of Criminal Justice, 37,* 627–635.

Williams, L. S., Alvarez, S. D., & Andrade Hauck, K. S. (2002). My name is not María: Young Latinas seeking home in the heartland. *Social Problems, 49*(4), 563–584.

Xu, Q., Bekteshi, V., & Tran, T. (2010). Family, school, country of birth and adolescents' psychological well-being. *Journal of Immigrant & Refugee Studies, 8*, 91–110.

Zhou, M. (1997). Growing up American: The challenge confronting immigrant children and children of immigrants. *Annual Review of Sociology, 23*, 63–95.

Zhao, Y., & Qiu W. (2009). How good are the Asians? Refuting four myths about Asian-American academic achievement. *Phi Delta Kappan, 90*(5), 338.

Everyday Racial Interactions for Whites and College Students of Color

Leslie H. Picca

It is popularly believed that we are in a postracial society, highlighted by the election of a black U.S. President. The generation of young college students today is often characterized as celebrating diversity, for whom colorblindness is the norm (Bonilla-Silva, 2006; Gallagher, 2003). Legal segregation is ancient history for them (and even for some of their parents), and the Rev. Dr. Martin Luther King Jr.'s dream that we "will not be judged by the color of [our] skin but by the content of [our] character" appears to be a reality. They can rattle off successful people of color and role models in numerous facets of social life, from Tiger Woods to Condoleezza Rice to Oprah Winfrey.

On the surface, it seems that young adults today are in a better position to address issues of racial relations than past generations. Young adults are better equipped at dealing with public conversations: They have been raised with multicultural programming in schools and diverse images in the media, and they know how to not appear racist. Especially during President Barack Obama's first presidential campaign, he achieved "celebrity status" (often used against him by the opposing camps) among many white young adult supporters. Clearly this indicates the level of acceptance among young people today that we would not have seen decades ago.

While in the recent past overtly racist comments were tolerated and expected, now social pressures exist to avoid such racist statements (Feagin, 2006). However, subtle measures and tests in psychology and social psychology suggest a nonracist mask is covering an intact racist core, and that whites regularly underestimate the extent of their prejudice (Bonilla-Silva & Forman, 2000; Kawakami, Dunn, Karmali, & Dovidio, 2009). There is much social science literature on modern racism or colorblind racism: negative racial attitudes that haven't disappeared, they've just gone underground (Bonilla-Silva, 2006; Carr, 1997; Dovidio & Gaertner, 1991). Specifically, many argue that racism is hidden, subtle, and invisible, even if its consequences are not.

In order to further investigate this underground or subtle racism, Joe Feagin and I asked over 1,000 college students of all racial backgrounds across the U.S. to keep a journal or diary detailing their everyday racial interactions. We sought to examine if and how race impacts college students' daily lives. We published a book, *Two-Faced Racism: Whites in the Backstage and Frontstage* (Picca & Feagin, 2007) that examines the accounts of the 626 white college students; we're currently writing a second book on the experiences of the more than 400 students of color. The college students were recruited from across the United States, oversampling in the southeast and midwest, and the majority of the students were in the traditional age range (18 to 25).

Numerous white students in the sample said that racism was less of a problem among their generation, who were more accepting. Many white students wrote, "Racism will die when Grandpa dies," indicating that their generation is remarkably different than previous generations. However, analyzing the journals reveals that this is far from true. Grandpa's racism is still alive and well—it just looks different for young adults today.

We utilize the dramaturgical theoretical framework of the *backstage* and *frontstage* to illustrate how racial relations are impacted by what Erving Goffman would refer to as "the audience" (Goffman, 1959). Goffman states that in dramaturgy (dramatic composition for the theater) people use impression management and employ certain techniques in order to sustain a performance as actors on a stage. There are two structural features in dramaturgy: the frontstage and the backstage. In the frontstage, individuals or performance teams will perform a role that is appropriate for the audience to see. A classroom is likely a frontstage setting where the students (and faculty), are projecting an image that is appropriate for the setting (such as that of a good student who is paying attention and writing notes as the instructor speaks—even if the student is actually writing down a grocery list). The backstage is more informal; it is where performers can violate their expected norms, and also prepare for future frontstage interactions. Readers who have experience working in retail or service occupations have often experienced the differences between the frontstage interactions with the customers compared to the (often more relaxed) backstage among just coworkers. In this research project, we can examine how this frontstage and backstage setting can be applied to racial interactions.

JOURNALS BY WHITE COLLEGE STUDENTS

We found striking differences between interactions among whites only (family and friends, but also coworkers, employers, and strangers), compared to interactions involving people of color. Most young whites know it is not acceptable to be racist. In their student journals, when whites were around people of color (what we refer to as the frontstage), their interactions were characterized by a colorblind, nonracist appearance. White students would perform to prove they weren't racist, such as by acting extra polite, and avoiding anything that could be connected to race. However, when whites were in the company of other whites (the backstage), these frontstage pleasantries could be relaxed and openly contradicted. Racial and racist interactions were not only tolerated, but often sustained and encouraged.

The following account written by Becky, a white college student, illustrates the conflicting frontstage and backstage dimensions. Becky describes an interaction with some of her former high school friends who are all white:

> [My friend] Todd asked how school was going and then asked when I was going to let them come down and visit. I said, "I don't know guys, one of my suitemates is black, you would have to be nice to her." All the guys said, "Black!?!" Like they were shocked that I could actually live with someone of another color. Then David said, "Now why would you go and do that for?" Then they agreed that nothing would be said if they came to visit and then started to talk about some fight they had gotten into with some black kids in town. The conversation was short lived and I wasn't surprised by their comments or their reactions to Lisa (my suitemate). They are all really nice guys and I think if they came to visit that they would be respectful of Lisa. I know, however, that they would talk and make fun later about me living with a black girl. I know this summer I'm going to get shit from them about it. (Becky)

Becky's white friends openly admitted that they would be polite to the black woman to her face in the frontstage, fulfilling the expectations of a nonracist white public identity. However, in the all-white backstage, the men can behave very differently. In a secure all-white setting, the men can mock Becky and give her a hard time. The men clearly possess a level of awareness that their backstage interactions are inappropriate for the frontstage since they agree not to say anything.

In our data sample of white college students' journals, the most frequent theme that emerged was whites using racial joking in the backstage. Hundreds of whites reported regularly telling or hearing racist jokes in white-only groups. Consider the following journal entry written by Debbie, who was watching a movie with her four white friends when one of the white males made an aggressively racist joke:

> When we heard the joke, my one roommate Lillian said she thought that joke was "terrible." My other roommate Mike said, "It's true though." We all yelled at him and said he was the worst, etc., etc. However, none of us was really mad or really offended by what he said and we probably should have been. Instances like this make me realize that people have gotten too used of people making jokes about minorities. We are too willing to accept people making inappropriate comments about minorities. I feel like I'm so used to people saying jokes like that, that I don't even take them seriously anymore. The strange thing is that I don't think any of my friends are actually racist, they just sometimes say inconsiderate things that they don't really mean. (Debbie)

Like hundreds of whites in our sample, Debbie comments on the normalization of hearing racist jokes by her white friends. Many of the jokes are said in white-only social networks, and in private conversations away from people of color. Due to spatial racial segregation (notably in neighborhoods and schools), most whites said they largely interacted only with people who looked like them. They didn't have to worry about getting caught telling racist jokes. For many whites, using racist epithets is not a problem; it only becomes a problem if it is said in the wrong context. This tells us that there are acceptable contexts for using racist epithets, such as when the target is not around.

Debbie clearly recognizes that such racist humor is wrong, yet, no white person here gets offended by the jokes. There are no negative consequences for their actions—racism is just part of the fun. Examining the media context that young people are immersed in illustrates the supposedly light-hearted nature of racism. They listen to comedians who joke about racism. The hip-hop music that whites listen to regularly features racist epithets (Hurt, 2006). Comedy and music are powerful tools to subvert the racial hierarchy; however, with an uninformed audience, it can be a dangerous method of perpetuating the same old stereotypes. For example, comedians like Dave Chappelle often utilize racial stereotypes and racist epithets in order to dismantle their power. However in the white student journals, whites would often argue, "If Dave Chappelle can say the word nigger, why can't I?" without recognizing that the social context matters. The meaning changes if a racist epithet is used to perpetuate the racial hierarchy versus to subvert the racial hierarchy.

Everything around today's youth is digital, immediate, and appearance-oriented. Like the quick tap of a smartphone or computer tablet, there is a limited depth of processing that dominates the media world. This lack of reflection translates into racial interactions and stereotypes, where jokes are supposedly just jokes. In the backstage, there never has to be any deeper acknowledgement or questioning why making fun of people of color is normalized. There is no consciousness about the meaning or consequences of their fun. We can blame the whitewashed education that children receive, where they have minimal understanding of our racial pasts, and certainly no comprehension of how this legacy still has immediate effects today (Lewis, 2003). However, they understand enough as evident in the behavior change when they are around people of color. Like previous generations, young people today still largely interact in racially segregated spaces (Massey, Rothwell, & Domina, 2009). Many whites commented they didn't have to practice frontstage pleasantries but could remain in their comfortable backstage settings.

Debbie, like most whites in our sample, claims that her friends who tell racist jokes are not actually racist. For many whites, it isn't viewed as a racial slur if it isn't said directly to a person of color. For many young whites, real racists are the Klansmen who wear white robes and burn crosses; these white college students are just having fun. Of course, we know the subtle and hidden forms of racism behind the scenes can be just as damaging (some argue more) compared to the overt and in-your-face forms (Yamato, 1987). Racism is often reduced to the individual actions of a few bigots, rather than as systemic and institutionalized into every social institution. Racial relations impact every major decision a person makes—and how you're treated: where you live, what schools you attend, where you work and shop, the quality of health care and well-being, interactions with the police (Blank, 2009). Part of white racial privilege is the luxury to take their advantageous experiences as the norm, and deny that racial injustices (beyond those perpetrated by racial extremists like the Klan) still exist today (Johnson, 2006).

Certainly, white college students are not inventing racial stereotypes or racist jokes. They rely on stereotypes that have been passed down through generations, and stereotypes that were created (by whites) to legitimize slavery, legal segregation, lynchings, and other atrocities. There is an intergenerational component that has been inherited by young people, even if they claim to celebrate diversity. What young whites call fun in a private backstage has real and serious consequences that preserves and perpetuates old racist stereotypes, contributing to and maintaining larger racial hierarchies (as evident in higher education, health care, the legal system, housing) that whites have the privilege to ignore (Collins, 2000). There never has to be any acknowledgement of how their everyday micro-interactions sustain the macro-interactions of institutional racism.

On the whole, the accounts from the white college students focused on backstage interactions that could relax frontstage expectation. Backstage joking was the most prevalent and common theme reported in the tens of thousands of journal narratives we collected from white college students. Some white students speculated in their journals that "it must go both ways" where they suspected that students of color sit around telling racist jokes against whites. A white student, Samuel, notes in his journal after hearing racist jokes in an all-white context:

> One of my buddies just told us [a joke] with a racial punch line. It was odd to look at such a normal occurrence as a sociologist, but I realized that everyone was laughing. It was then that I realized how much we take our whiteness for granted. Then I got thinking whether people of color tell white jokes, and concluded that they must, but that they're probably about specific white people, like southerners, etc. When I asked my friends what they thought, one said sarcastically, "I'm sure they do; we did oppress them for 150 years[1] [*sic*]!"

In addition to collecting the narratives of over 600 white students across the country, we also collected over 400 journals written by students of color. The next section describes some of the prevalent themes written by these students, which are strikingly different than the journals written by their white peers.

JOURNALS BY COLLEGE STUDENTS OF COLOR

While it's true that there are some accounts of students of color making antiwhite comments as Samuel (above) suggests, the nature of the comments is vastly different as they are not nearly as common, vicious, or damaging. First, the comments are not nearly as frequent as the antiblack, anti-Latino, anti-Arab American, and anti-Asian comments we see in the white student journals. Many of the white students who kept a journal reported their surprise at how often they heard racist comments that often slip under the radar of consciousness unless they are asked to pay attention. For the students of color, there was no parallel reaction, as very few of them proportionally wrote about antiwhite, or anti-other-racial-group comments.

Second, the overwhelming majority of antiwhite comments are based on a reaction to a specific event. For example, one black woman reported seeing a white woman leave a public bathroom without washing her hands, and made a comment to her friends that "white people are dirty." Although generalizing negative comments to an entire group is never a good thing, there is a difference when the comment initiates from direct experiences (as is the case with many students of color) compared to common stereotypes and a lack of direct interaction (as is the case with many white students) (Hraba, Brinkman, & Gray-Ray, 1996; Pettigrew, 1985).

Finally, the comments made by students of color lack the institutional support to have any real negative consequences. The pejorative words used against whites are not equal to the pejorative words used against people of color. The stereotypes we have for whites (such as white people cannot dance, or play certain sports) do not have nearly as many negative consequences as the stereotypes we have for people of color

---

[1]Samuel's friend either illustrates a lack of knowledge on racial history or a tendency to minimize it. Oppression under the American slave trade and enforced legal segregation lasted 360 years, not 150 years.

(such as blacks are criminal and lazy, and Latinos are all illegal immigrant Mexicans), which have very real damaging consequences, such as on the job market or in securing housing (Lipsitz, 1995). For example, a number of white students wrote in their journals about instructions they received at work from their white bosses and managers to discriminate against people of color (see Picca & Feagin, 2007, chapter 4), such as not accepting their employment applications or monitoring them for possible shoplifting. In the journals we received from students of color, none of them discussed discriminating against whites, which is not surprising as people of color often lack the institutional support to enact it.

The everyday journals collected by students of color were vastly different because the accounts focused on differential treatment that they (or their racial minority friends) experienced. Especially true for students of color attending a predominately white institution, the students wrote about their interactions with campus police, with white professors and students (at social gatherings, in the classroom, in public campus spaces), and around the campus community such as at work. In our sample, white students regularly interacted in white-only social spaces away from people of color in a secure backstage. This was not true for students of color who had fewer opportunities in the backstage away from whites (Feagin, 1991). A black male wrote about his experiences attending a party during their university's parents weekend (which often involves parents socializing and drinking with the college students):

> I went to a house party with my white roommate to link up with my other white roommate and some friends (all white). We arrived at the party and there were about 100 people of all ages drinking and enjoying each other's company. I didn't feel out of place at all until this somewhat random person, which was talking to our group of parents and friends, stopped mid-conversation and asked "are you the token black person." I was shocked and had no clue as to how to positively respond. I thought to myself that I can't be a token black person because I was there on my own free will. I thought that regardless of me being there, the party would be the same. Even though I was telling myself that I wasn't the token black person, I jokingly told them that I was because I didn't know what else to say that wouldn't take from or negatively add to the party. I just internalized my feelings and eventually went home. (Len)

Students of color attending non-HBCUs (historically black colleges and universities) often remarked upon being the only or one of a few racial minorities in their college classes or at parties. Their presence at the university and achievements such as scholarships and selection into prestigious positions, were often attributed to fulfilling a racial quota rather than to individual merit and hard work (Wise, 2005). Additionally, there is typically an added layer of surveillance placed upon students of color compared to white students (Feagin, Vera, & Imani, 1996; McIntosh, 1998). For example, students of color often remarked that whenever the topic of race is mentioned in class, the other students will immediately turn to look at their reaction.

As noted previously, white students often made racial jokes in private backstage settings, but it was not uncommon for whites to "slip" and say it in the company of people of color (see chapter 5 of *Two-Faced Racism* [Picca & Feagin, 2007]). The reaction of students of color, who likely did not ask to be placed in an awkward situation, can have serious consequences for future interactions. Consider Len's account of being referred to as the "token black person" above. Len could have reacted in anger, by laughing it off, educating the white person, or simply walking away. Len was put on the spot. He mentioned that he was in such disbelief of the comment that he did not pursue the conversation further. Whatever Len decided might have had consequences for how white students treated him in the future: confronting a comment might make him seem too sensitive about racial issues, yet ignoring the comment or laughing it off might be perceived as accepting that hurtful comments were no big deal (Frye, 1998). Len also noted that he did not want to disrupt the social situation so he internalized his feelings and left. Many scholars have documented the impact of the additional stress and negative health consequences in dealing with racist interactions (Feagin & McKinney, 2003; Randall, 2006).

While many white college students believe racism is not a significant issue at their campus or nationwide (Feagin, Vera, & Imani, 1996), many students of color in our sample detailed painful narratives of hostile racial interactions. Alex, a biracial man, begins one of his journal entries, describing the frequency which he is referred to as a racist epithet:

> This is one of those sad and angry nights for me. Tonight marks the third time since the beginning of the school year that I've been called a nigger by a bunch of white students on a Saturday night, or weekend more in general. At first I used to wonder where they actually take the time in their heads to separate me from everyone else by the color of my skin. I used to just blame alcohol consumption for their obvious ignorance and racist attitudes, but I have since stopped trying to make excuses for them. . . . Sometimes it seems that if I am around all white people, then I become nothing more than a token Black "exhibit" for their amusement. . . . The saddest thing however, is that these people, these COLLEGE STUDENTS are supposed to be the supposed crème de la crème, the future business and political leaders. They are supposed to be the brightest of the brightest, but then again I guess ignorance can't be masked by book smarts. (Alex)

The pain and sadness are especially apparent in Alex's narrative, which has a very different feeling than the lighthearted nature of many of the white students' journal entries. In their journals, most whites reported reserving racial comments for the backstage, away from the presence of people of color. However, Alex reminds us that even in the frontstage, people of color may still be confronted with racist comments, which may increase at certain times of the day or week. Alex notes that at evenings and weekends, the frequency of racist comments increases, which are also the times when college students are more likely to consume alcohol excessively. Indeed, in the white students' journal entries, many pointed at alcohol use as an excuse for racist comments and interactions. Alcohol is frequently used as an excuse by whites to downplay racist activity. In our book, Joe Feagin and I discuss "two-beers racism" (Picca & Feagin, 2007, p. 72), where consuming significant amounts of alcohol can relax the social pressures against openly expressing racist ideas. While alcohol can loosen inhibitions, it cannot create racist sentiments that are not already there.

Alex refers to the social construction of racial categories when he wonders why he is separated from his peers based just on his skin color. In the social construction of race and ethnicity, race is not a fixed biological fact, but is a social agreement. While biology determines our physical phenotypes, it is society that determines the meanings we give to arbitrary traits like skin color, eye shape, and hair texture. Earlier in his journal, Alex notes that he has one black parent and one white parent. He identifies himself as biracial, even though he writes that he is often identified as just a "token Black exhibit." Alex is also referred to as one of the harshest of racist epithets, a term with a long and violent history that is usually reserved for blacks (Kennedy, 2003). Racial categorizations depend on not only what an individual identifies for him or herself, but also depend upon what identities other people impose upon the individual as well.

Racist individuals who use the n-word often conjure up the image of a neo-Nazi skinhead or uneducated working-class person (the latter type best characterized by the 1970s television character, Archie Bunker). Alex emphasizes that the persons instigating racial insults are educated, college students who make up the next generation of our nation's leaders. While education is believed to be the great equalizer of racial relations, many scholars suggest that our nation's schools maintain and perpetuate racial inequalities both in structure and in content (Lewis, 2003; Loewen, 1995).

In their journals, students of color in our sample reported that they were often assumed to fit the stereotype of their racial group. Asian students were asked by classmates they did not know to help with math homework. Latinos were asked if they were in this country legally. Students of Middle Eastern descent were referred to as terrorists. Many black men wrote about their interactions with campus police, where they were assumed to have engaged in violent crimes, or presumed by other students to be untrustworthy. For example, Brian wrote about whites, especially white women, who openly avoid interacting with him on their university campus:

> This morning I was walking to my 10:30 class. I was running a few minutes late and I saw another student, a white female, walking toward me. She was about 50 yards down the street from me on [Main Street]. I saw her look up at me, then she crossed the street and walked on the other side. She walked for about another 20 yards then crossed back to the side she was originally on. Now, I don't know if that was really that racist but the implication to me was that she was afraid of me. (Brian)

Brian gives this white female the benefit of the doubt that she was not behaving in a racially motivated manner, but he senses that she fears him. Other black male college students in our sample detailed the hurt they felt when their fellow students do not feel comfortable walking along the university streets next to them. After detailing a similar experience to Brian's journal entry above, Todd, a black man, wrote, "I tried to come up with other possible reasons for her actions [crossing the street to avoid him then crossing back after they passed], but the only logical conclusion I can come up with is that she encountered a black male, a threat she felt required quick evasive action." Brian and Todd are reminded that they are not equal in the minds of their fellow students, but are someone to be viewed with suspicion and caution.

A common theme in the white student journals, particularly written by white women, was fearing violence from people of color (most often black and Latino men), yet very few of the white journal writers wrote about experiencing violence at the hands of people of color. The opposite was true for the journals written by students of color. Regarding interracial violence, fewer students of color wrote in their journals about fearing violence from whites. However, proportionately more wrote about experiencing violence at the hands of white people. For example, Kris, a Latino college student wrote in his journal:

> Freshman year I lived in [the residence hall] with Eduardo. We went to high school together. It was a cold Friday night, and I remember we were at this party [on-campus]. I left early because I was tired, and then later on that night, Eduardo comes into our dorm

room bleeding in his hands and face. I asked what the hell had happened to him. He told me the story of how he got beat up by three white males on his way back to the dorm. The reason why he got beat up was because he was fighting on the phone with his girlfriend of the moment, screaming out in Spanish while he walked back. The white guys that beat him up told him that, "This is America, and we speak English only" and beat him up. I think that this experience was ridiculous. It's absurd to beat someone up because he was speaking in another language. I had a similar experience on my freshman year, too, where I was called a "Spic." I almost lost it and I'm glad I was with a friend of mine that just pushed me in the other direction because if not I would have tried to fight the guy. (Kris)

This account of Eduardo and Kris's experiences with racialized violence evokes the same pain and sadness that we see in Alex's journal entry, which is a much more common feeling in the journals written by students of color compared to the white student journals. Similar to Alex's entry, Kris's journal reveals that this incident of racial violence occurs on a weekend evening, and the perpetrators were college students. Kris's journal entry cannot be dismissed as a mere isolated event: College and university settings are the third most common place for hate crimes to occur (following residences and on streets), and anti-Latino hate crimes are on the rise (Southern Poverty Law Center, 2008).

Students of color wrote that when they confronted their peers about racial stereotypes, they were labeled as being too sensitive about race or playing the race card. Jordan wrote in her journal about a recent shopping trip where a stranger commented about her appearance:

I was buying windshield wipers at Walmart today and this man told me I reminded him of Lucy Liu. It's been the hundredth time that someone has told me that I look like Lucy Liu. I look nothing like Lucy Liu. [My friend] says I should take it as a compliment because Lucy Liu is hot, but that's not the damned point. The only reason why they think I look like her is because I'm Asian and have long black hair. . . . How is it a compliment when it has nothing to do with your "self" and everything to do with your race? I'm sick of being told I look like Connie Chung, Zhang Ziyi, Kaity Tong and . . . Lucy Liu. What sucks is that every time I go off on a tirade about it I get pissed on for having a bad attitude. The same question pops up, "why can't you take a compliment?" I try to explain that it is not a compliment but people don't understand why not. (Jordan)

From the tone of Jordan's narrative, we get a sense of the frustration she feels. Jordan resists the assumption that she should see her comparison with an attractive actress as a compliment. We can speculate that she may be referencing the stereotype of Asian American women as being docile and submissive, when she says she gets "pissed on for having a bad attitude" and not agreeing with the supposed compliment. Jordan's comparison to the "hot" Lucy Liu references another stereotype of the exotic, erotic sexualization of Asian women (Chou & Feagin, 2008; Feng Sun, 2003). She recognizes that the comparison has less to do with her appearance, and more with her being lumped into the category of an Asian woman, where her individuality is ignored. People of color often all look alike to people outside their race, referred to as the *other-race effect* in psychology. The homogenous view of individuals in other-races has been attributed to having more experience looking at faces of one own's race (Chiroro & Valentine, 1995). However, studies also suggest that it relates to prejudice, because prejudiced individuals are focused on racial stereotypes and ignore individual differences (Ferguson, Rhodes, & Lee, 2001).

Conclusion

Many students of color at predominately white campuses endure added layers of complexity in their everyday interactions, compared to their white peers. Most white students do not have to contend with negative racial stereotypes.[2] White students' admission to the university and their subsequent successes and failures are not viewed through the lens of their racial identity. When a white student receives a scholarship, it is perceived to be based on hard work and the effort of an individual's accomplishment. The parallel is not true for students of color, who are often presumed to receive preferential treatment at the expense of white students, even when there is no evidence to suggest this is true (Wise, 2005). Students of color, especially on predominately white campuses, are all too often reminded that their actions impact, for better or worse, racial stereotypes. White students can be just individuals and their race is largely ignored. For these students, using racial stereotypes and racist humor, especially in the backstage, is just fun without any negative consequences.

Although we can celebrate the racial progress we've made in the early 21st century, we still have a lot of work to do. I offer two starting points: First, we need to increase the awareness of how racial interactions impact everyone, and bring these conversations into an open dialogue. This can start with something as simple as asking students to pay attention to their interactions. To account for the normalization of racist interactions, many whites commented in their journals that they never paid attention to it until they were asked to keep a daily journal. Numerous whites said they were shocked by how often negative comments slipped under the radar of consciousness, indicating that part of white racial

transparency is the privilege to ignore it. The good news is that when the white journal writers noted persisting racism, many of them felt called to challenge it in their lives. Consider the narrative written by Kyle, a white male, who ended his journal on this note:

> As my last entry in this journal, I would like to express what I have gained out of this assignment. I watched my friends and companions with open eyes. I was seeing things that I didn't realize were actually there. By having a reason to pick out of the racial comments and actions I was made aware of what is really out there. Although I noticed that I wasn't partaking in any of the racist actions or comments, I did notice that I wasn't stopping them either. I am now in a position to where I can take a stand and try to intervene in many of the situations. (Kyle)

Kyle discusses how invisible and normal racist actions and comments can seem, and that now that he is able to recognize this, he can move on to actively resisting the racial hierarchy.

Second, as seen in Kyle's journal, we need to encourage whites to hold other whites accountable. Too often, the burden of responsibility rests with people of color to educate whites about racism. Whites need to recognize that racist comments made in private settings directly contribute to racial hostilities in the larger society. There are numerous tools whites can use to diffuse racist comments, such as using humor (sarcastically saying, "Gee, I didn't know you were a racist."), or pleading ignorance ("Can you please explain that comment to me? I don't understand what you mean."). Even to the most ignorant person, racist jokes are not funny if you have to explain them.

Substantially improving our cultural racial climate, particularly on college campuses, is critical for many reasons. Racial and ethnic

---

[2] Researchers suggest that racism from the myth of the model minority leads to increased academic and social pressure on Asian American college students, who are more likely to commit suicide compared to their white peers (Leong, Leach, Yeh, & Chou, 2007).

diversity can create an intellectually stimulating environment that can be used as an educational tool to promote the learning and development of all students (Milem, Chang, & Antonio, 2005). A core characteristic is not simply to add people of color and stir or just to increase the numbers of racially diverse individuals. Students accrue the educational benefits of diversity (benefits ranging from enhanced self-confidence, deeper critical thinking, and educational aspirations to greater cultural awareness) by being exposed to a wider range of perspectives on issues which improves the quality of intellectual advancement (Chang, 1999; Milem, 2003).

In addition to benefiting the broader campus climate, a commitment to improving the racial climate benefits individuals of all racial groups. Taking an other-oriented approach, it is the decent and fair thing to do. Even from a self-interested standpoint, given the competitive global economy that today's college students will likely enter, and the demographic shifts in the United States, it is critical for students to be prepared to work with people who are not like them. Indeed, one national study indicates that employers' highest priority in hiring college graduates is their ability to collaborate with others in diverse group settings (Peter D. Hart Research Associates, 2006).

Regardless if students utilize the other or the self-benefit position, it is clear that racial issues and racial diversity are critically important, and that we still have much work to do. We need your student voices in the dialogue.

References

Blank, R. M. (2009). An overview of trends in social and economic well-being, by race. In C. A. Gallagher (Ed.), *Rethinking the color line* (pp. 39–49). New York, NY: McGraw-Hill.

Bonilla-Silva, E. (2006). *Racism without racists: Colorblind racism and the persistence of racial inequality in the United States* (2nd ed.). Lanham, MD: Rowman & Littlefield.

Bonilla-Silva, E., & Forman, T. A. (2000). "I am not a racist but . . . ": Mapping white college students' racial ideology in the USA. *Discourse and Society, 11,* 50–85.

Carr, L. G. (1997). *"Colorblind" racism.* Thousand Oaks, CA: Sage.

Chang, M. J. (1999). Does racial diversity matter? The educational impact of a racially diverse undergraduate population. *Journal of College Student Development, 40,* 377–395.

Chiroro, P., & Valentine, T. (1995). An investigation of the contact hypothesis of the own-race bias in face recognition. *Quarterly Journal of Experimental Psychology, 48A,* 879–894.

Chou, R. S., & Feagin, J. R. (2008). *The myth of the model minority.* Boulder, CO: Paradigm.

Collins, P. H. (2000). *Black feminist thought: Knowledge, consciousness, and the politics of empowerment.* New York, NY: Routledge.

Dovidio, J. F., & Gaertner, S. L. (1991). Changes in the expression and assessment of racial prejudice. In H. J. Knopke, R. J. Norell, & R. W. Rogers (Eds.), *Opening doors: Perspectives on race relations in contemporary America* (pp. 119–150). Tuscaloosa: University of Alabama Press.

Feagin, J. R. (1991). The continuing significance of race: Antiblack discrimination in public places. *American Sociological Review, 56,* 101–116.

Feagin, J. R., & McKinney, K. D. (2003). *The many costs of racism.* New York, NY: Rowman & Littlefield.

Feagin, J. R., Vera, H., & Imani, N. (1996). *The agony of education: Black students at white colleges and universities.* New York, NY: Routledge.

Feng Sun, C. (2003). Ling Woo in historical context: The new face of Asian American stereotypes on television. In G. Dines & J. M. Humez (Eds.), *Gender, race, and class in media* (pp. 656–664). Thousand Oaks, CA: Sage.

Ferguson, D. P., Rhodes, G., & Lee, K. (2001). "They all look alike to me": Prejudice and cross-race face recognition. *British Journal of Psychology, 92,* 567–577.

Frye, M. (1998). Oppression. In P. S. Rothenberg (Ed.), *Race, class, and gender in the United States: An integrated study* (4th ed., pp. 146–149). New York, NY: St. Martin's Press.

Gallagher, C. (2003). Color blind privilege: The social and political functions of erasing the color line in post-race America. *Race, Gender, & Class, 10,* 22–37.

Goffman, E. (1959). *The presentation of self in everyday life*. New York, NY: Anchor Books.

Hraba, J., Brinkman, R., & Gray-Ray, P. (1996). A comparison of black and white prejudice. *Sociological Spectrum, 16,* 129–157.

Hurt, B. (director, producer, narrator). (2006). *Hip-hop: Beyond beats and rhymes.* [Motion picture.] United States: Media Education Foundation and God Bless the Child Productions.

Johnson, A. G. (2006). *Privilege, power, and difference* (2nd ed.). New York, NY: McGraw-Hill.

Kawakami, K., Dunn, E., Karmali, F., & Dovidio, J. F. (2009). Mispredicting affective and behavioral responses to racism. *Science, 323,* 276–278.

Kennedy, R. (2003). *Nigger: The strange career of a troublesome word.* New York, NY: Vintage Books.

Leong, F. T. L., Leach, M. M., Yeh, C., & Chou, E. (2007). Suicide among Asian Americans: What do we know? What do we need to know? *Death Studies, 31,* 417–434.

Lewis, A. E. (2003). *Race in the schoolyard: Negotiating the color line in classrooms and communities.* New Brunswick, NJ: Rutgers University Press.

Loewen, J. W. (1995). Lies my teacher told me: Everything your American history textbook got wrong. New York, NY: Simon & Schuster.

Lipsitz, G. (1995). The possessive investment in whiteness: Racialized social democracy and the "white" problem in American studies. *American Quarterly, 47,* 369–387.

Massey, D. S., Rothwell, J., & Domina T. (2009). The changing bases of segregation in the United States. *Annals of the American Academy of Political and Social Science, 626,* 74–90.

McIntosh, P. (1998). White privilege and male privilege: A person account of coming to see correspondence through work in women's studies.

In M. L. Andersen & P. H. Collins (Eds.), *Race, class, and gender: An anthology* (pp. 94–105). Belmont, CA: Wadsworth.

Milem, J. F. (2003). The educational benefits of diversity: Evidence from multiple sectors. In M. J. Chang, D. Witt, J. Jones, & K. Hakuta (Eds.), *Compelling interest: Examining the evidence on racial dynamics in higher education* (pp. 126–69). Stanford, CA: Stanford University Press.

Milem, J. F., Chang, M. J., & Antonio, A. L. (2005). *Making diversity work on campus: A research-based perspective.* Washington, DC: Association of American Colleges and Universities.

Peter D. Hart Research Associates. (2006). How should colleges prepare students to succeed in today's global economy? Retrieved from http://aacu.org/leap/documents/Re8097abcombined.pdf

Pettigrew, T. F. (1985). New black-white patterns: How best to conceptualize them? *Annual Review of Sociology, 11,* 329–346.

Picca, L. H., & Feagin, J. R. (2007). *Two-faced racism: Whites in the backstage and frontstage.* New York, NY: Routledge.

Randall, V. R. (2006). *Dying while black.* Dayton, OH: Seven Principles Press.

Southern Poverty Law Center. (2008). Hate crimes: Anti-Latino hate crime up for fourth year. *Intelligence Report, 132.* Retrieved from http://www.splcenter.org/get-informed/intelligence-report/browse-all-issues/2008/winter/hate-crimes

Yamato, G. (1987). Something about the subject makes it hard to name. In G. Anzaldúa (Ed.), *Making face, making soul/haciendo caras: Creative and critical perspectives by feminists of color* (pp. 20–24). San Francisco, CA: Aunt Lute Books.

Wise, T. J. (2005). *Affirmative action: Racial preference in black and white.* New York, NY: Routledge.

12

The College Hookup Culture

Why Participation Varies

Kathleen Bogle

Over the past decade, there have been countless stories in the media about the hookup culture on campus. In many cases, the media focused on college students going to wild parties and engaging in casual sex. These stories match popular culture images of college students as sex-crazed. These indelible portraits would have Americans believing that this is what all students are like, that all students are the same. In fact, today's college students are not a homogenous group. Sociologists and other researchers have found that although the hookup culture exists on many campuses, not everyone participates. And, among those who do participate, very few students match the image the media would have us believe. When researchers analyze college students' social lives, they find that it is not just a matter of some individuals choosing to participate in hooking up and some choosing not to. Rather, the demographic categories students belong to, including race, sexual orientation, and gender as well as the groups they join (e.g., fraternities and sororities and religious organizations), affect the likelihood of students forming relationships via hooking up and how they feel about the hookup culture pervading campus life.

In order to understand the contemporary hookup culture on campus, it is helpful to place it in historical context. College students did not always hook up. In fact, it was not long ago that college students formed sexual and romantic relationships via traditional dating. Over time, changes in society led to changes in how students date and mate.

NEW ERA ON CAMPUS

In any time period, in any particular culture, there are norms for how men and women form sexual and romantic relationships. The norms of that particular culture tell young men and women who initiates getting together, where the couple should meet, how they should get to know each other, and when the relationship should escalate sexually or romantically. Sociologists call this a *script* (Simon & Gagnon, 1984). Just as television and movie actors have a script that tells them what role to play, sociologists believe we, as members of a particular culture, are drawing from the scripts available to us for forming relationships. In the United States, from the 1920s through the mid-1960s, most college students utilized the traditional dating script (Bailey, 1988). Men asked women on dates, took them to places like restaurants, movie theaters, or dance halls, paid for the food and entertainment, and took them home (or back to their dorm) afterwards. Although premarital sex was considered taboo during this period and college men and women were forbidden from entering each other's dorm rooms, it was common for dating partners to "neck" (i.e., kiss or "make out") or "pet" (i.e., "fool around" without having oral sex or intercourse).

For most of these four decades, dating was the centerpiece of college social life. But during the late 1960s and throughout the 1970s, the script started to change (Bailey, 1988). The sexual revolution was going on, and birth control, including "the pill," became increasingly available. College students also began to rebel against campus rules, such as strict curfews and single-sex dorms. This rebellion occurred while more Americans were going to college than ever before and an increasing number were living on campus. As more young people went to college, the age at first marriage increased significantly. (Today, women get married on average at age 26 and men get married at age 28. During the 1950s, it was 20 and 22, respectively.) With so many young people living together in close quarters without parental supervision and with no plans to marry for years to come, the stage was set for the hookup script to emerge on campus (Bogle, 2007).

In the 1970s instead of going on formal dates every weekend, more college students were socializing by "hanging out" with large groups of friends at parties and bars and pairing off to form sexual and romantic relationships (Moffatt, 1989). By the early to mid-1980s, the term "hooking up" was being widely used as a slang term for having a physical encounter with someone—anything from kissing to sex—without going on a formal date first (Eble, 1996).

This new hooking up era differs from the norms of the dating era in several important ways. First, although college students in both the dating and hooking up eras were interested in forming sexual and romantic relationships with the opposite sex, when the script changed from dating to hooking up the order of events changed as well. In the dating era, students would date and get to know one another first, which might or might not ever lead to something sexual happening. In the hookup era, students engage in sexual activity first, which might or might not ever lead to dating. Second, while the couple was the focus of the dating era, "hanging out" in large groups is more common in the hooking up era. Along with the group dynamic, alcohol consumption has become a central feature of socializing in the hookup era (Bogle, 2008).

RESEARCH ON HOOKING UP

Although traditional dating was no longer the centerpiece of the college social scene beginning in the late 1960s and the term hooking up has been used since the 1980s, researchers did not begin studying the hookup culture until the turn of the 21st century (Bogle, 2008; Eshbaugh & Gute, 2008; Glenn & Marquardt, 2001; Hamilton & Armstrong, 2009; Lambert, Kahn, & Apple, 2003; Paul & Hayes, 2002; Paul,

McManus, & Hayes, 2000). In 2001, Glenn and Marquardt conducted a national study on college women's sexual attitudes and behaviors. They found that hooking up is a very common practice, so much so that the researchers concluded that this form of interaction is dominating male–female interaction on the modern college campus (Glenn & Marquardt, 2001). In the quantitative portion of their study, they found that 91% of college women believed hook ups occurred "very often" or "fairly often" on their campus. Further, 40% of the college women sampled said they had personally engaged in a hookup encounter since coming to college. Glenn and Marquardt concluded "hooking up, a distinctive sex-without-commitment interaction between college men and women, is widespread on-campuses and profoundly influences campus culture" (2001, p. 4).

Other studies reveal further evidence that hooking up is a hallmark of the college experience. In a representative study of undergraduate students at a college in the Northeastern part of the United States, 78.3% of the men and women sampled had hooked up. Paul and colleagues (2000) found that the participants' total number of hook up partners ranged from 0–65 with an average of 10.8 and a median of 6. Paul and colleagues (2000) concluded that "some students were hooking up on a weekly basis" (p. 84).

One of the largest quantitative studies on hooking up was conducted by Paula England and her research team. England surveyed over 14,000 students at 19 colleges and universities in the United States. Like previous researchers, she found a high percentage of students had hooked up at least once (72%). Among students who had ever hooked up, 40% had done so three or fewer times, 40% had done so four to nine times and only 20% had more than ten hookup partners. When taken together, that means approximately 80% of college students hook up on average less than once per semester (Armstrong, Hamilton, & England, 2010). When these findings are coupled with data from the National College Health Association, which shows that approximately 25% of college students in the United States are virgins, it is clear that media images to the contrary are misleading (American College Health Association, 2008).

Just as the media has hyped the image of college students having high numbers of sexual partners, they also have fueled the image that most hookup encounters involve sexual intercourse. However, research shows that is not the case. In one major representative study on the east coast, 78% of the students surveyed had hooked up, but only 38% of those same students ever had sexual intercourse during a hookup encounter (Paul et al., 2000). Similarly, in England's national study she asked about students' most recent hookup experience and found that only about one third of students had sexual intercourse the last time they hooked up. And, for those who did have sex, they were more likely to have done so with someone they had hooked up with repeatedly, that is, not a one-night stand (Armstrong et al., 2010).

In addition to the hookup culture being less wild than is commonly believed, some students opt out of the hookup scene altogether. The flip side of the statistics cited above indicating that between 72% and 78% of college students have hooked up is that between 22% and 28% have never done so. Although some students opt out of the alcohol-driven hookup culture, it does not necessarily mean that they are not sexually active or in romantic relationships. It just means that they are not using the hookup script in order to meet potential sexual or romantic partners.

MY STUDY

The quantitative research that has been conducted has helped people understand whether college students are hooking up, how often they do so, and what type of sexual activity they engage in during a hookup encounter. But, I wanted to learn more than just how many students were engaging in certain types of behavior. To this end, in 2001, while working on my doctoral degree in sociology, I began a qualitative research study on how contemporary men and women form sexual and romantic relationships both during college and after.

I knew I would have to interview a lot of people so that I did not just get one perspective. So, over the next several years I interviewed 76 people, 51 college students (ages 18–23) and 25 young alumni (ages 23–30). I interviewed people from two different types of universities, so I did about half my interviews at a large state school and the other half at a smaller Roman Catholic college. I talked to men and women from all grade levels and social circles (i.e., those who were in fraternities and sororities or athletic teams and those who were not, those who drank alcohol and those who did not). Most of the people I spoke to were white and heterosexual, but I also sought out minority students and gay/lesbian/bisexual students to get their perspectives. My research on minority and gay/lesbian/bisexual students was exploratory, given that they represented only a small percentage of my overall sample.

My research confirmed that the hookup culture was a fundamental part of college social life. But, through in-depth interviews, I was able to understand why participation in hooking up varies. Although some students do not hook up for individual reasons, such as already being in an exclusive relationship or having a shy personality, what is interesting to sociologists is the patterns that exist among certain groups. I found that the *groups students are born into* (e.g., race, sexual orientation,[1] and gender) and the *groups students choose to be a part of* (e.g., fraternities or sororities, religious organizations) affect their involvement in and reactions to the hookup culture.

WHO IS HOOKING UP?

There are many aspects of college life that converge to make hooking up the dominant script for initiating sex and relationships on campus, but students participate to varying degrees. Despite the disparity in individual involvement, the hook up culture transcends gender, grade level, and institution. Both men and women on the college campuses I studied took part in the hook up system. Additionally, hooking up was not limited to any particular grade level, although a few students suggested that it was more prevalent freshmen year. The hook up script was also not confined to one particular campus; in fact, it was pervasive on both campuses I studied.

The universities I studied had some important differences: one is a large state-sponsored university, which I refer to as "State University," with a diverse population in terms of religion; the other is a smaller faith-based institution, which I refer to as "Faith University," where the student body is largely Roman Catholic. Fraternities and sororities exist on both campuses. However, Greek life seemed much more visible

---

[1] I realize that not all scholars agree that sexual orientation is something you are born with, but addressing that debate is beyond the scope of this chapter.

and central to the experience of students at State University. Despite the differences between the two universities, hooking up is very much a part of the social landscape on both campuses. In my interviews with students at Faith University, I asked whether they thought the religious affiliation of the school had any effect on hooking up on campus. Most students insisted it was completely irrelevant.

KB: Do you think Faith University is different in any way because of being a Catholic school?

LYNN: No.

KB: So, Faith would be the same as state schools or wherever?

LYNN: With like hooking up, yeah . . . the Catholic school part doesn't really have [anything] to do with hooking up. Hooking up I think is across the board, it would happen at any college. (Sophomore, Faith University)

KB: Do you think male-female interaction would be the same no matter what school you went to?

TRENT: Yeah.

KB: So, if you went to [a larger state school] or anywhere it would be the same?

TRENT: Yeah, the same thing just a different size.

KB: Do you think there's anything different about this school because it's a Catholic school? Does that matter?

TRENT: Not really.

KB: So, Catholic or public or state or whatever, the same thing?

TRENT: Yeah. (Senior, Faith University)

These students may be correct that the hookup culture is just as dominant at Roman Catholic universities. In fact, one national quantitative study found that "women attending colleges or universities affiliated with the Catholic Church are almost four times as likely to have participated in hooking up compared to women at secular schools" (Burdette, Ellison, Hill, & Glenn, 2009, p. 10). Similarly, Freitas (2008) found that hooking up was common at both the Roman Catholic and secular colleges and universities she studied; however, hooking up was less common at evangelically affiliated institutions.

In my study, although hooking up was commonplace among the student body at both Faith and State Universities, there were certain circumstances that affected one's degree of involvement in the hookup scene, including clique membership and alcohol use. A student's circle of friends, or clique, was a good predictor of how entrenched he or she was in hooking up. The students I talked to who belonged to popular groups on campus, such as fraternities or sororities and athletic teams, were more likely to be heavily involved in hooking up. Fraternity men in particular believed that finding hooking up partners was very easy.[2] They suggested a typical number of different hook up partners would be 20–25 during a semester when they were unattached (i.e., not in

---

[2] The fact that fraternity men are among the most sexually active on campus can be explained by Martin and Hummer (1989). They found that the selection process for gaining entry into a fraternity ensures that the most macho, athletic, and womanizing men will be admitted to brotherhood, while those who do not live up to these standards are more likely to drop out during the pledge process or never attempt to pledge in the first place.

an exclusive relationship). Kyle, a senior at State University, mentions how his fraternity brothers can have sex whenever they want to, while this may not be the case for nonfraternity men on campus.

KYLE: The majority of students probably don't have sex as much as they would like to. My friends have sex, they can and they do when they want to, most nights.

The ease with which fraternity men find hook up partners is not surprising given their notorious involvement with hosting alcohol-driven parties on campus.[3] Greek members are typically at the center of social life on campus; therefore, they are frequently in situations conducive to hooking up.[4]

For students in non-Greek friendship circles, involvement in hooking up was varied. Many students flock to fraternity parties or other events featuring alcohol even though they do not actually belong to a fraternity or sorority. These students seemed to have no difficulty finding a hook up partner for the evening.

It is important to understand why alcohol plays such a major role in the hook up script. Typically, hookups are initiated during alcohol-centered socializing. According to the college students I spoke to, alcohol makes initiating sexual encounters easier by setting a tone of "kicking back," "letting loose," or "partying."

KB: Say you weren't in a relationship, how would you get together with girls?

LARRY: Probably like you're hanging out with a group of male friends, let's say you go to a bar and you're going to meet people obviously from [Faith U]. Around here, the bars are packed with [Faith] people . . . You know you basically meet them at bars, you're drinking, you're dancing . . . you go [to bars or parties] and [girls] come up and give you a big hug and kiss and the conversation just gets into everything, like crazy things, it really changes from when you're on campus to an outside social experience, it really does change, I feel it really does.

At bars and parties, college students may be in an environment where they can meet potential hookup partners, but the alcohol helps facilitate the interaction between potentially interested parties. Without alcohol as a social lubricant, the series of nonverbal cues (e.g., eye contact, body language, and so on) used to determine if a potential partner is interested in a hook up could be rather nerve-racking. College students also firmly believed that alcohol lowers their inhibitions and makes them want to hook up.

VIOLET: When I drink I get like in the mood to hook up and I just want to go and meet as many different people as I can. And I think that is the way that I react when I drink and I am more likely to hook up . . . when I am drinking. (Junior, State University)

Since students believed that alcohol is almost a necessary component to hooking up, students who did not drink alcohol, or at least did not feel comfortable drinking

---

[3] See Martin and Hummer (1989) for more on how fraternity members use alcohol in sexual situations.

[4] See Boswell and Spade (1996) for a discussion of how the characteristics of certain fraternities make them more conducive to the sexual exploitation of women.

in a party atmosphere, had more difficulty following the hookup script than the more party-focused cliques.

Just as one's social circle predicts a student's level of participation or enthusiasm for the hookup scene, so too does gender affect feelings about hooking up. While clearly both men and women are participating in the hookup culture, many women I interviewed conveyed their misgivings about hooking up. One of their concerns was they wished hookup encounters would more often lead to "something more" (i.e., some semblance of a relationship).

LISA: As time goes on, it gets kind of old [the whole hook up scene] and you're like: "Alright, I'm sick of just kissing random people; it's not really that fun; it doesn't mean anything." And I think people, *at least girls*, as they progress through college they start to really want, I know a lot of them really want to find someone that they really like and have a real relationship.

KB: Do you think that is something they will be able to find or is that something that's hard for them to find?

LISA: I don't know, I mean it is kind of hard to find in college. (Sophomore, State University)

DIANE: Girls are like very predictable . . . if they're hooking up with someone for a while, they're going to want a relationship. They're going to want like some type of like title, not title but like . . .

KB: Commitment or something?

DIANE: Right. Exactly, commitment. And usually guys don't want it.

KB: Why don't they want it?

DIANE: Because they don't. They're in college, they don't want a girlfriend. They basically just want to get ass.

KB: So girls are looking more for relationships? Guys are looking more for a sexual relationship?

DIANE: Yeah. (Sophomore, Faith University)

Given that men's and women's goals in the hookup scene are often at odds, with men being more focused on sex and women being more focused on relationships, there is often a battle of the sexes fought on college campuses over commitment. And, college women were very bothered that men seemed to control whether a hookup encounter evolved into an ongoing relationship or not.

KB: So, [from what you are saying] it seems like the guys decide [when it is a relationship or not]?

MARIE: I feel like they do, I definitely feel like they do because most of the girls I know are looking for *something*, you know someone, even if it's not serious, someone that is there to hang out with and talk to, [girls want] a feeling of being close to someone and I don't know if it's even guys don't want that, it's just they don't care if they have that, it's like: "Whatever." It could be any other girl any night and you know that's fine with them. [emphasis by interviewee] [Senior, State University]

The hookup culture on campus puts women in a double bind. On one hand, many women want to be part of the social scene on campus and to do so they are expected to hook up. Since hooking up is seen as the pathway to a relationship, women feel they have to participate to find boyfriends. On the other hand, most hookup encounters do not lead to exclusive relationships and men seem to hold most of the cards for deciding when (or if) the relationship will escalate romantically. This leaves many college women as active, but disgruntled, participants in hooking up.

In addition to women not getting what they want from the hookup culture, there are also serious problems experienced by some women who participate in hookups. First, research has shown that there is a double standard for sexual behavior in the hookup culture. While men are encouraged to acquire new sexual partners, the behavior of women is scrutinized. If women are seen as hooking up too often, they can be labeled a "slut" by their peers. In my study, students spoke of women who were ostracized by peers for being too active in the hookup culture. Second, socializing in the hookup scene can put women at risk for sexual assault. Several research studies have found that in some cases hookup encounters can be coerced or forced against a woman's will (see Armstrong, 2006; Flack et al., 2007; Kimble, Neacsiu, Flack, & Horner, 2008). Thus, women may be participating in the hookup culture, but their feelings about hooking up and the risks they encounter are quite different from those of their male peers.

WHO IS NOT HOOKING UP?

Although the hookup culture seemed to permeate many groups on campus, I also interviewed students who did not partake in the hookup scene. One student I spoke to, Hannah, a junior at State University, abstained from hooking up due to her religious beliefs. Hannah believed her Christian faith was a central part of who she is and what she does; religion was not just another demographic category, something in the back of her mind. She possessed a very active faith; it was a central part of her identity and her daily activities. Hannah rejected the dominant hookup culture on campus because she believed hooking up was immoral.

> HANNAH: The people I hang out with aren't really those kind of people who just have a one-night thing. I think of hooking up as a one-night kind of thing and myself and people I know don't do that.

Hannah was not a part of the alcohol-centered, party lifestyle; instead, she socialized within a close-knit group of friends who were also very religious.

> HANNAH: I don't really feel comfortable spending time with people who don't think in a similar fashion to me.
>
> KB: Do you consider yourself part of the mainstream of State University in terms of what students do socially?
>
> HANNAH: No.
>
> KB: What do you think of as mainstream and how are you different from that?
>
> HANNAH: Mainstream [means] the weekend starts on Thursday, you know, you go out drinking and partying, that kind of thing.
>
> KB: That's what you feel most students do?
>
> HANNAH: A lot do that and it kind of overshadows those of us who have a mellow weekend.

Hannah and her friends were interested in finding serious relationships. Although she found a relationship with someone who shared her religious beliefs, she said that many of her friends had difficulty finding "mature" relationships on campus.

Other studies have confirmed my findings regarding religious students like Hannah. One national quantitative study found that students who were more involved with religious activities, such as attending religious services on campus, were less likely to hook up (Burdette et al., 2009).

In addition to religiosity affecting involvement in the hookup culture, race is also an important factor to examine. Although most of the participants in my study were white, I did interview a few minority students.[5] These men and women recognized that hooking up was very common on campus; however, they did not engage in this practice. Lannette, a black student at Faith University, knew what hooking up meant, but did not say it or do it herself.

> KB: Is [hooking up] a term you use or is that a term you just more heard?
>
> LANNETTE: Um, I don't really use the term "hooked up" so it's more what I hear. Like if someone said: "Yeah I hooked up with him," I understand what they're talking about. But, me personally, I wouldn't say [it].
>
> KB: Are you involved in . . . the hook up scene at all?
>
> LANNETTE: No, cause I mean . . . I'm not really the type that just goes around and hooks up with random people. That's just not my . . . you know, that's not who I am. . . . Even if I'm interested in a boy, I won't just hook up with [him] randomly. . . . Like, I want to get to know him first and all that. That's just not my thing; so I'm not really in that whole category, just hookups. (Sophomore, Faith University)

Instead of hooking up, she indicated that she generally met men through friends or local "hangouts" at home. Once she met someone of interest, she would start "talking" to him. During the process of getting to know one another, the two might go out on something resembling a traditional date or they might "just chill" together at someone's home. Lannette, and other minority students I spoke to, used the term *talking* somewhat differently than did their white counterparts.

> KB: What about the . . . word, I think you mentioned it —"talking." If someone says "we're talking" what does that mean?
>
> LANNETTE: It means like I guess um, when you're interested in someone, I guess you want to, if you don't already know them you know you want to get to know them so you know you're I guess "talking" to get to know the person. Um, you're not necessarily with them or . . . so you might think: "Okay it's possible that we would become . . . a boyfriend or girlfriend, but you know maybe not." So it's like kind of like

---

[5] In terms of racial diversity, I conducted interviews with two black students (one male, one female) and two Asian American students (one male, one female). Although the number of interviews with students from diverse backgrounds was too small to state anything conclusively, my findings do confirm what others have found. That is, how men and women meet, interact, and form sexual or romantic relationships varies by race. See Glenn and Marqurardt (2001) and Williams (1998).

a beginning stage of a possible relationship. Um, talking to someone is pretty much just getting to know them. . . . If you already do know them, like if . . . you're friends for a while and you start talking—it's more like: "Okay I realize that I might want to be with you." So you spend more time with them and you kind of limit talking to other guys or girls.

For the minority students I spoke to, particularly blacks, "talking" preceded being "with" someone as an exclusive couple. Although talking often involved some degree of sexual intimacy, it was thought of differently from just hooking up because there was an understanding that the two people were contemplating a romantic relationship. Hookups were seen as more casual, even though some hookups led to relationships also.

Lannette also indicated that her minority friends on campus do not participate in the hookup scene on campus. Their decision to abstain was not necessarily a moral one, but perhaps is based on other considerations. First, research has shown that minority students are significantly less likely to binge drink (Wechsler, Davenport, Dowdall, Moeykens, & Castillo, 1994). Given the central role alcohol plays in facilitating hooking up, this fact may decrease their participation. Second, the people I spoke to said many minority students are not interested in sexual encounters and relationships with white students (and vice versa). Therefore, on campuses that are overwhelmingly white, minority students often socialize among themselves on campus and keep close ties with friends from home.

One major quantitative study that examined race found a more complex portrait of how minority students navigate the hookup culture on campus. Similar to my study, this study found black students tended to date and mate with people of the same race; however, they found variation by gender, with black women being the least likely to utilize the hookup script in favor of other methods of dating and mating (see McClintock, 2010, for a full discussion of how race factors into how students choose hookup and dating partners).

In addition to speaking to a handful of minority students, I also talked to a few gay and lesbian students.[6] Like minorities, homosexuals were not involved with the dominant hookup culture on campus. These students often struggled to reveal their sexual identity to fellow classmates and, therefore, had difficulty finding other gay and lesbian students for potential sexual and romantic relationships.

> KB: So for meeting someone . . . of the same sex or socially interacting, how does all of that work for you? How does it work if you're not . . . heterosexual . . . [at Faith University]?
>
> Timothy: You're like: "Is he [gay] or is that just wishful thinking?" [laughing] I wish I had glasses I could like put on and people would appear; it's like my glasses would be blue if they see people who are blue that means they're gay.

Unlike heterosexual students who had a system in place to find partners, homosexual students were more or less on their own in their quest to find potential partners.

---

[6] I interviewed two gay men and one bisexual woman in a focus group at Faith University.

TIMOTHY: It's harder to meet anyone, other than like to go to a bar that you know specifically everyone's gay or most people are because there are straight people, a few, that go to gay clubs and stuff. But um, you don't know on campus [who is gay].

JONATHAN: No one at the gay bar is going to smack you on the head because you're like: "Hey you want to dance?" and they're like: "No I'm straight, I'm sorry." Nobody's going to freak out at you at the gay bar because you asked them to dance because *you're at a gay bar.* But on campus . . . you couldn't just be like: "Hey do you want [to get] a drink?" or something. (emphasis by interviewee)

Given the discrimination gay and lesbian students face on campus, many stay "in the closet" among their straight peers. Therefore, it is difficult for homosexual students to identify potential sexual or romantic partners at campus parties and bars that revolve around the heterosexual hookup scene. As a result, gay and lesbian students look for off-campus alternatives for socializing and forming relationships.

Conclusion

Just as social life on college campuses throughout much of the twentieth century was defined by dating, the centerpiece of social life on today's college campuses is alcohol-centered socializing and hooking up. Messages from television, movies, and reports from news media support the notion that being in college and being part of the hookup culture goes hand-in-hand. Although the media is correct that hooking up is the primary means by which students get together for sexual or romantic relationships, all students do not participate. And even among those who do participate, there is a great deal of variation in level of involvement and feelings about the hookup scene. Interestingly, researchers have found that much of the variation in the hookup culture can be accounted for by analyzing the groups one is born into (e.g., race, sexual orientation, and gender) and the groups one chooses to belong to (e.g., fraternities or sororities and religious groups). In order to fully understand the hookup culture and its alternatives, one must take into account the diversity of the student body.

Future research should include more diverse samples of college students in order to better analyze variation in the way students form sexual and romantic relationships. Factors that should be considered include: race, class, gender, religion, religiosity, and students with disabilities. There are many other factors that researchers could consider as well. For example, does being a first generation college student affect one's likelihood of participating in the hookup scene? What is the experience of students who are not born in the United States? Does being a resident versus a commuter matter? In addition to these individual factors, researchers must consider how the type of college one attends affects how students form sexual and romantic relationships. For example, is the hookup scene prevalent at historically black colleges? How do heterosexual students meet potential partners if they attend a single-sex institution? What happens at community colleges and other institutions where all the students commute? Does the geographic location of the college or university itself make a difference? When all these factors are taken into account, a more complex portrait of college student social life will emerge.

References

American College Health Association (2008, Fall). *American College Health Association: National College Health Assessment (ACHA-NCHA) Reference group report*. Retrieved from http://www.acha-ncha.org/docs/ACHA-NCHA_Reference_Group_Report_Fall2008.pdf.

Armstrong, E. (2006). Sexual assault on campus: A multi-level, integrative approach to party rape. *Social Problems, 53*, 483–499.

Armstrong, E. A., Hamilton, L., & England, P. (2010). Is hooking up bad for young women? *Contexts, 9*, 22–27.

Bailey, B. L. (1988). *From front porch to back seat: Courtship in twentieth-century America*. Baltimore, MD: Johns Hopkins University Press.

Bogle, K. A. (2007). The shift from dating to hooking up in college: What scholars have missed. *Sociology Compass, 1*(2), 775–788.

Bogle, K. A. (2008). *Hooking up: Sex, dating, and relationships on campus*. New York: New York University Press.

Boswell, A. A., & Spade, J. Z. (1996). Fraternities and collegiate rape culture: Why are some fraternities more dangerous places for women? *Gender & Society, 10*, 133–147.

Burdette, A. M., Ellison, C. G., Hill, T. D., & Glenn, N. D. (2009). Hooking up at college: Does religion make a difference? *Journal for the Scientific Study of Religion, 48*, 535–551.

Eble, C. (1996). *Slang and sociability: In-group language among college students*. Chapel Hill: University of North Carolina Press.

Eshbaugh, E., & Gute, G. (2008). Hookups and sexual regret among college women. *Journal of Social Psychology, 148*, 77–90.

Flack, W. F., Jr., Daubman, K. A., Caron, M. L., Asadorian, J., D'Aureli, N., Kiser, S., Hall, A., Gigliotti, S., & Stine, E. (2007). Risk factors and consequences of unwanted sex among university students: Hooking up, alcohol, and stress response. *Journal of Interpersonal Violence, 22*, 139–157.

Freitas, D., & Winner, L. (2008). *Sex and the soul: Juggling sexuality, spirituality, romance and religion on America's college campuses*. New York, NY: Oxford University Press.

Glenn, N., & Marquardt, E. (2001). *Hooking up, hanging out and hoping for Mr. Right: College women on dating and mating today*. An Institute for American Values Report to the Independent Women's Forum. AmericanValues.org. Retrieved from http://www.americanvalues.org/Hooking_Up.pdf

Hamilton, L., & Armstrong, E. A. (2009). Gendered sexuality in young adulthood: Double binds and flawed options. *Gender & Society, 23*, 589–616.

Kimble, M., Neacsiu, D., Flack, W. F., Jr., & Horner, J. (2008). Risk of unwanted sex for college women: Evidence for a "red zone." *Journal of American College Health, 57*, 331–337.

Lambert, T. A., Kahn, A. S., & Apple, K. J. (2003). Pluralistic ignorance and hooking up. *Journal of Sex Research, 40, 129–133*.

Martin, P. Y., & Hummer, R. (1989). Fraternities and rape on campus. *Gender & Society, 3*(4), 457–473.

McClintock, E. A. (2010). When does race matter? Race, sex, and dating at an elite university. *Journal of Marriage and Family, 72*, 45–72.

Moffatt, M. (1989). *Coming of age in New Jersey: College and American culture*. New Brunswick, NJ: Rutgers University Press.

Paul, E. L., & Hayes, K. A. (2002). The casualties of casual sex: A qualitative exploration of the phenomenology of college students' hookups. *Journal of Social and Personal Relationships, 19*, 639–661.

Paul, E. L., McManus, B., & Hayes, A. (2000). Hookups: Characteristics and correlates of college students' spontaneous and anonymous sexual experiences. *Journal of Sex Research, 37*, 76–88.

Simon, W., & Gagnon, J. H. (1984). Sexual scripts. *Society, 22*, 53–60.

Wechsler, H., Davenport, A., Dowdall, G., Moeykens, B., & Castillo, S. (1994). Health and behavioral consequences of binge drinking in college: A national survey of students at 140 colleges. *Journal of the American Medical Association, 272*, 1672–1677.

Williams, K. M. (1998). *Learning limits: College women, drugs, and relationships*. Westport, CT: Bergin & Garvey.

13

What Does Mainstream Media Tell Us about Whites' Racial Behavior?

Chavella T. Pittman

The mass media is a major influence in U.S. society. Newspapers, magazines, the internet, music, movies, and other forms of mass media all communicate what is normal and expected in society. While we are not often aware of it, mass media has a large impact on what individuals believe and do. Socialization is the process by which individuals learn how to become members of their society (Bandura & Walters, 1963; Cooley, 1983; Goffman, 1959; Mead, 1934). Agents of socialization—family, school, religion, peers, work, and media—do so by teaching society members how to think, feel, and behave. Some refer to the mass media as a *superpeer*, given its pervasiveness and socializing abilities above and beyond those of friends, family, peers, schools, religion, and so on (Gray, 2008; Strasburger & Kadin, 1995). There are a multitude of theories that explain how these agents teach societal lessons to their members. However, as summarized by Dixon (2008), popular theories for explaining how media socializes individuals include cultivation (e.g., Gerbner, Gross, Morgan, & Signorielli, 1986), framing (e.g., Iyengar & Kinder, 1978), and social cognition theories about priming and stereotypes (Domke, McCoy, Torres, 1999; Gorham, 1999).

A few hypothetical situations illustrate the ways in which media may influence and socialize individuals. A small boy watches a television show appropriate for his age which consistently displays boys and girls with different clothing and interests. As a result of constant exposure to persistent gender messages (cultivation of norms) on television, this boy refuses to wear pink or play with dolls. A teenager notices that the same topics appear frequently via trending, most viewed, and popular searches on social media. She draws conclusions that these are the important issues given their frequent and highlighted media portrayals (framing) instead of other potentially important issues with less media focus and exposure. An adult regularly watches and reads the news which overrepresents Latinos as undocumented criminals. This shortcut yet stereotyped information from the news guides this adult's policy preferences on immigration and crime (i.e., social cognition). While these theories are complicated by active or passive processes, contextual factors, and social identities (Fiske, 2011), each offers compelling evidence that mass media shapes our thoughts, feelings, and behaviors across the life course.

Researchers demonstrate that mass media influences individuals' attitudes and beliefs (Fiske, 2011; Gray, 2008; Holz & Wright, 1979; McQuail, 1985). Mass media is influential in providing its audience with information that is then used to form opinions and beliefs (Gamson, Croteau, Hoynes, & Sasson, 1992; Gilliam, 1999; Hunt, 2005). In fact, some researchers have argued for decades that people in the United States are dependent upon media as a major source of knowledge they have about the world, especially when an individual has no or limited experience with the topic (e.g., Ball-Rokeach & DeFleur, 1976; Entman, 1989; Gray, 2008). Mass media also influences the attitudes and emotions (Ball-Rokeach, Grube, & Rokeach, 1981; Gray, 2008; Park, Yun, McSweeney, & Gunther, 2007; Pidgeon, Kasperson, Slovic, 2003; Ross, 2009; Wirth & Schramm, 2005; Yanovitzky, 2002) we have toward everything from social groups (e.g., women) to events (e.g., presidential elections or natural disasters). Beyond attitudes and opinions, media also influences a range of behaviors from voting to antisocial acts (Anderson & Bushman, 2001; Dalton et al., 2003; Gray, 2008; Hennesey, Bleakley, Fishbein, & Jordan, 2009; McQuail, 1985; Paik & Comstock, 1994). Given all of this, it is clear that the mass media's influence upon individuals is immense as it affects their beliefs, attitudes, emotions, and behaviors.

One mechanism by which mass media influences individuals is by maintaining and creating norms (e.g., cultivation theory). A norm is the perception of behaviors as common or uncommon (i.e., descriptive), or acceptable or unacceptable (i.e., injunctive) (Ajzen, 1991; Cialdini & Trost, 1998; Deutsch & Gerard, 1955). For example, a social norm tells you that most people stand in line to purchase a ticket for a movie. It also tells you that you should wait in line, too. That is, a social norm also informs you that you should not walk to the front of the line ahead of other waiting people. In simple form, norms tell you how others are or should be behaving, thinking, and feeling. Several media researchers (Fiske, 2011; Gamson et al., 1992; Holz & Wright, 1979; McQuail, 1985) argue that more research should be done on the broader norms transmitted by media instead of focusing on individual effects. That is, research should examine media's messages about social norms as part of a larger socialization process of defining and constructing reality (Gamson et al., 1992; Gray, 2008; Lippmann, 1922; McQuail, 1985). This constructed reality is what provides individuals with the meaning to both interpret and behave in their world (Gamson et al., 1992; Gerber, 1999; Gray, 2008; Lippmann, 1922).

What is the constructed reality mass media presents about race? How are individuals encouraged to interpret and, more important, act regarding race? In line with research on the broader norms communicated by mass media, this chapter examines media's norms about race. It concisely describes racial oppression in the United States as well as suggestions for understanding it better. Next it briefly discusses prior research on mass media and race as well as what is missing from that research. The majority of the chapter fills that gap by presenting mass media's norms for white racial behavior. Each norm description is followed by a discussion of the implications of these norms for racial oppression in the United States. The chapter closes with a brief discussion about how mass media's influence can be minimized and redirected to address racial oppression.

RACIAL OPPRESSION

Diversity (inclusive of racial diversity) has many positive benefits for society. Broadly, diversity produces varied opinions, feelings, and behaviors regarding a full spectrum of issues and situations. The inclusion of diverse perspectives avoids groupthink or narrow behavior choices, and results in higher quality thinking and actions (Rink & Ellemers, 2010). Diversity in the workplace can result in higher productivity and more products and services relevant to diverse groups (e.g., Herring, 2009). Research also indicates that diversity is important for increasing critical thinking, problem solving, and coping with change (e.g., Gurin, Dey, Hurtado, & Gurin, 2002). While there are many more positive benefits of diversity, these few demonstrate the importance of examining and improving interpersonal and structural relations between racial groups.

While a common belief is that we are living in a postracial society, evidence demonstrates that we are not (Metzler, 2008). In 2011 there were 2,495 antiblack, 507 anti-Latino, and 167 anti-Asian hate crimes (Federal Bureau of Investigation, 2012). Structural markers of racial oppression also run contrary to perceptions of improving race relations (Feagin, 2006; Massey, 2005; Pager & Shepherd, 2008). For example, black women are 2.37 times more likely to experience infant mortality than white women (Mathews & MacDorman, 2011). Native American infants die from SIDS at 2.5 times the rate of white infants (National Conference of State Legislatures, 2012). Latinas have rates of cervical cancer as twice that of white women. Asian Americans have disproportionate rates of several forms of cancer, tuberculosis, and hepatitis B (Russell, 2010). U.S. Census Bureau figures reveal that the median household net worth for whites was $110,729 in 2010, in contrast to $69,560 for Asians, $7,424 for Latinos, and $4,995 for blacks (Luhby, 2012). In line with these data showing whites' wealth at 22 times that of blacks, it is no surprise that blacks also earn significantly less income and exist disproportionately below the poverty level in comparison (DeNavas-Walt, Proctor, & Smith, 2010). This racial wealth gap widened in the recent economic downturn such that Asians, Latinos, and blacks lost 60% of their net median household income between 2005–2010 and whites only lost 23% (Luhby, 2012).

Despite an assumed postracial era, racial segregation for whites remains high in the United States. Even with reductions of racial segregation between 1980 and 2010, whites continue to exhibit high levels of segregation from other racial groups (Logan, Stults, & Farley, 2004; Wilkes & Iceland, 2004). For example, in 2000, the Index of Dissimilarity (weighted for percent of minority population) for segregation of whites in all U.S. metropolitan areas from Asians was 42.2%, Latinos 51.6%, blacks 65.2% (Logan et al., 2004). This means that 42% to 65% of whites would have to move to new neighborhoods to have racial integration. In 2010, the unweighted dissimilarity indices for whites were 37.2% from Asians, 40.1% from Latinos, and 53.5% from blacks (Frey, 2011). This pattern of high racial segregation holds true in metropolitan (Logan et al., 2004; Wilkes & Iceland, 2004), rural, and small town areas (Lichter, Parisi, Grice, & Taquino, 2007). In fact, in 2010, the average white person lived in a neighborhood that was primarily (75%) white with very few people of color (Logan & Stults, 2011). These segregation details are especially important for this chapter because they reveal that whites lack real-life experience with people of color. Therefore, the media is a primary source of whites' constructed racial reality and behavior norms.

MASS MEDIA AND RACE

What does mass media tell us about the persistence of racial oppression in the United States? What is the constructed reality mass media presents about race? How are individuals encouraged to interpret race? Several decades of research on media and race address these questions. They demonstrate that mass media portrays race in ways that maintain racial oppression. Native Americans are portrayed as vicious or noble savages, helpless victims (e.g., alcoholics), or loyal but unintelligent helpers to whites (Holtzman, 2000; Larson, 2006; Miller & Ross, 2004). Asians are characterized as gang members, dangerous or criminal foreigners, and model minorities in the media (Chen, 2013; Holtzman, 2000; Larson, 2006). The media portrays Latinos as violent and both Latinas and Latinos as overly sexualized (Larson, 2006). Blacks are presented as criminals, uneducated, in low status (e.g., subservient) jobs, and highly sexual (Dixon & Linz, 2000; Entman & Rojecki, 2000; Gilliam, 1999; Gilliam & Iyengar, 2000; Larson, 2006). When media portrays middle-class people of color, its images, storylines, and characters construct a (false) reality of racial equality and equal opportunity (Busselle & Crandall, 2002; Holtzman, 2000; Hunt, 2005). Thus, media obscures the current realities of racial and social class oppression through racial and social class portrayals that suggest reforms are not needed (Busselle & Crandall, 2005; Butsch, 2011).

These media messages about race influence individuals' racial opinions, judgments, attitudes, and policy preferences (Domke, 2001; Domke et al., 1999; Downing & Husband, 2005; Gilliam, 1999; Gilliam, Nicholas, & Beckmann, 2003; Jhally & Lewis, 1992; Mastro, Lapinski, Kopacz, & Behm-Morawitz, 2009; Oliver & Fonash, 2002; Ramasubramanian, 2011a, b). They also affect individuals' emotions about race (Dixon, 2009; Entman & Rojecki, 2000; Gray, 2008; Ramasubramanian, 2010; Surlin, 1978). In these ways mass media has real-world consequences upon individuals' attitudes, opinions, feelings toward and policy preferences regarding race in the United States.

The above research demonstrates that media messages influence the racial attitudes, opinions, and feelings of individuals. As mentioned previously, mass media also influences behavior (Anderson & Bushman, 2001; Gray, 2008; Larson, 2006; McQuail, 1985). So what are the media messages regarding racial behavior? Researchers have not examined media messages for racial behavior despite the recognition that behaviors maintain racial oppression (e.g., voting on race-related policies, racist joking, and discriminatory hiring practices). We assume racial attitudes lead to behaviors despite the fallacy of this assumed attitude–behavior correspondence (Kraus, 1995; LaPiere, 1934; Schuman & Johnson, 1976). Thus, to understand racial oppression we must focus on understanding the racial behaviors that create and maintain it. Everyday behaviors can reveal how racial oppression is "done", produced, and reproduced (Essed, 1991; Goffman, 1959; West & Fenstermaker, 1995). With this in mind, the next section examines media messages regarding whites' racial behaviors.

MASS MEDIA'S MESSAGES ABOUT WHITE RACIAL BEHAVIOR

Prior research on mass media and race examines the portrayal of people of color and the resultant effect on individuals' racial attitudes, opinions, and beliefs. This section instead focuses on the racial behaviors portrayed by the mass media. We use television situation comedies (sitcoms) in particular because at least one television is in 114.9 million U.S.

households, with the average person watching for five hours per day (www.nielsen.com). Indeed, television has been argued as one of the most pervasive and influential forms of mass media (Gray, 2008; Hunt, 2005; McQuail, 1985). Additionally, situation comedies are a convenient media source to examine for messages about racial behavior. While drama, reality, or other types of plots might exist across many episodes, occluding the context for behavior, the plots for situation comedies tend to conclude within one episode.

The analyses focused on primetime situation comedies with all-white casts, given that they represent the reality of racial segregation and interaction for whites in the United States (Frey, 2011; Logan & Stults, 2011). Beyond residential segregation, whites may have many opportunities to interact with people of color at work, school, grocery stores, while shopping, and by inviting them into their homes as friends. The analyses aim to examine how these *cross-race interactions* are portrayed in primetime situation comedies. The varying histories of and attitudes toward racial minorities in the United States likely impact the behaviors whites have toward them. For example, whites may behave toward Native Americans as alcoholics, Asians as model minorities, and Latinos as illegal aliens. For this reason, the analyses focus on one racial group—blacks—as we cannot assume that whites' racial behavior toward different racial minorities would be the same.

As will be discussed further, both systematic and exploratory analyses were necessary. Systematic and exploratory refers to the sampling methods for the episodes analyzed. The systematically chosen episodes were selected on the basis of television ratings to reduce bias in the analyses. Exploratory sampling was necessary as the systematic sampling did not produce many episodes to be analyzed (i.e., no cross-race interaction). Exploratory sampling was not systematic but was random and resulted in a selection of episodes that could be analyzed (i.e., including cross-race interaction).

For both the systematic and exploratory analyses, each episode was analyzed by at least two coders. The first round of coding examined each sitcom episode for cross-race interaction. In the second round of coding, the scene surrounding the cross-race interaction was examined for media messages regarding racial behavior. In simple form, the coder asked, "What is this scene telling me is expected and/or common racial behavior for whites?" In the text that follows, the media message about racial behavior uncovered by the systematic examination is described. After this is a description of the most common racial behaviors revealed via an exploratory media message analysis.

Systematic Analysis: Whites do not Interact with Blacks

The situational comedies with the highest primetime ratings were examined in the systematic analysis of media messages. The highest rated primetime sitcom 2008–2010 was *Two and a Half Men* (www.nielsen.com). An additional highly rated primetime sitcom with an all-white cast was *How I Met Your Mother*. The *Two and a Half Men* plot revolves around a wealthy, philandering bachelor (Charlie) whose dentist brother (Alan) and young nephew (Jake) move in with him. *How I Met Your Mother* centers on a group of five young middle-class friends (Ted, Lily, Marshall, Barney, and Robin) living in New York City as one friend (Ted) searches for love. Seasons 6 and 7 of *Two and a Half Men* (2008–2010) and season 5 of *How I Met Your Mother* (2009–2010) were included in the systematic analyses.

What did a systematic examination of these highly rated sitcoms reveal about white racial behavior? Interestingly, but not surprisingly, this analysis revealed that cross-race interaction with blacks rarely occurs. On the rare occasions that blacks (and people of color generally) were present, they were in the background (e.g., walking down the street, sitting in a café). In other cases they were the service person (e.g., mover, waiter). Hence the media communicates that racial behavior with blacks (and people of color) is uncommon and novel.

This media message is damaging in that it reinforces racial segregation between whites and blacks. This mass media portrayal of (a void of) racial behavior does not problematize the current high segregation between these racial groups. Instead it presents this lack of cross-race interaction as normal and expected behavior. In doing so, it communicates to whites that they do not need to know how to interact regarding and with blacks as the norm is to only expect interactions with other whites.

Even more important, this systematic analysis of media presents a message of cross-race behaviors as novel and uncommon. Segregation research details that, in fact, whites are having very little interaction with blacks (Frey, 2011; Logan et al., 2004). Together these facts further the idea of behaviors regarding and with blacks as novel. Research demonstrates that social norms (i.e., what is common and expected) are an even more powerful influence upon behavior when a situation is novel (Crano & Prislin, 2008; Festinger, 1954; Haney, Banks, & Zimbardo, 1973; Sherif, 1937). This means that the behavior norms presented by media become the primary guidance whites will use for how to behave in cross-race interactions. That is, because whites have few interactions with blacks, whites are likely to use norms to guide their behavior. They are likely to look to norms to get a feel for how others are behaving in similar situations and to figure out how they should behave. Thus whites will use norms to determine: What are other whites doing in their racial behaviors with blacks? How should I behave regarding blacks? Given that this systematic analysis of highly rated primetime situation comedies demonstrated a lack of racial behavior, an exploratory examination of primetime situation comedies was conducted.

Exploratory Analysis

A social norm communicated about behavior that is novel is particularly important, powerful, and influential (Crano & Prislin, 2008; Festinger, 1954; Haney et al., 1973; Sherif, 1937). The systematic analyses revealed that the dominant mass media message about racial behavior is that whites do not interact with blacks. Thus, this complementary exploratory analysis is necessary to identify norms for whites' novel behaviors with blacks. The following sections describe the media messages about norms for whites' racial behavior. These norms were identified in an exploratory examination of episodes of situation comedies aired on primetime television across a 15-year period (1994–2008). These episodes, viewed randomly over time and not initially analyzed, were what inspired the systematic analysis. However, once the systematic analyses revealed the episodes' primary normative message regarding racial behavior (cross-racial behavior does not and is not expected to occur), it became important to examine the novel examples of cross-race interaction for media norms of racial behavior.

As with the systematic analysis, only situation comedies with all-white major characters were included in the exploratory analysis since they reflect the reality of most whites' novel behaviors regarding blacks. The resultant nine episodes (see the Appendix at the end of this chapter for details) contained media messages that communicated norms for whites' racial behavior. Again, these episodes were identified from casual television watching. That is, they were not identified systematically nor by an avid viewer of these situation comedies. The viewer knew neither the characters, nor the prior nor the future plots. In fact, these episodes were identified randomly, often while the television was on in the background or a viewer was flipping past a channel. Yet, the social norm communicated to whites about their racial behavior was able to reach even its most casual media viewer (Gray, 2008). This attests to the effectiveness and potency of these situation comedies' ability to communicate norms for racial behaviors to both their casual and loyal white viewers. Below are the novel, yet influential, messages these media examples communicated about white racial behavior.

ACTING "BLACK". A clear and common norm for racial behavior involved whites "acting black." In fact this white racial behavior appeared in 19 instances across six of the nine episodes. This social norm displayed whites engaged in behaviors reflecting stereotypes of black mannerisms, vernacular, and attire. *Everybody Loves Raymond* is about Raymond, a successful middle-class sports reporter whose parents and policeman brother (Robert) live in the same neighborhood. In one episode of *Everybody Loves Raymond*, Robert appears dressed in a brightly colored suit with a longer than average jacket length. He poses leaned over to the side to look "cool." In one scene he says to Sergeant Judy (his black policewoman partner):

> Yeah, well, see, [Raymond] never had soul food before, and when I told him where I was going, he begged me to come along, and *he got all up in mine*, I couldn't say *no to the brotha, ya know what I'm saying*?

The italicized text represents some of the black jargon he speaks all the while using stereotypically black inflection. In addition to the above scene, throughout the episode, he says such phrases as "put salt in my game," "aiiight," "gonna hook you up," and "you all that," all with a black intonation. Robert's behavior results from his recent socializing with black friends. Interestingly, he believes that acting in this (stereotypical) manner will endear him to his black friends. Raymond points out the error of his ways in the following conversation:

> ROBERT: You think *you all that*.
>
> RAYMOND: All right, see, that's the problem. That's what Judy [the black friend] wanted to talk about.
>
> ROBERT: What is?
>
> RAYMOND: You! *"All that"*!
>
> ROBERT: What?
>
> RAYMOND: [The black friend] doesn't want to go out with you because you're black, Robert. Judy [the black friend]—her and her [black] friends, they think that you're just—you're putting on some kind of act.

Instead of endearing him to blacks, Robert's behaviors parody blacks in a way that alienates them from him.

Reba is a middle-class "soccer mom" whose life has been turned upside down when her dentist husband (Brock) gets his hygienist (Barbara Jean) pregnant. Barbara Jean's behaviors similarly communicate a norm of whites engaging in black mannerisms, vernacular, and appearance. To interact with a black family, Barbara Jean has her hair corn-rowed and dresses in an athletic jumpsuit and gold chains. Her speech includes "sup" (short for "what's up?"), "I feel ya," "know what I'm saying," "chill girlfriend," and "oh no she didn't." She speaks all of these phrases with stereotypical black inflections, neck rolling, and hand gestures. Again, instead of assisting her interactions with blacks, it makes them leery of her. In fact, at the end of this episode the black family specifically requests that Barbara Jean not come along when Reba's family travels to visit them in Louisiana.

As a final media example from recent years, *How I Met Your Mother* also evidences an "act black" norm for whites' racial behavior. In *How I Met Your Mother*, Lily engages in a black performance when Michelle (her black female friend) is around:

> "That my girl Michelle [black friend]? . . . How she livin'? . . . Large! Oh, girl, you gots to get your drink on up in here."

In this episode, Lily changes her behavior in order to relate to her black friend. Her adjusted behavior includes improper grammar as well as the colloquialisms above and "fo' real," "you feel me?," and "scrub." It also includes a stereotypical black inflection and swaggering walk. After Lily swagger-walks away from the table, her other [white] friends engage Michelle [the black friend] in a conversation. Interestingly and humorously, the black friend does not engage in the black behaviors that Lily performs in interactions with her. In fact, the black friend is a doctoral student in psychology at Columbia University who begins to explain Lily's "raced" behaviors as "associative regression . . . [involving] neural pathways."

The media norm for whites to "act black" may appear harmless but it is not. These behaviors are harmful in several ways. First, they maintain the racist idea that all blacks behave in these stereotypical ways. These messages encourage negative interpersonal interactions with blacks by positing them as not speaking, dressing, and behaving in a mainstream manner. More important, these stereotyped messages about blacks affect their ability to find housing, employment (Pager & Shepherd, 2008) and to receive adequate health care (Dovidio et al., 2008).

Second, this media norm suggests to whites that this racist behavior ("acting black") is appropriate camaraderie and relationship-building behavior for interactions with blacks. Instead, these behaviors harm whites' relations with blacks. By "acting black," whites communicate their racist stereotypes of blacks. Thus, this parodying behavior is offensive to blacks. In each of the examples described above the black friend of the white character is offended and rejects them. For example, in *How I Met Your Mother*, the black friend explains Lily's behavior as pathological (i.e., associative regression). In short, white people "acting black" offends and alienates blacks.

The final harmful feature of this media norm about racial behavior is that other whites do not problematize the character's racist performances of "black" behavior. In only three of the nineteen instances of "acting black" did another white person directly reference the stereotypically black behavior. For example, Raymond says to his brother, "We're Italian, Robert, okay?" Reba tells her ex-husband's wife, Barbara Jean, "You're the whitest person in Texas. Stop talking like that." Charlie tells his nephew Jake, in *Two and a Half Men*, "You're a pasty white kid. Start acting like one." Other white characters discouraged the behavior on the basis that the individual is not black. However, they never mentioned "acting black" as inherently racist. Overall, by "acting black" whites contribute to the creation and maintenance of racism by perpetuating stereotypes about blacks and alienating them in such a manner that would deter cross-racial interaction and understanding.

DON'T APPEAR RACIST.   Another common norm is that media tells whites to engage in behaviors to not *appear* racist. That is, media demonstrates a range of behaviors whites do to avoid looking racist. For example, in an episode of *Roseanne* (a show about the life of a working-class family of two parents and three children), Roseanne discovers that her young son, DJ, does not want to kiss a girl in his school play because she is black. She tells her husband, Dan: "We've got to make him kiss her, or everybody will think we're racists." You might assume that in this first interaction with her husband about this that she would be concerned about her son, DJ, being a racist. As this incident illustrates, her concern is not to appear to others as racist. Throughout the episode there are several additional incidents in which appearing racist to others is Roseanne's major concern versus actually addressing or dealing with potential racism in her family. Roseanne is not alone in the racial behavior of not appearing racist. Dan tells Roseanne "I'm not a racist" despite defending and upholding DJ not wanting to kiss a black girl. Beyond telling Roseanne he is not a racist, he further tries to shake off the racist label in this interaction with his white male poker buddies:

> DAN [TO WHITE MALE POKER BUDDIES]:   You think I'm a bigot? . . .
>
> WHITE MALE POKER BUDDY: I probably would have felt the same way you did.
>
> DAN: That makes me feel better.

Rather than examine the behavior in question for its somewhat obvious racism, Dan defensively tells Roseanne he is not a racist. He is visibly relieved that he does not appear racist to his white male poker buddies. They, in fact, cosign his behavior by saying they would have done the same (racially problematic) behavior. In a later scene Roseanne and her sister, Jackie, are startled to see and then afraid to open their restaurant (a public business) door to a black man. They only let him in once he, ironically, identifies himself as the father of the little black girl DJ does not want to kiss. Jackie quickly says to him, "(We) didn't do that because you're African American." Instead of taking the time to critically examine their behavior, Jackie's immediate priority was to not appear racist.

Frasier chronicles the interactions of a pompous upper-class radio psychiatrist (Frasier) with his coworker Roz, fellow psychiatrist brother Niles, his live-in former cop dad (Martin), and the dad's nurse, Daphne. This show similarly engages in a range of behaviors to avoid appearing racist. In one episode, a black woman (Mary) is temporarily working as Frasier's radio show producer. Frasier encourages her to speak up on the show. Mary obliges but speaks up more than Frasier intends and likes. The exchange below occurs while Frasier is complaining to his family about Mary talking too much on his radio show:

> MARTIN [FRASIER'S DAD]:   I don't know what the big deal is. If she's talking too much, just tell her to shut her big bazoo.

> FRASIER: Oh really? How do you suggest I accomplish that without sounding like a complete bigot?

As with the *Roseanne* examples, Frasier does not want to sound like a racist. This norm is apparent in other exchanges in the same episode. That is, Frasier continues to be tortured by the idea that his behaviors toward the black woman might make him appear like he is a racist. Frasier denies to his friends and family that he modifies his behavior toward the black woman to keep from looking racist. However, the final few minutes of the episode hilariously confirm this as the motivation for his behavior. Frasier finally tells the black woman that she talks too much on his show:

> MARY [BLACK WOMAN]: I . . . I had no idea. Well why didn't you just say something before?
>
> FRASIER: [uncomfortable pause] Well, it's because you're black. And the truth is that I was afraid that if I said something critical of you, you might react the wrong way . . . and I just feel terrible about it.

Interestingly enough, in an earlier part of this episode Frasier mimics the black woman by behaving how he thinks she will respond if he asks her to stop talking so much on his radio show. His portrayal of her was indeed racist. Frasier used "black" slang, rolled his neck, and wagged his finger in the "sassy" manner black women are stereotyped as behaving. So while, his behaviors in the episode were racist, he spent the entire episode trying to not appear as such.

At first glance it may seem great that whites behave to not appear racist. It may seem reasonable that their behavior aims to reduce being mistaken for people who really are racist. Unfortunately, similar to the prior media behavior norm, this one is also harmful. Whites focused so much on not appearing racist that they were unable to address actual racism. For example, Frasier was so focused on not appearing racist that he could not see the problem with assuming that blacks are oversensitive and prone to conflict regarding race. He also could not see the inherent racism present in his stereotyped portrayal of black women. Similar to the characters described above, his concern with not being racist distracted his attention away from actual racism. Because of the shift in focus, the racism portrayed does not get analyzed or examined. The characters focus on how to not appear racist instead of reflecting upon how to not be racist. By doing so, they mask the problems of racism. Without critical examination and reflection upon their behaviors, whites will continue to create and maintain interpersonal and structural racism (e.g., relying and acting upon assumptions and stereotypes about blacks).

RACE TALK IS TABOO The final common media norm about racial behavior discussed in this chapter is that whites should not talk about race. That is, talking about race is taboo behavior. In many of the episodes, whites were obviously uncomfortable and did their best to avoid talking about race (or anything perceived as a race topic). *Seinfeld* was a show about the adventures of a neurotic middle-class comedian (Jerry) and his equally neurotic best friends (George, Elaine, and Kramer) all of whom lived in New York City. In an episode of *Seinfeld*, Jerry assumes Elaine's boyfriend Darryl is black. Elaine is not sure of Darryl's race and a line of questioning ensues between her and Jerry about it. George interrupts their discussion with his discomfort of race talk:

JERRY: I think he's black.

GEORGE: Should we be talkin' about this?

ELAINE: I think it's okay.

GEORGE: No, it isn't.

JERRY: Why not?

GEORGE: Well, it would be okay if Darryl [Elaine's boyfriend] was here.

JERRY: If he's black.

In the above exchange, George's stern and worrisome tone of speech communicates that he feels talking about race is inappropriate. In fact, everyone's discomfort with this race topic is comically evident when they rapidly and awkwardly empty their wallets to give a huge tip to their waitress, who is black.

In an episode of *Monk* (show about an obsessive compulsive middle-class detective and his working-class nurse Sharona), Adrian and Sharona do their best to avoid talking about race. Upon meeting a group of white people, Adrian shakes each of their hands. A black man walks up and is also introduced to Adrian, who shakes his hand. However, after shaking the black man's hand, Sharona passes a wet wipe to Adrian who uses it to anxiously clean his hands. Hilarity ensures as both the newly introduced whites and black man assume that Adrian Monk is a racist who does not want to touch blacks:

WHITE WOMAN: We're all just people, Mr. Monk.

ADRIAN MONK: Of course we are. I . . . I [nervous stuttering] . . . [pauses uncomfortably] I always have to [another awkward pause] . . . I'm not [pause seemingly due to uncertainty about what to say] . . .

SHARONA: Oh, no. He's not.

What the whites and the black man do not know is that Adrian is a germaphobe. That is, he is afraid of touching anything and anyone out of extreme fear of contracting germs. Sharona was fumbling in her bag all along looking for wet wipes for Adrian to clean his hands after he shook the whites' hands. It was comical timing that she did not find nor give him the wipe until after he shook the black man's hand. Adrian is mortified that these individuals perceived him as a racist, however, he avoids talking about race. This is what this dialogue should have looked like:

WHITE WOMAN: We're all just people, Mr. Monk.

ADRIAN MONK: Of course we are. I am not *a racist*.

SHARONA: Oh, no. He's not *a racist*.

In this incident, talking about race is essential. However, both Adrian and Sharona avoid it by omitting the word "race" or "racist." Throughout the episode, these whites treat Adrian negatively as a result of his interaction with the black man. Though Adrian and Sharona do their best to address the seemingly racist incident, they continue to avoid talking about race by using words like "rainbow":

ADRIAN MONK: Yes, ma'am. I [nervous stuttering] . . . I'm a big rainbow guy.

SHARONA: [enthusiastically agrees] He loves rainbows.

In the above dialogue, Adrian and Sharona continue to deny racism, but since talking about race is taboo, they instead use code words to talk about race.

In a final example from *Roseanne*, Roseanne's husband Dan and his white poker buddies are having a typical "locker room" type of exchange. However, their behavior makes it clear that this raced conversation is different and taboo:

WHITE MALE POKER BUDDY 1:   Any of you guys ever been with a black woman?

WHITE MALE POKER BUDDY 2:   [leans forward conspiratorially and talks in a quiet voice] Well, there was this one girl in Atlantic City. One time. Looked just like that nurse used to be on television, you know, that Julia? I mean, this girl had legs that went on forever—[black male walks in]

WHITE MALE POKER BUDDY 3:   [quickly interrupts and cuts off white male 2's story] Hey, Chuck.

ALL THREE WHITE MALE POKER BUDDIES: [nervously] Chuck. Hey. Chuck. Hey.

BLACK MALE POKER BUDDY [CHUCK]:   So, go on . . . legs that go on for ever and ever.

WHITE MALE POKER BUDDY 2:   [looks around nervously] She was a very lovely woman, and we had a very nice time.

BLACK MALE POKER BUDDY: You're a wild man, Marvin.

The only difference between their normal locker room talk and the above exchange is that they were talking about a black woman. The way the white men leaned forward and spoke in quiet voices illustrated that race is a taboo topic. This taboo topic was immediately cut off once the black man (Chuck) entered the room. The black man goaded them to continue the delectable woman story. Instead the white men shared cues (e.g., interrupting one another, nervous shifting in their seats, editing the story content) that this topic was not okay and they would not continue to talk about race.

The above examples demonstrate that for whites talking about race is taboo in their interactions with each other and with blacks. From explicitly asking if this is an appropriate topic to nervousness to avoidance of the words "racism" or "racist" when obviously necessary, talking about race is a taboo topic resulting in discomfort for whites.

This media norm to avoid race talk is problematic. As the research mentioned earlier suggests, we are not living in a postracial society (Metzler, 2008). Whites are still segregated from other racial groups and racial minorities suffer inequality in all aspects of life. Unfortunately, racism cannot be acknowledged nor addressed if there is a taboo against talking about race. Instead of discussing race openly, whites experience discomfort and sweep the issue under the rug. Surprisingly, this occurs not merely in cross-race interactions but also in all white settings. If whites cannot talk among themselves to develop an understanding of and to develop allied strategies to reduce racism, racial oppression will persist in U.S. society. Thus, this media message norming race talk as taboo behavior is harmful.

Summary

The systematic and exploratory analyses of primetime situation comedies reveal several norms about white racial behavior. The dominant mass media norm is that cross-racial interactions regarding and with blacks do not occur. However, there are rare instances in which these racial behaviors do occur. In these instances, the media norms are that it is common and expected for whites to behave by "acting black," not appearing racist, and avoiding talking about race. Presenting these norms using humor can help make them visible and thus available for discussion and challenge. At the same time, we must be careful to not view the norms themselves as funny. This is important because, to reiterate briefly, these media norms perpetuate racial segregation, encourage unchallenged racist performances, and obscure racism through a focus on appearances and a taboo on discussing it.

These findings are important in the context of prior research that identifies the negative and stereotypical messages the mass media presents about blacks as well the influence of these messages on whites' racial attitudes, feelings, and policy preferences (Dixon, 2009). This research fills a gap and complements these works by focusing explicitly on media's norms about racial behaviors. In doing so, these findings present a fuller picture of how racial oppression is created and maintained via racial behaviors. In fact, the media messages communicated by these primetime television situation comedies did indeed promote norms of white behavior that promote racial oppression.

These media messages are important given research on norms and behavior. Social norms are an important determinant of individual behavior (Cialdini & Trost, 1998; La Piere, 1934), including racial behaviors. For example, Fendrich (1967) notes that norms influenced whites' 1) avoidance of blacks, 2) being photographed with a black person, and 3) participation in race riots against blacks. Norms were also predictive of how whites reacted to hostile jokes about racial minorities (Crandall, Eshelman, & O'Brien, 2002). One of my studies (Pittman, 2008) demonstrates that norms were related to whites' willingness to engage in behaviors that challenged racial oppression and promoted racial equality. Another study (Pittman, 2010) revealed that whites report that norms influence their 1) antiracist, 2) racist, and 3) race-avoidant behaviors. These works show that the media role in positing norms is an important factor for understanding racial behaviors and racial oppression.

In summary, media's messages about whites' racial behavior are powerful, given the 1) influence of the media, 2) strength of norms in novel situations, and 3) relationship between norms and racial behavior. The media delivers social norms that encourage behaviors that create and maintain racial oppression.

POTENTIAL SOLUTIONS?

To counter the media's influence on whites' racial behavior individuals must develop media literacy. As a superpeer, mass media's messages are far reaching and influential (Anderson & Bushman, 2001; Gray, 2008; McQuail, 1985; Strasburger &

Strasburger & Kadin, 1995). This is particularly true of media messages about novel situations or those with which individuals have little or no personal experience (Crano & Prislin, 2008; Gray, 2008; Sherif, 1937). As such, individuals must become savvy consumers of mass media to offset its normative power at perpetuating behaviors that contribute to racial oppression. Media literacy aims to develop an individual's critical thinking skills in relation to media (Feuerstein, 1999). Specifically, advocates of media literacy (Feuerstein, 1999; Kellner & Share, 2005; Lind, 2013; Livingstone, 2004) believe that individuals should be aware that the mass media communicates messages. This awareness should result in asking the following questions about media messages: Is this message valid? What are the implications of this message? What does this message mean? An individual's reflection upon the answers to these questions should guide resulting behaviors in relation to the media message. In the context of this chapter, media literacy might result in whites thinking critically about media that portrays racial segregation versus accepting it as normal. Media literacy skills might also encourage the type of thinking necessary to recognize "acting black" as a behavior that leads to racial distance versus camaraderie.

Additionally, the power of the media could be used to develop interventions that use norms to reduce racially oppressive behaviors and increase those that promote racial equality. The *Rock the Vote* (www.rockthevote.org/) and *Vote or Die* ad campaigns both encouraged young people to vote in U.S. elections. More recently, *Changing the Game* (sports.glsen.org/game-changers/nba-glsen-and-ad-councils-official-think-b4-you-speak-psa/) launched an ad campaign to discourage homophobic behaviors. In one scene of the ad, an athlete uses a gay slur to "trash talk" with another athlete. The use of this slur is responded to negatively by every athlete in the ad. In doing so, the ad identified specific homophobic behaviors as unacceptable and antihomophobic behaviors as cool. Thus, this ad campaign used the media to communicate and create social norms for particular behaviors. Indeed, there is a body of evidence that demonstrates that this social norm strategy is an effective mechanism for influencing both experimental and real-world behaviors and attitudes (Beatty, Syzdek, & Bakkum, 2006; Beaudoin & Thorson, 2007; Beeghley, Bock, & Cochran, 1990; Chernoff & Davison, 2005; Donovan & Lievans, 1993; Slater, Lawrence, & Comello, 2009). Despite the effectiveness of norms for producing behavior, they have not been fully examined as a media strategy for reducing (versus maintaining) racial oppression. In the context of this chapter, if the media showed more whites challenging other whites for "acting black" it could create a norm for this antiracist behavior. Media images with whites talking about race can contribute to a norm where having racial discussions is both common and expected. Changes of these sorts in racial behavior could have an impact on reducing racial oppression.

Finally, a critical piece of the socialization process is who gets to socialize and to whose norms (Fiske, 2011). People of color are underrepresented in media ownership, production, and performers (Campbell, 2005; Gray, 2008; Hunt, 2005; Larson, 2006). This limits their ability to influence the messages and norms in media portrayals of people of color and related racial behaviors. Increasing the representations of people of color in all aspects of mass media may lessen problematic and increase useful norms to produce racial behaviors that reduce racial oppression.

Conclusion

Individuals in the United States watch an average of five hours of television every day (www.nielsen.com; Roberts, Foehr, & Rideout, 2005). While this could be viewed as a simple leisure activity, television watching is so much more. As discussed, the mass media both contributes to our views of the world and guides our behaviors in it. This chapter asked: What is the constructed reality mass media presents about race? How are individuals encouraged to interpret and, more important, act regarding race? The analyses revealed that the mass media constructs a reality in which whites segregate from blacks such that cross-race interaction is novel. The mass media encourages white individuals to engage in behavior that mocks, avoids, and occludes racial oppression. The common thread of these media norms is that whites are discouraged from analyzing or examining racism. As such, the answers to these questions are troubling in that the media promotes white racial behaviors that maintain racial oppression.

References

Anderson, C. A., & Bushman, B. J. (2001). Effects of violent games on aggressive behavior, aggressive cognition, aggressive affect, physiological arousal, and prosocial behavior: A meta-analytic review of the scientific literature. *Psychological Science, 12,* 353–358.

Ajzen, I. (1991). The theory of planned behavior. *Organizational Behavior and Human Decision Processes, 50,* 179–211.

Ball-Rokeach, S. J., & DeFleur, M. L. (1976). A dependency model of mass-media effects *Communication Research, 3*(1), 3–21.

Ball-Rokeach, S. J., Grube, J. W., & Rokeach, M. (1981). "Roots: The next generation"—Who watched and with what effect? *Public Opinion Quarterly, 45*(1), 58–68.

Bandura, A., & Walters, R. H. (1963). *Social learning and personality development.* New York, NY: Holt, Rinehart & Winston.

Beaudoin, C. E., & Thorson, E. (2007). Evaluating the effects of a youth health media campaign. *Journal of Health Communication, 12*(5), 439–454.

Busselle, R., & Crandall, H. (2002). Television viewing and perceptions about race differences in socioeconomic success. *Journal of Broadcasting and Electronic Media, 46*(2), 265–282.

Butsch, R. (2011). Ralph, Fred, Archie, and Homer: Why television keeps recreating the white male working-class buffoon. In G. Dines & J. M. Humez (Eds.), *Gender, race, and class in media: A critical reader* (3rd ed., pp. 101–109). Thousand Oaks, CA: Sage.

Campbell, C. P. (2005). A myth of assimilation: "Enlightened" racism and the news. In D. M. Hunt (Ed.), *Channeling blackness: Studies on television and race in America* (pp. 137–153). New York, NY: Oxford University Press.

Cialdini, R. B., & Trost, M. R. (1998). Social influence: Social norms, conformity, and compliance. In D. Gilbert, S. Fiske, & G. Lindzey (Eds.), *The handbook of social psychology* (pp. 151–192). New York, NY: McGraw-Hill.

Chen, C. H. (2013). "Outwhiting the Whites": An examination of the persistence of Asian American model minority discourse. In R. Lind (Ed.), *Race/gender/class/media 3.0: Considering diversity across audiences, content, and producers* (pp. 148–154). Upper Saddle River, NJ: Pearson.

Cooley, C. H. (1983). *Social organization: A study of the larger mind.* New Brunswick, NJ: Transaction.

Crandall, C., Eshleman, A., & O'Brien, L. (2002). Social norms and the expression and suppression of prejudice: The struggle for internalization. *Journal of Personality and Social Psychology, 82,* 359–378.

Crano, W. D., & Prislin, R. (2008). *Attitudes and attitude change.* New York, NY: Psychology Press.

Dalton, M. A., Sargent, J. D., Beach, M. L., Titus-Ernstoff, L., Gibson, J. J., Ahrens, M. B., Tickle, J., & Heatherton, T. F. (2003). Effect of viewing smoking in movies on adolescent smoking initiation: a cohort study. *Lancet, 362*(9380), 281–285.

DeNavas-Walt, C., Proctor, B. D., & Smith, J. C. (2010). *U.S. Census Bureau, current population reports, P60–238, income, poverty, and health insurance coverage in the United States: 2009,* Washington, DC: U.S. Government Printing Office.

Deutsch, M., & Gerard, H. B. (1955). A study of normative and informational social influence upon individual judgment. *Journal of Abnormal and Social Psychology, 51,* 629–636.

Dixon, T. L. (2008). Network news and racial beliefs: Exploring the connection between national television news exposure and stereotypical perceptions of African Americans. *Journal of Communication, 58*(2), 321–337.

Dixon, T. L. (2009). "He was a Black guy": How news' misrepresentation of crime creates fear of Blacks. In R. A. Lind (Ed.), *Race/gender/media: Considering diversity across audiences, content, and producers* (2nd ed., pp. 24–29). Boston, MA: Pearson Education.

Dixon, T. L., & Linz, D. (2000). Overrepresentation and underrepresentation of African Americans and Latinos as lawbreakers on television news. *Journal of Communication, 50*(2), 131–154.

Domke (2001). Racial cues and political ideology: An examination of associative priming. *Communication Research, 28*(6), 772–801.

Domke, D., McCoy, K., & Torres, M. (1999). News media, racial perceptions, and political cognition. *Communication Research, 26*(5), 570–607.

Donovan, R. J., & Lievans, S. (1993). Using paid advertising to modify racial stereotype beliefs. *Public Opinion Quarterly, 57*(2), 205–218.

Dovidio, J., Penner, L., Albrecht, T., Norton, W., Gaertner, S., & Shelton, J. (2003). Disparities and distrust: The implications of psychological processes for understanding racial disparities in health and health care. *Social Science & Medicine, 678,* 478–486.

Downing, J., & Husband, C. (2005) *Representing 'race': Racisms, ethnicities and media.* London, UK: Sage.

Entman, R. M. (1989). How the media affects what people think: An information processing approach. *Journal of Politics, 51,* 347–370.

Entman, R. M., & Rojecki, A. (2000). *The Black image in the White mind: Media and race in America.* Chicago, IL: University of Chicago Press.

Essed, P. (1991). *Understanding everyday racism: An interdisciplinary theory.* Newbury Park, CA: Sage.

Feagin, J. (2006). *Systemic racism: A theory of oppression.* New York, NY: Routledge.

Federal Bureau of Investigation. (2012). *Hate crime statistics, 2011.* Retrieved from http://www.fbi.gov/news/stories/2012/december/annual-hate-crimes-report-released/annual-hate-crimes-report-released

Fendrich, J. M. (1967). Perceived reference group support: Racial attitudes and overt behavior. *American Sociological Review, 32,* 960–970.

Feuerstein, M. (1999). Media literacy in support of critical thinking. *Journal of Education Media, 24*(1), 43–55.

Festinger, L. (1954). A theory of social comparison processes. *Human Relations, 7,* 117–140.

Fiske, J. (2011). *Television culture* (2nd ed.). New York, NY: Routledge.

Frey, W. H. (2011). Brookings Institution and University of Michigan Social Science Data Analysis Network's analysis of 1990, 2000, and 2010 Census Decennial Census tract data. Retrieved from http://www.psc.isr.umich.edu/dis/census/segregation2010.html and http://censusscope.org/2010Census/

Gamson, W. A., Croteau, D., Hoynes, W., & Sasson, T. (1992). Media images and the social construction of reality. *Annual Review of Sociology, 18,* 373–393.

Gerber, G. (1999). Cultivation analysis: An overview. *Mass Communication & Society. 1*(3/4), 175–194.

Gerbner, G., Gross, L., Morgan, M., & Signorielli, N. (1986). Living with television: The dynamics of the cultivation process. In J. Bryant & D. Zillman (Eds.), *Perspectives on media effects* (pp. 17–40). Hilldale, NJ: Lawrence Erlbaum Associates.

Gilliam, F. D. (1999). The "welfare queen" experiment. *Nieman Reports, 53*(2), 49–53.

Gilliam, F. D., & Iyengar, S. (2000). Prime suspects: The impact of local television news on the viewing public. *American Journal of Political Science, 44*(3), 560–573.

Gilliam, F. D., Nicholas, V., & Beckmann, M. (2003). Where you live and what you watch: The impact of racial proximity and local television news on attitudes about race and crime. *Political Research Quarterly, 55*(4), 755–780.

Goffman, E. (1959). *The presentation of self in everyday life.* New York, NY: Doubleday.

Gorham, B. W. (1999). Stereotypes in the media: So what? *Howard Journal of Communications, 10*(4), 229–247.

Gray, J. (2008). *Television entertainment.* New York, NY: Routledge.

Gurin, P., Dey, E., Hurtado, S., & Gurin, G. (2002). Diversity and higher education: Theory and impact on educational outcomes. *Harvard Educational Review, 72*(3), 330–366.

Haney, C., Banks, C., & Zimbardo, P. (1973). Interpersonal dynamics in a simulated prison. *International Journal of Criminology & Penology, 1*(1), 69–97.

Hennesey, M., Bleakley, A., Fishbein, M., & Jordan, A. (2009). Estimating the longitudinal association between adolescent sexual behavior and exposure to sexual media content. *Journal of Sex Research, 46*(6), 586–596.

Herring, C. (2009). Does diversity pay?: Race, gender, and the business case for diversity. *American Sociological Review, 74*(2), 208–224.

Holtzman, L. (2000). *Media messages: What film, television, and popular music teach us about race, class, gender, and sexual orientation.* New York, NY: Sharpe.

Holz, J. R., & Wright, C. R. (1979). Sociology of mass communications. *Annual Review of Sociology, 5,* 193–217.

Hunt, D. M. (2005). *Channeling blackness: Studies on television and race in America.* New York, NY: Oxford University Press.

Iyengar, S., & Kinder, D. R. (1978). *News that matters.* Chicago, IL: University of Chicago Press.

Jhally, S., & Lewis, J. (1992). *Enlightened racism: The Cosby show, audiences and the myth of the American dream.* Boulder, CO: Westview Press.

Kellner, D., & Share, J. (2005). Toward critical media literacy: Core concepts, debates, organizations and policy. *Discourse: Studies in the Cultural Politics of Education, 26*(3), 369–386.

Kraus, S. J. (1995). Attitudes and the prediction of behavior: A meta-analysis of the empirical literature. *Personality and Social Psychology Bulletin, 21,* 58–76.

LaPiere, R. T. (1934). Attitudes versus actions. *Social Forces, 13,* 230–237.

Lichter, D. T., Parisi, D., Grice, S. M., & Taquino, M. C. (2007). National estimates of racial segregation in rural and small-town America. *Demography, 44*(3), 563–581.

Lind, R. A. (2013). *Race/gender/class/media 3.0: Considering diversity across audiences, content, and producers.* Upper Saddle River, NJ: Pearson.

Lippmann, (1922). *Public opinion.* New York, NY: Harcourt, Brace.

Livingstone, S. (2004). Media literacy and the challenge of new information and communication technologies. *Communication Review, 7*(1), 3–14.

Logan, J. R., Stults, B. J., & Farley, R. (2004). Segregation of minorities in the metropolis: Two decades of change. *Demography, 41*(1), 1–22.

Luhby, T. (2012, June 21). Worsening wealth inequality by race. *CNN Money.* Retrieved from http://money.cnn.com/2012/06/21/news/economy/wealth-gap-race/index.htm

Massey, D. (2005). Racial discrimination in housing: A moving target. *Social Problems, 52*(2), 148–151.

Mastro, D., Lapinski, M., Kopacz, M., & Behm-Morawitz, E. (2009). The influence of exposure to depictions of race and crime in TV news on viewer's social judgments. *Journal of Broadcasting & Electronic Media, 53,* 615–635.

Mathews T. J., & MacDorman, M. F. (2011). Infant mortality statistics from the 2007 period linked birth/infant death data set. *National Vital Statistics Report, 59*(6), 1–30.

McQuail, D. (1985). Sociology of mass communication. *Annual Review of Sociology, 11,* 93–111.

Mead, G. H. (1934). *Mind, self, and society.* Chicago, IL: University of Chicago Press.

Metzler, C. J. (2008). *The construction and rearticulation of race in a post-racial America.* Bloomington, IN: AuthorHouse.

Miller, A., & Ross, S. D. (2004). They are not us: Framing of American Indians by the Boston Globe. *Howard Journal of Communications, 15,* 245–259.

National Conference of State Legislatures. (2012). Disparities in health. Retrieved from http://www.ncsl.org/research/health/health-disparities-overview.aspx

Nielsen. (n.d.). Reports and top tens and trends. Retrieved from http://www.nielsen.com/us/en/reports.html and http://www.nielsen.com/us/en/top10s.html

Oliver, M. B., & Fonash, D. (2002). Race and crime in the news: Whites' identification and misidentification of criminal suspects. *Media Psychology, 4,* 137–156.

Pager, D., & Shepherd, H. (2008). The sociology of discrimination: Racial discrimination in employment, housing, credit, and consumer markets. *Annual Review of Sociology, 34,* 181–209.

Paik, H., & Comstock, G. (1994). The effects of television violence on antisocial behavior: A meta-analysis. *Communication Research, 21,* 516–546.

Park, S. Y., Yun, G. W., McSweeney, J. H., & Gunther, A. C. (2007). Do third-person perceptions of media influence contribute to pluralistic ignorance on the norm of ideal female thinness? *Sex Roles, 57*(7–8), 569–578.

Pidgeon, N. F., Kasperson, R. E., & Slovic, P. (2003). *The social amplification of risk.* New York, NY: Cambridge University Press.

Pittman, C. (2008). The relationship between social influence and social justice behaviors. *Current Issues in Social Psychology, 13*(20), 243–254.

Pittman, C. (2010). Moving from attitudes to behavior: Using social influence to understand interpersonal racial oppression. In G. Cassano, & R. Dello Buono (Eds.), *Crisis, politics, and critical sociology* (pp. 143–160). Boston, MA: Brill.

Ramasubramanian, S. (2010). Television viewing, racial attitudes, and policy preferences: Exploring the role of social identity and intergroup emotions in influencing support for affirmative action. *Communication Monographs, 77*(1), 102–120.

Ramasubramanian, S. (2011a). Television exposure, model minority portrayals, and Asian-American stereotypes: An exploratory study. *Journal of Intercultural Communication*. Retrieved from http://www.immi.se/intercultural/nr26/ramasubramanian.htm

Ramasubramanian, S. (2011b). The impact of stereotypical versus counterstereotypical media exemplars on racial attitudes, causal attributions, and support for affirmative action. *Communication Research, 38*, 497–516.

Rink, F., & Ellemers, N. (2010). Benefiting from deep-level diversity: How congruence between knowledge and decision rules improves team decision making and team perceptions. *Group Processes & Intergroup Relations, 13*(3), 345–359.

Roberts, D. F., Foehr, U. G., & Rideout, V. (2005). Generation M: Media in the lives of 8–18 year-olds. *Kaiser Family Foundation Report*. Retrieved from http://kff.org/other/event/generation-m-media-in-the-lives-of/

Ross, K. (2009). *Gendered media: Women, men and identity politics*. Lanham, MD: Rowman & Littlefield.

Russell, L. (2010, December 16). Fact sheet: Health disparities by race and ethnicity. Center for American Progress. Retrieved from http://www.americanprogress.org/issues/healthcare/news/2010/12/16/8762/fact-sheet-health-disparities-by-race-and-ethnicity/

Schuman, H., & Johnson, M. P. (1976). Attitudes and behaviors. *Annual Review of Sociology, 2*, 161–207.

Sherif, M. (1937). An experimental approach to the study of attitudes. *Sociometry, 1*(1/2), 90–98.

Slater, M. D., Lawrence, F., & Comello, M. L. (2009). Media influence on alcohol-control policy support in the U.S. adult population: The intervening role of issue concern and risk judgments. *Journal of Health Communication, 14*(3), 262–275.

Strasburger, V. C., & Kadin, A. E. (Eds.) (1995). *Adolescents and the media*. Thousand Oaks, CA: Sage.

Surlin, S. H. (1978). Roots research: A summary of the findings. *Journal of Broadcasting, 22*(3), 309–320.

West, C., & Fenstermaker, S. (1995). Doing difference. *Gender & Society, 9*(1), 8–37.

Wilkes, R., & Iceland, J. (2004). Hypersegregation in the twenty-first century. *Demography, 41*(1), 23–36.

Wirth, W., & Schramm, H. (2005). Mass media and emotions. *Communication Research Trends, 24*(3), 3–39.

Yanovitzky, I. (2002). Effect of news coverage on the prevalence of drunk-driving behavior: Evidence from a longitudinal study. *Journal of Studies on Alcohol, 63*, 342–351.

Appendix

- Roseanne, Season 7, Episode 9, "White Men Can't Kiss," aired Wednesday, November 16, 1994
- Seinfeld, Season 9, Episode 15, "The Wizard," aired February 26, 1998
- Everybody Loves Raymond, Season 3, Episode 15, "Robert's Date," aired February 1, 1999
- Frasier, Season 7, Episode 16, "Something About Dr. Mary," aired February 17, 2000
- Monk, Season 1, Episode 8, "Monk and the Marathon Man," aired September 13, 2002
- Reba, Season 5, Episode 5, "No Good Deed," aired October 14, 2005
- How I Met Your Mother, Season 2, Episode 10, "Single Stamina," aired November 27, 2006
- Two and a Half Men, Season 4, Episode 17, "All I Did Was Sleep with a Commie," aired February 26, 2007
- How I Met Your Mother, Season 3, Episode 16, "Sandcastles in the Sand," aired April 21, 2008

14

Patriarchy.Com

Adult Internet Pornography and the Abuse of Women*

Walter S. DeKeseredy

INTRODUCTION

> Technology is occupying an increasingly important role in everybody's life, regardless of ethnicity, social status, gender, preferences, nationality, and even technology literacy or Internet connectivity. (Vargas Martin, Garcia-Ruiz, & Edwards, 2011, p. xxi)

For those who can afford them, information technologies, such as the Internet and the iPhone 5, are part-and-parcel of many people's daily lives. There are pluses and minuses associated with such new means of communication. Some positive features are: keeping in touch visually and verbally with friends and relatives in other countries without paying long-distance telephone fees, quick access to scholarly sources on websites, and listening to international radio stations. On the other hand, scores of people, especially those who work for government agencies and large corporations, view their BlackBerry or iPhone, as a leash. This is because they can be contacted "24/7" by their managers or bosses. Additionally, numerous communications devices are equipped with geographical positioning systems (GPS) that enable employers to monitor their staff's whereabouts. Note, too, that college professors are inundated with e-mail and find it stressful keeping up with it.

Not everyone experiences the same technology-related problems, and some troubles are more harmful to certain groups of people than are others. One obvious one is Internet child pornography. Large numbers of people, mostly men, consume and share electronic depictions of the sexual abuse of children. For example, the UN Report of the Special Rapporteur on the sale of children, child prostitution, and child pornography states there are close to 500,000 sites dedicated to child pornography around the world, and most

*I would like to thank Raquel Kennedy Bergen, Molly Dragiewicz, Louise Moyer, Claire Renzetti, and Martin D. Schwartz for their helpful comments.

are used for commercial purposes (Ibrahim, 2011). Nevertheless, there is widespread outrage and anger about Internet child pornography, which is why some criminologists define it, like murder and robbery, as a *consensus crime* (DeKeseredy, Ellis, & Alvi, 2005; Hagan, 1994). This means that members of all or most social groups share norms and values that call for legally prohibiting the production and consumption of child pornography, and they want to impose the most severe penalties on those who engage in these behaviors. Criminal justice officials are responsive to these norms and values because arrests and prosecution for child pornography possession and production in the United States have substantially increased over the past few years. In fact, arrests for child pornography production more than doubled from 402 in 2000–2001 to 859 in 2006 (Wolak, Finkelhor, Mitchell, & Jones, 2011).

Societal reactions are not as punitive when it comes to the "pornification" of women once they turn 18 years old (Nikunen, Paasonen, & Saarenmaa, 2007). Thousands of legal cyberporn sites "childify" adult women and typing "teen porn" into Google generates over nine million hits, giving users a choice of thousands of sites (Dines, 2010). There are also thousands of sites explicitly featuring adult women being degraded and abused. Actually, a common feature of new pornographic videos is painful anal penetration, as well as men slapping or choking women or pulling hair while they penetrate them orally, vaginally, and anally (Bridges, Wosnitzer, Scharrer, Sun, & Liberman, 2010; Dines & Jensen, 2008).

Most people's idea of pornography resembles what is depicted in *Playboy Magazine* centerfolds (Dines, 2010). However, the reality is that we now live in a post-*Playboy* world (Jensen, 2007), where Internet pornography has become normalized or mainstreamed (Jensen & Dines, 1998), despite becoming increasingly more violent and racist (DeKeseredy, 2011a). For instance, Doghouse Digital is a company that produced the film *Black Bros and White Ho's*, which offers stereotypical images of "the sexually primitive black male stud" (Jensen, 2007, p. 66). Another example is the interracial film *Blacks on Blondes*, which features a white man in a cage watching black men have sex with his wife (Dines, 2006).

Black men and women are by no means the only people to be racially exploited by pornographers. There is, as pointed out by Dines (2010) and other leading experts in the field (e.g., Jensen, 2007), much consumer demand for "hot blooded Latinas," "submissive Far East nymphos," and middle-eastern women. Most, if not all, anti-pornography feminists would agree with Dines' claim that, "Irrespective of the ethnic group, the framing of the narrative is exactly the same—the women's race makes them that bit sluttier than 'regular,' white porn women" (p. 131).

Lower-class rural people, too, are routinely stereotyped in pornography. The rural women featured in thousands of pornographic websites typically have large breasts, wear halter tops and frayed denim short-shorts, and are usually portrayed as farmers' daughters. As well, similar to characters in scores of rural horror movies (e.g., *The Hills Have Eyes*), rural people featured in cyberporn comics are often characterized as inbreds or "hicks." Actually, incest is a common theme that runs throughout numerous rural farm girl porn cartoon sites. One prime example is Jab Comix's cartoon *Real Hicks Get Naughty*, which depicts a nephew having sexual intercourse with his aunt and then having anal sex with his sister. Furthermore, the characters generally have stereotypical southern Appalachian names that imply they are illiterate, like Jezebel, Boo, Clem, and Luke (DeKeseredy, Muzzatti, & Donnermeyer, 2012).

Different forms of oppression intersect in pornography. The main objective of this chapter, then, is threefold: (1) to offer a brief description of the current state of the Internet pornography industry, (2) to examine sociological empirical and theoretical work on the linkage between heterosexual adult Internet pornography and woman abuse, and (3) to suggest feminist means of reducing much pain and suffering caused by the "dark side" of new information technologies. First, though, it is necessary to define pornography.

WHAT IS PORNOGRAPHY?

The term *pornography* translates from Greek to mean "writing about prostitutes" (Katz, 2006, p. 188). Women's bodies are at the forefront of heterosexual Internet and other types of pornography, which is not surprising in a male-dominated culture. Although many women consume adult pornography, it is created primarily for generating sexual arousal in heterosexual men (Bridges & Jensen, 2011). Nevertheless, defining adult pornography is subject to much debate. Those who produce it, consume it, or oppose prohibiting it typically refer to harmful, sexually explicit material as erotica (DeKeseredy & Olsson, 2011). But there is a major difference between erotica and adult pornography. Erotica refers to "sexually suggestive or arousing material that is free of sexism, racism, and homophobia and is respectful of all human beings and animals portrayed" (Russell, 1993, p. 3). On the other hand, in adult pornography, women are sexually objected, portrayed as sexual slaves to men, routinely verbally abused, and are physically assaulted in ways that few of us could possibly imagine (Longino, 1980).

Pornography hurts women, as well as men (Katz, 2006). Also, from the standpoint of many feminist scholars (e.g., DeKeseredy, 2009; Dworkin, 2004), pornography, regardless of whether it appears on the Internet, on television, in literature, or in other media is also a variant of hate-motivated violence. As stated previously, what men and boys watch on adult pornographic Internet sites are not simply "dirty pictures that have little impact on anyone" (Funk, 2006, p. 165). Rather, the images typically endorse "women as second-class citizens" and "require that women be seen as second-class citizens" (Funk, 2006, p. 165). Consider what Gail Dines (2010) discovered while studying cyberporn:

> A few more clicks and I was at GagFactor.com owned by JM Productions, a much-talked-about site in the porn trade magazines. When I clicked on it I was invited to "Join us now to Access Complete Degradation." On the site there are hundreds of pictures of young women with penises thrust deep into their throat. Some are gagging, others crying, and virtually all have faces, especially their eyes covered in semen. The user is bombarded with images of mascara running, hair being pulled, throats in a vicelike grip, nostrils being pinched so the women can't breath as the penis fills the mouth, and mouths that are distended by either hands pulling the lips apart or penises inserted sideways.

What makes Dines' observation even more disturbing is that there is a huge market for these images. Moreover, there is ample evidence supporting the claim that men who do not consume pornography in our society are atypical. Every second, over 28,258 Internet users view pornography (DeKeseredy & Olsson, 2011; Zerbisias, 2008), and the vast majority of them are men and boys. Indeed, cyberporn is big business and has moved "from the backstreet to Wall Street" (Dines, 2010, p. 47).

THE PORNOGRAPHY INDUSTRY

As difficult as it is to believe, pornography is, in large part, responsible for giant advances in communication technology (Dines & Jensen, 2008). The Internet would not have grown so quickly without pornography, and the popular news channel CNN would have great difficulties broadcasting news clips without the video streaming software developed for pornography sites (Barss, 2010). Pornography, too, is the chief catalyst behind "tweeting" and DVD technology (Hauch, 2011). Moreover, large numbers of people watch sexual images at home by themselves, and this market started to drive the home entertainment industry (Jordan, 2006). Internet pornography has eliminated more traditional means of distributing and consuming degrading images of people. For example, in 2000, a man referred to as the Smut Peddler reported that he used to sell about 100 VHS pornographic tapes to fraternities per year, but after 15 years in the business, he witnessed a dramatic decline in sales due to Internet viewing (Claus, 2000). Twelve years later, it is logical to assume that this man has probably pursued another career because of Internet technology, which provides fraternity brothers easy and constant accessibility that cannot be offered by the Smut Peddler (Dines & Jensen, 2008).

It cannot be emphasized enough, however, that the relationship between sex and technology is not new. As Attwood (2010) puts it, "technologies have always been adapted for sexual purposes, and it is regularly claimed that sex drives technological development" (p. 8). Still, what modern technologies do today is allow for pornography consumption to be part of what Attwood refers to as a "multitasking mode" involving users moving between "socializing, buying commodities and searching information, chatting, peeping, cruising, masturbating, and maintaining friendships" (Jacobs, 2004, p. 45). As well, webcam technologies enable a very large but unknown number of amateur performers to produce their own pornography at home and to profit from downloads of their videos. Consider that amateurs who post their material on XTube (an Internet site that allows users to share cyberporn with one another) receive 50% of the net profit for every download of their videos or photosets (Mowlabocus, 2010).

There are over four million pornography sites on the Internet (Dines, 2010), with as many as 10,000 added every week (DeKeseredy & Olsson, 2011; Funk, 2006). Hence, worldwide pornography revenues from a variety of sources (e.g., Internet, sex shops, and hotel rooms) recently topped $97 billion. This is more than the revenues of these famous technology companies combined: Microsoft, Google, Amazon, eBay, Yahoo!, Apple, Netflix, and EarthLink (Zerbisias, 2008). What Schwartz and DeKeseredy (1997) stated 15 years ago still holds true today: rare are men who are not exposed to pornographic images. Even if people go out of their way to avoid pornography, it frequently pops up on people's monitors while they are working or surfing the web for information that has nothing to do with sex (Dines & Jensen, 2008).

More recent evidence of the growth of pornography is the emergence of "tubes," video sites such as YouPorn, XTube, and PornoTube, all based on the widely used and popular YouTube paradigm. YouPorn had 15 million users after launching in 2006 and was growing at a monthly rate of 37.5% (DeKeseredy, In press; Mowlabocus, 2010). Undoubtedly, cyberporn is "the quietest big business in the world" (Slayden, 2010, p. 57).

Pornography consumption is a widespread problem that is intensifying every day because of easy access offered by the Internet and devices such as the iPhone and iPad. Take into account that:

- Every second, $89.00 is spent on cyberporn.
- "Sex" is the most searched word on the Internet.
- Thirty-five percent of all Internet downloads are pornographic. (Slayden, 2010, p. 54)

Regardless of whether researchers ever obtain accurate estimates of the percentage of males who consume adult cyberporn, most leading experts in the field agree that it is a routine activity for millions of people around the world. Actually, almost all northern European boys have been exposed to pornography and 42% of Internet users ages 10 to 17 in the United States have viewed cyberporn (Hammaren & Johansson, 2007; Mossige, Ainsaar, & Svedin, 2007; Wolak, Mitchell, & Finkelhor, 2007). A study done in Alberta, Canada, found that one in three boys aged 13 to 14 accessed sexually explicit media content on digital or satellite television, video and DVD, and on the Internet. More than one third of the boys reported viewing pornography "too many times to count" and a sizeable minority of the boys in the sample planned social time around viewing porn with their male friends (Betowski, 2007, p. 10).

Pornography is a lucrative business, but it is a cruel one for women, and they do not last long in the industry (Bridges & Jensen, 2011, p. 136). The average employment period for "porn stars" only ranges from six months to three years and they often end their careers without money saved in the bank (Calvert & Richards, 2006). It is also common, as described in a previous section, for female actors to be humiliated, degraded, and abused in the process of making cyberporn and other types of pornography. Pornography hurts other women (Funk, 2006), including the thousands who are romantically involved with men who use it or who have left such men.

PORNOGRAPHY AND WOMAN ABUSE IN INTIMATE HETEROSEXUAL RELATIONSHIPS

Men's consumption of, and addiction to, Internet pornography can negatively affect their intimate partners in a variety of ways, such as the following described by Bridges and Jensen (2011):

> Partners of identified "sexual addicts" reported feelings of hurt, betrayal, lowered self-esteem, mistrust, anger, feelings of being unattractive and objectified, feeling their partners ha[ve] less interest in sexual contact, pressure from the partner to enact things from the online fantasy, and a feeling that they could not measure up to the women online. . . . (p. 144).

Pornography consumption is also a powerful correlate of male physical and sexual violence in dating, marriage or cohabitation, and during and after separation or divorce. In fact, one study found that a male partner's pornography consumption doubles the risk that a battered woman experiences sexual assault (Shope, 2004). However, many people contend that pornography is not a key correlate of woman abuse because most men who consume it are not violent. As Russell (1998) puts it:

> This is comparable to arguing that because some cigarette smokers don't die of lung disease, there cannot be a causal relationship between smoking and lung cancer. Only members of the tobacco industry and some seriously addicted smokers consider this a valid argument today. (p. 150)

North American research consistently challenges the notion that pornography does not contribute to violence against women. For example, of the 1,638 women who participated in the Canadian National Survey on Woman Abuse in University/College Dating (CNS) and who both dated and answered a question about pornography, 137 (8.4%) stated that they were upset by their dating partners trying to get them to do what they had seen in pornographic media (DeKeseredy & Schwartz, 1998). This is very similar to the 10% figure that Russell (1990) uncovered from asking a random sample of 930 women in the San Francisco area a similar question.

What is more important here is that the CNS found a significant relationship between being upset by men's attempts to imitate pornographic scenes and sexual victimization. Of those who were sexually abused, 22.3% had also been upset by attempts to get them to imitate pornographic scenarios. Only 5.8% of the women who were not victimized reported not being upset by pornography. The relationship also holds for physical violence. Of the female CNS respondents who reported being physically abused in a dating relationship, 15.4% also reported being upset by pornography. Only 4.5% of those who were not physically victimized reported being upset. These findings mirror the pornography-related abuse reported by married and formerly married women (Bergen, 1996; Bergen & Bogle, 2000; Harmon & Check, 1989).

South of the Canadian border, DeKeseredy and Schwartz's (2009) more recent qualitative study of separation or divorce assault in rural Ohio also found a strong relationship between men's consumption of pornography and woman abuse. Sixty-five percent of the male estranged partners of the 43 women interviewed used pornography, and 30% of those interviewed reported that pornography was involved in sexually abusive events they experienced. This figure and other data show that some men use "pornography as a training manual for abuse" (Bergen & Bogle, 2000, p. 231). Gathered by feminist scholars who view pornography as deeply oppressive, these statistics also challenge Weitzer's (2011) claim that "those who adopt the oppression paradigm substitute ideology for rigorous empirical analysis" (p. 666). Keep in mind, too, that pornography use is often a secretive event. Therefore, it is possible that most female study participants who state that their partners do not view pornography are probably unaware of the men's consumption of it (DeKeseredy & Olsson, 2011). In other words, data presented here and elsewhere, already alarming, are underestimates.

The correlation between pornography and violence against women is not only found in North America. In Italy, for example, one study of high school students uncovered strong associations between sexually harassing or raping peers and pornography consumption (Bonino, Ciairano, Rabaglietti, & Cattelino, 2006). Additionally, CNS data reported above compare well with Itzin and Sweet's (1992) report of the British *Cosmopolitan* Survey, which was administered to over 4,000 readers of this women's magazine and was one of the first large-scale sources of information on women's experiences with pornography in the United Kingdom. However, more research is necessary to conclusively determine if pornography use contributes to woman abuse around the world.

While we know that pornography use is associated with woman abuse, why do many men enjoy watching cyberporn and assault the women they love or are sexually involved with? The most common answer is they must be sick or mentally ill. How could a normal person watch the images described in this chapter? How could a normal person force his intimate partner to imitate what he had seen at a pornographic website? The truth is that there is no reliable evidence linking personality disorders, biological factors, or alcohol or drug abuse to Internet porn use (DeKeseredy & Olsson, 2011; Stack, Wasserman, & Kern, 2004). Similarly, a large literature shows that most men who abuse female intimates are "less pathological than expected" (Gondolf, 1999, p. 1), with only 10% of all incidents of intimate violence resulting from mental disorders (DeKeseredy & Schwartz, 2011; Gelles & Straus, 1988).

If only a handful of men watched cyberporn or beat, hit, raped, and killed their female partners, it would be easy to accept nonsociological accounts of their behavior. The reality, though, is that violence against women and cyberporn use is deeply entrenched in our society and so is patriarchal male peer support, which is attachments to male peers and the resources these men provide that perpetuate and legitimate male-to-female abusive behaviors (DeKeseredy, 1990). For example, in North America, annually, at least 11% of women in marital or cohabiting relationships are physically assaulted by their male partners (DeKeseredy, 2011a), and large- and small-scale surveys of college students consistently show that 25% of North American female undergraduates experience some variation of sexual assault every year (DeKeseredy & Flack, 2007). Further, there is ample quantitative and qualitative evidence to support what Lee Bowker (1983) said more than 25 years ago about all-male patriarchal subcultures of violence:

> This is not a subculture that is confined to a single class, religion, occupational grouping, or race. It is spread throughout all parts of society. Men are socialized by other subculture members to accept common definitions of the situation, norms, values, and beliefs about male dominance and the necessity of keeping their wives in line. These violence-supporting social relations may occur at any time and in any place. (pp. 135–136)

The contribution of Internet pornography to woman abuse is related to male peer support (DeKeseredy & Olsson, 2011). Some men learn to sexually objectify women through their exposure to pornographic media (Dines, 2010; Katz, 2006), and they often learn these lessons in groups, such as at pornographic video showings at men's homes (DeKeseredy, 2011a). Such strengthening of male misogynist bonds is not a recent phenomenon (Lehman, 2006, pp. 4–5). Cinematic pornography originated in 16 mm silent films, which were:

> usually shown in private all-male "smokers" in such contexts as bachelor parties and the like. Within such a context, the men laughed and joked and talked among themselves while watching the sexually explicit films about women, who though were absent from the audience, were the likely butt of the jokes, laughing, and rude remarks. (Lehman, 2006, p. 4)

Similarly, a study done nearly 20 years ago uncovered that university fraternity brothers also generally went to pornographic theaters in groups (Sanday, 1990). Now, due to the Internet and other new technologies, these men and others who want to consume pornography can watch it at a peer's house, which also enables them to drink excessive amounts of alcohol without the risk of stigmatization. Such gatherings are common and are salient contemporary expressions of patriarchy (DeKeseredy, 2011a; Jensen, 2007). There are various definitions of patriarchy. For simplicity, though, following Eisenstein (1980), it is defined here as "a sexual system of power in which the male possesses superior power and economic privilege" (p. 16).

Some men abuse female intimates and consume pornography, but do not see it in groups gathered at one particular place. Additionally, they may not directly interact with abusive or sexist peers on a face-to-face basis (DeKeseredy & Olsson, 2011). This is not to say, though, that they are not influenced to consume cyberporn or victimize women by male peers. Further, new cyberspace technology enables men to engage in the online victimization of women. This involves men "virtually assaulting," "virtually raping," or "cyber stalking" women who use the Internet (Kendall, 2003; Tucker, Fraser, & Shulruff, 2008). Sadly, there are Internet rape sites and video games such as RapeLay, in which players direct a man to sexually assault a mother and her two young daughters at an underground station before raping a selection of other females (Kome, 2009).

Pro-abuse cyberspace male peer support groups are also emerging (DeKeseredy & Olsson, 2011; Kendall, 2003). Although the precise number is unknown, some research shows that many men, most of whom probably never had face-to-face contact with each other, share pornographic material with other men through the Internet (Doring, 2009). Also, there is evidence suggesting that an undetermined number of these consumers and distributors are "part of a broader subculture of sexual deviance that legitimizes various forms of deviant sexuality" (Stack et al., 2004, p. 85).

Male peer support theorists argue that the sharing of cyberporn helps create and maintain sexist male peer groups (DeKeseredy & Olsson, 2011). This sharing reinforces attitudes that reproduce and reconstitute ideologies of male dominance by approving presenting women as objects to be conquered and consumed. Such sharing also makes it difficult for users to separate sexual fantasy from reality and assists them in their attempts to initiate female victims and break down their resistance to sexual acts (Dines, 2010; Dines & Jensen, 2008).

In sum, given the widespread nature of woman abuse, cyberporn, and male peer support, how can people claim that these problems are committed by sick or pathological individuals? Even if this were the case, one would have to spend a great deal of time looking at the social structure and culture of a country that produces more sick or pathological individuals than many other countries (DeKeseredy, 2011a; DeKeseredy & Schwartz, 1996). Nevertheless, there are some people who have biological or psychological problems that factor into their decision to assault women or view degrading, violent pornography. Consequently, it is incorrect to completely reject individualistic explanations, but it appears that they can account for only a very small number of violent perpetrators. Consider, too, that there are other sociological accounts of pornography's negative effects (see Bridges & Jensen, 2011), but it is beyond the scope of this chapter to review them.

WHAT IS TO BE DONE ABOUT INTERNET PORNOGRAPHY?[1]

At London, Ontario's Fanshawe College, on September 26, 2008, University of Western Ontario scholar Dr. Helene Berman gave a powerful presentation at a conference titled "Overcoming Violence in the Lives of Girls and Young Women: Stories of Strength and Resilience." She asked the audience to imagine what an anthropologist from outer space would see if she or he came to study Canadian society. As well as the beautiful landscape, people involved in scholarly and athletic activities, and many other positive things, the anthropologist would be hard pressed not to notice an alarming amount of pornographic

---

[1] This section includes modified parts of work published previously by DeKeseredy (2011, 2012).

images on television, on the Internet, in video outlets, and elsewhere, many of them including children. Pornography today has, as Robert Jensen told *London Free Press* journalist Ian Gillespie (2008), "become as common as comic books were for you and me" (p. A3). Related to this point is Gail Dines' (2010) reflection: "We are so steeped in the pornographic mindset that it is difficult to imagine what a world without porn would look like" (p. 163).

What is to be done? Some feminists, such as Anna Gronau (1985) assert that pornography, even its violent forms, should be freely available in private and public places because it functions to remind women of the patriarchal forces that victimize and exploit them. If it is banned, then it is much more difficult for women to struggle against hidden patriarchy than it is to fight against the blatant and extreme forms of sexism found in pornography. There are other feminists with different perspectives, like those who embrace the postmodernist view that pornography can be subversive and liberatory (Williams, 1989). As well, some sex-positive feminists assert that pornography is just as important to women as to men, and that there is nothing inherently degrading to women about such media (McElroy, 1995; Strossen, 2000). Most feminists, however, including me, view pornography as purposely designed to humiliate and degrade women and that efforts to make it socially unacceptable are necessary. They do not advocate the elimination of all sexually explicit media, only those that objectify and hurt people in ways described in this chapter and elsewhere.

The porn industry is an economic juggernaut and is not easy to defeat (Dines, 2010). Still, a number of strategies can put chinks in its armor until radical change transpires. One obvious way of dealing with pornography is to simply not view it, read it, or participate in any public or private events that involve pornographic words, behaviors, or images. Yet, it is clearly not enough to change our own behavior. As Jensen (2007) states, "That's a bare minimum. Such change must be followed by participation in movements to change the unjust structures and the underlying ideology that supports them" (p. 182).

Another strategy is to complain to hotel managers and owners about offering customers pay-per-view "adult films." I frequently travel and stay in hotels. Upon arrival at the front desk I often say to the clerk, "Your company is proud to offer a smoke-free environment, but you offer movies that harm women. I find this offensive and would like to speak to the manager." The typical response I get is something like this, "Well Sir, it is your choice not to watch it and what TV services we offer are beyond my control." After I return home, my usual routine is to write a formal complaint. So far, I have never received an official response.

One collective strategy that could make a difference is to take the advice of a close friend of mine who works in the Ontario provincial government. She suggests that organizations planning large conferences should make explicit in their negotiations for discount group rates that they will not book rooms in hotels that provide pornographic media. This strategy is currently being used by the Minnesota Men's Action Network: Alliance to Prevent Sexual and Domestic Violence and is referred to as the Clean Hotel Initiative.[2] Additionally, groups of men and women should collectively expose and criticize injurious media coverage of woman abuse (e.g., news reports that blame women for their victimization) and boycott companies that profit from pornography.

It is also essential for those involved in the feminist antiporn movement to express their views in the mainstream media. That articles and letters written by feminists are

---

[2] For more information on the Clean Hotel Initiative, go to www.peacemakers.org/programs/mnman/hotels.

periodically published by the mainstream press and that some feminists appear on CNN serves as evidence that the orthodox media do not totally dismiss struggles against patriarchal oppression (Caringella-MacDonald & Humphries, 1998; DeKeseredy, 2011b). For example, pioneering feminist Gloria Steinem's critique of the NBC television series *The Playboy Club* recently appeared in the widely read Canadian newspaper the *Toronto Star*. She stated:

> The question is the attitude of the film or series. Is it aggrandizing the past in a nostalgic way, or is it really showing the problems of the past in order to show that we have come forward and continue to come forward? I somehow think the Playboy shows are maybe not doing that. There are other shows that do. I feel dismay that young men especially are being subjected to that and made to feel that's a mark of masculinity. (Cited in Salem, 2011, p. 1)

For educators, it is essential to recognize that student consumption of pornography is a widespread problem that will get worse due to easy access offered by the Internet. For example, one U.S. study of undergraduate and graduate students ages 18 to 26 around the country uncovered that 69% of the male and 10% of the female participants view pornography at least once a month (Carroll et al., 2008). Although hardly a reliable statistic, also note that at least 50 out of about 65 students in my 2009 violence against women class estimated that between 75% and 80% of male students enrolled at my university view Internet pornography. What, then, is to be done by feminist men and women on campus?

One answer to this question is to give workshops and presentations that encourage critical thinking and that begin by asking questions such as the following graphic ones suggested by feminist male educator Rus Funk (2006). These are designed to humanize women in the pornography industry:

- Does the woman in pornography really like that?
- Does she like the names that men in pornography call her?
- Does she really like being ejaculated upon, probably several times? Does she really like double or triple penetration?
- Would she want her sister or daughter doing the same things?
- Would they (the male audience members) want their sister, mother, daughter, or girlfriend to be in the pornography they watch? (p. 168)

A cautionary note, however, is required here. As Funk (2006) correctly points out, many men in the audience may be titillated by images used in workshops and are likely to answer these questions with a "resounding yes" (p. 168). Even when feminist male educators attempt to generate "honest talk and careful hearing" (Jensen, 1995, p. 52), such events can turn into celebrations of male sexual and patriarchal power (DeKeseredy & Schwartz, 1998; Sanday, 1996). Thus, Funk recommends that educators engage men in the audience who oppose pornography and facilitate a conversation and debate among men who disagree with each other. Again, the goal is to promote critical thinking and perhaps a number of men will leave the workshop or presentation with a different way of thinking about pornography.

One more cautionary note is necessary. Educators and activists must be very careful when using pornographic images to make points about the harm they cause. Some instructors show these images in some courses (e.g., a course on woman abuse sponsored by a women's studies program) and understand their use as educational tools in the right environment. Nonetheless, many women have not been exposed to pornography and are unaware of the level of antiwoman hatred embedded in many Internet sites and other pornographic media (Granau, 1985). Showing pornographic media, then, may cause some women much discomfort or trigger painful memories. Therefore, educators need to work closely with counselors on campus to prepare for possible traumatic outcomes.

The progressive solutions suggested here constitute just the tip of the iceberg. Many more could easily be provided, including methods of responding to pornography advocates' freedom of speech arguments.[3] Antipornography feminists and others opposed to hurtful sexual media are often accused of censorship and this issue warrants some attention here. Why is it in the United States, Canada, and elsewhere we have very strong reactions against movies showing approvingly the mass execution of Jews by the Nazis in World War II but find it appropriate, or at least a free speech issue, to allow films approvingly showing women being beaten, raped, and degraded in a myriad of ways that are difficult if not impossible for the average person to comprehend? Here, informed by my earlier policy work on pornography (see DeKeseredy & Schwartz, 1998), I am not calling for censorship. Rather, I argue that in a better, equitable society, it would be considered morally reprehensible to view or show pornography, just as it is now for nondocumentary films advocating proslavery violence and Nazi killings (DeKeseredy & Olsson, 2011; Schwartz, 1987).

Most people would never dare to praise or support musicians, filmmakers, or actors who say hateful things about people's ethnic or cultural backgrounds or spirituality. Nonetheless, that cyberporn and other types of pornography constitute a multibillion dollar industry reveals that our media, politicians, and society in general do not find violent, racist, and degrading images of women offensive. As is often asked, "What's wrong with this picture?" Robert Jensen (2007), one of the world's leading feminist experts on pornography reminds us that "We have a lot of work to do" (p. 184).

Conclusion

The rapid growth of the Internet has globalized access to violent and degrading pornographic materials on women and other potentially vulnerable groups in converged online and offline environments. Such media can be diffused to millions of people in only seconds due to faster ways of disseminating digital media productions, and the Internet facilitates access for those seeking pornographic content, whether it is legally recognized or not. What used to be rather difficult to access and a secret phenomenon is now accessible for larger groups and has subsequently become a huge industry with operations around the world. The Internet not only facilitates access to previously inaccessible materials, but it has also helped create an environment that normalizes hurtful sexuality and racism.

Internet pornography also contributes to woman abuse in heterosexual intimate relationships and is a highly injurious symptom of patriarchy. What will the future bring? Internet and other types of porn are already so brutal that it

---

[3] See DeKeseredy (2011b), DeKeseredy and Schwartz (1998), and Funk (2006) for more in-depth suggestions about how to respond to claims of censorship.

is hard to imagine that violent and racist images, as well as their negative effects, could get worse. However, the future looks bleak because so much money is being made by pushing the cruelty line (Jensen, 2007). On the other hand, it is possible that the porn industry might cross a line that results in outraging most people and politicians, leading to strict regulation and highly punitive responses (Bridges & Jensen, 2011).

We don't know for sure what will happen next, but what we definitely know is that pornography has changed substantially over the past two decades and that many people continue to be hurt by it (Katz, 2006). And, as Dines (2010) notes, "What we do know is that we are surrounded by images that degrade and debase women and that for this the entire culture pays a price" (p. 163).

References

Attwood, F. (2010). Porn studies: From social problem to cultural practice. In F. Attwood (Ed.), *Porn. com: Making sense of online pornography* (pp. 1–13). New York, NY: Peter Lang.

Barss, P. (2010). *The erotic engine: How pornography has powered mass communication, from Gutenberg to Google.* Toronto, Canada: Random House.

Bergen, R. K. (1996). *Wife rape.* Thousand Oaks, CA: Sage.

Bergen, R. K., & Bogle, K. A. (2000). Exploring the connection between pornography and sexual violence. *Violence and Victims, 15,* 227–234.

Betowski, B. (2007). 1 in 3 boys heavy porn users: Study shows. Retrieved from http://www.eurekalert.org/pub_releases/2007-02/uoa-oit022307.php

Bonino, S., Ciairano, S., Rabaglietti, E., & Cattelino, E. (2006). Use of pornography and self-reported engagement in sexual violence among adolescents. *European Journal of Developmental Psychology, 3,* 265–288.

Bowker, L. H. (1983). *Beating wife-beating.* Lexington, MA: Lexington Books.

Bridges, A. J., & Jensen, R. (2011). Pornography. In C. M. Renzetti, J. L. Edleson, & R. Kennedy Bergen (Eds.), *Sourcebook on violence against women* (2nd ed., pp. 133–148). Thousand Oaks, CA: Sage.

Bridges, A. J., Wosnitzer, R., Scharrer, E., Sun, C., & Liberman, R. (2010). Aggression and sexual behavior in best-selling pornography videos: A content analysis. *Violence Against Women, 16,* 1065–1085.

Calvert, C., & Richards, R. D. (2006). Porn in their words: Female leaders in the adult entertainment industry address free speech, censorship, feminism, culture, and the mainstreaming of adult content. *Vanderbilt Journal of Entertainment and Technology Law, 9,* 255–299.

Caringella-MacDonald, S., & Humphries, D. (1998). Guest editors' introduction. *Violence Against Women, 4,* 3–9.

Carroll, J. S., Padilla-Walker, L. M., Nelson, L. J., Olson, C. D., Barry, C. M., & Madsen, S. D. (2008). Generation XXX: Pornography acceptance and use among emerging adults. *Journal of Adolescent Research, 23,* 6–30.

Claus, M. (2000, December 12). Internet changes porn scene at DePauw U. *High Beam Research, 1.* Retrieved from http://www.highbeam.com/doc/1P1-37925753.html

DeKeseredy, W. S. (1990). Male peer support and woman abuse: The current state of knowledge. *Sociological Focus, 23,* 129–139.

DeKeseredy, W. S. (2009). Male violence against women in North America as hate crime. In B. Perry (Ed.), *Hate crimes: The victims of hate crime* (Vol. 3, pp. 151–172). Santa Barbara, CA: Praeger.

DeKeseredy, W. S. (2011a). *Violence against women in Canada.* Toronto, Canada: University of Toronto Press.

DeKeseredy, W. S. (2011b). *Contemporary critical criminology.* London, UK: Routledge.

DeKeseredy, W. S. (2012). Ending woman abuse on Canadian university and community college campuses: The role of feminist men. In J. Laker (Ed.), *Canadian perspectives on men and masculinities: An interdisciplinary reader* (pp. 70–89). Toronto, Canada: Oxford University Press.

DeKeseredy, W. S. (In press). Pornography and violence against women. In C. Cuevas & C. M. Rennison (Eds.), *Wiley-Blackwell handbook on the psychology of violence.* New York, NY: Wiley-Blackwell.

DeKeseredy, W. S., Ellis, D., & Alvi, S. (2005). *Deviance and crime: Theory, research and policy.* Cincinnati, OH: LexisNexis.

DeKeseredy, W. S., & Flack, W. F., Jr. (2007). Sexual assault in colleges and universities. In G. Barak (Ed.), *Battleground criminal justice* (pp. 693–696). Westport, CT: Greenwood.

DeKeseredy, W. S., Muzzatti, S. L., & Donnermeyer, J. F. (2012, November). *Mad men in bib overalls: Media's horrification and pornification of rural culture.* Paper presented at the annual meeting of the American Society of Criminology, Chicago.

DeKeseredy, W. S., & Olsson, P. (2011). Adult pornography, male peer support, and violence against women: The contribution of the "dark side" of the Internet. In M. Vargas Martin, M. A. Garcia Ruiz, & A. Edwards (Eds.), *Technology for facilitating humanity and combating social deviations: Interdisciplinary perspectives* (pp. 34–50). Hershey, PA: Information Science Reference.

DeKeseredy, W. S., & Schwartz, M. D. (1996). *Contemporary criminology.* Belmont, CA: Wadsworth.

DeKeseredy, W. S., & Schwartz, M. D. (1998). *Woman abuse on campus: Results from the Canadian national survey.* Thousand Oaks, CA: Sage.

DeKeseredy, W. S., & Schwartz, M. D. (2009). *Dangerous exits: Escaping abusive relationships in rural America.* New Brunswick, NJ: Rutgers University Press.

DeKeseredy, W. S., & Schwartz, M. D. (2011). Theoretical and definitional issues in violence against women. In C. M. Renzetti, J. L. Edleson, & R. Kennedy Bergen (Eds.), *Sourcebook on violence against women* (2nd ed., pp. 3–20). Thousand Oaks, CA: Sage.

Dines, G. (2006). The white man's burden: Gonzo pornography and the construction of black masculinity. *Yale Journal of Law and Feminism, 18*, 296–297.

Dines, G. (2010). *Pornland: How porn has hijacked our sexuality.* Boston, MA: Beacon Press.

Dines, G., & Jensen, R. (2008). Internet pornography. In C. M. Renzetti & J. L. Edleson (Eds.), *Encyclopedia of interpersonal violence* (pp. 365–366). Thousand Oaks, CA: Sage.

Doring, N. (2009). The internet's impact on sexuality: A critical review of 15 years of research. *Computers in Human Behavior, 25*, 1089–1101.

Dworkin, A. (1994). Pornography happens to women. Retrieved from http://www.nostatusquo.com/ACLU/dworkin/PornHappens.html

Eisenstein, Z. (1980). *Capitalist patriarchy and the case for socialist feminism.* New York, NY: Monthly Review Press.

Funk, R. E. (2006). *Reaching men: Strategies for preventing sexist attitudes, behaviors, and violence.* Indianapolis, IN: JIST Life.

Gelles, R. J., & Straus, M. A. (1988). *Intimate violence: The causes and consequences of abuse in the American family.* New York, NY: Simon & Schuster.

Gillespie, I. (2008, June 11). Nowadays, it's brutal, accessible; pornography. *London Free Press*, A3.

Gondolf, E. W. (1999). MCMI-III results for batterer program participation in four cities: Less "pathological" than expected. *Journal of Family Violence, 14*, 1–17.

Gronau, A. (1985). Women and images: Feminist analysis of pornography. In C. Vance & V. Burstyn (Eds.), *Women against censorship* (pp. 127–155). Toronto, Canada: Douglas and McIntyre.

Hagan, J. (1994). *Crime and disrepute.* Thousand Oaks, CA: Pine Forge Press.

Hammaren, N., & Johansson, T. (2007). Hegemonic masculinity and pornography: Young people's attitudes toward and relations to pornography. *Journal of Men's Studies, 15*, 57–71.

Harmon, P. A., & Check, J. V. P. (1989). *The role of pornography in woman abuse.* Toronto, Canada: LaMarsh Research Program on Violence and Conflict Resolution, York University.

Hauch, V. (2011, June 16). Porn the catalyst behind tweeting, DVD technology. *Toronto Star*, A4.

Ibrahim, A. (2011). Child pornography and IT. In M. Vargas Martin, M. A. Garcia Ruiz, & A. Edwards (Eds.), *Technology for facilitating humanity and combating social deviations: Interdisciplinary perspectives* (pp. 20–32). Hershey, PA: Information Science Reference.

Itzin, C., & Sweet, C. (1992). Women's experience of pornography: UK magazine survey evidence. In C. Itzin (Ed.), *Pornography: Women, violence and civil liberties* (pp. 222–235). New York, NY: Oxford University Press.

Jacobs, K. (2004). Pornography in small places and other spaces. *Journal of Cultural Studies, 18*, 67–83.

Jensen, R. (1995). Pornographic lives. *Violence Against Women, 1*, 32–54.

Jensen, R. (2007). *Getting off: Pornography and the end of masculinity.* Cambridge, MA: South End Press.

Jensen, R., & Dines, G. (1998). The content of mass-marketed pornography. In G. Dines, R. Jensen, & A. Russo (Eds.), *Pornography: The production and consumption of inequality* (pp. 65–100). New York: Routledge.

Jordan, Z. (2006). *A view at cyberporn and its influence on aggression against women.* (Unpublished manuscript). Iowa State University, Ames.

Katz, J. (2006). *The macho paradox: Why some men hurt women and how all men can help.* Naperville, IL: Sourcebooks.

Kendall, L. (2003). Cyberporn. In M. S. Kimmel & A. Aronson (Eds.), *Men and masculinities: A social, cultural, and historical encyclopedia* (Vol. 1, p. 193). Santa Barbara, CA: ABC-CLIO.

Kome, P. J. (2009). Amazon declines to sell "Rapelay" video game. Retrieved from http://www.telegraph.co.uk/scienceandtechnology/technology/46I11161/rapelay-virtual-rape-game-banned-by-Amazon.html

Lehman, P. (2006). Introduction: "A dirty little secret": Why teach and study pornography? In P. Lehman (Ed.), *Pornography: Film and culture* (pp. 1–24). New Brunswick, NJ: Rutgers University Press.

Longino, H. (1980). What is pornography? In L. Lederer (Ed.), *Take back the night: Women on pornography* (pp. 40–54). New York, NY: William Morrow.

McElroy, W. (1995). *XXX: A woman's right to pornography.* New York, NY: St. Martin's Press.

Mowlabocus, S. (2010). Industry, social practice, and the new online porn industry. In F. Attwood (Eds.), *Porn.com: Making sense of online pornography* (pp. 69–87). New York, NY: Peter Lang.

Nikunen, K., Paasonen, & Saarenmaa, L. (Eds.). (2007). *Pornification: Sex and sexuality in media culture.* Oxford, UK: Berg.

Russell, D. E. H. (1990). *Rape in marriage* (2nd ed.). Bloomington: Indiana University Press.

Russell, D. E. H. (1993). *Against pornography: The evidence of harm.* Berkeley, CA: Russell.

Russell, D. E. H. (1998). *Dangerous relationships: Pornography, misogyny, and rape.* Thousand Oaks, CA: Sage.

Salem, R. (2011, August 1). The sway of the '60s playboy. *Toronto Star,* E1.

Sanday, P. R. (1990). *Fraternity gang rape.* New York: New York University Press.

Sanday, P. R. (1996). *A woman scorned: Acquaintance rape on trial.* New York, NY: Doubleday.

Schwartz, M. D., & DeKeseredy, W. S. (1997). *Sexual assault on the college campus: The role of male peer support.* Thousand Oaks, CA: Sage.

Shope, J. H. (2004). When words are not enough: The search for the effect of pornography on abused women. *Violence Against Women, 10,* 56–72.

Slayden, D. (2010). Debbie does Dallas again and again: Pornography, technology, and market innovation. In F. Attwood (Eds.), *Porn.com: Making sense of online pornography* (pp. 54–68). New York, NY: Peter Lang.

Stack, S., Wasserman, I., & Kern, R. (2004). Adult social bonds and use of internet pornography. *Social Science Quarterly, 85,* 75–88.

Strossen, N. (2000). *Defending pornography: Free speech, sex and the fight for women's rights.* New York: New York University Press.

Vargas Martin, M., Garcia-Ruiz, M. A., & Edwards, A. (2011). Preface. In M. Vargas Martin, M. A. Garcia Ruiz, & A. Edwards (Eds.), *Technology for facilitating humanity and combating social deviations: Interdisciplinary perspectives* (pp. xxii–xxvii). Hershey, PA: Information Science Reference.

Weitzer, R. (2011). Pornography's effects: The need for solid evidence. *Violence Against Women, 17,* 666–675.

Williams, L. (1989). *Hard core: Power, pleasure and the "frenzy of the visible."* Berkeley: University of California Press.

Wolak, J., Finkelhor, D., Mitchell, K. J., & Jones, L. M. (2011, July 22). Arrests for child pornography production: Data at two time points from a national sample of U.S. law enforcement agencies. *Child Maltreatment,* 1–12.

Wolak, J., Mitchell, K. J., & Finkelhor, D. (2007). Unwanted and wanted exposure to online pornography in a national sample of youth Internet users. *Pediatrics, 119,* 247–255.

Zerbisias, A. (2008, January 26). Packaging abuse of women as entertainment for adults: Cruel, degrading scenes "normalized" for generation brought up in dot-com world. *Toronto Star,* L3.

IV

Communities and the Environment

A standard definition of *community* is a group of people living together in the same place or area. But for sociologists, the notion of *community* also embodies a sense of belonging, which goes beyond simply being in the same place at the same time. The members of a community usually share common characteristics. One of these is socioeconomic status. Income determines, to a large extent, the community or neighborhood in which one lives. Race and ethnicity, which are closely related to income, also affect where people live. But there is, in a sense, a reciprocal relationship between the characteristics of a community and residents' quality of life, for the characteristics of the community in which they live may certainly impact their life chances, including the likelihood that they will live in a different type of community or neighborhood than the one in which they grew up.

In Chapter 15, Susan Clampet-Lundquist discusses how growing up in a poor urban neighborhood affects residents' life chances. As she points out, the urban neighborhood has been a focus of sociological research since the development of sociology in the United States in the late 1800s. Clampet-Lundquist traces the trajectory of sociological research on urban neighborhoods to the present, discussing studies of the impact of residential segregation and the concentration of poverty. This research, along with her own in Baltimore, Maryland, demonstrates that place matters. After controlling for other potential contributing factors, the research indicates that neighborhood characteristics contribute to a variety of outcomes in residents' lives, including their likelihood of being arrested; of being violently victimized, even killed; of dropping out of high school; and of being a single parent. But these effects are not uniform across residents of a specific neighborhood; as Clampet-Lundquist shows, for example, the age and gender of the residents also matter, demonstrating yet again the significance of intersecting inequalities.

The characteristics of one's neighborhood are also related to residents' chances of owning their own homes. In Chapter 16, Anna Maria Santiago, Amy Restorick Roberts, and Eun-Lye Lee explore the meaning of home ownership and neighborhood in low-income communities. Home ownership has long been a primary component of the American dream. In their research with former public housing residents in Denver, Colorado, Santiago, and her colleagues found that owning a home represented more than just a financial asset to this racially and ethnically diverse group of residents. Additional meanings of home ownership that emerged in their study were personal pride in achieving the status of home owner: a sense of belonging to a community; and a feeling of privacy, autonomy, or control over one's life and living conditions. Ties to one's community emerged as an important factor in the study, with home owners talking about knowing their neighbors and the children living in the neighborhood, as well as feeling that neighbors looked out for one another. A picture of strong social cohesion emerged from this study, leading Santiago and her colleagues to urge policy makers to continue to provide resources to promote home ownership among low-income groups. As the authors emphasize, the benefits of home ownership extend beyond the financial realm, and even beyond the specific neighborhoods of the home owners, benefitting the entire society.

Some problems within communities may be hidden or invisible. For instance, when we think of hunger, we usually think of communities in economically undeveloped countries, where the majority of the population is too poor to buy enough food to provide adequate nutrition for themselves and their family members. But we don't tend to think of hunger as a serious problem in the United States. Keiko Tanaka, Patrick Mooney, and Brett Wolff disabuse us of this belief in Chapter 17. Their focus is on food insecurity in the United States. *Food insecurity* refers to the problem of not being able to provide adequate food for the members of a household due to insufficient resources. As Tanaka and her colleagues note, this problem affects about one in seven households in any given year in the United States. Their research addresses four aspects of food insecurity: accessibility, availability, affordability, and adequacy. And as they show, while the problem is largely one of social class, social class inequality cannot be analyzed in isolation from gender, race, ethnicity, age, and disability, which together produce varying experiences of food insecurity, which require diverse solutions depending on the needs of a specific group. Tanaka, Mooney, and Wolff's chapter makes visible a problem hidden in the midst of what most of us consider the land of plenty.

While much community sociology has focused on urban areas, Shannon Bell draws our attention to rural communities in central Appalachia (southern West Virginia, eastern Kentucky, southwest Virginia, and eastern Tennessee). Bell refers to these communities as "energy sacrifice zones." This region of the country is rich in coal, which is used by coal-burning power plants to provide electricity. To keep the coal-burning plants running, the health and well-being of the residents of these central Appalachian communities, as well as their natural environment, is sacrificed through commercial exploitation. As Bell reports, for example, homes are frequently damaged from flooding caused by mountaintop removal to access coal; roads have become unsafe because of the heavy and fast-moving trucks transporting the coal; and residents suffer from higher rates of illness and mortality related to exposure to pollutants. Residents of these communities, along with the natural environment, appear to be viewed by the coal companies as expendable. They are very poor—indeed, central Appalachia is one of the poorest regions in the United States—and they have low levels of educational attainment compared with the U.S. population as a whole. This does not mean, however, that the residents of these communities are passive victims. Bell's chapter documents the activism and resistance of community residents, particularly groups of women, as they attempt to force the powerful coal companies to address the health and environmental hazards posed by the industry. Although this appears to be a David versus Goliath scenario, the courage and perseverance of the residents Bell interviewed should remind all of us of the power of collective activism to bring about social change, even when the odds are stacked against the activists. This is truly a fitting—and inspirational—way to end a book that has as its goals the celebration of diversity while overcoming inequality.

15

Growing Up in Poor Neighborhoods

Susan Clampet-Lundquist

How does growing up in a poor neighborhood affect your life chances? What larger economic, political, and social forces shape what urban neighborhoods are like today? When I was working with children and teens in low-income neighborhoods in Philadelphia, PA, just after graduating from college, these were the questions that intrigued me and ultimately led me to graduate school and research in urban sociology. This chapter will briefly describe the key factors that sociologists examine when studying urban neighborhoods, explain how neighborhoods may affect residents, and use interviews from a qualitative study in Baltimore, MD, to illustrate the role of neighborhoods in the lives of low-income teenagers.

URBAN SPACE

Urban neighborhoods have long held a fascination for sociologists in the United States, and the Chicago [IL] School researchers led the way in the early 1900s with their research on life in ghettoes (inhabited by European immigrants at the time), juvenile delinquency, gangs, mental illness, and other topics, all situated within a particular urban space (see Drake & Cayton, 1945; Park, Burgess, & Mackenzie, 1925; Wirth, 1928; Zorbaugh, 1929). For example, in 1942, Shaw and McKay examined the relationship between juvenile delinquency rates and neighborhood characteristics such as unemployed men and families receiving public aid. Based on their analysis of several cities, they concluded that there is a direct relationship between local community conditions like unemployment and the delinquency rate. They claimed that "Delinquency . . . has its roots in the dynamic life of the community" (Shaw & McKay, 1942, p. 315). In recent decades, urban sociologists have used their methodological tools to disentangle how racial residential segregation and concentrated poverty intersect in urban space to create struggling communities.

Many of the sociologists from the early years of the Chicago School espoused the view that there was a rational process of human settlement at work whereby people and groups were distributed across the city's space in a natural way not unlike vegetation and wildlife around a stream or meadow. From this urban ecological viewpoint, an issue such as racial residential segregation—where racial or ethnic groups live separated from one another—is simply a natural phenomenon wherein people from similar backgrounds want to live next to one another (Gottdeiner & Feagin, 1988).

Over time, sociologists, some of whom came from a Marxist paradigm, focused more on how powerful actors shape urban neighborhoods. This approach looks at a variety of forces and policies that affect how space in cities is arranged, critically examining "the marriage of public policy and private interests [and] whose interests are being served" (Flanagan, 1993, p. 74). Scholars from this perspective point to how federal legislation, local policies, and deindustrialization have shifted the middle-class and upper-class population out of central cities and into the suburbs, concentrating poverty in cities and in certain neighborhoods. At the same time that Veterans Administration loans and Federal Housing Administration loans were fueling massive home construction in the suburbs but not the cities after World War II, the Federal-Aid Highway Act passed in 1956 constructed interstate highways that made commuting from the suburbs to central cities easier, opening up those areas to real estate development for those who could afford it. In the process, these highways tore through city neighborhoods, destroying communities (Teaford, 1990). Suburban municipalities offered tax breaks to businesses to relocate from central cities to the suburbs, and with cheaper land prices in the suburbs, this move made financial sense for many businesses. Finally, the factories that had offered millions of lower-educated people jobs moved out of cities into suburbs, then into southern states, and finally into developing countries, in search of the lowest labor costs possible (Bluestone & Harrison, 1982).

In terms of residential segregation, sociologists coming from this critical perspective would argue that instead of simply individual preferences guiding residential choices, which then led to our segregated metropolitan areas—with predominantly white suburbs and predominantly black central cities—racialized space has been shaped by structural forces and the individual preferences of many whites who would rather live in all-white neighborhoods (Charles, 2003; Massey & Denton, 1993). The structural forces include redlining, which starved majority black neighborhoods of real estate financing for a few decades while financing the housing dreams of white suburbanites, and other discriminatory real estate practices such as geographic steering and more favorable loan packages for whites than for blacks or Latinos (Massey & Denton, 1993; Squires, 1994; Turner & Ross, 2006).

The racial and ethnic distribution across metropolitan areas has shifted over the last two decades, as blacks have moved to the suburbs and as Latinos and Asians have become a more substantial part of the U.S. population. Measures of segregation for Latinos and Asians have always been lower than for blacks, especially as minority income levels rise. In the last two decades, we have witnessed a gradual decline in black–white segregation across metropolitan areas; however, we still see high levels of segregation between blacks and whites, particularly in older cities such as Chicago and Philadelphia (Logan & Stults, 2011).

Until the civil rights movement, the population shift from the cities to the suburbs was almost wholly white. However, with the passage of the Fair Housing Act in 1968, which prohibited racial discrimination in housing, and as the violence that often met black families trying to move to the suburbs began to fade, the black middle class left segregated city neighborhoods for better opportunities elsewhere. As William Julius Wilson (1987) has argued, the combination of these factors has led to urban neighborhoods characterized by concentrated poverty. These concentrated high-poverty neighborhoods are those in which 40% or more of the residents are poor. To put this into perspective, around 15% of the U.S. population is poor, so these neighborhoods represent poverty levels that are not experienced by most Americans. High-poverty neighborhoods usually lack amenities such as decent grocery stores or quality public schools. Signs of physical and social disorder, including abandoned buildings, trash, and crime are common. Though there was an increase in concentrated poor neighborhoods from 1970–1990, the 1990s witnessed a decline in the number of people living in concentrated poor neighborhoods as individuals cycled out of poverty and as people moved from high-poverty neighborhoods to lower-poverty neighborhoods (Wagmiller, 2011).

NEIGHBORHOOD EFFECTS RESEARCH

Given these larger forces which have contributed to residential segregation and concentrated poverty, how does growing up in a poor neighborhood affect kids? After a long hiatus in research on neighborhood effects, William Julius Wilson opened up research into this area with the publication of his book, *The Truly Disadvantaged*, in 1987. Over the next decade, his thesis about concentrated poverty neighborhoods evolved into one that focused on the role that joblessness plays in poor black neighborhoods. Wilson's narrative went as follows: previously, the black middle class had lived side by side with poor families in segregated communities, providing role models for kids and supplementing neighborhood institutions (such as churches) with resources. Earlier, too, adults with lower levels of education could find work in factories. With the massive move of factories out of cities, these jobs were no longer available. Instead of neighborhoods being segregated but buzzing with people going to work, they were still segregated but characterized by astoundingly high rates of jobless adults (Wilson, 1996). According to Wilson (1996), when children grow up in neighborhoods high in unemployment, they miss out on seeing working role models and instead are negatively affected by their physical and social neighborhood environments in several ways.

When researchers explore how neighborhoods affect those who live in them, they try to isolate the effects of the neighborhood from other factors, such as family or individual characteristics. For example, a parent's socioeconomic status (income, education, and occupation) affects the child's educational performance. Therefore, if a researcher wants to document the relationship between dropping out of high school and neighborhood poverty, she or he will need to control for the parent's education in the statistical equation, in order to try to measure just the impact of neighborhood poverty. Although it is difficult to disentangle individual and family-level variables from the neighborhood-level context, the basic concept of neighborhood effects is powerful in terms of providing a comprehensive framework for the impact of concentrated urban poverty. Numerous studies have indicated the importance of community on individual behaviors, including adolescent sexual behaviors (Billy, Brewster, & Grady, 1994; Brewster, Billy, & Grady, 1993; Brooks-Gunn, Duncan, Klebanow, & Sealand, 1993; Coulton & Pandey, 1992; Crane, 1991; Hogan & Kitagawa, 1985; Ku, Sonenstein, & Pleck, 1993), the physical home environment (Klebanow, Brooks-Gunn, & Duncan, 1994), child maltreatment (Coulton, Korbin, Su, & Chow, 1995) and the likelihood of dropping out of high school (Brooks-Gunn et al., 1993; Coulton & Pandey, 1992; Crane, 1991).

Essentially, the research over the past three decades indicates that neighborhoods matter for children and teens in several ways. Sociologists have also explored how neighborhood-level variables like unemployment or poverty actually affect individuals— basically trying to understand the mechanisms at work. Children may be influenced by older teens or adults on their block who are working or not working, or they may be more strongly influenced by same-age peers (Harding, 2010; Jencks & Mayer, 1990; Leventhal & Brooks-Gunn, 2000; Sampson, Morenoff, & Gannon-Rowley, 2002; Wilson, 1996). Neighborhood collective efficacy, which represents whether adults in a community trust one another and work together for the common good, may affect individual outcomes, particularly those related to delinquency and crime (Sampson, Raudenbush, & Earls, 1997). The presence and quality of neighborhood institutions like schools and recreation centers may play a major role in affecting individual outcomes such as completing high school and avoiding teen pregnancy (Sampson et al., 2002; Small, 2004).

Another way of looking at how neighborhoods matter for children and teens is through the concept of an *opportunity structure*. The opportunity structure is defined by Galster and Killen (1995) as how markets, service delivery systems, institutions, and local social networks shape outcomes affecting social advancement. How adolescents perceive or are shaped by the opportunity structure in their neighborhoods can be a powerful influence on whether they engage in illegal activities, graduate from high school, or have a child as a teen. People base their prospects on their individual characteristics, backgrounds, and on their "subjective perceptions of how the opportunity structure will judge and transform these attributes" (1995, p. 9). Galster and Killen (1995) claimed that the opportunity structure varies geographically within a metropolitan area. They argued that adolescents make rational decisions based on the perceived costs and benefits of their actions. Due to disparate spatial variations in opportunity, an adolescent in a low-income, low-resource neighborhood will have a different set of opportunities from which to choose compared to a teen in an affluent neighborhood.

In his ethnographic study of three New York neighborhoods, Sullivan (1989) documented how the illegal and legal money-earning opportunities for young men were shaped by their neighborhoods, as Galster and Killen (1995) also point out. Sullivan (1989) described how the job opportunities of teen males in three different neighborhoods affected their involvement in illegal activities. White teens from a working-class neighborhood had relatively easy access through their local social networks to blue-collar jobs, and as they moved into this work, they decreased their involvement in crime. The black and Puerto Rican teen males in his study, on the other hand, were isolated from networks that eased their way into steady employment right after high school. With this absence, and the lack of informal social control in their communities, they continued to be involved in street crime which generated income.

MOVING TO OPPORTUNITY

The flurry of activity in neighborhood effects research had an impact on housing policy in the early 1990s. The Department of Housing and Urban Development, with input from sociologists and economists, implemented the Moving to Opportunity (MTO) Fair Housing demonstration in Baltimore, Chicago, New York, Boston, and Los Angeles.

Families living in public housing (developments managed by a local housing authority, reserved for low-income families) in neighborhoods where over 40% of people were poor could sign up for MTO. Unusually for public policy, MTO was designed as an experiment so that policy makers could document whether this housing policy was effective, and so that researchers could understand more about how neighborhoods affect the well-being of families. To that end, the families who signed up were then randomly assigned to one of three groups. Those in the low-poverty treatment group received a Housing Choice Voucher (HCV) which could only be used in a neighborhood that was less than 10% poor as defined by the 1990 U.S. Census. This voucher would allow them to rent in the private housing market and the federal government would pay a portion of their rent, based on their income. They also received budget counseling and assistance in finding an eligible apartment. Those in the regular treatment group received a voucher but could use it in any neighborhood. The remainder was assigned to a control group and they received no change in their housing through MTO.

In 2002, the MTO Interim Survey (Orr et al., 2003) attempted to interview all household heads in the MTO experiment, as well as their school-aged children and teens, to determine what effect the treatment had on a variety of adult and youth outcomes. Five to seven years after random assignment, the survey found that the low-poverty treatment group families were still living in significantly less poor neighborhoods, on average, than families in the control group. In addition, survey findings revealed that the intervention had a significant and positive effect on a number of other important outcomes. For example, adults in the low-poverty group felt safer and perceived less neighborhood disorder than those in the control group (Kling, Liebman, & Katz, 2007). Moreover, low-poverty group adults reaped substantial positive mental health benefits relative to control group adults. Yet contrary to expectation, the survey did not detect beneficial effects on other important adult outcomes such as employment or welfare receipt.

The most surprising results of the MTO demonstration, however, were the sharply divergent treatment effects for adolescent boys and girls. While there were significant mental health gains for girls in the low-poverty treatment group, who scored much lower than control girls on psychological distress and generalized anxiety, the survey found no effect on boys' mental health (Kling et al., 2007). Striking gender differences in teens' risk behaviors were evident as well (Kling et al., 2007). Girls in the low-poverty treatment group were less likely to report smoking marijuana in the past month than control girls, but boys in the low-poverty treatment group were significantly more likely to report smoking cigarettes or drinking alcohol in the past month than their control-group counterparts. Boys in the low-poverty treatment group were also more likely to self-report behavior problems relative to control group boys (Kling, Ludwig, & Katz, 2005).

To understand why girls might have benefited more from a move to a low-poverty neighborhood than boys, I, along with three others, analyzed in-depth interviews of a subsample of 86 Baltimore and Chicago MTO teens from families who moved to low-poverty neighborhoods, as well as teens from control families. We found that gender differences in daily routines worked in favor of girls fitting into lower-poverty neighborhoods in an easier way than boys. Whether they were living in a high-poverty or low-poverty neighborhood, girls were more likely to hang out with their friends on front porches, in their homes, at a mall, or downtown. Boys, on the other hand, were used to hanging out on corners or on basketball courts. While the street corner or playground style of hanging out was the norm in the high-poverty neighborhoods, it did not fit in as well in low-poverty neighborhoods. This might also have been due to negative stereotypes that the new neighbors or police held against young black males (Brunson & Miller, 2006). Almost all of our sample in Baltimore and Chicago were black, and while they moved to predominantly black neighborhoods, these neighborhoods were middle class and had different expectations for the daily routines of teenagers. As evidence of this clash in norms, males in the low-poverty treatment group were more likely than those in the control group to describe being harassed by police or their neighbors for simply hanging out.

Families who moved to a low-poverty neighborhood with a voucher only had to remain there for one year. They were then free to use the housing voucher to move wherever they desired. Over time, families moved back to poorer neighborhoods. This return to higher-poverty neighborhoods was due to several factors. At a practical level, it was difficult for families who did not have a car to live in an area that was not well-served by public transportation, so those in low-poverty neighborhoods without bus lines struggled to get around. Some people decided to move back to poorer neighborhoods to be near their extended families and friends. Low-income families rely on their social networks to get by even more than other families, and being geographically close to those networks makes it easier to drop off one's kids for child care, borrow money, or come by for a meal. Furthermore, landlords who accept government housing vouchers are more likely to be situated in poor neighborhoods.

Moving back to poorer neighborhoods might have put the boys in the low-poverty treatment group at a particular disadvantage. Different neighborhoods require different neighborhood navigational skills (Anderson, 1990; Young, 1999). Knowledge about which areas to avoid and understanding whom to hold close as a friend and whom to mistrust can be the difference between life and death in some neighborhoods high in crime. These boys moved out of a high-poverty area into a neighborhood where one did not have to worry as much about watching one's back—in fact, some teens described their low-poverty neighborhoods as bereft of people their age. In their narratives, the boys in the control group were much more likely to describe how they stayed to themselves, or how they made decisions about which parts of their neighborhoods they avoided than the boys in the low-poverty treatment group, despite the fact that many of those in the latter group had moved back to poor neighborhoods. These navigation strategies are important for girls as well; however, given the difference in delinquency rates and homicide rates between males and females, having a gap in this skill set appears to be more deleterious for males than females. This research points out the importance of understanding how the mechanisms through which neighborhoods influence teens can be very different by gender (Clampet-Lundquist, Edin, Kling, & Duncan, 2011).

INDIVIDUALS AND NEIGHBORHOODS

These gender differences in the MTO study point out the seemingly obvious: neighborhoods do not affect every individual in the same way. Even as we take into consideration the importance of the neighborhood environment on the well-being of children and adolescents, we cannot forget the *agency* of the individuals in that environment. That is, not every kid who grows up in a poor neighborhood ends up dropping out of school. Nor, for that matter, does every kid who grows up in a pampered existence in an affluent suburb finish college. The sociological theory of *structuration,* developed by Anthony Giddens (1984), argues that structure (in this case, the neighborhood environment) and agency shape and are shaped by one another. Though growing up in a neighborhood with few resources may have a negative impact on average on such outcomes as finishing high school or juvenile delinquency, we know that individuals still have agency within this environment, and some may be better poised to respond to this deprivation in neighborhoods.

There are a variety of protections that may help kids buffer their exposure to community violence and concentrated poverty in their neighborhoods. Sampson and Laub (1994) suggested that parenting practices like supervision and attachment mediate the effects of neighborhood poverty and can potentially reduce the odds of their teens' involvement in delinquent behavior. *Resiliency theory* points out that the balance of risk and promotive factors in an individual's life can affect his or her well-being. Note that this conceptualization of resiliency encompasses factors within the individual (personality, self-efficacy, and so on) and outside the individual (family, peer, community, and so on). Risk factors include exposure to community violence, family conflict, and substance use. Parental monitoring, and attitudes on violence and self-efficacy are examples of promotive factors. In a sample of adolescents in one of the most violent cities in the United States, Stoddard and colleagues (2012) found that lower levels of violent behavior were associated with higher levels of promotive factors that "moderated the negative effects of cumulative risks on youth violent behavior" (p. 62).

Psychologists have recently found a way to measure an individual attribute they identify as *grit*, and this concept is relevant to thinking about how youth from struggling neighborhoods strive. Duckworth, Peterson, Matthews, and Kelly (2007) define grit as "perseverance and passion for long-term goals" (p. 1087). Their research documented how even with IQ included in the model, grit accounted for a significant amount of the variance of an individual's success outcomes ranging from performance in the National Spelling Bee, completing West Point's summer training program, to college GPA. Striving toward goals, despite barriers, little positive feedback, and failure along the way may be a quality that buffers young people from negative effects of growing up in a high-poverty neighborhood.

The concept of grit is included in set of *essential character strengths* that Duckworth and her colleagues (2007) put together so that educators could experiment with teaching "character" to children and adolescents in their schools. While character may be viewed as an innate quality, many researchers and educators claim that it is actually malleable, and can therefore be taught (Tough, 2012). In fact, there has been a shift in policy discussion among sociologists, psychologists, and economists. Rather than thinking about how to mitigate the negative effects of neighborhoods by relocating families to less-poor neighborhoods or improving the neighborhoods themselves, policy discussion has started revolving around how to strengthen individuals such that they can weather high-poverty environments that have few resources. Concluding his book on how children succeed—especially those from poor backgrounds, Paul Tough (2012) argued that "[t]here is no antipoverty tool we can provide for disadvantaged young people that will be more valuable than the character strengths that [teens interviewed in his book] possess in such impressive quantities" (p. 195).

We know that neighborhoods do not affect everyone living in them the same way. They are not deterministic; or, thinking about it through the lens of Giddens (1984), it is not all about structure. But this character or grit discussion puts much of the onus on individuals: it is all about agency. Policy-wise, would we do low-income kids a disservice if we ignored their neighborhoods and simply strengthened their characters?

To illustrate the role that neighborhood can play in the lives of low-income teens and to inject real people into this discussion of agency and structure, I will describe four teens—two males and two females—who live in the Baltimore metropolitan area, who lived in high-poverty public housing throughout part of their childhood, and who are part of the MTO sample. Keep in mind that their experiences are not representative of all black teens or all low-income teens. The adults who signed up for MTO came from some of the most disadvantaged families in Baltimore in terms of poverty, health, and education. Their names and other details have been changed to protect their confidentiality. Regardless of the MTO treatment group that their families were in, these teens moved through a few neighborhoods throughout their childhood and adolescence. We interviewed all but one of them at least two separate times over the last seven years, and interviewed the mothers of all but one as well.

TEENAGERS AND NEIGHBORHOODS: FOUR TALES

Malcolm was 15 when we interviewed him. When he was a child, his mother was a drug addict. They lived in a Baltimore neighborhood where drugs were easily accessible, and drug paraphernalia littered the sidewalks. Malcolm started selling drugs when he was 12, moving from marijuana to cocaine because he could make three times the money each week. Unlike other people in our sample who sold drugs, Malcolm was able to save quite a bit of money. He was saving it for a unique goal—to move his family out of his neighborhood, called the "Avenue"—where drugs were easily accessible, and into the suburbs, with the hope of helping his mother kick her habit. So, one day, he came up to his mom and said, "'Ma, I'm tired of living on the [Avenue]' She was like, 'Well, what you wanna—why you saying it to me or whatever.' I was like, 'It's time to move.' Then I just pulled out the bag of cake [money]. . . . That was the best day of my life . . . because just to see the expression on my mother's face." With this money from drug profits, they moved out of the Avenue into the suburbs. After moving to the suburbs, he commuted back to the city to sell drugs until he was arrested. His mother eventually quit using drugs, but ended up dying of AIDS when he was 14.

During the months that his mother was dying, Malcolm and his family lived with one aunt in a county about an hour away from Baltimore. This was what he referred to as the "county-county" and it was far from what he had grown used to in his high-poverty Baltimore neighborhood. It was a low-density suburb and Malcolm felt isolated geographically and socially, illustrating how a simple switch of neighborhood environments can actually be quite complicated. After his mother died, he moved in with another aunt who lived in an inner-ring suburb that shared a border with Baltimore, where he felt more comfortable. This suburban area is generally referred to as "the county." He had a sociologist's eye for details for differences in norms across neighborhoods and socioeconomic status. Describing his aunt's low-density suburb, Malcolm stated, "Everybody out there was rich . . . I wasn't fitting in too good." Malcolm went on to explain that people at his school in the affluent suburb could not understand his speech, because "they talked proper." He continued to describe his isolation: "I just ain't like it. Wasn't nobody from the hood, I couldn't bond with nobody out there."

Until this point in his life, Malcolm has had to survive in difficult neighborhood circumstances. Sociologists such as William Julius Wilson (1987, 1996) and Doug Massey (1993) describe the social isolation that can exist in concentrated poor, racially segregated neighborhoods such as the one where Malcolm grew up. But within this social isolation, kids create ways of getting by and surviving, using a wide range of individual and social resources. Malcolm has used entrepreneurial skills out on the corner selling drugs; he has been arrested several times; he has been turned over to the police in a sting operation by a drug kingpin; he has watched his mother waste away from drug addiction and AIDS; and he has accomplished all of this by learning the necessary strategies of negotiating his neighborhood environment. One might say he has grit; certainly he displays perseverance.

When he compares himself to the boys in his aunt's affluent suburb or even to those in his other aunt's inner-ring suburb, he recognizes that they come from different worlds and it is hard to bridge this gap. Malcolm describes boys his age who live in his current inner-ring suburb:

> They be trying to be thugs. They not, so they act like they're thugs . . . they're from the county but they wanna be city boys . . . They hate on dudes that come from the city, like me . . . They treat us like, you know what I'm saying, we bad, like we ain't used to stuff like this, which we're not. But, you know, we don't let them know that we ain't used to stuff like this.

This gap may be more difficult to overcome for males than females, given the different perception that society has of young black males relative to females. Despite his struggles fitting in, Malcolm recognizes the resources that this suburb has relative to his old neighborhood. When asked where he would like to raise his children (hypothetically, as he does not have any yet), he replied that he would like to raise them in the suburb next to the city, but he would take them back to his old neighborhood, to "let them know where they're from, where their father is from."

Juvon was 16 when we first met him. He had grown up in public housing in East Baltimore, but had moved out to a row house about 10 minutes away, still on the east side. Juvon spent a lot of time in his house, but sometimes ventured out to play ball at a neighborhood basketball court. People sold drugs in his neighborhood, but he compared it favorably to the public housing he grew up in where he would regularly hear gunshots and he was beaten up. In spite of his separation from the drugs and delinquency in his neighborhood, Juvon was not protected from police surveillance. Undercover police tried to pin a crime on him when he was standing in front of his church one day, because he "fit the description." Only intervention by his pastor and stepfather, who were standing nearby and vouched for Juvon's innocence (he was in a church meeting during the incident) protected him from being hauled in.

Juvon was an unusual young man for our sample. He wrote poetry, wore skull rings, and listened to punk rock. Juvon had placed into one of the city's magnet high schools; however, during his sophomore year, his world fell apart with the divorce of his stepfather and mother, and the demise of his first romantic relationship. His grades suffered as a result, and Juvon had to transfer to his neighborhood high school, one of the lower performing schools of Baltimore. He was bored at this school so he pleaded with his teachers to give him more work, and he petitioned the school administration to put him in more difficult classes. While Juvon found a group of friends who shared his nonconformist interests, other kids at the school engaged in regular fights, often stemming from rivalries between neighborhoods. Juvon recognized that the identity he shaped for himself was opposite to that which society had marked out for young black men from urban neighborhoods:

> Society has this outlook on us as though, well I am black and I am supposed to do this. I am supposed to be bad and do that and things like that. I don't want to be like that; I don't want to be a stereotype. So, of course, I am not; I am different as you can see by you know how I am and what I wear.

At age 16, Juvon had clear aspirations and plans to attend college, and saw college as a first step to finding a place where he belonged: "I definitely want to go to college. I want to move away from Baltimore. I cannot wait to leave here because there's nothing—there's no opportunity for me here at all because I am so different." However, when we interviewed him again, at age 19 and age 23, Juvon had still not made it to college, though he still had the desire. Years of low-wage work, and no person in his life who could help him figure out how to apply to college and for financial aid, left him adrift. In the meantime, Juvon struggled to stay out of trouble in his neighborhood, where his brother was an active drug dealer who physically threatened him on two occasions with a gun because he suspected Juvon was talking to the police about him. The neighborhood he lived in when he was 19 was a heavily drug-trafficked neighborhood, with a good deal of police activity. Juvon explained the constraints of this neighborhood environment,

> I know there are good people in the neighborhood, but it's really, really hard for them especially with you know you got the police running out every day . . . You know you got all this yelling all hours of the night; it's really hard to get any sleep.

Later in the interview, Juvon stated, "my neighborhood does make me feel down. [I worry about my safety] all the time. That's why I try to get out of here as fast as I can."

Juvon's story highlights the tenuous nature of opportunities in poor neighborhoods. Most teens mess up at some point—their grades fall, or they do something stupid in terms of delinquency. But when one's opportunities are so fleeting, there is no safety net to fall back on to, and second chances are rare. If Juvon had attended a well-resourced school in an affluent suburb and his grades had fallen during his parents' divorce, he would have been able to remain at that school. Moreover, a student who is able to handle advanced math classes and maintain a decent grade point average at a suburban high school would have guidance counselors to offer him step-by-step instructions for applying to college, even if his parents had no experience with college. Juvon had none of these opportunities because he did not have access to quality neighborhood institutions. And so, at age 23, he is working for minimum wage at a coffee shop, still maintaining his unique identity to separate himself from the drugs, violence, and poverty that surround him.

Clarice lived on a block just off one of Baltimore's main drug corridors when we first interviewed her. Technically, the row house she lived in was situated within a low-poverty neighborhood, because the U.S. Census boundaries included a nearby wealthy gated community. Nonetheless, Clarice and her family were quite literally walled off from the resources of that neighborhood. Despite this exclusion, the block still represented a vast improvement from the public housing high-rise they had moved from seven years prior to our interview. In fact, her mother told us that when she moved to this neighborhood, she had been inspired by seeing her hard-working neighbors—so much so that she quit her years-long addiction to heroin. Fifteen-year-old Clarice and her mother had typical teenage daughter and mother conflict, which was exacerbated by the mother's disapproval of Clarice dating girls. A couple months before our first interview, Clarice had just returned home from living with her father for a month.

Clarice attended a high school on the other side of town, using her grandmother's address, since her neighborhood high school was an academically weaker and more volatile school. Though Clarice didn't get involved in fights, fights happened at her school between kids from West Baltimore versus those from East Baltimore. Clarice explained that these fights broke out over "where you from . . . [and] who got the most guns and just stupid stuff." Her block, however, was fairly calm, though a street gang existed two blocks away where she said "it could be dangerous." Unlike other teens we interviewed, police did not harass Clarice and her friends, and as she described one of the local officers, she stated that "we talk to him. We got an alright relationship with the police officer that be in this area." People on her block looked out for one another, and Clarice mentioned that "some of them, like the people next door, I consider them like family." She spent a lot of time sitting on her porch, playing cards, smoking weed, talking with an elderly neighbor, or playing basketball in a friend's yard with a crate rigged up.

By the time we interviewed Clarice three years later, she had graduated from high school. She and her mother had reconciled, and she credited staying in school to the support of her mother:

> I was just giving up. I wasn't even gonna go back to school in my senior year and what made me go back was my mother. I was not gonna let my mother down cause that's all she was asking for, just to graduate.

She had been kicked out of her original school for fighting and ended up graduating from the neighborhood school she had previously avoided. She had worked a few jobs, and was in the process of applying to a trade school for electrician training.

A year after our first interview, Clarice and her family moved to a quieter neighborhood further out to the edge of the city. When she described her previous neighborhood, it sounded as if the quality of life on the block had declined:

> We was hanging out around there. I think if my mother wouldn't have moved us from around there I would probably be one of those statistics, locked up. I mean that's just how the neighborhood was, and if she wouldn't have moved us from out of there, who knows what would happen.

In her new neighborhood, she did not play basketball, or engage in many other activities, because it was necessary to have a car to go to places. She also did not know many neighbors, and there were no people her age on her street. Clarice drew a sharp contrast between people in her current and previous neighborhood:

> It's just a different area, period. I mean, people's carrying stuff around there [in the previous neighborhood]. I wouldn't say that I could bring the friends that I got over [in the previous neighborhood] around here. If I brought them around here they probably would try to evict us or something. Yeah, because the neighborhood is not like that, it's not a, you know, it's different, different environment.

Clarice engaged in a few high-risk behaviors in her previous neighborhood. She told us that teens stole a lot of cars there, and while she did not steal any, she drove a couple of stolen cars. In addition to selling marijuana, Clarice also had a gun. She did not keep the gun or her stash in her house, for fear that her mother would know what she was doing. Being in that environment stressed her out, and she told us that, "When I was over on [previous neighborhood], I was stressing, seeing how much money I'm a get tonight. Being outside over there, something would be going on. I'm here [in new neighborhood], I'm just chill cause I be home, so laid back, watch TV, talk on the phone." She no longer sold drugs, and attributed this change to her move:

> I'm pretty sure if I was to move back over there I'd be back at it again . . . I'd give myself a week. Cause I know it's guaranteed I could get some money around there. You know, I don't know this area, you know what I'm saying? I know the police, how they operate around there. What they drive in, what they sell. But see around here I can't say the same.

Similar to Clarice, Keala moved from a public housing high-rise to neighborhoods that were less and less poor, eventually ending up in the suburbs of Baltimore. Her mother, Peaches, initially moved into public housing because she had two children, and was trying to make ends meet while also attending community college. She was not happy with the neighborhood environment in public housing and had dreams of moving out soon:

> And I can remember just a whole lot of days I would sit on that fourteenth floor cause you could see everything, the whole city from the fourteenth floor. And I would sit out on the balcony and just look over the whole city and I used to say, "God, my house is out there, somewhere. My future is out there somewhere, you know. Just when is it going to happen?" But, you know, like I said I just kept my mind on the big picture.

So, how was Peaches able to aspire to this "big picture" and actually succeed in a way that many of her other public housing neighbors weren't? We can attribute much of this ability to move out of early disadvantage to something within Peaches that stubbornly pursued education so that she could attain better employment. Moreover, Peaches was encouraged and supported in this pursuit by her mother, who had to raise three kids on her own after her husband died an early death, and her two siblings, both of whom completed their bachelor's degrees. These factors would be what sociologists would consider individual-level and family-level variables. But encouragement and perseverance alone may not be enough to push a single mother of three out of a high-crime and high-poverty public housing project. The instrumental factor in getting her out of the projects and into a neighborhood environment that matched her personal ambitions was Moving to Opportunity.

When they moved into a low-poverty Baltimore neighborhood with the MTO voucher, Peaches considered it "neat, clean and well-kept and quiet and peaceful." While Peaches was already motivated to improve her situation, such as attending community college, she said that moving into this neighborhood "motivated me to get more" by seeing how her neighbors lived, since most of them worked and were "doing something positive." With a certificate she earned from school and eventually an associate's degree, Peaches landed a job at a hospital where she was making double the wages she had made at her previous job. After a few years, Peaches started feeling discouraged about the negative influence of the teens in the neighborhood on her own children, and they ended up moving out to the suburbs.

This move offered a real change to the school environment for Keala who had just finished her first year of high school before they moved. Previously, even though she had been in a low-poverty neighborhood, she was still attending a public high school within the financially strapped Baltimore city school district. Her high school in Baltimore was chaotic and fights frequently broke out. Switching to a public high school in the suburbs offered Keala a chance to attend a school where she could concentrate on academics and not be distracted by fights in the hallway. A counselor at the school took a special interest in Keala and not only helped in her transition, but also continued to work with her to take more challenging classes and graduate early. Keala's mother recognized how the better-resourced suburban high school along with a quieter neighborhood affected Keala, putting it in terms similar to the research discussed earlier about character:

> Her character has changed, you know? I don't know whether it's because she's growing up or the atmosphere of her mind yet, but she speaks a whole lot better compared to when we were down in the city. She takes her time, her thoughts are more clearer. She's more focusing on what she's saying. It's a difference—it's definitely an improvement and I owe it to the school and the environment.

Keala worked extra hard to achieve her educational goals, showing the grit within her. For example, she struggled in math class, but she finally ended up with a B. Even with math as a weak point, she took up accounting in community college. She has used her work experience to help her with her accounting classes. She said, "I have high expectations for myself. And I set a goal, the goal has to be met, no matter how long it takes me."

Keala's mom encouraged her to go to college "as soon as I got out of high school." Keala's aunt and uncle, both of whom obtained bachelor's degrees, also provided encouragement about continuing in higher education. Both Keala's neighborhood environment with a strong public school and her family put her on the path to higher educational attainment. When we interviewed her in 2010, Keala, now 22 years old, was about to start attending community college in the suburbs, and was working on an accounting degree, so she could take her CPA exam. She had already finished one year at a community college in the city, but stopped for a while after having her son. Even in high school, Keala always combined work and school, and she was working for two temporary agencies in 2010.

Conclusion

These four individuals were all on the path to young adulthood when we interviewed them. Making decisions in the domains of education, early family formation, employment, and illegal activities are all part of this transition (Arnett, 2000, 2005; Furstenberg, Kennedy, McLoyd, Rumbaut, Settersten, 2004). In the U.S. context, there are important variations by social class in the transition to early adulthood. For affluent young people, adult roles can be postponed during early adulthood to allow time for college, graduate study, and career launch. However, for disadvantaged youth such as those whose parents participated in the MTO demonstration, early adulthood is often a time of great difficulty as young people often falter in high school or postsecondary education, have difficulty establishing stable employment, may engage in risky behaviors that can lead to incarceration, and may take on the roles of partner and parent as well (Furstenberg, 2008).

The stories of these four teenagers reflect different ways that growing up in poor neighborhoods can affect young people negatively and how a switch to a neighborhood with more resources may change an individual's pathway. Moreover, these stories highlight how individual agency interacts with the environment. All four had to navigate crime in their neighborhoods, and Clarice's story highlights how living in one neighborhood makes it easier to get into selling drugs compared to another neighborhood. Juvon's story shows how institutions, such as schools, can lack the resources and tools to guide students who aspire to college to make this a reality. Malcolm's analysis of the subtle differences in norms between the city and the suburbs offers insight into how neighborhood environments can influence the outward presentation of self and create divisions and stigma among youth. Finally, Keala's story reflects how institutional quality (more specifically schools) varies across metropolitan areas such that her suburban high school offered her much better resources than her city high school. Moreover, we read about how her mother's perseverance in setting higher aspirations for herself and her family was assisted with a voucher which allowed her to move to a low-poverty neighborhood.

These stories show that it is crucial that we find creative ways to provide supports for children and teens within high-poverty neighborhoods to help them succeed. Building up character strengths such as grit may not be enough for children who attend schools in a bankrupt school district or who are exposed to community violence on a regular basis. Moving to low-poverty neighborhoods doesn't necessarily improve the well-being of all children either, especially when these moves are short-lived and families move back to poorer communities. But we see in these stories and in the survey data from MTO that for some kids, this type of sustained move can make a huge difference for them relative to what their outcomes might have been without the subsidized move.

Juvon, Keala, Malcolm, and Clarice are all following the rules of mainstream society in varying ways. They have worked to graduate from high school, and in some cases like Juvon and Keala, they have taken on advanced classes to accelerate this process. Unassisted by the MTO voucher, Malcolm figured out his own way to move his family to a less-devastated suburban environment to get his mother away from drugs. And Keala is working her way through community college, juggling to balance work, family, and school with fewer supports than most middle-women, on whom this debate often focuses, have. The important takeaway point here is that there is no single policy that can fix things for young people in poor neighborhoods. Their well-being is a function of a unique package of individual, family, and neighborhood factors, and we need to be flexible in meeting their needs. But there are some key basics that should provide an institutional floor below which their quality of life does not fall, such as quality public schools. Having this institutional safety net of good schools with caring counselors and energetic teachers could go a long way in promoting social mobility for these teens, regardless of their family background. Investing creatively in low-income neighborhoods such that low-income residents can stay and reap the benefits of improved amenities and job opportunities, rather than be displaced by a more affluent population represents another set of policy tools.

References

Anderson, E. (1990). *Streetwise: Race, class, and change in an urban community*. Chicago, IL: University of Chicago Press.

Arnett, J. J. (2000). Emerging adulthood: A theory of development from the late teens through the twenties. *American Psychologist, 55*(5), 469–480.

Arnett, J. J. (2005). The developmental context of substance use in emerging adulthood. *Journal of Drug Issues, 35*(2), 235–254.

Billy, J. O. G., Brewster, K. L., & Grady, W. R. (1994). Contextual effects on the sexual behavior of adolescent women. *Journal of Marriage and the Family, 56*, 387–404.

Bluestone, B., & Harrison, B. (1982). *The deindustrialization of America: Plant closings, community abandonment, and the dismantling of basic industry*. New York, NY: Basic Books.

Brewster, K. L., Billy, J. O. G., & Grady, W. R. (1993). Social context and adolescent behavior: The impact of community on the transition to sexual activity. *Social Forces, 71*, 713–740.

Brooks-Gunn, J., Duncan, G. J., Klebanow, P. K., & Sealand, N. (1993). Do neighborhoods influence child and adolescent development? *American Journal of Sociology, 99*, 353–395.

Brunson, R., & Miller, J. (2006). Gender, race, and urban policing: The experience of African-American youths. *Gender & Society, 20*, 531–552.

Charles, C. Z. (2003.) The dynamics of racial residential segregation. *Annual Review of Sociology, 29*, 67–207.

Clampet-Lundquist, S., Edin, K., Kling, J., & Duncan, G. (2011). Moving teenagers out of high-risk neighborhoods: How girls fare better than boys. *American Journal of Sociology, 116*(4), 1154–1189.

Coulton, C. J., Korbin, J. E., Su, M., & Chow, J. (1995). Community level factors and child maltreatment rates. *Child Development, 66*, 1262–1276.

Coulton, C. J., & Pandey, S. (1992). Geographic concentration of poverty and risk to children in urban neighborhoods. *American Behavioral Scientist, 35*, 238–257.

Crane, J. (1991). The epidemic theory of ghettos and neighborhood effects on dropping out and teenage childbearing. *American Journal of Sociology, 96*, 1226–1259.

Drake, St. Clair, & Cayton, H. R. (1945). *Black metropolis*. New York, NY: Harcourt, Brace.

Duckworth, A. L., Peterson, C., Matthews, M. D., & Kelly, D. R. (2007). Grit: Perseverance and passion for long-term goals. *Journal of Personality and Social Psychology, 92*(6), 1087–1101.

Flanagan, W. G. (1993). *Contemporary urban sociology*. Cambridge, UK: Cambridge University Press.

Furstenberg, F. F. (2008). The intersections of social class and the transition to adulthood. *New Directions for Child and Adolescent Development, 119*, 1–10.

Furstenberg, F. F., Jr., Kennedy, S., McLoyd, V. C., Rumbaut, R. G., & Settersten, R. A., Jr. (2004). Growing up is harder to do. *Contexts, 3*(3), 33–41.

Galster, G. C., & Killen, S. P. (1995). The geography of metropolitan opportunity: A reconnaissance and conceptual framework. *Housing Policy Debate, 6*(1), 7–43.

Giddens, A. (1984). *The constitution of society*. Cambridge, UK: Polity Press.

Gottdeiner, M., & Feagin, J. (1988). The paradigm shift in urban sociology. *Urban Affairs Quarterly, 24*(2), 163–187.

Harding, D. (2010). *Living the drama: Community, conflict, and culture among inner-city boys*. Chicago, IL: University of Chicago Press.

Hogan, D. P., & Kitagawa, E. M. (1985). The impact of social status, family structure, and neighborhood on the fertility of black adolescents. *American Journal of Sociology, 90*, 825–855.

Jencks, C., & Mayer, S. (1990). The social consequences of growing up in a poor neighborhood. In L. E. Lynn, Jr, & G. H. McGeary (Eds.), *Inner city poverty in the United States*, (pp. 111–186). Washington, DC: National Academy Press.

Klebanow, P. K., Brooks-Gunn, J., & Duncan, G. J. (1994). Does neighborhood and family poverty affect mothers' parenting, mental health, and social support? *Journal of Marriage and the Family, 56*, 441–455.

Kling, J. R., Liebman, J. B., & Katz, L. F. (2007). Experimental analysis of neighborhood effects. *Econometrica, 75*(1), 83–119.

Kling, J. R., Ludwig, J., & Katz, L. F. (2005). Neighborhood effects on crime for female and male youth: Evidence from a randomized housing voucher experiment. *Quarterly Journal of Economics, 120*(1), 87–130.

Ku, L., Sonenstein, F. L., & Pleck, J. H. (1993). Neighborhood, family, and work: Influences on the premarital behaviors of adolescent males. *Social Forces, 72*, 479–503.

Leventhal, T., & Brooks-Gunn, J. (2000). The neighborhoods they live in: The effects of neighborhood residence on child and adolescent outcomes. *Psychological Bulletin, 126*(2), 309–337.

Logan, J. R., & Stults, B. (2011). *The persistence of segregation in the metropolis: New findings from the 2010 Census.* Census Brief prepared for Project US2010. Retrieved from http://www.s4.brown.edu/us2010/Data/Report/report2.pdf.

Massey, D. S., & Denton, N. A. (1993). *American apartheid: Segregation and the making of the underclass.* Cambridge, MA: Harvard University Press.

Orr, L., Feins, J. D., Jacob, R., Beecroft, E., Sanbonmatsu, L., Katz, L. F., Liebman, J. B., & Ling, J. R. (2003). *Moving to opportunity: Interim impacts evaluation.* Washington, DC: U.S. Department of Housing and Urban Development.

Park, R., Burgess, E., & Mackenzie, R. (1925). *The city.* Chicago, IL: University of Chicago Press.

Sampson, R., & Laub, J. (1994). Urban poverty and the family context of delinquency: A new look at structure and process in a classic study. *Child Development, 65*(2), 523–540.

Sampson, R., Morenoff, J., & Gannon-Rowley, T. (2002). Assessing "neighborhood effects": Social processes and new directions in research. *Annual Review of Sociology, 28,* 443–478.

Sampson, R., Raudenbush, S., & Earls, F. (1997, August 15). Neighborhoods and violent crime: A multilevel study of collective efficacy. *Science, 277*(5328), 918–924.

Small, M. (2004). *Villa Victoria: The transformation of social capital in a Boston barrio.* Chicago, IL: University of Chicago Press.

Squires, G. (1994). *Capital and communities in Black and White: The intersections of race, class, and uneven development.* Albany: State University of New York Press.

Stoddard, S. A., Whiteside, L., Zimmerman, M. A., Cunningham, R. M., Chermack, S. T., & Walton, M. A. (2013). The relationship between cumulative risk and promotive factors and violent behavior among urban adolescents. *American Journal of Community Psychology, 51,* 57–65.

Sullivan, M. (1989). *Getting paid: Youth, crime and work in the inner city.* Ithaca, NY: Cornell University Press.

Teaford, J. (1990). *The rough road to renaissance: Urban revitalization in America, 1940–1985.* Baltimore, MD: Johns Hopkins University Press.

Tough, P. (2012). *How children succeed: Grit, curiosity, and the hidden power of character.* New York, NY: Houghton Mifflin Harcourt.

Turner, M. A., & Ross, S. (2006). How racial discrimination affects the search for housing. In X. de Souza Briggs (Ed.), *The geography of opportunity: Race and housing choice in metropolitan America.* Washington, DC: Brookings Institution Press.

Wagmiller, R. (2011). Why did poverty become less geographically concentrated in the 1990s? *Social Science Quarterly, 92*(3), 710–734.

Wilson, W. J. (1987). *The truly disadvantaged: The inner city, the underclass, and public policy.* Chicago, IL: University of Chicago Press.

Wilson, W. J. (1996). *When work disappears: The world of the new urban poor.* New York: Vintage Books.

Wirth, L. ([1928] 1956). *The ghetto.* Chicago, IL: University of Chicago Press.

Young, A., Jr. (1999). The (non)accumulation of capital: Explicating the relationship of structure and agency in the lives of poor black men. *Sociological Theory, 17*(2), 201–227.

Zorbaugh, H. (1929). *Gold coast and the slum.* Chicago, IL: University of Chicago Press.

16

Not Just Buying a Home

The Meaning of Home, Homeownership, and Neighborhood in Low-income Communities*

Anna Maria Santiago, Amy Restorick Roberts, and Eun-Lye Lee

INTRODUCTION

*And then there's the American Dream—if you work hard, you'll get ahead.
Half of Americans say the old adage still holds true—perhaps not all that
bad, given the economy's condition. But 43 percent say this basic principle of
grade-school civics once was true, and isn't any more.*

—GARY LANGER, ON POLITICS, ECONOMY AND THE AMERICAN DREAM

*"It feels like the American Dream is not attainable to a lot of us,"
a participant in a town hall meeting with Obama said. "Is the American
Dream dead for me?"*

—SUNLEN MILLER, OBAMA'S ECONOMIC TOWN HALL

During the past 20 years, a growing number of scholars and policy makers (e.g., McKernan & Sherraden, 2008; Sherraden, 1991) have encouraged the use of asset-based policies, including policies promoting homeownership, as long-term strategies for the social and economic development of individuals, families, and communities. Drawing attention to the longstanding use of asset-based subsidies that have increased the wealth of more affluent residents in the United States (see Quigley, 2008), current policy debates stress the need for a parallel set of policies and programs that will serve as asset-building tools for

*The research reported in this chapter is supported by grants from the Ford Foundation and the MacArthur Foundation. The views expressed in this chapter are the authors' and do not necessarily reflect those of these foundations or the Board of Trustees at Case Western Reserve University. We also express our gratitude to the Denver Housing Authority for their support of this research, particularly Ismael Guerrero, Stella Madrid, and Renee Nicolosi.

low-income individuals and families. In this chapter, we examine how homeownership has emerged as one of the primary vehicles for building economic and noneconomic assets among low-income Latino and black households.

Political support for homeownership as an asset-building tool is not new; such support has fueled the American Dream for multiple generations of American homeowners. Dating back to the 1940s, federal housing policies that encouraged owner-occupancy over rental tenure using Federal Housing Administration (FHA) and Veteran's Administration (VA) mortgage loans were the major catalysts of the post-World War II housing boom in suburban America (Galster, 2008; Shlay, 2006; Stegman, Quercia, McCarthy, Foster, & Rohe, 1991). During the last 30 years, however, federal policies have encouraged households of increasingly lower incomes to become homeowners (Rohe & Watson, 2007; Shlay, 2006). Starting with the Reagan administration in the 1980s, the U.S. Department of Housing and Urban Development (HUD) piloted a homeownership program that sold public housing units to their occupants. In 1992, Congress enacted the Federal Housing Enterprises Financial Safety and Soundness Act to make it easier for potential homebuyers to acquire mortgages in traditionally underserved low-income and minority urban neighborhoods. Further, Congress mandated the Federal National Mortgage Association (Fannie Mae) and the Federal Home Mortgage Corporation (Freddie Mac) to buy a minimum share of mortgages in underserved neighborhoods and to offer mortgages to low-income borrowers regardless of location. Additional innovations in low down payment mortgage instruments, such as Affordable Gold mortgages, further expanded access to low-income borrowers (Bostic & Lee, 2008; Gramlich, 2007; Immergluck, 2008). By the 1990s, the Clinton Administration established national homeownership goals. In the 2000s, the Bush Administration made the expansion of low-income and minority homeownership a priority within HUD's mission (U.S. Department of Housing and Urban Development, 2002). Over the last several decades, Congress also has enacted pilot programs for homeownership education and counseling, individual development accounts for asset building, and the use of Housing Choice Vouchers for home-buying (Grinstein-Weiss et al., 2008; Locke et al., 2006; Rohe, Quercia, & Van Zandt, 2002). Under the Obama administration, Congress adopted the American Recovery and Reinvestment Act in 2009, which provided refundable tax credits for home purchases by low- and moderate-income households.

As a result of this consistent policy emphasis favoring homeownership and the generally favorable economy that existed in prior decades the United States experienced considerable growth in homeownership rates for low-income and minority households from the mid-1980s through the mid-2000s (Allen, 2002; Boehm & Schlottman, 2003; Kochhar et al., 2009; Retsinas & Belsky, 2002). An estimated 800,000 low-income households bought their first home in the 1990s (Retsinas & Belsky, 2002), raising homeownership rates of non-elderly households in the lowest income group from 22% in 1989, to 28% by 2001, to 38% by 2006 (Bostic & Lee, 2008; Nothaft & Chang, 2005). Between 1993 and 1999, the number of mortgage loans to low-income borrowers almost doubled (Pitcoff, 2003), increasing the share of all home-purchase loans to such borrowers from 14% to 19% (Wiranowski, 2003). Further, the average real value of home equity held by low-income households rose sharply from $67,683 in 1985, to $76,505 in 1995, to $96,011 by 2001 (Nothaft & Chang, 2005). At the height of the housing bubble in the mid-2000s, both homeownership rates and home equity continued their unprecedented rise.

Two arguments have been used to support the continued use of low-income homeownership as an asset building tool (see Galster & Santiago, 2008). The first promotes homeownership because of its links to increased wealth, prestige, stability, control, life satisfaction, and well-being experienced by the homeowners themselves (Rohe & Watson, 2007; Rossi & Weber, 1996). Other supporters stress the benefits homeownership offers to children who are able to grow up in homes owned by their parents (Galster, Marcotte, Mandell, Wolman, & Augustine, 2007; Green & White, 1997; Harkness & Newman, 2003; Haurin, Parcel, & Haurin, 2002). Still others argue that homeownership provides benefits to the larger society through enhanced home mainte-nance, greater civic engagement, and stronger attachment to community (DiPasquale & Glaeser, 1999; Englehardt et al., 2010; Galster, 1987; Hoff & Sen, 2005).

An alternate view emphasizes the antipoverty effects of low-income homeowner-ship. As the antipoverty debate changed to one emphasizing building assets instead of income support (McKernan & Sherraden, 2008; Shapiro & Wolff, 2001; Sherraden, 1991), the center of attention has shifted to the wealth-building potential of homeown-ership through home appreciation and the potential deductibility of mortgage interest and local property taxes (Stegman et al., 2007). For most American homeowners, home equity is the most important, if not sole, component of wealth; this is particularly true for low-income households. Although the amount of assets held by low-income homeowners may be modest relative to that of more affluent owners, low-income homeowners hold significantly higher assets than people who continue renting. For instance, the median net worth of homeowners earning less than $20,000 per year was $72,750 in 2001, compared to $900 for renters in this income range (Belsky, Restsinas, & Duda, 2005). Further, while low-income and minority homeowners saw net gains in home appreciation during the 1990s averaging $1,712 each year, renters experienced no gain in nonhousing wealth over the same time period (Boehm & Schlottmann, 2004).

Unlike the idealized vision of the American Dream, homeownership does not necessarily guarantee benefits for low-income households. Since the beginning of the housing and financial crisis in the mid-2000s, both homeownership rates and property values, particularly for low-income and minority owners, have fallen sharply. Five potential reasons might have contributed to these losses (Galster & Santiago, 2008). First, low-income homebuyers might have invested more in housing than was best compared to other assets (Goetzmann & Spiegel, 2002). Second, low-income homeown-ers lost opportunities for wealth-building because they are less likely to prepay their mortgages through refinancing when interest rates decline (Nothaft & Chang, 2005). Third, unexpected major home repairs or loss of income through illness, injury, or layoff might have created unsustainable financial stresses that led to subsequent mortgage delinquency and default and associated costs in terms of psychological damage, loss of home equity, and destruction of consumer credit ratings (Haurin & Rosenthal, 2005). Fourth, homes purchased by low-income and minority buyers, like those of higher incomes, might not have appreciated or might even have declined in value, especially if they were located in distressed neighborhoods (Woldoff & Ovandia, 2009). The financial returns from homeownership and the probability of mortgage default are highly sensi-tive to fluctuations in mortgage interest rates and price movements between purchase and sale dates (Belsky et al., 2005; Bocian, Li, Reid, & Quercia, 2011; Turner & Smith, 2009). Fifth, low-income and minority homeowners were at greater risk of victimization by predatory lenders, including disproportionate purchases of adjustable rate and balloon payment mortgages, leading to the loss of equity through excessive refinancing fees or, in the worst case, default and foreclosure (Bowdler, Quercia, & Smith, 2010; Lutes Fuentes, 2009; Renuart, 2004).

The explosion of home foreclosures and underwater mortgages during the past five years has raised questions about the wisdom of low-income homeownership policies, focusing on the high risks and potentially low returns associated with such ownership (Bostic & Lee, 2008; Van Zandt & Rohe, 2011). The ongoing housing crisis challenges the notion that homeownership leads to increased housing stability and wealth. Even in studies pre-dating the crisis, low-income and minority households were much less likely than higher-income white ones to maintain ownership (Boehm & Schlottmann, 2004). As a result of these legitimate concerns, the policy discussion has evolved from considering how more low-income households can attain homeownership (e.g., Listokin, Wyly, Schmitt, & Voicu, 2002) to considering how more low-income and minority households can sustain homeownership (Herbert & Belsky, 2006; Shlay, 2006), to more recent debates as to whether we should discontinue support for low-income homeownership altogether (Florida, 2010; Kaus, 2011; Lerman, 2011).

Yet, relatively little is known about the noneconomic benefits of homeownership amassed by low-income buyers and how such benefits contribute to the long-term sustainability of homeownership. What is the meaning of home for low-income owners? How does homeownership shape the meaning of neighborhood and community for these owners? How are the meaning of home, neighborhood, and community shaped by the intersection of gender and ethnicity?

These are the key questions that this chapter addresses, using data gathered about the home-buying experiences of 232 former public housing residents who purchased homes in the Denver, CO, metropolitan area during the period between 1995 and 2009. We begin by looking at the meaning of home, paying particular attention to what is known about low-income homeowners' experiences, concerns, perceptions, and expectations. We then briefly describe the Denver context and the low-income homeowners we studied. The rest of the chapter narrates the experiences of our sample of low-income homeowners, identifying areas of similarity and difference across gender and ethnic lines. We conclude the chapter with a discussion of the implications of our findings for U.S. housing policy.

LITERATURE REVIEW

The Meaning of Home for Low-income Owners

There are multiple meanings attached to home (e.g., Easthope, 2004; Mallett, 2004; Manzo, 2003). Kearns, Hiscock, Ellaway, and Macintyre (2000) describe home in terms of a haven, the site of autonomy and source of status. Home becomes a place of belonging and safe refuge where individuals not only have control over their environment but also enjoy the freedom to be and express themselves without outside surveillance (Saunders & Williams, 1988). Homeownership deepens this sense of refuge by providing individuals with a source of personal identity and status as well as personal and familial security (Mallett, 2004). This sense of status and identity conferred via homeownership was described by Peter Marcuse (1975):

> The average home owner is higher status, better paid, better educated, richer, and more middle class. . . . Consequently the change from tenant to homeowner increases the likelihood that the individual will be taken to be well paid, well educated and middle class. (p. 184)

Further, it has been argued that homeownership provides more autonomy because owners are capable of modernizing and personalizing their dwellings, which adds to their perception of home (Kearns et al., 2000). Unfortunately, we do not know the extent to which low-income individuals—homeowners or renters—view their homes as havens, places of autonomy, or sources of status. Nonetheless, given the extensive history of discriminatory lending practices in poor and minority neighborhoods (see for example, Reid, 2010; Schwartz, 2006; Turner & Skidmore, 1999; Turner et al., 2002; Wyly & Hammel, 2004) and documented concerns about predatory lending targeting such neighborhoods in the midst of the current housing crisis (e.g., Bocian et al., 2011; Lutes Fuentes, 2009) low-income and minority owners may not achieve a feeling of security in their homes if they are concerned about the possibility of repossession or relocation (Rohe & Stegman, 1994a,b). For owners teetering on the brink of losing their homes, the freedom and control often associated with homeownership may instead become a proverbial ball and chain of hopelessness and despair (McCormack, 2012).

THE SOCIAL BENEFITS OF HOMEOWNERSHIP FOR LOW-INCOME HOUSEHOLDS

During the past several decades, considerable attention has been given to the economic benefits of homeownership for low-income owners; significantly less attention has been given to the social benefits gained from homeownership. In a study of low-income homeowners and renters in Baltimore, MD, Rohe and Basolo (1997) found that owning a home did not increase self-esteem or perceived sense of control even after three years of homeownership. However, they found that homeowners were more likely than renters to interact with their neighbors and participate in neighborhood or block club meetings. Yet, owning a home did not increase participation in other social, school, or political organizations and actually decreased attendance at meetings of church-affiliated groups. Mitchell and Warren (1998) discovered that the most common benefits of homeownership expressed by low-income, Habitat for Humanity homeowners were pride, increased stability, and increased feelings of security about their tenure. Further, they found that respondents believed that homeownership was having a positive impact on their families, especially through increased stability and privacy for their children. In a subsequent study by Rohe and Quercia (2003), one in five NeighborWorks Program homebuyers identified the increased "sense of independence" as the most important benefit. They also found that homebuyers were more satisfied with their lives and had larger social support networks than continuing renters. However, they found no differences in levels of participation in voluntary associations, neighborhood satisfaction, self-esteem, or perceptions of opportunity. In contrast, Manturuk, Lindblad, and Quercia's (2010) study of nearly 3,000 Community Advantage Program (CAP) participants found that compared to renters, homeownership provided owners with a different opportunity structure—one that fostered greater neighborhood involvement.

Further, they argue that through increased neighborhood involvement, homeowners had opportunities to expand their social networks and interact with others in their local communities. The researchers speculate that homeownership offers a distinctive pathway to social wealth for low- and moderate-income families. These previous studies suggest that, for most low-income or minority families, owning a home proves to be a positive experience psychologically, socially, and economically—at least in the short run. However, little is known about whether these social benefits of homeownership persist over longer periods of homeownership.

THE CONTEXT: DENVER AND THE DENVER HOUSING AUTHORITY'S HOMEOWNERSHIP PROGRAM

The meaning of *homeownership* for our low-income owners needs to be understood within the context of the Denver metropolitan area housing market during the period from 1995 through 2009. Following a decade of depressed housing prices, the mid-1990s marked the beginning of the most recent housing market boom in Denver, which lasted through 2005. Responding to a growing economy, increased housing demand fueled the construction of thousands of new housing units and the rapid rise of median home values from $71,500 in 1995 to $224,700 in 2001, peaking at $254,600 in 2005 (Joint Center for Housing Studies, 2011). This housing construction boom opened up new neighborhoods to low-income and minority homeowners located on the fringes of the metropolitan area. With the bursting of the housing bubble in 2006, Denver experienced a tsunami of foreclosures—the number of foreclosure filings placing it in the top five cities in 2006. Although Denver no longer is among the nation's leaders in foreclosures, Colorado remains among the top ten states (RealtyTrac, 2011). Presently, Denver's overall foreclosure rate is 0.93%, approximately one third the national rate of 2.8% (CoreLogic, 2013; Joint Center for Housing Studies, 2011).

It was within this context of improving economic and housing markets and the initial push toward using subsidized housing as a springboard to economic self-sufficiency that DHA began its HomeOwnership Program (HOP). Operating since 1995 in conjunction with its federally funded Family Self-Sufficiency (FSS) program, and since 2001 with its Resident Opportunities for Self-Sufficiency (ROSS) program, HOP has provided services to more than 1,600 subsidized housing residents. The goal of HOP is to assist DHA residents in improving their human, financial, and social capital, with the ultimate goal of them buying their own home. From 1995 through 2007, all DHA residents and Housing Choice Voucher (HCV, formerly known as Section 8) recipients were eligible to participate in HOP, regardless of whether they were living in DHA's conventional public housing, scattered-site units, or HCV-subsidized units. Since 2007, HOP homeownership counseling services have been extended to include non-DHA residents, although the majority of participants are still DHA residents.

In the initial phase of the program, participants are eligible for homeownership assessments, free credit reports, credit repair and money management counseling, and classes on a wide variety of topics (e.g., housing finance, home repairs, and shopping for real estate and mortgages). DHA residents also can open individual development accounts with 1:1 matches up to $1,500, and for FSS program participants, rent escrow accounts where increases in DHA rents associated with increasing tenant income are placed into escrow for use for a down payment. Working with program case management staff, HOP participants develop individual training and service plans outlining the steps needed to realize their self-sufficiency and homeownership goals. Also during this initial phase of the program, participants file monthly updates with their HOP technician and their overall plans are reassessed quarterly to ascertain client progress toward goals and compliance with program requirements.

During the final stage of the HOP, participants who are within a year of being able to purchase a home, have at least $500 in savings, and have employment stability are invited to join the Homebuyer's Club (HBC). The primary purpose of the HBC is to prepare participants for the purchase of a home. Participants are required to attend monthly HBC classes, which provide intensive real estate and financial literacy training, presentations by housing industry representatives, and peer support. Membership in HBC provides additional benefits such as lower interest rates, discount fees, down payment and closing cost assistance, and second mortgage assistance.

Since 1995, enrollment in HOP has averaged 400 to 450 participants annually. In any given year, between 5% and 10% of HOP participants are in the Homebuyer's Club. As of 2009, a total of 292 participants had reached this final stage of the HOP. By the end of 2009, slightly more than half (52.4%) of all HBC participants had graduated from the program and purchased homes; approximately 24% had dropped out but went on to purchase homes outside the program; 20% had dropped out and did not purchase homes; and 3% were still in the program.

Slightly less than one third of the 232 homeowners in our study had graduated and purchased their homes as part of HOP, nearly one in six were HOP dropouts, and the remainder were homeowners who never were in HOP (55%). Almost six out of ten study participants (56%) were Latino, 24% were black, about 11% were Vietnamese, and the remaining 9% were white. Slightly more than one third of the homeowners were immigrants. The average age of homeowners at time of home purchase was 38.4 years. Approximately 75% of the homeowners were female and 60% of home buying households were headed by single parents. The average number of children or grandchildren under 18 residing in the household was 2.0. At time of home purchase, the median annual household income was $26,282.

THE MEANING OF HOME FOR LOW-INCOME HOMEOWNERS

Homebuyers in our study were asked an array of questions about their experiences. Several questions asking specifically about the meaning of home and homeownership elicited a total of 401 distinctive responses from study participants. We analyzed their responses to identify themes (see Braun & Clarke, 2006, and Fereday & Muir-Cochrane, 2006, for descriptions of this kind of analysis). Four primary themes about the meaning of home surfaced from our analyses of the data (Kearns et al., 2000). We organized our low-income homeowners' perceptions of home as follows:

1. *home as a haven* providing owners with a sense of security, stability, and privacy;
2. *home as the site of autonomy* providing owners with a sense of control over their dwellings, including the freedom to do what they wanted (e.g., personalize their dwelling space) as well as freedom from doing other things (e.g., not having to respond to the demands of a landlord) within their homes;

3. *home as a source of status or identity* including pride of ownership; and
4. *home as an asset.*

One of the economic benefits of homeownership—home as an asset—stems directly from our study participants' understandings of their homes as representing much more than a roof over their heads. Each of these depictions of home is summarized in Table 16-1 and described in detail below.

Home as a Haven

One of the black HOP graduate homebuyers—a married mother of four—summarized the sense of home as haven as "appreciating the fact that I have a home, having a place that really feels like home." Slightly more than one third of all of the homeowners described their homes as havens, highlighting the sense of security, stability, and privacy that homeownership afforded to them and their families. The importance of security and stability of housing, particularly for households that have experienced significant housing instability and frequent moves, cannot be underestimated. One of the HOP graduates—a black mother of two—described the benefits of owning versus renting as a buffer against housing instability and especially the constant fear that renters faced of losing their home and being forced to move:

> It's like uhh . . . [Renting] That's not stability, that's not security. That's somebody else's stuff. They can say get out any day. And that's the other thing, you know, that as long as you are able to work, that [the house] it's yours.

Table 16-1	The Meaning of Home for Low-income Homeowners
	All homeowners
	Number of responses (% of all responses)
Home as a haven	138 (34.4)
Home as a source of security and stability	82 (20.4)
Home as a source of privacy	56 (14.0)
Home as a site of autonomy	114 (28.4)
Home as status or identity	84 (20.9)
Home as an asset or financial good	65 (16.2)
Total number of responses	401 (100.0)
Total number of respondents	232

Source: Qualitative data derived from the *Denver Housing Study* Retrospective Homeowner Survey. Study participants could identify more than one response on the meaning of home.

Percentages are calculated based on the total number of responses. For example, 34% of all responses described home as a haven, 28% described home as a site of autonomy, 21% described home as a source of status and identity, and the remaining 16% of the responses described home as an asset.

Security, however, meant more than just housing stability to our respondents; it was also financial security. Homeownership protected owners from unexpected or unusually large annual increases in rents while also serving as a mechanism for wealth building as expressed by these homeowners:

> Financially secure in knowing that the mortgage is gonna be pretty much the same. They're not gonna be able to raise it a hundred dollars every single year. (black HOP graduate, mother of one)

> Security, knowing that my hard-earned money is going into my own pocket. (Latina HOP graduate, mother of two)

Denver homeowners also identified security in terms of enhanced personal safety for them and their children. Reflecting on the differences between living in DHA and now in her own home, one Latina HOP graduate who headed a multigenerational family of five quickly responded: "The privacy, the safety of my own place," noting how subsidized housing offered little privacy and varying degrees of safety depending on the tenants and neighborhood where one lived. The perceived lack of safety in subsidized housing led many of our respondents to keep their children indoors. So in describing the meaning of home, another Latina homebuyer who was never in HOP describes the sense of safety she and her two children have derived from their new neighborhood: "My kids play outside and I don't worry that something will happen to them."

Along with security and stability, privacy is a key component of the perceptions of home as haven. In contrast to their experiences in public housing, where DHA staff had access to housing units to conduct mandatory inspections or maintenance tasks, one in seven homeowners reveled in the degree to which they could maintain a sense of privacy. As one black HOP graduate homebuyer noted, "I don't have to answer the door. You know, no more inspections. It's a pleasure knowing that not every year, someone is going to call me and come inspect my house, and I have to be there." This sense of privacy also extends to relations with neighbors. A Latina HOP graduate said, "It's my own place. I don't have to deal with neighbors." Another black homebuyer who purchased outside of the program further underscored this sense of privacy for herself and her two children when not having to contend with neighbors surrounding you on all sides: "[I] can do whatever I want to it. No neighbors above, right next to, or below me."

Home as a Site of Autonomy

Given the context of subsidized housing environments that are highly structured and regulated, it is quite understandable that our sample of low-income homeowners, who have spent considerable time in subsidized housing, would cite autonomy—control over one's dwelling—as one of the primary meanings of home and homeownership. Specifically, owners perceived exclusive control of their environments and expressed the freedom to make choices and do as they pleased without the constraints of requesting permission from anyone.

Approximately 28% of the homeowners in the study cited such control over their dwellings as the key benefit of homeownership. Summing up the experience of many of our low-income homeowners, several owners related their experiences with homeowning and the freedom to both do and to not do things in their homes:

> Being able to make changes, upgrading house. Nobody tells me who could come and go. (black HOP graduate, mother of two)

> I so enjoy not being told what I have to do inside my house. (Latina HOP graduate, mother of five)

> But, it's great! I'm loving it because I know that, you know, they can't put me out and I can do whatever I want to increase my home's value. (single black HOP graduate)

One of the most enjoyable experiences described by our low-income homeowners is the ability to personalize their own space without having to ask permission of the housing authority or landlord. Participants expressed a deep personal satisfaction regarding decorating their own homes and, more commonly, painting the walls any color they wanted. As one black HOP graduate homebuyer and head of a multigenerational family of three explained, "Well for me the most wonderful thing is knowing that I now get to explore my sense of style and decorating. Because I can redo stuff the way I want to." This enjoyment extends to the rest of the family. According to one of the HOP graduate homeowners: "It's nice. It's made my family feel good because they can personalize their house now. They can personalize their room. . . . When we were living in DHA you can't do nothing to 'em" (white father of one).

This heightened sense of autonomy remained primary in the minds of homeowners not only during the initial years of homeownership but also in subsequent years. Our respondents expressed this sense of control in a variety of ways:

> Knowing that it's yours and need no one's permission to make changes. (Latina HOP graduate with five children)

> Just being able to do anything, anytime we want. (Latino father with two kids who never participated in HOP)

Thus, homeownership enabled low-income buyers to regulate and modify their own surroundings in ways that were prohibited in subsidized or rental housing.

Home as Status and Identity

The low-income homeowners in our study recognized how much of one's sense of identity is tied to their home. For 20% of our homeowners, their homes were associated with a sense of pride they felt in becoming homeowners and, in particular, reaching their goal of homeownership. One HOP graduate homebuyer—a black mother of two—describes this sense of pride in accomplishing her goal of homeownership on her own, particularly when confronted by skeptical family members:

> I got my own (home). I did this, and I did it by myself, you know. And um, it just gives me a real sense of strength and pride in being able to accomplish something so big, and to do it on my own. . . . And um, every once in a while my brother, 'cause he's the only one, he'll go off on his little tangents about how everybody's worthless, how nobody's worth anything. And, you know, I just say "You know what, your opinion about me doesn't matter because I own my own home. I own my own car. All the things that I have accomplished, I have accomplished them on my own. Nobody handed me nothing." And, um, for me, what I've done and what I've been able to accomplish, really has strengthened who I am as a person, on the inside. Because it helps to believe in a dream. If you can accomplish something this big, what else can you accomplish if you put your mind and your heart into it?

For some of our participants, this sense of pride in attaining a major goal was accompanied by an increasing sense of self-worth. As this black grandmother and HOP graduate homebuyer noted,

> But, for me it's like they said pride in owning your own and being able to accomplish the goal of owning your own. And the self-esteem that goes with knowing that you know you succeeded at a really big goal. You know? I mean like I said it's not like going out and buying a new car. Or you know you got a new appliance or you got that new big screen TV. You know you're talking about qualifying and being able to buy something in the hundreds of thousands of dollars and you were able to pull it off.

According to a number of the respondents, this sense of identity and pride affected every member of the household and especially the children. In describing this effect on children, one black mother of one, who graduated from the HOP program emphasized:

> One other good thing about being a homeowner is you're showing your children, that, you know, get somewhere and be stable and save your money. Buy your own house, buy you a condo. . . . So you're teaching your children stability, and you're teaching them how to save and you're showing them that you're trying to do better. That you didn't want them raised in what you used to call projects. . . . You know that you didn't want them, you wanted to show them there's a better side of life than just living off the government.

Further, in the eyes of other community members, homeownership conveyed a new sense of identity and status to our study participants. As homeowners, participants who once struggled to obtain modest amounts of financing were deluged with mail and telephone offers for additional sources of credit. Yet, creditors were not the only ones to acknowledge their change in status. As one non-HOP homeowner—a black mother of three—reports, "People in general looked and conversed with me differently (since I became a homeowner)." For many, social status was further enhanced by where they lived. Another of the black HOP graduates described the neighborhood where she purchased a townhome:

> I live in [an] upper crust neighborhood. I mean seriously. The townhome community is surrounded by three, four, five hundred thousand dollar homes. Easy. They just put up a house up around the corner from me . . . and it's got a 6 car garage, okay. No the neighborhood is extremely nice. I mean it's a very, very nice neighborhood.

She went on to note how others treated her and her children differently on the basis of where she now lived.

Home as an Asset

Low-income homeowners were cognizant of the financial benefits associated with homeownership and thus had a sense of home as an asset (see further discussion of these benefits in Santiago et al., 2010a,b). The 16% of homeowners in the study who described their homes as assets acknowledged the potential for increased equity, access to credit, and the tax benefits associated with owning. Study participants viewed homeownership as a much better use of their money relative to continuing to rent. As one non-HOP Latina homebuyer explained, "[I'm] not throwing money away on rent. [I'm] putting money into something that is ours." Another black non-HOP homebuyer caring for her infirm mother noted the long-term benefits of homeownership, particularly as an inheritance for their children: "The money we're putting into it benefits us and those who get it after us."

Despite the housing crisis that permeated the Denver market at the time we interviewed our homeowners, they expressed continued optimism about the potential to build home equity, an optimism that was partially supported by our earlier findings on the financial characteristics of study participants. Moreover, some of the homeowners in the study found that homeownership and holding equity served as a springboard for other opportunities. As mentioned earlier, homeownership opened the floodgates to access more credit. According to this HOP graduate homebuyer—a white mother of one, "[I now have] access to more credit, more lending power . . . [and] feel more secure financially." Moreover, some homeowners, like this Latina HOP program exiter, identified the availability of additional credit "if I were to need it." For some, access to credit strengthened their self-esteem, since more credit appeared to be linked to perceptions of greater worth personally and financially. As another HOP graduate—a black grandmother heading a multigenerational family—described, "[I have] more credit available to me. It has made my self-esteem greater. I am self-sufficient and proud of it!"

Numerous homeowners identified the wealth-building potential of mortgage interest deductions. According to this Latina HOP graduate homebuyer and mother of one, "[The house is a] tax write-off. I can do whatever I want to invest in my home. I have a monetary investment that I can take with me." While they recognized this potential, none of the homebuyers mentioned if they used any tax refunds to actually generate wealth. Moreover, relatively few homebuyers mentioned any other specific wealth-building strategies.

Based on the responses of our study participants to questions regarding the benefits associated with owning a home, it is clear that noneconomic benefits were salient among low-income homeowners. Increased control or autonomy, pride in their identity as homeowners, and increased security and privacy were more important to the homeowners in our study than the financial benefits. Realizing what might have seemed an unreachable goal led many homeowners to a sense of empowerment and belief in their ability to attain other goals in their lives. After purchasing her home, this black mother of one described what keeps her setting new goals:

> My motto in life is to always go forwards, never go backwards. You've already been there so you gotta keep going forward. I guess you gotta constantly keep having goals, you know. I actually started classes in June for nursing school. I'm at the top salary at my job, and I know that I cannot live off of what I make right now. You know the way things are changing in this world, this type of money is not going to work for me forever and I've got to have more options. And I've been stuck before in my life. I'm not stuck anymore and I refuse to just move from this point to this point and then just be at this point. I always want to be able to, I always want to be able to call the shots in my life.

We found relatively few ethnic or gender differences in the meaning of home for our low-income homebuyers. Compared to the low-income men we interviewed, black and Latina women were more likely to express the importance of home as a place providing autonomy, safety, security, stability, and privacy, signaling perhaps the ways in which homeownership served to break down gender barriers in access to housing. Further, they also recognized the effects that homeownership had on increasing their assets and access to credit, also reflecting the differential access to financial resources experienced by minority women.

THE NEIGHBORHOOD CONTEXT OF LOW-INCOME HOMEOWNERSHIP

In this next section of the chapter, we examine the perceptions held by low-income homeowners about their new neighborhoods and communities. To provide a context for their perceptions, we begin with an overview of the actual neighborhood conditions at time of purchase. All low-income homeowners regardless of gender or ethnic background experienced significant improvements in neighborhood quality with the purchase of their homes, when compared to the neighborhoods they lived in as residents of public housing or as holders of Housing Choice vouchers. In addition to moving to more ethnically diverse neighborhoods with higher fractions of white neighbors, low-income homeowners also moved to neighborhoods with fewer children per household and fewer households headed by women. Also, low-income buyers, on average, moved into more affluent neighborhoods with higher percentages of homeowners and newer housing, as well as lower rates of poverty, unemployment, and vacant housing. Nonetheless, when compared to black, white, and Vietnamese homebuyers, Latinos experienced the greatest improvements in neighborhood quality (for further discussion see Santiago, Galster, Tucker, Santiago-San Roman, & Kaiser, 2011).

LOW-INCOME HOMEOWNER PERCEPTIONS OF THEIR NEIGHBORHOODS

As shown in Table 16-2, the vast majority of low-income homeowners (70%) felt that their new homes were located in neighborhoods that were better than their last DHA or Housing Choice Voucher neighborhood. Yet, 23% said that the two neighborhoods were about the same and another 7% said they moved into worse neighborhoods. This last scenario was more likely to occur for homeowners who had lived in either dispersed housing units or units subsidized through the Housing Choice Voucher program. In both cases, the owners had opportunities to rent in neighborhoods that would be financially out of reach for them as homebuyers. Given the economic uncertainties of the Great Recession and housing crisis, homeowners in the study had mixed feelings about the future of their homes and neighborhoods. More than half of the homeowners in our study (56%) anticipated declining quality of life in their neighborhoods and 46% expressed concerns about continuing decreases in property values over the next few years. There were no significant gender or ethnic differences in these perceptions of neighborhood quality.

Homeowners were then asked about a wide range of potential neighborhood concerns that ranged from changes in the characteristics of neighbors, to issues with neighbors and neighborhood children, to criminal activity in the neighborhood. Relatively few homeowners (12% or fewer) reported serious concerns about changing demographics in their neighborhood, including high concentrations of low-income people, the wrong kind of people moving into the neighborhood, or problems with ethnic group conflict. Homeowners also expressed relatively few concerns about the behaviors of neighborhood adults and children. Issues with neighbors generally were not considered to be serious concerns. The most bothersome problems identified were loud music and problem neighbors; however, only one out of seven homeowners considered even these issues as serious neighborhood

Table 16-2 Low-income Homeowners' Perceptions of their Neighborhoods	
	All homeowners (*n* = 232)
Perceptions of current vs. last DHA neighborhood	
Percent reporting new neighborhood is better	70.2
Percent reporting new neighborhood is about the same	23.2
Percent reporting new neighborhood is worse	6.6
Percent anticipating declining quality of life in the neighborhood	55.7
Percent anticipating declining property values	46.2
Percent reporting that neighborhood issue is a serious concern:	
Demographic issues	
Different racial or ethnic groups who do not get along	8.8
Too high concentration of low-income people	6.3
Wrong kind of people moving into neighborhood	11.5
Issues with neighbors	
People hanging out and making a nuisance	11.5
Loud music	14.2
People who bother or insult others on the street	5.8
Neighbors who cause trouble	14.1
Issues with neighborhood children	
Kids dropping out of school	11.1
Teenage girls getting pregnant before marriage	18.6
Many children and teens getting into trouble	14.0
Criminal activity in neighborhood	
Gang activity in the neighborhood	14.4
People selling drugs in the neighborhood	11.8
People engaged in criminal activity	7.5
Homes being burglarized	13.5
People being robbed or mugged	7.4
People getting beaten or raped	3.9

Source: *Denver Housing Study* Retrospective Homeowner Survey. Statistics compiled by authors.

problems. Between 11% and 19% of low-income homeowners identified issues with children as serious neighborhood problems, particularly out-of-wedlock teen childbearing and children getting into trouble. Compared to white and Asian home-buyers, Latinos were particularly concerned about the problem of teen childbearing outside marriage.

Few homeowners identified criminal activity to be a serious concern in the neighborhoods where they purchased their homes. According to the homeowners in the study, the most frequent of these illegal activities were gang activity (14%), home burglaries (14%), and drug dealing (12%). Thus, it would appear that both objective and subjective indicators of neighborhood quality support low-income homeowners' overall perceptions of improved neighborhood quality as one of the returns of homeownership. However, for a small group of these homeowners, the presence of these harmful neighborhood conditions diminished the quality of life.

LOW-INCOME HOMEOWNERS AND THEIR TIES TO THE NEIGHBORHOOD

What perceptions do low-income homeowners have about their neighbors and neighborhoods in terms of social relationships? To what extent do low-income homeowners interact with their neighbors? In order to address these questions we asked homeowners to describe the kinds of connections that they had with neighbors in terms of membership or inclusion, shared values, social cohesion, collective efficacy, resources, intra-neighborhood (within neighborhood) social networks, and extra-neighborhood (outside neighborhood) social networks. A summary of their responses is shown in Table 16-3.

Table 16-3 Low-income Homeowners' Social Ties to their Neighborhoods	
	All homeowners (_n_ = 232)
Percent agreeing	
Inclusion or membership	
Very few of my neighbors know me	60.3
Parents know their children's friends	66.8
Adults know the local children	79.5
Easy to identify strangers	65.9
Shared values	
People in this neighborhood do not share the same values	31.4
There's no point in making the neighborhood nice because others let things go	12.7
Social cohesion	
I care about what my neighbors think of my actions	66.9
People in this neighborhood don't get along with one another	6.5
Collective efficacy	
I have no influence over what the neighborhood is like	25.7
People in the neighborhood can get together to solve neighborhood problems	75.6
Neighborhood resources	
Presence of adult role models for respondent in the neighborhood	67.2
Presence of adult role models for children in the neighborhood	73.0

(Continued)

Table 16-3   (*Continued*)

	All homeowners (*n* = 232)
Adults watch out for children in the neighborhood	76.8
Respondent could borrow $30 from a neighbor in an emergency	47.2
Neighbors watch out for others' property	87.3
Neighbors would shop for groceries if respondent was ill	51.1
Number of individuals	
Extra-neighborhood social networks	
Number of relatives in Denver	5.0
Number of friends in Denver	8.0
Number of total people respondent could ask for ride	3.1
Number of total people respondent could talk re: personal issue	2.8
Number of total people good source of job info	2.2
Number of total people respondent admires for achieving major goal	2.4
Intra-neighborhood social networks	
Number of relatives in neighborhood	1.0
Number of friends in neighborhood	2.0
Number of neighborhood adults respondent recognizes by sight	7.5
Number of neighborhood children respondent recognizes by sight	7.0
Number of people in neighborhood respondent could ask for ride	1.5
Number of people in neighborhood could talk re: personal issue	0.7
Number of people in neighborhood good source of job info	0.3
Number of people in neighborhood respondent admires for achieving major goal	0.2

Source: Denver Housing Study Retrospective Homeowner Survey. Statistics compiled by authors.

INCLUSION OR MEMBERSHIP.   Inclusion or membership refers to the extent to which people feel a part of the larger group within their local neighborhood or community. Overall, nearly eight out of ten low-income homeowners reported that neighborhood adults knew the local children and two thirds of the parents knew their children's friends. Nearly two thirds of the homeowners also indicated that it was easy to identify strangers in their neighborhoods. Yet, this sense of membership within the larger community group appears to be relatively superficial. Six out of ten homeowners indicated that very few of their neighbors actually knew them beyond sight recognition.

SHARED VALUES.   Fewer than one third of the homeowners felt that their neighbors did not share the same values. Still fewer (13%) felt that it was useless to improve their neighborhoods because others would not keep up the neighborhood. Thus, one would expect ties among neighbors would be more extensive in neighborhoods with high perceived levels of shared values.

SOCIAL COHESION.   Social cohesion reflects the sense of connectedness and commitment to a community. Study participants report high levels of social cohesion in their neighborhoods. Most homeowners described their relationships with neighbors as cordial, with only 7% indicating that neighbors did not get along with each other. Further, two thirds expressed concern about how they are viewed by their neighbors, suggesting that they might modify their behaviors in order to meet the perceived expectations of neighbors.

COLLECTIVE EFFICACY.   Collective efficacy reflects the shared beliefs that community members have in their capabilities to achieve an intended goal. Approximately three out of four low-income homeowners in the study reported that they and their neighbors could successfully engage in collective efforts to improve neighborhood conditions or resolve neighborhood problems.

NEIGHBORHOOD RESOURCES.   Neighborhood resources represent the financial, material, or human assets available to members of a given neighborhood. The most frequently mentioned neighborhood resource available to low-income homeowners was that of having neighbors who would watch out for their neighbor's property (87%). In addition, more than three out of four homeowners reported that adults in the neighborhood watched out for neighborhood children; nearly that same fraction of owners reported the presence of adult role models for children in the neighborhood. Two thirds of the homeowners noted the presence of neighborhood role models for them as well. Yet when it came to more intimate relationships with neighbors, the low-income homeowners in our study were much more reluctant to utilize the help of neighbors in emergency situations. Only about half of the homeowners would count on the assistance of neighbors to help purchase groceries and less than half indicated that they would or could borrow $30 from a neighbor if needed.

EXTRA-NEIGHBORHOOD SOCIAL NETWORKS.   We asked the homeowners in our study about the social networks they had developed with people outside their immediate neighborhood. As shown in Table 16-3, homeowners reported an average of eight friends and five relatives residing in the larger Denver metropolitan area. When asked about the number of individuals in these extra-neighborhood networks who could provide them with assistance, information, or advice, homeowners sought such help from a relatively small number of individuals ranging from two people in their networks who could provide job information or whom they admired for achieving personal goals to three individuals they would ask for rides or if they needed to talk to someone about personal issues. This suggests that our low-income homeowners typically did not form extensive social networks outside of their immediate family members and friends.

INTRA-NEIGHBORHOOD SOCIAL NETWORKS.   We posed the same questions about the networks they developed within their neighborhoods. Homeowners had relatively few ties to their neighbors beyond recognizing by sight about seven neighborhood adults or children, on average. Few family members or friends resided in their neighborhoods and, for the most part, homeowners in the study had even fewer neighbors they would use as resources. Very few had any neighbors that they admired or who could provide job information. This would suggest that even the long-term, low-income homeowners in the study generally kept to themselves within their neighborhoods and were reluctant to form close relationships with neighbors.

THE CIVIC ENGAGEMENT OF LOW-INCOME HOMEOWNERS

Given the relatively low interactions with immediate neighbors, to what extent are low-income homeowners involved in neighborhood and community organizations? We asked study participants to identify their participation or attendance at block club or neighborhood meetings, political party organizations, school-related groups, church-related groups, community-based social clubs, and sports teams of other groups. Their responses to these questions are summarized on Table 16-4.

Slightly more than half of the homeowners were involved in any neighborhood or community organization while 48% were not. Given the relatively low rates of civic participation that exist at the neighborhood level in the United States (estimated to be between 10% and 30%, depending on residents' education, income, and ethnicity), it does appear that high fractions of these homeowners are involved in neighborhood activities. We found that homeowners engaged in neighborhood or community organizations were most likely to be participating in church (35%) or school-related (23%) groups. About one in eight participated in neighborhood block club meetings and one in nine was active in community social clubs, sports teams, or other women's or men's groups. Only 2% reported attending political party meetings. Black, Latino, and Asian homeowners were less likely to participate in PTA meetings than were whites. However, the lack of reliable estimates of civic engagement among homeowners, and among low-income homeowners in particular, makes it difficult to place these patterns of participation within a larger context.

Table 16-4 Civic Engagement of Low-income Homeowners in Neighborhood and Community	
	All homeowners (*n* = 232)
Participation in neighborhood or community organizations	
Percent attending block club or neighborhood group meetings	12.8
Percent attending political party organizations	2.2
Percent attending PTA or school-related groups	22.9
Percent attending social clubs, sports teams, women's or men's groups	10.6
Percent attending church-related groups	35.2
Percent not involved in any neighborhood or community organizations	48.5
Percent involved in one neighborhood or community organization	30.0
Percent involved in 2 or more neighborhood/community organizations	21.5

Source: Denver Housing Study Retrospective Homeowner Survey. Statistics compiled by authors.

Conclusion

Since the 1990s, federal programs have encouraged ever lower-income households to buy homes. Because of the current economic and housing market crisis in the United States, concerns have been raised regarding the desirability of continuing support of low-income homeownership policies. Given the current economic constraints on the financial returns of homeownership, particularly for less affluent owners, we underscore the need to consider the social benefits of homeownership when assessing the potential costs and risks to low-income buyers. We assessed the social returns of homeownership by investigating the homeowning experiences of a group of very low-income homeowners in Denver. This sample of homeowners is unique since it is comprised of former recipients of housing subsidies, half of whom voluntarily participated in a multiyear homeownership counseling and asset-building program. The other half consisted of subsidized housing residents who purchased on their own.

Based on the experiences of these participants, our findings suggest that low-income homeownership confers an array of social benefits that has been rarely discussed in the literature (e.g., Shlay, 2006) to a population that long has been marginalized within U.S. society. These benefits include:

- Autonomy, security, stability, and privacy, as well as social status and identity.
- Pride and accomplishment for homeowners and their entire families.
- Higher social status and benefits such as access to more credit.
- Sense of membership and cohesion with their neighbors.
- Connections to neighborhood or community organizations, primarily church or school-related groups.

We also found that some of these benefits accrued differently for women than men as well as across ethnic groups (McCall, 2005). However, it would appear that there were more similarities of experience than differences based on the class positions that these low-income homeowners held within the larger society.

In sum, our findings suggest that there may be multiple social benefits associated with public policies and programs aimed at supporting low-income homeownership—benefits that need to be considered when evaluating such policies and programs. During this time of economic uncertainty, programs designed to help keep the American Dream alive for low-income homeowners by helping them remain in their homes may also enable them to keep the social benefits they have acquired.

References

Allen, B. L. (2002). Race and gender inequality in homeownership: Does place make a difference? *Rural Sociology, 67,* 603–621.

Belsky, E. S., Retsinas, N. P., & Duda, M. (2005). *The financial returns to low-income homeownership.* Cambridge, MA: Harvard University.

Bocian, D. G., Li, W., Reid, C., & Quercia, R. G. (2011, November). *Lost ground, 2011: Disparities in mortgage lending and foreclosures.* Chapel Hill: University of North Carolina, Center for Responsible Lending.

Boehm, T. P., & Schlottman, A. M. (2003). The dynamics of race, income, and homeownership. *Journal of Urban Economics, 55,* 113–130.

Boehm, T. P., & Schlottman, A. M. (2004). *Wealth accumulation and homeownership: Evidence for low-income households.* Washington, DC: U.S. Department of Housing and Urban Development, Office of Policy Development and Research.

Bostic, R. W., & Lee, K. O. (2008). Mortgages, risk, and homeownership among low- and moderate-income families. *American Economic Review: Papers and Proceedings, 98,* 310–314.

Bowdler, J., Quercia, R., & Smith, D. (2010). *The foreclosure generation: The long-term impact of the housing crisis on Latino children and families.* Washington, DC: National Council of la Raza.

Braun, V., & Clarke, V. (2006). Using thematic analysis in psychology. *Qualitative Research in Psychology, 3*, 77–101.

CoreLogic. (2013, April). *National foreclosure report.* Retrieved from http://www.corelogic.com/research/foreclosure-report/national-foreclosure-report-April-2013.pdf

DiPasquale, D., & Glaeser, E. (1999). Incentives and social capital: Are homeowners better citizens? *Journal of Urban Economics, 45*, 354–384.

Easthope, H. (2004). A place called home. *Housing, Theory and Society, 21*, 128–138.

Englehardt, G. V., Erikson, M. D., Gale, W. G., & Mills, G. B. (2010). What are the social benefits of home-ownership? Experimental evidence for low-income households. *Journal of Urban Economics, 67*, 249–258.

Fereday, J., & Muir-Cochrane, E. (2006). Demonstrating rigor using thematic analysis: A hybrid approach of inductive and deductive coding and theme development. *International Journal of Qualitative Methods, 5*, 1–11.

Florida, R. (2010, June 7). Homeownership is over-rated. *The Wall Street Journal*, p. A17.

Galster, G. (1987). *Homeowners and neighborhood reinvestment.* Durham, NC: Duke University Press.

Galster, G. (2008). Scholarship on U.S. housing, planning, and policy: The evolving topography since 1968. *Journal of the American Planning Association, 74*, 1–12.

Galster, G., Marcotte, D., Mandell, M., Wolman, H., & Augustine, N. (2007). The impacts of parental homeownership on children's outcomes during early adulthood. *Housing Policy Debate, 18*, 785–827.

Galster, G., & Santiago, A. M. (2008). Low-income homeownership as an asset-building tool: What can we tell policymakers? In M. A. Turner, H. Wial, & H. Wolman, (Eds.), *Urban and regional policy and its effects* (pp. 60–108). Washington, DC: Brookings Institution Press.

Goetzmann, W. N., & Spiegel, M. (2002). Policy implications of portfolio choice in underserved mortgage markets. In N. P. Retsinas & E. S. Belsky (Eds.), *Low-income homeownership: Examining the unexamined goal* (pp. 257–274). Washington, DC: Brookings Institution Press.

Gramlich, E. M. (2007). *Subprime mortgages: America's latest boom and bust.* Washington, DC: Urban Institute Press.

Green, R. K., & White, M. J. (1997). Measuring the benefits of homeowning: Effects on children. *Journal of Urban Economics, 41*, 441–461.

Grinstein-Weiss, M., Lee, J., Greeson, J., Han, C., Yeo, Y., & Irish, K. (2008). Fostering low-income homeownership through Individual Development Accounts: A longitudinal, randomized experiment. *Housing Policy Debate, 19*, 711–740.

Harkness, J. M., & Newman, S. J. (2003). Differential effects of homeownership on children from higher- and lower-income families. *Journal of Housing Research, 14*, 1–19.

Haurin, D. R., Parcel, T. L., & Haurin, R. J. (2002). Impact of home ownership on child outcomes. In N. P. Retsinas & E. S. Belsky (Eds.), *Low income homeownership: Examining the unexamined goal* (pp. 427–446). Washington, DC: Brookings Institution Press.

Haurin, D. R., & Rosenthal, S. S. (2005). *The growth of earnings of low-income households and the sensitivity of their homeownership choices to economic and socio-demographic shocks.* Washington, DC: U.S. Department of Housing and Urban Development, Office of Policy Development & Research.

Herbert, C. E., & Belsky, E. S. (2006). *The homeownership experiences of low-income and minority families: A review and synthesis of the literature.* Cambridge, MA: Abt Associates.

Hoff, K., & Sen, A. (2005). Homeownership, community interactions, and segregation. *American Economic Review, 95*, 1167–1189.

Immergluck, D. (2008). From the subprime to the exotic: Expanded mortgage market risk and implications for metropolitan areas and neighborhoods. *Journal of the American Planning Association, 73*, 59–76.

Joint Center for Housing Studies. (2011). *The state of the nation's housing.* Boston, MA: Joint Center for Housing Studies, Harvard University.

Kaus, M. (2011, April 3). Push low-income home purchases? Not again? Retrieved from https://google.com/#q=Kaus+push+low-income+home+purchases%3Fpurchases-not-again/

Kearns, A., Hiscock, R., Ellaway, A., & Macintyre, S. (2000). "Beyond four walls" The psycho-social benefits of home: Evidence from West Central Scotland. *Housing Studies, 15*, 387–410.

Kochhar, R., Gonzalez-Barrera, A. & Dockterman, D. (2009, May). *Through boom and bust: Minorities, immigrants and homeownership.* Washington, DC: Pew Hispanic Center.

Langer, G. (2010, September 21). On politics, economy and the American Dream. Retrieved from http://abcnews.go.com/Politics/Polling/abc-newsyahoo-news-poll-reality-check-politics-economy/story?id=11662904

Lerman, R. (2011, March 30). Fighting the last war on homeownership. Urban Institute, MetroTrends Blog. Retrieved from http://blog.metrotrends.org/2011/03/fighting-the-last-war-on-homeownership/

Listokin, D., Wyly, E. K., Schmitt, B., & Voicu, I. (2002). *The potential and limitations of mortgage innovation in fostering homeownership in the United States.* Washington, DC: Fannie Mae Foundation.

Locke, G., Abbenante, M., Ly, H., Michlin, N., Tsen, W., & Turnham, J. (2006). *Voucher homeownership study: Cross-site analysis* (Vol. 1). Washington, DC: U.S. Department of Housing and Urban Development, Office of Policy Development and Research.

Lutes Fuentes, N. (2009). Defrauding the American Dream: Predatory lending in Latino communities and reform of California's lending law. *California Law Review, 97,* 1279–1335.

Mallett, S. (2004). Understanding home: A critical review of the literature. *Sociological Review, 52*(1), 62–89.

Manturuk, K., Lindblad, M., & Quercia, R. (2010). Friends and neighbors: Homeownership and social capital among low- to moderate-income families. *Journal of Urban Affairs, 32,* 471–488.

Manzo, L. C. (2003). Beyond house and home: Toward a revisioning of emotional relationships with places. *Journal of Environmental Psychology, 23,* 47–61.

Marcuse, P. (1975). Residential alienation, home ownership and the limits of shelter policy. *Journal of Sociology and Social Welfare, 3,* 181–203.

McCall, L. (2005). The complexity of intersectionality. *Signs: A Journal of Women in Culture and Society, 30*(3), 771–800.

McCormack, K. (2012). Comfort and burden: The changing meaning of home for owners at-risk of foreclosure. *Symbolic interaction, 35,* 421–437.

McKernan, S., & Sherraden, M. (2008). *Asset building and low-income families.* Washington, DC: Urban Institute Press.

Miller, S. (2010, September 20). Obama's economic town hall: "Is the American Dream dead for me?" Retrieved from http://www.freerepublic.com/focus/news/2593009/pos

Mitchell, M., & Warren, S. P. (1998). Making home ownership a reality. In *Survey of Habitat for Humanity International (HFHI), Inc., homeowners and affiliates.* Washington, DC: U.S. Department of Housing and Urban Development, Office of Policy Development and Research.

Nothaft, F. E., & Chang, Y. (2005). Creating wealth in low-income communities: Refinance and the accumulation of home equity wealth. In N. P. Retsinas & E. S. Belsky (Eds.), *Building assets, building credit: Creating wealth in low-income communities* (pp. 71–102). Washington, DC: Brookings Institution Press.

Pitcoff, W. (2003, January/February). Has homeownership been oversold? National Housing Institute, *Shelterforce Online* (No. 127). Retrieved from http://www.nhi.org/online/issues/127/homeownership.html

Quigley, J. M. (2008). Housing policy in the United States. In S. N. Durlauf & L. E. Blume (Eds.), *The New Palgrave dictionary of economics online* (2nd ed.). Palgrave Macmillan. Retrieved from http://www.dictionaryofeconomics.com/article?id=pde2008_H000098

RealtyTrac. (2011, January 12). Record 2.9 million U.S. properties receive foreclosure filings in 2010 despite 30-month low in December. Retrieved from http://www.realtytrac.com/content/press-releases/record-29-million-us-properties-receive-foreclosure-filings-in-2010-despite-30-month-low-in-december-6309

Reid, M. (2010). Gender and race in the history of housing policy and research: From industrialization to Hurricane Katrina. *Sociology Compass, 4,* 180–192.

Renuart, E. (2004). An overview of the predatory lending process. *Housing Policy Debate, 15,* 467–502.

Retsinas, N. P., & Belsky, E. S., (Eds.) (2002). *Low income homeownership: Examining the unexamined goal.* Washington, DC: Bookings Institution Press.

Rohe, W., Quercia, R., & Van Zandt, S. (2002). *Supporting the American Dream of home ownership: An assessment of the Neighborhood Reinvestment's Home Ownership Pilot Program.* Chapel Hill: Center for Urban and Regional Studies, University of North Carolina Press.

Rohe, W., & Stegman, M. (1994a). The effects of home ownership on the self-esteem, perceived control, and life satisfaction of low-income people. *Journal of the American Planning Association, 60,* 173–184.

Rohe, W., & Stegman, M. (1994b). The impact of home ownership on the social and political involvement of low-income people. *Urban Affairs Quarterly, 30,* 152–172.

Rohe, W. M., & Basolo, V. (1997). Long-term effects of homeownership on the self-perceptions and social interaction of low-income persons. *Environment and Behavior, 29*, 793–819.

Rohe, W. M., & Quercia, R. G. (2003). *Individual and neighborhood impacts of Neighborhood Reinvestment's Homeownership Pilot Program.* Chapel Hill: University of North Carolina, Center for Urban and Regional Studies.

Rohe, W. M., & Watson, H. L., (Eds.) (2007). *Chasing the American Dream: New perspectives on affordable homeownership.* Ithaca, NY: Cornell University Press.

Rossi, P. H., & Weber, E. (1996). The social benefits of homeownership: Empirical evidence from national surveys. *Housing Policy Debate, 7*, 1–35.

Santiago, A. M., Galster, G. C., Kaiser, A. A., Santiago-San Roman, A. H., Grace, R. A., & Linn, A. T. H. (2010a). Low income homeownership: Does it necessarily mean sacrificing neighborhood quality to buy a home? *Journal of Urban Affairs, 32*, 171–198.

Santiago, A. M., Galster, G. C., Santiago-San Roman, A. H., Tucker, C. M., Kaiser, A. A., Grace, R. A., & Linn, A. T. H. (2010b). Foreclosing on the American Dream? The financial consequences of low-income homeownership. *Housing Policy Debate, 20*, 707–742.

Santiago, A. M., Galster, G. C., Tucker, C. M., Santiago-San Roman, A. H., & Kaiser, A. A. (2011). Be it ever so humble, there's no place like home: The experiences of recent, low-income homebuyers. In K. Patterson & R. Silverman (Eds.), *Fair and affordable housing policy in the United States: Trends, outcomes, and future directions* (pp. 289–342). Leiden, NL, and Boston, MA: Brill, Studies in Critical Social Science.

Saunders, P., & Williams, P. (1988). The constitution of the home: Towards a research agenda. *Housing Studies, 3*, 81–93.

Schwartz, A. F. (2006). *Housing policy in the United States: An introduction.* New York, NY: Routledge.

Shapiro, T. M., & Wolff, E. N. (2001). *Assets for the poor: Benefits and mechanisms of spreading asset ownership.* New York, NY: Russell Sage.

Sherraden, M. (1991). *Assets and the poor: A new American welfare policy.* Armonk, NY: M. E. Sharpe.

Shlay, A. B. (2006). Low-income homeownership: American Dream or delusion? *Urban Studies, 43*, 511–531.

Stegman, M. A., Quercia, R. G., & Davis, W. (2007). The wealth-creating potential of homeownership: A preliminary assessment of price appreciation among low-income homebuyers. In W. M. Rohe & H .L. Watson (Eds.), *Chasing the American dream: New perspectives on affordable home ownership* (pp. 271–292). New York, NY: Cornell University Press.

Stegman, M. A., Quercia, R. G., McCarthy, G. W., Foster, M., & Rohe, W. M. (1991). Designing better homeownership assistance programs using the Panel Study of Income Dynamics (PSID): An exploratory analysis. *Journal of Housing Research, 2*, 39–85.

Turner, M. A., & Skidmore, F. (1999). *Mortgage lending discrimination: A review of existing evidence.* Washington, DC: Urban Institute Press.

Turner, M. A., Freiberg, F., Godfrey, E., Herbig, C., Levy, D. K., & Smith, R. R. (2002). *All other things being equal: A paired testing study of mortgage lending institutions.* Washington, DC: U.S. Department of Housing and Urban Development.

Turner, T. M., & Smith, M. T. (2009). Exits from homeownership: The effects of race, ethnicity and income. *Journal of Regional Science, 49*, 1–32.

U.S. Department of Housing and Urban Development. (2002). *Barriers to minority homeownership.* Washington, DC: Author.

Van Zandt, S., & Rohe, W. M. (2011). The sustainability of low income home-ownership: The incidence of unexpected costs and needed repairs among low income buyers. *Housing Policy Debate, 21*, 317–341.

Wiranowski, M. (2003). *Sustaining home ownership through education and counseling.* Boston, MA: Fellowship Program for Emerging Leaders in Community and Economic Development, Neighborhood Reinvestment Corporation, Joint Center for Housing Studies of Harvard University.

Woldoff, R. A., & Ovandia, S. (2009). Not getting their money's worth: African-American disadvantages in converting income, wealth, and education into residential quality. *Urban Affairs Review, 45*, 66–91.

Wyly, E. K., & Hammel, D. J. (2004). Gentrification, segregation, and discrimination in the American urban system. *Environment and Planning, 36*, 1215–1241.

Food Insecurity in the United States

Who's Hungry?

Keiko Tanaka, Patrick H. Mooney, and Brett Wolff

INTRODUCTION

Modern media has given us ready images of hungry people: hungry children with potbellies and big teary eyes in Africa, hungry mothers in Bangladesh rocking their bodies with babies in their arms, or a line of men in front of a soup kitchen door in New York. These images of individuals privately struggling to get food contrast with, and complement, discussions of hunger as a public issue: policy decisions, international aid in the face of famine, and the impacts of a globalized food system.

According to the Food and Agriculture Organization of the United Nations (FAO) (2010), 925 million people (or approximately 13.4%) in the world are estimated to be *undernourished* or *hungry*. Only 2% of the world's hungry lives in developed countries. The FAO defines undernourishment (often used interchangeably with hunger) as the condition when people's caloric intake falls below the minimum dietary energy requirement necessary to engage in light activities and sustain a minimum acceptable weight and height (FAO, 2010). Hundreds of millions more are *malnourished*; they may be obtaining enough calories but those calories are nutritionally inadequate to sustain their health.

Food security is another term related to hunger. According to the U.S. Department of Agriculture (USDA), 14.9% (17.9 million) of U.S. households experienced food insecurity, or difficulty in providing enough food for all its members because of a lack of resources, at some time during the year of 2011 (Coleman-Jensen, Nord, Andrews, & Carlson, 2012). In this so-called nation of plenty, with the world's largest economy, with food exports of $13 billion and food imports valued at $8 billion (USDA Foreign Agricultural Service, 2013), how is it possible that one in every seven households does not get enough food?

This chapter will examine hunger as a social problem that reflects unequal relations among diverse populations in the United States. We present hunger as a critical class issue that intersects with gender, race, ethnicity, age, and disability to create a diverse array of food insecure people that defy any simple, one-size-fits-all solutions. We focus on *food insecurity*, rather than undernourishment. We will discuss food insecurity as an important sociological concept with four inter-related dimensions, including: *accessibility, availability, affordability,* and *adequacy.* The first section briefly reviews some basic current demographic data on food insecurity in the United States. The second discusses each of the four dimensions of food security introduced above in light of social inequalities in the increasingly diverse population of the United States. In the third section, we present key findings from our ongoing study that synthesizes research, instruction, and service in the Lexington Community Food Assessment (LCFA) of the University of Kentucky College of Agriculture, Food and Environment (see http://uky.ag/lcfa/). This local illustration of food insecurity in Lexington-Fayette County, Kentucky, sheds light on what food insecurity looks like in one particular community. We conclude with examining a set of myths about the private and public components of food insecurity addressed through the LCFA. Particularly we address the ways in which: (a) certain at-risk groups have become even more vulner-able to food-related problems, and (b) groups traditionally not considered vulnerable are having their first experiences with food insecurity.

HOUSEHOLD FOOD INSECURITY IN THE UNITED STATES

Let us briefly look at the current state of household food security in the United States. Keep in mind that such data are important in shaping nutritional supplement and anti-hunger programs and policies at the national and state levels.

The USDA broadly defines a food insecure household as one that at some point dur-ing the last year could not claim to "have consistent, dependable access to enough food for active, healthy living" (Coleman-Jensen et al., 2012, p. v). Since the mid-1990s, the Economic Research Service (ERS) of the USDA has collected annual data on food security through its Current Population Survey. An 18-item questionnaire determines whether a household was considered "food insecure" during the last year. Of these 18 questions, eight relate specifically to feeding children in the household. The topics covered include the lack of money to buy food, skipping meals, and whether or not this was a temporary (monthly) occurrence or a chronic problem. Most food-insecure households, especially in developed nations such as the United States, are only food-insecure for a brief time period, such as a period of unemployment, or when a family member becomes ill and health care costs put extreme pressure on family budgets. Other households tend to suf-fer hunger temporarily, but recurrently, such as at the end of each month, or annually, due to regular seasonal fluctuations in employment. The USDA further breaks food inse-curity down into "low food security" and "very low food security." The "low food secu-rity" label applies to households who indicate food access issues (reported three to five food insecure conditions) in their surveys, but who have not had to make drastic changes in their food intake as a result. Those households exhibiting "very low food security" (reported six or more food insecure conditions) have presumably made changes and reductions in their food intake as a result of the food access issues they have indicated.[1]

---

[1]Before 2006, these categories were called "food insecure without hunger," and "food insecure with hunger."

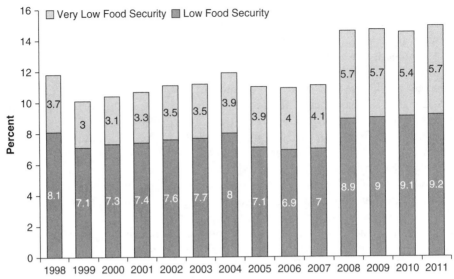

FIGURE 17-1 Prevalence of Household-Level Food Insecurity, 1999–2011: Low Food Secure versus Very Low Food Secure Households.

Source: Coleman-Jensen, Nord, Andrews, & Carlson (2012)

Let us first examine some numbers from the 2011 Household Food Insecurity Report, published by the USDA Economic Research Service (Coleman-Jensen et al., 2012). When reading these numbers, it is very important to understand differences between households and individuals as a unit of analysis, among various demographic categories used to break down the aggregate data, and among three categories of food security ("food secure," "low food insecurity," and "very low food insecurity").

Between 1999 and 2011, the prevalence of household food insecurity in the United States increased from 10.1% to 14.9% (see Figure 17-1), or an increase of roughly 7.3 million households. Over the same period, the number of individuals living in food-insecure households increased from 36 million to 50 million. Although the rate of food-insecure households declined in 2004 and 2005, the proportion of households with "very low food insecurity" among food-insecure households rose from 29.7% in 1999 to 32.8% in 2004 and then to 35.5% in 2005. By 2008, the proportion of "very low food security" within the overall food-insecure population was 39%. A nearly 2% increase in both categories of the food insecure was particularly noticeable in 2008, indicating that economic situations for many American households and individuals deteriorated over the 12 months from December 2007. This indicates two important trends. First, the overall prevalence of food insecurity has increased. Second, the relative severity among food-insecure households has also increased.

Household food insecurity varies by ethnicity. As shown in Table 17-1, non-Hispanic black and Hispanic households experience food insecurity at a disproportionate rate relative to whites. In absolute numbers, white households constitute the largest single food insecure group, but it is clear from the population proportions that the burden is disproportionately distributed by race and ethnicity.

Another very vulnerable group is children. According to the same USDA-ERS report, 20.6% of households with children were food insecure at some point in 2011

Table 17-1 Household Food Security, by Race, by Food Security Status of Household, 1999 versus 2011

Year	Total households		White, non-Hispanic		Black, non-Hispanic		Hispanic		Other	
	1,000	%	1,000	%	1,000	%	1,000	%	1,000	%
Food secure										
1999	94,154	89.9%	73,451	93.0%	9,936	78.8%	7,285	79.2%	3,482	89.8%
2011	101,631	85.1%	73,823	88.6%	11,066	74.9%	10,829	73.8%	6,113	87.3%
Food insecure										
All										
1999	10,529	10.1%	5,546	7.0%	2,680	21.2%	1,907	20.8%	396	10.2%
2011	17,853	14.9%	9,481	11.4%	3,699	25.1%	3,781	26.2%	892	12.7%
Low food security										
1999	7,420	7.1%	3,873	4.9%	1,866	14.8%	1,406	15.3%	275	7.1%
2011	11,014	9.2%	5,689	6.8%	2,155	14.6%	2,583	17.9%	587	8.4%
Very low food security										
1999	3,109	3.0%	1,673	2.1%	814	6.4%	502	5.5%	121	3.1%
2011	6,839	5.7%	3,792	4.6%	1,544	10.5%	1,198	8.3%	305	4.4%

Sources: Andrews, Nord, Bickel, & Carlson (1999); Coleman-Jensen, Nord, Andrews, & Carlson (2012)

while only 12.2% of those without children reported problems. Single-parent households experienced disproportionate levels of food insecurity. While 24.9% of households with children headed by a single man experienced food insecurity, 36.8% of those headed by single women were food insecure.

Keep in mind that these numbers reflect certain social and economic transformations in American society, to which we will now turn our attention.

Context

According to the National Bureau of Economic Research (NBER), the United States was in recession between March and November 2001, and then in the Great Recession between December 2007 and June 2009 (Sum & Khatiwada, 2010). According to the U.S. Department of Labor, Bureau of Labor Statistics (BLS), unemployment climbed to 6.3% in June 2003, and to 10.1% in October 2009 (U.S. Bureau of Labor Statistics, 2011). During the same period, the consumer price index (CPI) for food in urban areas[2] steadily rose, with the largest jump, 10.9%, between 2007 and 2008. In other words, food became increasingly more expensive as more individuals became unemployed. This increased uncertainty with the nation's economy forced more households to make difficult spending choices.

These types of aggregate data are useful in assessing how macro level socioeconomic and political factors might have shaped everyday lives of individuals and understanding how personal troubles such as hunger and food insecurity may be part of broad societal trends which affect a large number of individuals and households at the county, state, regional, and national scale. Among numerous research bureaus and agencies within the U.S. government that offer such data, the USDA Food Environment Atlas (http://www.ers.usda.gov/foodatlas/) is a powerful tool for investigating how environmental factors, including proximity to food stores and restaurants, food prices, the availability of food and nutrition assistance programs, and community characteristics, may affect people's choices for food, and consequently the quality of their diet. This interactive site, which became available in 2010, allows for analysis of county-level indicators to examine the level of food insecurity and the creation of maps to compare geographical differences.

It is important to recognize some limitations of these aggregate data in order to avoid overgeneralization, and worse, stereotyping of certain social groups while over-looking other groups. First, aggregate data are very good at showing trends among individual categories, but mask variations within them. All people of a given racial group or living situation are not the same and neither is their relationship with food, but data at the large scale do not tell us about these differences. Second, these trend data alone are not sufficient to explain why a given social phenomenon (e.g., unemployment, food CPI increase) may produce different outcomes (e.g., low food security versus very low food security) among similar households within a given geographical area. To address a social problem, it is critically important to understand its causes. Unfortunately, most social problems are results of complex interactions of numerous factors, which may or may not be effectively measured. As a result, simple linear patterns of causation are nearly impossible to construct. However, correlations among a spectrum of factors such as unemployment, poverty, and food security can help us to understand the changes we observe in these phenomena. Finally, measures through which data are collected always include

---

[2] Food CPI in rural areas was not available on the BLS website.

some assumptions while excluding others. The above-mentioned food security questionnaire used by USDA-ERS can be examined as an example of what exactly are included and excluded as key variables empirically measuring food security. The choices we make about how to measure a problem have broad, often hard-to-see consequences for how we understand it. In the next section, we focus on food security as a sociological concept with four different, though closely interrelated, dimensions. By dissecting the concept, we will demonstrate that the ERS's Current Population Survey questionnaire overemphasizes certain dimensions, while neglecting others (Wolff, 2012). It should also become more apparent why food insecurity as a social problem is very difficult to measure effectively.

FOUR DIMENSIONS OF FOOD SECURITY

The term food security is used in varied ways by many different organizations and interest groups. The FAO's Committee on World Food Security defines food security as "when all people, at all times, have physical, social and economic access to sufficient safe and nutritious food that meets their dietary needs and food preferences for an active and healthy life" (FAO Committee on Food Security, 2011, n.p.). We can break this general definition down to four dimensions of food security: availability, accessibility, affordability, and adequacy. We consider these four dimensions of food security as conceptually distinct, but they overlap in most actual situations. Below we compare some of those micro–macro differences as we discuss these four dimensions.

At the macro level, availability refers to whether a society (usually a nation) simply has enough food to sustain the lives of its entire population. Busch and Lacy (1984) argue that this depends on an agricultural and food distribution system that: (a) can produce enough food in the short run; (b) is sustainable in the long run; (c) does not place undue risks on agricultural producers; and (d) responds rapidly to disruptions in the food supply due to natural disasters (e.g., earthquakes, hurricanes), civil disturbances (e.g., wars), environmental imbalances (e.g., climate change, soil loss), or other causes. Today, most developed nations depend extensively on the world market to correct short-run imbalances and disruptions in the food supply in particular places.

Many critics of the food system contend, however, that the more serious problem is the long-term sustainability of our industrialized agriculture production and food distribution system, which are both highly dependent on oil and other forms of energy to produce and to move food long distances from farm to market. These concerns have been enhanced in recent years as increasingly more agricultural land and production are being directed to producing biofuels rather than food. While this development has raised farm commodity prices (as well as rent and land prices) for many farmers, it has also, of course, led to higher food prices for consumers here and abroad. In several countries (e.g., Yemen, Haiti, Egypt, Pakistan, Indonesia, Ivory Coast, and Mexico), food price increases due to the restructuring of agriculture toward biofuels have actually led to food riots (Bailey, 2008).

At the micro level, we might consider availability as management of seasonal and regional variations of food to meet the nutritional needs of household members. Before transportation and refrigeration technology expanded the geographical and temporal availability of food at the macro level, households largely relied on various processing techniques for food preservation (e.g., drying, fermentation, pickling, smoking), which were handed down over generations, to extend the availability of food during the winter months. Think of strawberries. Before refrigerators became a common household appliance, many households preserved strawberries in the form of jams and preserves. Today, fresh or frozen strawberries are available for us all year round in the United States, regardless of location. Ironically, as the food economy has overcome geographical and temporal specificities of agricultural production through global trade of diverse food products, much of the knowledge and skills for gardening and food preservation, such as growing strawberries and making strawberry jams, have become lost or a tradition to be rediscovered and learned through formal training.

Accessibility refers to all members of society being able to obtain the food they need. At the macro and mid-range levels, this issue has become particularly significant in terms of what have become known as *food deserts*: large spatial areas within urban or rural areas where there are few, if any, grocery stores or other establishments that sell food, and residents have difficulty purchasing that food. There are, of course, also areas where there are food retailers, but the choices are quite limited. In most of these cases, the problem is particularly one of an absence of fresh foods, especially fruits and vegetables. Significantly, not all food deserts are identical. A recent report to Congress (Ver Ploeg et al., 2009) analyzed food deserts and found that urban food deserts are, not surprisingly, characterized by high levels of racial segregation and poverty. In rural food deserts, accessibility is also associated with poverty but especially with inadequate transportation infrastructure. Measuring food deserts usually involves identifying urban neighborhoods that are more than one mile (walkable distance, according to Ver Ploeg et al., 2009, p. 3) from supermarkets and grocery stores. In rural areas, a distance of more than 10 miles from a supermarket or grocery store has been used as a measure (Morton, Bitto, Oakland, & Sand, 2005) of a rural food desert. Of course, the latter assumes that every rural household has access to a vehicle since very few rural areas in the United States have public transportation between communities or across the countryside. Community-level case studies can help us better understand the unique dynamics (e.g., urban bus routes, residential segregation) and characteristics (e.g., locations of different types of food stores) of specific food deserts. However, such studies require considerable time and expense to gather data.

In places where there are limited retail outlets for food, the prices customers must pay are usually high. That leads us to recognize that, for some analysts, accessibility necessarily includes affordability. As Busch and Lacy (1984) noted, "simply making food available is not enough; one must also be able to purchase it" (p. 2). This dimension of food insecurity is perhaps most easily observed and understood at the micro or household level. Indeed, this is the most common level of measurement by most government agencies and other organizations in surveys. Affordability problems can also be recognized at macro levels of entire nations that can neither produce nor import enough food. Ironically, in some cases, nations that export many agricultural products also have large portions of their populations (including farmers) who are food insecure. This is especially the case when a nation's agriculture is dedicated to the production of non-staple products such as coffee, cotton, or cut flowers, or to the export of meat products that consume much of the grain that might otherwise be available for human consumption.[3]

Adequacy refers to the provision of balanced diets for the nutritional needs of various segments of the population and implies that food is free from disease and toxic

---

[3] Many food assistance programs that provide surplus agricultural products to "hungry" nations can impede the development of that nation's long-term food security by depressing local prices for their own farmers, rendering agricultural production of staple products for the domestic market an unsustainable occupation.

substances. It may also include a number of cultural or personal preferences regarding what foods should be included in an adequate diet. Busch and Lacy (1984) contend that a "secure food system should not impose undue social, economic or health costs" on any particular segments of the population (p. 2). Measurement of adequacy is, perhaps, the most contentious aspect of food security. Experts often disagree about what foods are *safe* (e.g., with regard to chemical pesticides, herbicides, genetically modified organisms [GMOs]) and *healthy* to eat. There is also the question of the possibility of households obtaining a culturally adequate diet based on ethnic, religious, and ideological reasons. We might consider, for example, recent immigrants who can only obtain access to a portion of the foods typical of their familiar culture. While they can find some familiar foods, they are often unable to find all of the foods that made up the traditional and possibly more nutritionally balanced diets in their country of origin. Other cultural or subcultural norms may be considered with respect to adequacy. Some religious beliefs, such as eating kosher (Judaism) or halal (Islam) dictate particular dietary needs. Many Americans also have particular religious, moral, political, or health interests such as moral or religious objections to GMO products, concerns with animal rights, vegetarian needs, issues with chemical contamination, or apparently increasing problems of allergic reactions to food that inform their understanding of the adequacy of the food supply.

One problem with global and national measures of availability and adequacy is that some measures can hide food insecurity (Kimura, 2013). The United Nations and World Bank, for instance, often measure food security as the number of calories consumed in a particular nation. Some nations, such as the United States, would appear under such a measurement to have plenty of available food. In this case, the extremely high level of calorie consumption by many Americans will, in measures of average or per capita consumption, statistically obscure that portion of the population that might be deprived of an adequate number of calories. Such statistics would incorrectly suggest food security where extreme inequalities could hide a food-insecure underclass even in terms of minimal caloric intake.

Such measures can also be problematic at the household level in terms of adequacy. We might say that, in a sense, all calories are not created equal. We can conceive of a household that consumes an abundance of high-calorie soft drinks, fried foods, and sweets. This household may easily reach the minimum recommended caloric intake but have a nutritionally inadequate diet. Indeed, most health professionals in the United States today recognize that a somewhat invisible form of food insecurity or malnutrition is constituted not by low caloric intake but a high intake of nutritionally inadequate calories (Carolan, 2011). Although popular press accounts often attribute this problem to poor choices on the part of individuals, examination of the problem of accessibility reveals a public issue insofar as choices for many food-insecure people are limited by the types and quality of food available in those food deserts where the local market is inadequate to serve those neighborhoods or communities, who, even collectively, cannot effectively participate in it.

Responses to Food Insecurity as a Public Issue

There are a number of attempts currently underway in the United States to deal with the problem of food insecurity. Some of these remedies involve government programs and policies, others are found in civil society associated with voluntary organizations (e.g., churches, social clubs, activist organizations). Most of the best-known programs have existed for some time.

GOVERNMENT PROGRAMS. What is commonly known as the food stamp program or, more recently as SNAP (Supplemental Nutrition Assistance Program), is nearly 50 years old. Originally begun, in part, as a means to increase consumption of agricultural surplus, this program (still administered by USDA, rather than by Health and Human Services) provided benefits to 44.7 million Americans (14% of individuals) in an average month in 2011 with an average benefit of $134 per person per month (Coleman-Jensen et al., 2012). Since much food insecurity is temporary due to monthly or annual cycles as indicated above, many citizens would be affected by this program. In 2011, the total federal expenditures for this program were $75 billion.

More recent complements to this program include: the Special Supplemental Nutrition Program for Women, Infants, and Children (also known as WIC) that provides funds to states for distribution of food as well as nutrition education to low-income pregnant women and mothers of children under the age of five. In 2011, WIC served a monthly average of 9 million women with an average contribution of $47 per month in food vouchers (Coleman-Jensen et al., 2012).

Another recent innovation is related to USDA's interest in expanding the role of direct marketing of agricultural products via local farmers' markets. In 2010, the Farmers' Market Nutrition Program (FMNP) provided additional benefits to 2.15 million WIC recipients in the form of coupons to be used to buy fresh fruits and vegetables from farmers, farmers' markets, or roadside stands that have been approved to accept FMNP coupons. There is a parallel program that provides FMNP coupons to low-income senior citizens. These are relatively small programs with benefits ranging from only $10 and $30 per year, per recipient, although state agencies may supplement the federal benefit (Nord, Coleman-Jensen, Andrews, & Carlson, 2010).

The National School Lunch (NSL) program also has a relatively long history. Begun in 1946, in part due to the recognition by military authorities of the poor nutritional health of potential draftees, this program now provides annual funding of $53.6 billion for meals in over 100,000 public and private schools (Levine, 2010). Low-income students receive free or reduced-price lunches. In 2011, 58% of all the lunches served in the U.S. were free, while an additional 8% were provided at reduced prices. On each school day, an average of 31.8 million children benefitted from the NSL program (Coleman-Jensen et al., 2012). This program is a vital element in reducing the levels of food insecurity in households with children, often providing the only certain meal of the day for those from impoverished families. In recent years, the content of these meals has become quite controversial, with much debate about their nutritional adequacy. "Farm-to-school" movements to provide school cafeterias with locally produced food have been one response.

NONGOVERNMENT PROGRAMS. Recent years have seen a significant increase in the number of Americans seeking food assistance from a variety of emergency food programs such as food pantries, emergency kitchens, and shelters. Regardless of their level of organization, these programs depend heavily on volunteers and donations. A nearly exhaustive sample of 181 food banks (food banks obtain donated food for distribution to those agencies that directly serve food insecure clients) in the Feeding America network (Mabli, Cohen, Potter, & Zhao, 2010) indicated that they worked with nearly 50,000 additional charitable organizations that operated or co-operated approximately 30,000 food pantries (food pantries distribute nonprepared food and, sometimes, fresh foods) to individual clients; 4,453 emergency kitchens (which serve prepared meals to clients who are not resident on the premises); and food assistance in 3,576 shelters (where food assistance is usually a secondary function to providing temporary housing for the homeless, substance abuse programs, victims of intimate partner violence, and others). Feeding America estimated that, in 2009, their pantries served 33.9 million people, their kitchens served 1.8 million people, and their shelters served 1.3 million people (Mabli et al., 2010). Significantly, they estimate that this is an increase of approximately 46% since 2005. This increase is likely associated with the economic recession that continued into 2009 as indicated by significant monthly increases in newcomers—clients who were making their first visit to a pantry or kitchen during this time period.

There are considerable differences between those who utilize food pantries and those who use emergency kitchens and shelters, with the latter being far more likely to be single individuals, while pantries tend to serve households of two or more people, usually including children and the elderly. Pantry clients are more likely to be women (67%) while emergency kitchen clients and shelter clients are more likely to be men, 62% and 75%, respectively. Nine out of 10 clients at all three institutions are U.S. citizens (Mabli et al., 2010).

This increase in utilization of emergency food assistance programs is not simply a problem of unemployment in the current recession. Feeding America found that approximately a third of clients qualifying for help at food pantries and kitchens had at least one adult household member employed. Minimum wage or subminimum wage jobs have been unable to keep pace with recent increases in food prices. Many people might also be surprised to know that 65% of pantry clients, and 70% or more of kitchen and shelter clients have graduated from high school (Mabli et al., 2010).

More recently, through grants from private foundations and state and federal agencies (e.g., USDA Community Food Projects), more communities are tackling food insecurity with their own unique approaches, which build on the available resources and emphasize the capacity building of the poor and food insecure and the development of leadership in the community (Pothukuchi, 2007). Community gardening and urban community supported agriculture (CSA) organizations are examples of such efforts. These projects generally aim to help food-insecure residents build knowledge and skills to grow, cook, and preserve their own food and manage their health. Improved diet is facilitated by building raised-bed vegetable plots on empty parking lots for them to grow food and by using a community kitchen in a local Cooperative Extension Office for cooking and nutrition classes. The creation of food policy councils at the community, regional, and state level is another example (Winne, 2009). This usually focuses on building the community's capacity for democratic decision-making on food-related issues. Many such community-based projects also include activities for *community food assessment*, which generally entails collecting data on the current state of food access, availability, and affordability at the neighborhood level in the community and identifying specific challenges and needs of the food insecure population.

For the past eight years, we have developed an ongoing research project focused on the community food system in Lexington, Kentucky. One major part of this assessment has been mapping and investigating food insecurity in the city. The following gives a brief overview of the work and how it applies to the general principles of food security discussed above.

CASE STUDY: LEXINGTON COMMUNITY FOOD ASSESSMENT

Behind the translucent sheet of cloth in a shadow puppet theater, there are actual puppets and puppeteers telling us a story, yet we see nothing but shadows. In approaching food security, aggregate data are the shadows, while projects like the Lexington Community Food Assessment help us to see the puppets. You might not have realized a classmate sitting next to you in elementary school was experiencing difficulties in getting enough to eat at home. You might not have noticed that the retired couple who live next door are dependent on emergency food assistance. When most of us drive around our communities, we have little problem finding grocery stores, restaurants, and convenience stores. Food seems to be everywhere, so how do we go about studying food insecurity in our communities? In this section, we show how our students at the University of Kentucky, from freshmen to doctoral students, collected data on various aspects of food security in Lexington-Fayette County (hereafter Lexington), Kentucky, as part of our Lexington Community Food Assessment project (see Tanaka & Mooney, 2010).

With a population of 295,803, Lexington is the second largest city in Kentucky and 63rd largest city in the nation (U.S. Census Bureau, 2010). We can characterize Lexington as a racially and ethnically more diverse place than the state as a whole. Lexington is the home of several colleges and universities and three major hospitals and therefore has a substantially more highly educated population than the rest of the state and the nation in terms of percentages of college graduates. The median household income of Lexington residents is $46,386, considerably higher than that of the state ($40,061), though lower than the national median income of $50,221 (City-Data.com, 2012). However, Lexington's poverty rate for all ages is 17.4%, which is 3% higher than the national average. Between 1997 and 2007, the population of Lexington grew 13% while the number of food stores declined. The number of typical grocery stores declined nearly 20% and the number of supermarkets declined by 25% (U.S. Census Bureau, 1997, 2002, 2007). Although grocery stores and supermarkets are related, the former sells food while the latter is larger than most grocery stores and sells food and other household items. This implies a significant increase in the number of people served by fewer, albeit much larger, grocery stores.

In order to understand how food access is spatially distributed, since 2004 several different groups of our students have tackled four research questions:

1. What is the quality of food access in Lexington?
2. What challenges do Lexington residents face in accessing adequate quality food?
3. How does access to food relate to broader social problems of inequality in Lexington?
4. What political actions seem to be appropriate to address the problem of food insecurity in Lexington?

To address the first two questions, students focused on the location of major supermarkets and grocery stores such as Walmart and Kroger in relation to the distribution of households in poverty because these stores tend to offer a variety of food products that are nutritionally and culturally adequate at affordable prices. For the last two questions, our students examined what types of services are available to Lexington's food-insecure population.

Although students in each course, depending on the level and the learning objectives of the course, collected different kinds of data, all used at least three methodological techniques of community food assessment. First, guided by an incomplete list of food retailers and restaurants available from the Lexington Health Department, they walked and drove around an assigned geographical area to map all food stores and eateries. Second, market basket surveys were conducted to check the availability and prices (affordability) of 13 food items[4] (Cohen, 2002). Third, students completed semistructured interviews with community leaders, city council members, and residents. In some courses, additional methodological tools were used. For example, students carried out case studies of two neighborhoods with the highest rates of poverty by mapping food outlets as well as conducting focus group interviews with the residents. Ten undergraduate students completed participant observation at God's Pantry Food Bank while working as volunteers at its central intake office and two food pantries for the spring semester of 2001. They also helped God's Pantry carry out a biannual survey of its clients (God's Pantry Food Bank, 2011).

Through the data our students collected over the years, we have learned many *social facts*—as Emile Durkheim (1982) termed them—about hunger in Lexington that help us challenge seven myths about food access in the United States.

Myth 1. Food is Plentiful and Cheap for all in the United States

Mapping of food stores in urban Lexington revealed several food deserts with no grocery store within walking distance. More focused case studies of two neighborhoods with the highest rates of poverty confirmed that without any grocery store within walking distance the availability and affordability of food in these areas are limited. Of 35 food retailers in these two areas—mostly small-scale neighborhood grocery markets and convenience stores—none carried lettuce or frozen broccoli; apples and fresh broccoli were sold at one store each; and tomatoes were found in three stores. Only 14 stores had whole wheat bread, eggs, and 1% milk at the same time. Moreover, the market basket survey of 2006 and 2007 confirmed that the average prices of these latter three items in the case study neighborhoods were considerably (as much as three times) higher than those at chain grocery stores in Lexington. In other words, the variety (adequacy) and prices (affordability) of available food vary enormously among neighborhoods. Residents in food deserts are likely to experience difficulties in obtaining nutritionally and culturally adequate food at affordable prices. It is important to note that these food deserts tend to be located in the areas with high rates of poverty and low rates of household vehicle ownership.

Myth 2. A Higher Mean Market Basket Price in Low-income Areas Always Translates to Residents of those Areas Paying More for Food

Even without their own vehicle, residents in the food desert areas do indeed get to chain supermarkets and grocery stores by getting a ride from friends, family, public transportation services, or taxis. We compared prices of the market basket among 22 chain supermarkets and grocery stores in urban Lexington. The city was divided into six regions, each of which included two to five stores. The mean market basket price was lowest in the regions adjacent to the areas with the lowest socioeconomic profiles because two of the three chain discount stores, Sav-a-Lots, were located in this region. The third Sav-a-Lot is located in a neighborhood with a high concentration of Hispanic residents with low median household income. The highest mean market basket price was found in the region known for the most rapid urban sprawl. Unlike the neighborhoods with

---

[4] Market basket items include: apples (1 lb), fresh broccoli (1 lb), frozen broccoli (1 lb), lettuce (1 lb), potatoes (1 lb), tomatoes (1 lb), 1 % milk (1 gallon), cheddar cheese (1 lb), ground beef (1 lb), fryer whole or cut-up chicken (1 lb), large grade A eggs (1 dz), whole wheat bread (2 lbs), spaghetti (1 lb box).

low market basket prices, this is a relatively large area that is quite a distance from the downtown area, where residents must own vehicles to commute and shop for food. The socioeconomic profile of this region (e.g., median household income, poverty rate, education level) tends to be much higher than the low market basket regions (City-Data.com, 2012). These variations in market basket prices suggest that chain supermarket and grocery companies do indeed strategically choose the location of their stores based on the demographic characteristics of potential shoppers and that stores price products based on the willingness or ability of their shoppers to pay. We were not able to investigate qualitative differences of market basket products between stores.

Myth 3. As a Result of the Recent Surge of "Foodies" and their Calls for More "Local" and "Healthy" Food, Food Issues have become a Political Priority

Today more newspapers and TV programs seem to cover food-related topics than ever before. Farmers' markets are booming across the United States. Nonfiction, nonacademic books about food make it to best-seller lists. First Lady Michele Obama created a vegetable garden in the yard of the White House. Yet, as shown above, the number of residents affected by food insecurity has increased in the recent economic downturn. Lexington is no exception. However, a large proportion of community leaders contacted by our students for interviews showed very little enthusiasm or interest in tackling food insecurity as a public issue of importance. Indeed, of 15 city council members, only four agreed to be interviewed after repeated e-mail and phone requests by our students. Even the neighborhood leadership in high poverty areas tended to deny the lack of food access among their residents. They claimed that they could drive to the nearest Kroger or Walmart Supercenter. City council members cited the lack of requests by their constituents in their district as a reason for their own indifference in acting upon food access issues. Yet, at the same time, the local United Way's call center reported to us that a substantial proportion of their calls are in reference to issues of food access.

Community leaders and residents alike recognize that poverty in certain neighborhoods is a real, critical public issue to be tackled. However, they seem to have difficulty connecting poverty with food insecurity. To them, food access is a private matter of individuals deciding where to shop, how much to pay, and how to eat. Structural forces that constrain choices for individuals are often invisible to them, perhaps even more so than the invisibility of housing and health care insecurity and the vulnerability of the poor. More important, the very people who struggle most with hunger and food insecurity—children and the elderly—tend to have little voice in civic activities. In short, unless voices of the hungry can be heard in the public arena, there is little political incentive to address food insecurity as a public policy issue.

Myth 4. People Experiencing Hunger and Food Insecurity Come from Low Socioeconomic Background or are Racial and Ethnic Minorities

Numerous reports by government agencies and local community organizations consistently show that hunger disproportionately affects women, children, the elderly, and racial and ethnic minorities (e.g., God's Pantry Food Bank, 2011; Nord, 2009; Nord, Andrews, & Carlson, 2008;). According to God's Pantry Food Bank's (2011) most recent hunger survey of their Lexington clientele, which our students helped to carry out, single mothers with children, blacks, and the unemployed tend to be disproportionately more vulnerable than others. Of 450 clients visiting five food pantry locations in Lexington, 34% were black. Moreover, 61% walked, biked, or relied on family, friends, or public transportation to get to a pantry, suggesting that they do not own vehicles. However, the survey also reveals findings that contradict popular myths about the predominance of welfare mothers or poor blacks without education and skills that depend on handouts.

Instead, they tell more complex stories of so-called vulnerable social groups. When we compare the God's Pantry's survey data for 2007 and 2011 item by item, the impact of the current economic recession becomes apparent. In 2011, compared to the results from the 2007 survey (God's Pantry Food Bank, 2007), more white, more educated, and more unemployed people are seeking emergency food assistance. Despite rising food prices, the average household income declined from $8,943 in 2007 to $8,760 in 2011. Of 450 clients, 67% completed high school, and 27% even held a bachelor's and/or a graduate degree. Moreover, 23% of the adult clients served by the food emergency program were working full or part-time.

Based on the God's Pantry database, in absolute numbers more white Lexington residents are receiving services from God's Pantry than their black counterparts. In fact, 93% of all clients of God's Pantry Food Bank, which also serves largely rural central and eastern (Appalachian) Kentucky, are white; only 4% are black though 49% of whites and 34% of blacks participated in the 2011 survey of the city of Lexington itself. In working at God's Pantry, our students observed that the elderly were particularly vulnerable since their income is often fixed while the costs of food, medicine, and gasoline keep increasing. Many of these elderly were retirees who had had successful careers and a comfortable middle-class life style, and who had successfully raised children. Another group vulnerable to food insecurity is those who lost their jobs due to injuries or illness, including war veterans. Between the 2007 and 2011 surveys, clients who identified themselves as disabled or in poor health increased from 38% to 41%, although the number of clients without health insurance declined from 35% to 29%. So while certain racial and other minority groups are significantly more likely to bear the burden of food insecurity, they do not constitute the majority of those utilizing emergency food assistance.

Myth 5. There are Enough Services and Programs Available from Governmental Agencies and Community Organizations to Adequately Address and Solve the Problem of Food Insecurity in this Country

It is true that the USDA Food and Nutrition Service offers a series of nutritional assistance programs, described above, to provide children and needy families better access to food. State and local welfare offices often operate these programs. Food banks and pantries as well as soup kitchens also offer emergency food assistance to those in need, which are operated by nongovernmental community-based organizations, including churches. However, all these programs aim to provide temporary relief from hunger and offer better food access on a short-term basis. Many hungry people, especially the working poor (those who have full-time employment at low wages without benefits), often fall through the cracks because they are not eligible for these public assistance programs, don't know about them, are too proud to rely on them, or find the application process very cumbersome and confusing.

Most important, none of these public assistance programs tries to eliminate food insecurity. According to God's Pantry Food Bank (2007, 2011), 161,000 pounds of food was needed each month to distribute food to 1,600 households in 2011, up from 60,000 pounds in 2007. As one of our students pointed out, the increased need for capacity of food distribution by a food bank such as God's Pantry is an indication of worsening food insecurity as a social problem, rather than a success in addressing the problem. One challenge lies in the fact that most of these food and nutrition assistance programs treat food-insecure people as passive recipients of economically focused service, limiting room for these individuals to act (become agents) for change. Two contrasting examples of medium-to long-term approaches to addressing food insecurity in Lexington, a community gardening program offered by Seedleaf, a local organization that targets residents in one of our impoverished case study areas, and an annual food security symposium organized by the Sustainable Community Network to bring together community leaders. While the former aims to build the capacity of food insecure residents to grow and prepare their own food, the latter creates an opportunity for political and community leaders to gather and explore ideas for collective political action in order to address food insecurity.

Myth 6. A Big Grocery Store in Every Neighborhood will Solve the Problem of Food Insecurity

Bringing a chain grocery store such as Kroger into the food desert area was one of the most often cited solutions to food insecurity by community leaders in Lexington. Some faith-based organizations operate CSA programs in low-income neighborhoods in which participating households purchase a share (or subscription or membership) at a discount rate of the harvest that a farmer offers during the growing season. In the fall of 2010, a new farmers' market opened in a neighborhood with a high concentration of poverty. All these programs aim to improve the availability and accessibility of nutritionally adequate food, particularly fresh vegetables and fruits, for the poor on a medium- to long-term basis. These are important, and necessary, approaches to overcoming hunger. However, as our students pointed out after several interviews with community leaders in Lexington, it is often assumed that these approaches are what residents in the neighborhoods want and need and that building a supermarket closer to those residents will necessarily improve their diet. Sometimes the introduction of a grocery chain can be part of a gentrification process in the neighborhood, and consequently push out poorer residents, compounding their food insecurity with housing insecurity.

Myth 7. More Education is Needed about Food and Nutrition to Solve the Problem of Food Insecurity

Without a doubt, education is a crucial and necessary tool for addressing problems associated with hunger and food insecurity. For every social problem, "more education" is more often than not the first recommendation to be raised as a solution. When interviewed by our students, many of our community leaders and residents also emphasized the need to teach people how to grow food, showing them where and why to buy what they considered healthy food, and how to prepare it. Who should decide how food-insecure people are educated and with what knowledge? What constitutes a healthy or nutritionally adequate diet is a highly contested and politicized question (Nestle, 2003). Let us not forget the importance of cultural adequacy. It is important to recognize that by creating a boundary between teachers and students, education could potentially reproduce a hierarchical relationship between the haves and the have-nots of income, wealth, status, knowledge, and skills. People or organizations advocating for more education assume that food-insecure people are ignorant of what is good for them. This denies the possibility that their lack of economic resources forces them to purchase and consume food in an unhealthy way. This also increases the dependency of victims of a social problem on so-called experts.

Our case study of Lexington confirms that, "[f]ood is always available for those who can afford it" (Moore, 1998, n.p.). In the last decade, unfortunately, increasing numbers of people have been unable to afford food and have cut back their food expenditures (Nord, 2009b). According to the 2011 God's Pantry (2011) survey, many were forced to choose between food and other necessities (e.g., medicines, fuel). The survey found that in the previous year, 69% of clients had to choose between paying for food and paying for gasoline; 50% had to choose between paying for food and paying for their housing; and 43% had to choose between paying for food and paying for medicine or medical care. Food, medicine or medical care, and housing are all basic necessities for sustaining human lives. While working at God's Pantry, our students heard numerous tragic life stories of the food insecure, including: parents who skipped their meals to feed their children, an elderly woman who waited extra days to refill her prescriptions so she could feed grandchildren under her care, and a veteran who could not work because of his combat injury.

Through collecting and analyzing data about Lexington's community food security, our students have come to realize that hunger is not just an individual problem. The magnitude of hunger experienced often depends on the sociopolitical history, economic dynamics, and institutional arrangements of a community—all of which contribute to redistributing wealth, status, and political power among residents. The history of racial tension, strong anti-immigration sentiments, the availability of public transportation services, and the relative vitality of civic organizations are variables that affect how hunger is addressed as a public issue (Duncan, 1999; Putnam, 2000). All of these variables are variations on the theme of class inequality. Seeing both the shadows (public issues) and the puppets (private troubles) of this social problem helps us to build stronger and more nuanced attempts at addressing it.

Conclusion

Hunger and food insecurity are reflections of class inequality in a society; they are about differences between those who have food and those who do not, being able to feed themselves and their families. Asking the question, "Who's hungry?" is therefore critical in understanding how class intersects with gender, race, ethnicity, age, and disability in a given community to make certain social groups more vulnerable than others. In some ways, Lexington is a microcosm of the United States with regard to food security. Fayette County is itself a small-scale illusory land of plenty where most people have more than enough to eat. The food-insecure minority struggles while very few, regardless of their food-security status, easily translate personal troubles with hunger into public issues. However, research at the local level affords opportunities for a deeper understanding by local publics that is unavailable in generalized statements about food security in the

United States. It gives a face and a voice to those feeling the pinch of poverty, and makes their problems visible, tangible. We can see that for all the similarities of food insecurity across contexts, in each different place food insecurity plays out in some unique ways. Surely poverty anywhere shares many broad structural characteristics and causes, but it is important to also acknowledge that Lexington's food insecurity has many of its own local effects and its own local causes. In other words, food insecurity needs to be understood as the everyday experience of those who live in a given location—regardless of class, gender, race, ethnicity, age, disability, or any other social categories which sociologists may use.

Therefore in moving food insecurity and poverty from invisible to visible, and in conceiving of the transition from cause to effect, and from effect to solution, it is important to acknowledge the local. This means assessing how the local system might be changed to allow for a more equitable and healthy distribution of food resources. This entails talking to local people—both the food-insecure populations and important leaders in the area of food—to see what should be changed. Policies need to facilitate local solutions without dictating what the solutions might be. Both of these efforts—talking

to affected populations and changing policy to allow for democratic participation—reflect a grassroots approach to changing the food system. In many places in the United States, food policy councils are being created (in a wide variety of forms) to conduct this discussion among a diverse range of stakeholders, often in the name of food democracy (Mooney, Ciciurkaite, & Tanaka, 2012).

Academics, policy makers, and concerned citizens have often tried to enter a cultural and geographical context foreign to them in the hopes of solving the problem. It is our belief that lasting solutions will only come from those most familiar with the problem itself—the food insecure—and that the focus should be placed on creating a democratic process in which their diverse voices might be not only heard, but also respected. Food insecurity is not the only area in which food-insecure populations are marginalized—poverty hits a person in many different ways. Until those affected most by the problems we study believe that they can change their situations, solutions will continue to have only limited success. Until marginalized populations believe that their demands for a better life have a chance of being heard by those in power, change will remain painfully elusive.

References

Andrews, M., Nord, M., Bickel, & Carlson, S. (1999). *Household food security in the United States, 1999.* Washington, DC: USDA Economic Research Service.

Bailey, R. (2008) *The biggest green mistake: Biofuels and the global food crisis.* Reason.com. Retrieved from http://reason.com/archives/2008/04/08/the-biggest-green-mistake

Busch, L., & Lacy, W. B. (1984). *Food security in the United States.* Boulder, CO: Westview Press.

Carolan, M. (2011). *The real cost of cheap food.* London, UK, and New York, NY: Earthscan.

City-Data.com (2012). *Fayette County, Kentucky.* Retrieved from http://www.city-data.com/county/Fayette_County-KY.html

Cohen, B., Andrews, & Kantor, L. S. (2002, July). *Community food security assessment toolkit.*

(No. EFAN-02-013). Washington, DC: USDA Economic Research Service, Electronic publications from the Food Assistance & Nutrition Research Program.

Coleman-Jensen, A., Nord, M., Andrews, M., & Carlson, S. (2012). *Household food security in the United States in 2011.* Washington, DC: USDA Economic Research Service.

Duncan, C. (1999). *Worlds apart: Why poverty persists in rural America.* New Haven, CT, and London, UK: Yale University Press.

Durkheim, E. (1982). *The rules of sociological method and selected texts on sociology and its method.* New York, NY: Free Press.

Food and Agriculture Organization of the United Nations. (2010). *The state of food insecurity in the world: Addressing food insecurity in protracted crisis.* Rome, Italy: Author.

FAO Committee on Food Security (2011). CFS home. Retrieved from http://www.fao.org/cfs/en/.

God's Pantry Food Bank (2007). *Hunger in Fayette County.* Lexington, KY: Author.

God's Pantry Food Bank (2011). *Hunger in Fayette County.* Lexington, KY: Author.

Grey, M. A., Devlin, M., & Goldsmith, A. (2009). *Postville, USA: Surviving diversity in small-town America.* Boston, MA: Gemma Media.

Kimura, A. H. (2013). *Hidden hunger: Gender and the politics of smarter foods.* Ithaca, NY: Cornell University Press.

Levine, S. (2010). *School lunch politics: The surprising history of America's favorite welfare program.* Princeton, NJ: Princeton University Press.

Mabli, J., Cohen, R., Potter, F., & Zhao, Z. (2010, January). *Hunger in America 2010: National report prepared for Feeding America* (No. 06251-600). Princeton, NJ: Mathematica Policy Research.

Mooney, P. H., Ciciurkaite, G., & Tanaka, K. (2012, July–August). *The food policy council movement in North America: A convergence of alternative local agrifood interests?* Paper presented in Mini-Conference: Convergence: Alternative agrifood movements shaping the movement of our time? International Rural Sociological Association meeting. Lisbon, Portugal.

Moore, M. (1998). *12 myths about hunger.* Institute for Food & Development Policy, Food First. Retrieved from http://www.foodfirst.org/pubs/backgrdrs/1998/s98v5n3.html.

Morton, L. W., Bitto, E. A., Oakland, M. J., & Sand, M. (2005). Solving the problems of Iowa food deserts: Food insecurity and civic structure. *Rural Sociology, 70*(1), 94–112.

Nestle, M. (2003). *Food politics: How the food industry influences nutrition and health.* Berkeley and Los Angeles: University of California Press.

Nord, M. (2009a). *Food insecurity in households with children: Prevalence, severity, and household characteristics.* Washington, DC: USDA Economic Research Service.

Nord, M. (2009b). *Food spending declined and food insecurity increased for middle-income and low-income households from 2000 to 2007.* Washington, DC: USDA Economic Research Service.

Nord, M., Andrews, M., & Carlson, S. (2008). *Household food security in the United States, 2007. Measuring food security in the United States.* Economic Research

Report (No. ERR-66). Washington, DC: USDA Economic Research Service.

Nord, M., Coleman-Jensen, A., Andrews, M., & Carlson, S. (2010). *Household food security in the United States, 2009.* Washington, DC: USDA Economic Research Service.

Pothukuchi, K. (2007). *Community food security: Lessons learned from community food projects, 1999–2005.* Portland, OR: Community Food Security Coalition.

Putnam, R. D. (2000). *Bowling alone: The collapse and revival of American community.* New York, NY: Simon & Schuster.

Sum, A., & Khatiwada, I. (2010). The nation's underemployed in the "Great Recession" of 2007–09. *Monthly Labor Review, 133* (11), 3–15.

Tanaka, K., & Mooney, P. H. (2010). Public scholarship and community engagement in building community food security: The case of the University of Kentucky. *Rural Sociology, 75* (4), 560–583.

U.S. Bureau of Labor Statistics (2011, July 18). Labor force statistics from the current population survey. *Unemployment rate.* Retrieved from http://data.bls.gov/cgi-bin/surveymost

U.S. Census Bureau (1990). United States Census 1990. Retrieved from http://www.census.gov/main/www/cen1990.html

U.S. Census Bureau (1997). 1997 Economic Census. Retrieved from http://www.census.gov/epcd/www/econ97.html

U.S. Census Bureau (2000). United States Census 2000. Retrieved from http://www.census.gov/main/www/cen2000.html

U.S. Census Bureau (2002). 2002 Economic Census. Retrieved from http://www.census.gov/econ/census02/

U.S. Census Bureau (2007). 2007 Economic Census. Retrieved from http://www.census.gov/econ/census07/

U.S. Census Bureau (2010). United States Census 2010. Retrieved from http://www.census.gov/main/www/cen2010.html

USDA Foreign Agricultural Service (2011). Global Agricultural Trade System. Retrieved from http://www.fas.usda.gov/gats/default.aspx

Ver Ploeg, M., Breneman, V., Farrigan, T., Hamrick, K., Hopkins, D., Kaufmans, P., Lin, B.-H., Nord, M., Smither, T. A., Williams, R., Kinnison, K., Olander, C., Singh, A., & Tuckermanty, E. (2009, June). *Access to affordable and nutritious food: Measuring and understanding food deserts and their consequences.*

Report to Congress (No. AP-036). Washington, DC: USDA Economic Research Service.

Winne, M. (2009). *Closing the food gap: Resetting the table in the land of plenty*. Boston, MA: Beacon Press.

Wolff, B. (2012). *Meaning from method: An investigation of United States food security measurement tools* (Unpublished Master's Thesis). University of Kentucky, Lexington.

"Sacrificed So Others Can Live Conveniently"

Social Inequality, Environmental Injustice, and the Energy Sacrifice Zone of Central Appalachia

Shannon Elizabeth Bell

The way I feel about it, we've been discriminated against. We're being sacrificed here for energy for the rest of the world . . . To me, it's not the American way, it will never be the way of the America that I envision we're supposed to be here. It's horrible what they're letting happen, and it's just for greed. Why should we give up everything we own for somebody else to have cheap energy? For a world of people that's already pampered to death. It's the injustice of it. Honey, this is discrimination—and I don't use that word lightly, either.

—Pauline Canterberry, Environmental Justice Activist and Resident of Boone County, West Virginia (Quoted in Bell, 2013)

They say some people have to be sacrificed for the wealth of others, so others can live conveniently. To hell with those people . . . I've worked and paid for this house. This piece of land is mine . . . They say if we don't like it, why don't we leave? I'm sorry, but I was here first!

—Joan Linville, Environmental Justice Activist and Resident of Boone County, West Virginia (Quoted in Bell, 2013)

There are certain areas of the United States (and world) treated as *energy sacrifice zones,* regions where the people and the resources are exploited to allow corporations and consumers in the rest of the nation to have continued access to cheap energy. In these sacrifice zones, the true costs of energy are externalized onto local people and their environment in the form of pollution, destruction of the land, and limited economic opportunities. Examples of energy sacrifice zones in the United States include the Gulf Coast, which is sacrificed for oil resources (Haney, 2012), and Native American tribal land in the southwest, which is sacrificed for nuclear energy (uranium mining and radioactive waste storage) (Kuletz, 1998). The two people quoted at the beginning of this chapter—Pauline Canterberry and Joan Linville—live in southern West Virginia, which is part Central Appalachia, another highly exploited energy sacrifice zone (Fox, 1999; Lewis & Knipe, 1978; Scott, 2010). Composed of southern West Virginia, eastern Kentucky, southwest Virginia, and eastern Tennessee, Central Appalachia is one of the primary coal-producing areas in the United States. In 2012, coal-burning power plants produced 37.4% of the United States' electricity, more than any other electric utility, including natural gas (30.3%), nuclear (19.0%), hydropower (6.8%), and wind (3.4%) (U.S. Energy Information Administration, 2012). Because of its importance to the national economy, the coal industry is one of the most powerful industries in the United States.

The Central Appalachian region has a long history of exploitation, particularly by the coal industry, dating back more than 100 years. Much of the land in this area was practically (and sometimes outright) stolen from the local people by outside capitalists who knew of the rich mineral resources lying beneath the mountains (Gaventa, 1978). As Bell and York (2010) argue, the continued domination of Central Appalachia "has been achieved through corporate ownership of the majority of the land, effectively blocking other industries from entering the region in an attempt to maintain this part of Appalachia as a monoeconomy" for the coal industry (p. 119).

Many residents living in the coal-mining region of Central Appalachia maintain that their health and safety are threatened by mining activity in their communities (Bell, 2009, 2013; Bell & Braun, 2010; Bell & York, 2010; Fox, 1999). Particularly over the past two decades, an extremely destructive form of coal extraction known as *mountaintop removal mining* has become pervasive throughout this region. In this type of surface mining, mountains are blown apart to expose thin seams of coal, which are scraped from the newly flattened surface with massive earth-moving machines called draglines. The demolished earth above the coal, including rock, soil, and trees, is pushed into nearby valleys, creating *valley fills*, which bury streams, damage fragile ecosystems, and render nearby communities vulnerable to increasingly devastating flood events (Bell & Braun, 2010; Bell & York, 2010; Flood Advisory Technical Taskforce, 2002; Fox, 1999; Palmer et al., 2010; U.S. Environmental Protection Agency, 2005).

In addition to massive flooding in coal-mining communities, mountaintop removal has led to structural damage to homes; unsafe road conditions from overweight, speeding coal trucks; and losses in human life due to the myriad chronic health conditions coal extraction and processing causes (Bell, 2010). Researchers have found that in comparison with the rest of the nation, coal-mining areas of Appalachia suffer higher rates of hospitalization for certain respiratory and cardiovascular conditions, higher rates of mortality, and higher rates of chronic illnesses, even after controlling for such variables as income and education (Ahern & Hendryx, 2008; Hendryx, 2008; Hendryx & Ahern, 2008; Hendryx, Ahern, & Nurkiewicz, 2007). Health disparities appear to be even more extreme in communities exposed to mountaintop removal mining; in a 2011 study, Ahern and colleagues found that birth defects are significantly higher in mountaintop removal mining areas compared with non-mining areas, even after controlling for other causes. Hendryx and colleagues found in their door-to-door survey in a mountaintop removal mining–exposed community and a non-mining community that the self-reported cancer rate was twice as high in the community exposed to mountaintop removal mining compared with the non-mining community (Hendryx et al., 2012).

Like other sacrifice zones, a large portion of the population in Central Appalachia can be characterized as socially vulnerable. It is primarily class vulnerability that characterizes this region, much of which is white and working class (Scott, 2010; however, it is important to note that the region is not monolithically white[1]). Central Appalachia is one of the poorest areas in the nation. In 2000, more than 75% of Appalachian coal counties were classified as economically distressed by the Appalachian Regional Commission (Appalachian Voices, 2007). An examination of the eight top coal-producing counties in eastern Kentucky (Pike, Perry, Harlan, Letcher, Knott, Leslie, Martin, and Floyd) reveals that the poverty rate in each of these counties far exceeds the state's poverty rate of 18.4%. In fact, in five of the eight counties, the poverty rate is above 30% (U.S. Census Bureau, 2010b). Further, McDowell County, West Virginia, from which more tons of coal have been mined than any other county in the state (West Virginia Office of Miners' Health, Safety and Training, 2003), is not only the poorest county in West Virginia, but with a median household income of $22,222, it is the sixth poorest county in the entire United States (U.S. Census Bureau, 2010a). Forty-one percent of McDowell County's residents are living below the poverty line (U.S. Census Bureau, 2010a).

Equally alarming are the educational rates in much of Central Appalachia. In the eight coal-producing counties in Kentucky discussed above, the high school completion rate stands at only 66.7%, compared with a rate of 80.3% in Kentucky overall, and 84.6% nationally. Further, the percentage of the population with a bachelor's degree in these eight top coal-producing counties is only about half the overall rate in Kentucky (10.8% compared with 20.0%) (U.S. Census Bureau, 2010b).

ENERGY SACRIFICE ZONES AND PATTERNS OF ENVIRONMENTAL INJUSTICE

Energy sacrifice zones are part of a larger pattern of environmental inequality that exists within the United States and around the world. Environmental justice scholars argue that not all people share the burden of environmental hazards and pollutants equally. Those with the least political and economic power—communities of color, low-income communities, and people of the Global South (i.e., Latin America, Asia, and Africa)—bear a disproportionate share of the waste and pollution created by society (Bullard, 1990; Bullard et al., 2007; Čapek, 1993; Faber, 2008, 2009; Masterson-Allen & Brown, 1990; Pellow, 2004, 2007). In addition to the industries involved in natural resource extraction, there are many other highly profitable polluting industries, such as petrochemical plants and toxic waste facilities that disproportionately impact the most socially vulnerable communities and workers.

In 1986, the United Church of Christ Commission for Racial Justice undertook research on the racial and socioeconomic makeup of the communities where commercial

---

[1] For example, McDowell County and Kanawha County in West Virginia; Wise County, Virginia; and Harlan County, Kentucky, each have historically had substantial black populations. See Turner and Cabbell (1985), Lewis (1987, 1999) for the history of blacks in Appalachia.

hazardous waste facilities and uncontrolled toxic waste sites are located in the United States. The findings of the national study revealed that race was the most significant variable predicting where a commercial hazardous waste facility was placed (United Church of Christ Commission for Racial Justice, 1987). The study found that "three out of every five Black or Hispanic Americans lived in communities with uncontrolled toxic waste sites" and three out of the five largest commercial hazardous waste landfills in the nation, which accounted for 40% of the total landfill capacity in the country, were found to be located in black or Hispanic communities (United Church Christ Commission for Racial Justice, 1987, p. xiv). In 2007, a follow-up research study was conducted to assess whether progress had been made in the 20 years after the first study was conducted. Shockingly, the 2007 study found that racial disparities in the siting of hazardous waste facilities were even greater than previously reported. People of color were found to make up the "majority of those living in host neighborhoods within 3 kilometers (1.8 miles) of the nation's hazardous waste facilities" (Bullard et al., 2007, p. x). In addition, poverty rates in the host neighborhoods were found to be 1.5 times greater than non-host areas (Bullard et al., 2007, p. x).

People of color and low-income individuals not only disproportionately host hazardous waste facilities in their communities; their homes also shared geographical space with some of the most polluting manufacturing industries in the nation, such as petrochemical plants and oil refineries. One of the best-known examples of this pattern within the United States is Louisiana's Chemical Corridor, a 100-mile stretch of towns along the Mississippi River extending from Baton Rouge to New Orleans, where over 150 petrochemical plants and oil refineries are located. The plants in this area report the highest concentration of toxic emissions in the country (Dunn, 2000), and the people living in this area are primarily black and poor.

In his (2005) book *Diamond: A Struggle for Environmental Justice in Louisiana's Chemical Corridor*, Steve Lerner reveals the overwhelming impacts that the petrochemical industry has on the lives of the residents living in one community along the Chemical Corridor. The black neighborhood of Diamond, a subdivision of the town of Norco, is situated between a Shell Oil refinery and a Shell chemical plant. Diamond residents report a host of health problems, including decreased fertility, severe respiratory problems, rare forms of aggressive cancer, headaches, blurred vision, nausea, and shortened life spans. The story of Diamond is very similar to stories of other black communities throughout the south, where residents living proximal to such plants suffer great costs to their health and safety with little to no protection or compensation.

Why are any communities in the United States faced with dangerous living conditions because of pollution or extraction? Aren't there pollution-abatement technologies or lower impact methods of resource extraction that could be used to protect residents? The bottom line is that companies pollute and degrade the environment—both legally and illegally—because it is profitable (Faber, 2008). A hallmark characteristic of corporate capitalism is an unrelenting drive to increase profits and decrease costs. One of the easiest ways for corporations to decrease their costs is to *externalize* those costs (such as pollution) whenever possible (Brulle & Pellow, 2006; Schnaiberg, 1980). For example, rather than "internalize" the $10 million it would take to install a scrubber that would clean chemical pollutants from emissions, it is far cheaper for a chemical company to instead "'externalize' this expense onto society in the form of air pollution and other environmental health problems" (Faber, 2008; p. 24).

Similarly, it is far cheaper for a coal company to use explosives, a dragline, and a handful of workers to blow apart a mountain and scrape coal from the surface than it is to employ hundreds of workers to dig the coal from underground.

Almost as a rule, the people who are disproportionately affected by corporations' cost-externalization are those with the least political power: people of color, low-income individuals, and those living in nations of the Global South. As Faber (2008) so poignantly asserts, the "'disempowered' of America" are not only "effectively denied a voice in American society," they also serve as capitalism's "dumping ground" (p. 25).

THE ENVIRONMENTAL AND SOCIAL COSTS OF COAL POWER

The process of cost-externalization can be seen quite clearly in coal industry practices. Coal is an extremely cheap fuel, but it is only cheap because the unaccounted for costs of extraction, processing, and burning are externalized onto society. Coal was responsible for nearly 45% of global carbon dioxide emissions from energy consumption in 2010, an increase from 42% in 2006 (calculated from U.S. Energy Information Administration [2012] data). The coal industry—along with the capitalist world system that depends on the cheap energy it provides—holds a large share of the responsibility for rising global temperatures and the resulting harm that has already come (and will only intensify) in many geographically vulnerable nations.

In addition to its contributions to accelerating climate change, the coal industry also causes great ecological and social harm in its other industry activities. Throughout the entire life cycle of this fossil fuel—including the mining, processing, washing, and burning of coal—workers and nearby communities are endangered by industry practices. As one of the top coal-producing regions in the United States, Central Appalachian communities suffer long before this fossil fuel is ever burned. The land, water, and people of this region are forced to pay the cost of America's addiction to cheap electricity.

The story of living in an energy sacrifice zone is one that is best told by the people who have been forced to experience it firsthand. In the following section, five local activists tell—in their own words—the struggles they have faced. All of these narratives are excerpted from my book, *Our Roots Run Deep as Ironweed: Appalachian Women and the Fight for Environmental Justice* (University of Illinois Press, 2013), in which 12 Central Appalachian women activists share their stories of struggle and social change in the fight for environmental justice.[2]

LIVING IN AN ENERGY SACRIFICE ZONE

From 2006–2009, I conducted 13 months of field research in southern West Virginia to examine the social impacts of the coal industry on rural communities (see Bell, 2009, 2010, 2013; Bell & Braun, 2010; and Bell & York, 2010, for more on this research). As a part of my investigation, I conducted 20 interviews with a purposive sample of local coalfield residents (12 women and 8 men) who are working to hold the coal industry

---

[2] While an overview of the resistance efforts in Central Appalachia is outside the scope of this chapter, please see Bell (2010, 2013) and Bell and Braun (2010) for more detail on the movement to hold the coal industry accountable for irresponsible coal-mining practices.

and regulatory agencies accountable for irresponsible mining practices in Central Appalachia. Interviews ranged in length from 45 minutes to four hours. Each interview was audio-recorded, transcribed in full, and then coded thematically. As is the case with most grassroots environmental justice struggles, the majority of the local activists in this movement are women (Bell, 2013; Bell & Braun, 2010). For this reason, I oversampled male activists in order to ensure an adequate number of men for my analysis. All of the activists in this particular sample are local coalfield residents, individuals who have spent at least half of their lives or the majority of their childhoods in the coal-mining region and who have a family history of employment in the coal industry. While many people from across the nation have joined the struggle against irresponsible coal-mining practices in Central Appalachia (and I have also interviewed many of those individuals), I found it important to especially focus on local activists because they have had to overcome a conflicted identity as residents who have been ravaged by the industry that has likely put food on their tables at some point in their lives. In addition, many of these local activists have had to cope with backlash from family, friends, and neighbors who work for the coal industry.

When asked about the changes they have seen in their communities in recent years, many coalfield residents talk about the increase in severe flooding they have witnessed. Central Appalachia is home to some very steep mountain terrain, and in many coal-mining communities, most of the homes are built in *hollows*, which are narrow valleys between two mountains, often following a creek. As Bell and York (2010) describe, "When the mountains above these homes are deforested and flattened, there is nothing left to stop the rain from washing down the mountainsides and flooding the communities below" (p. 123). After massive flooding in 2001 devastated the homes of thousands of southern West Virginia residents (Loeb, 2003), the Flood Advisory Technical Taskforce of the West Virginia Department of Environmental Protection (2002) found that mining and timbering had, in fact, "[increased] surface water runoff and the resulting stream flows" during the heavy rain event. The flood of 2001 was only the beginning of a pattern of repeated flood events in the southern coalfields.

June 15, 2003, marked the beginning of Maria Gunnoe's awakening to the destruction that mountaintop removal coalmining was bringing to her community. On this day—her daughter's birthday—a nightmare of a flood threatened to wash away Maria's home and family.

> The evening of [my daughter's] birthday, it started raining—about 4:00 in the evening. And it was a really heavy rain. But honestly, though, we get heavy rains here in the spring—we always have. It started raining about 4:00, and by 7:00, the water was literally running from one hill to the other right here behind me. A stream that you could raise your foot and step over turned into a raging river in three hours' time. I've lived here my whole life, and I've never seen anything like that. And I hope and pray to God that I never see anything like that again. The stream come up, and when it come up, it just kept coming up, and up, and up. It washed away about five acres of our property. I lost two access bridges, and one of my dogs was killed right up there. He was tied outside the creek and it took him, just tumbled him down the middle of all that flood. My daughter was over here at a friend's house when the flooding first started. And within twenty minutes after it started raining, I left out of here. It was raining hard—I [had to] go get my baby, you know. I wasn't gone maybe fifteen, twenty minutes and we couldn't get back in.

I threw a rain slicker over her head and threw her over my shoulder and waded the water across. The water came up to my hips across that crossing. Once we got in here, there was no way out. We was surrounded by water. (Bell, 2013, p. 12)

Maria and her family spent the night awake, listening to the sounds of their property being destroyed and washing away:

All night long, you could hear our structures—pieces and bits of our structures that was on up the holler—you could just hear them twisting and maiming in the water. It was a night that I will never forget. If I live to be a hundred years old, I'll never forget that—because I mean it was hell—it literally was . . .

After I got my daughter back in here, the water was eating away at my sidewalk—the end of my sidewalk was standing out in mid-air. My family was in this house. And, I didn't know what else to do . . . We started up the mountain, and the mountain was sliding. So you can't, you can't put your kids on a sliding mountain. You know, at least inside the house, you're thinking, at least they're dry inside the house. There was no safe place to go. [Emergency] 911 could not get to me, I couldn't get to them. All I had to do at that point was to hit my knees right there in that sidewalk and pray to God that that water stopped. [Voice breaking] and thank God it did. Because if it wouldn't have, it would have taken the earth that my house was setting on—and me and my family in the process. (Bell, 2013, p. 13)

The flood had devastating effects on Maria's family, especially her young daughter, whom Maria asserts suffered from post-traumatic stress disorder as a result of that night. As Maria relates,

She would set up at night—if it was raining or thundering, or any weather alerts or anything like that going on on the news, my daughter would not sleep. And I, I didn't notice this to begin with. I was so overwhelmed with everything going on that I never even thought, "What's this putting my kids through?" Until one morning—I had noticed that she had been falling back in school, things wasn't going right in school. That was my first sign. And, one of her teachers said, "She sleeps in class." She'd been a straight-A student ever since she started school, so that was never a problem. I found out one morning at 3:00 in the morning, it was thundering and lightning, and I go in, and I find her sitting on the edge of her bed with her shoes and her coat and her pants [on]. [Pauses, deep breath, voice cracks.] And I found out then . . . [pauses] . . . what it was putting my daughter through. [Crying.] And that is what *pissed me off.* How *dare* they steal that from my child! The security of being able to sleep in her own bed. The coal companies now own that. They now own my child's security in her own bed. [Pauses.] And how can they expect me as a mother to look over that? How is it, what if I done this to their kids? What if I created *terror* in their children's lives? And that is what it has done to my children. (emphasis in original; Bell, 2013, pp. 13–14)

Flooding like what Maria Gunnoe and her family experienced is not the only cost of living in an energy sacrifice zone. After coal is mined, it must be chemically cleaned and crushed in order to prepare it for burning in coal-fired power plants. Often, these coal preparation plants are located on or near mountaintop removal mines. Communities neighboring such plants, such as the town of Sylvester in Boone County, West Virginia, contend with massive amounts of coal dust air pollution, making life unbearable for some residents.

Pauline Canterberry and Mary Miller, who are known as the "Sylvester Dustbusters" have been fighting coal dust for nearly a decade. In the excerpts below, they reveal the injustices they have had to endure because of a coal preparation facility that was built next to their community.

PAULINE:

Sylvester was a wonderful place to live up until Massey Energy decided to put in a [coal] preparation plant. They already had a facility over there—an underground mines.[3] They cut the bluff off [which was between the mine and the town of Sylvester] and put the processing plant right on top of the ridge where they had cut off the hillside—right in the direct airflow of the town . . .

Just as soon as they got it finished and it started into operation, which was in April of 1998, it *instantly* began to cover the town in coal dust. Within one month we were completely covered. It was horrible. We could walk outside here on [sunny] days like today and the sun looked like you was looking through a kaleidoscope, there was so much coal dust in the air. You couldn't do nothing outside—you couldn't have cookouts outside, you [couldn't] hang your clothes outside when you wash[ed] them. It just *plastered* our homes. And not only that, then it began to seep through your windows and inside your home. . . Our homes were just polluted completely with it . . .

. . . [I]t's not easy to sit and watch your home being destroyed, something you have worked for all your life . . . [The coal dust] just took the value completely away from it. We found out through our lawsuit—because we all had our homes appraised—that our homes have lost 90 percent of their value. (emphasis in original; Bell, 2013, pp. 28–29, 35–36)

Both Pauline and Mary's homes have lost nearly all of their resale value. In the 1990s, Mary's large brick home appraised for $144,000. After the preparation plant was built and had begun showering the town in coal dust, it appraised for only $12,000.

MARY:

I just think that's about the worst thing [that] could happen to somebody—when you see that you've worked all your life for this, and you're losing what you've loved and worked for. There's no inheritance. There's nothing, not even enough to bury us. Twelve thousand dollars wouldn't even build a garage, and like I said, it's certainly not going to bury us. If [we'd] ever have to go and borrow money, what have [we] got to put up for collateral? There's nothing there. Nothing. (Bell, 2013, p. 36)

In addition to coal dust, coal preparation plants also generate a great deal of liquid coal waste, which is called "slurry" or "sludge." The liquid waste is produced in the cleaning process and consists of water, small particles of coal, and chemicals that are used to wash the coal (Orem, 2006). Coal slurry can create a number of additional hazards for coal communities, such as slurry impoundment breaks and disasters (Eades, 2000; Erikson, 1976) and well water contamination (Orem, 2006).

Coal slurry is stored in one of two ways: either in massive impoundments on the surface of flattened mountaintops, or it is injected into abandoned underground coal mines (Orem, 2006). Often, the large impoundments end up situated directly above communities, threatening the residents below. The Buffalo Creek Disaster of 1972, which

---

[3] The use of the singular "a" with the plural "mines" ("a mines" or "an underground mines") is a common speechway throughout parts of Central Appalachia.

killed 125 people in Logan County, West Virginia, took place when a slurry impoundment burst, spilling 132 million gallons of coal waste onto Buffalo Creek Hollow (Erikson, 1976). In 2000, a slurry impoundment in Martin County, Kentucky, collapsed, discharging 250 million gallons of coal waste (20 times greater than the Exxon Valdez oil spill) and polluting more than 70 miles of West Virginia and Kentucky waterways, killing all wildlife it encountered (Scott et al., 2005). While there was very little national media coverage of the event, the EPA called it "one of the worst environmental disasters in the history of the Southeastern United States" (Sever, 2003).

The coal slurry that is injected into abandoned underground mines, rather than stored in surface impoundments, generates additional possibilities for damage to nearby communities, including well water contamination and certain health disorders that can result from such pollution. Liver and kidney cancers, colitis, skin disorders, gall bladder disease, and organ failure are some of the problems that have been documented to date (Bell, 2010; Orem, 2006; Wells, 2006).

Maria Lambert lives in the community of Prenter in Boone County, West Virginia. In 2008, Maria and other Prenter residents began to suspect that their well water was contaminated with coal slurry from a nearby underground slurry injection site. In the excerpt below, Maria shares the experience (and anger) of discovering her community's water was the cause of the health problems that plagued Prenter residents.

> We had well water, so [we thought] we didn't have to worry about having dirty water. We knew that they were mining back up there in the hollow, but it just didn't seem to be a bad thing, you know, because it had always been kind of clean and everything here. And Mommy started noticing that—she has a nose for everything—she noticed that her water didn't seem right, and she really hated using it. She had to clean her coffee pots really often, and she would have to go and *buy* new coffee pots often because they'd kind of quit working. So last fall, I don't know where they saw the flyer at, but somehow [my parents] found a flyer that said they were having a water meeting. And [my mom] said, "Maria, I really think that some of us needs to go to this meeting, because there's definitely something wrong with our water. It's not right, something is not right." So she and my dad and I, we went to the water meeting.
>
> Everybody was showing [samples of] their water. Different people stood up and told about their water and told about what they believed was happening, and told about the different illnesses—the brain tumors, the gall bladder problems, stomach problems, children's teeth falling out, and all of these things. (Bell, 2013, pp. 71–72)

During the meeting, Maria began making connections between the stories her neighbors were telling and what had been happening within her own family.

> . . . [I]t's like my whole life [was] flashing before my eyes, because my children had lost their teeth, my parents had had cancer, we'd had our gall bladders removed, and all of these things was, it's just like, oh no, it's not just us—it's the whole community, and we're not even blood related. There was Jennifer Massey, who had lost her brother to a brain tumor; Kathy Weikle who had a pituitary tumor; Terry Keith who has the triplets and another grandchild who has to bathe in the water, and they were having a rash and everything. They were having to mix their formula with the water and didn't realize it was bad. Oh gosh, let's see. Several people had kidney problems in their family. There's been two kidney transplants—one was a small child and one was an older gentleman—in the past four or five years. People dying from kidney disease, kidney dialysis patients. My mother had to

have a third of her lung removed from lung cancer—it wasn't in the bronchial tubes, it was in the fatty part of the lung, the tissuey part of the lung. And then my father come through thyroid cancer. And my husband and I both have had major stomach problems. My sister has major stomach problems and nerve problems, and there's a lot of neuropathy. . . . And I'm sure you've read the statistics on the gall bladders. Probably forty-six out of forty-eight people don't have a gall bladder. (Bell, 2013, p. 72)

Maria's health suffered greatly from the bad well water. Not long after the first community meeting, Maria had to go to the hospital because of intestinal bleeding. In the excerpt below, she describes her anger at discovering that the water was the cause of her health problems.

All summer long I had been on some medication, and my white blood [cell] count had dropped down to 2.5, and that is not good. They wanted me to go off of some of my medication to see if it could be that that was causing it. And I thought, "Well, since I'm going off of medication, I'm just going to go ahead and try to lose some of this weight," because I weighed over two hundred pounds. I lost fifty pounds by drinking water all summer long—our water—the water that we should not have been drinking. They tell you, "Drink lots of water," you know. So when I found out that what I thought was supposed to be a good thing [made me sick], I got so mad. It was just like an inferno inside of me that was just busting to get out. I was just really, really mad. . . .

I never really got that mad about anything [before this] . . . It just infuriated me to think that my husband had spent twenty-three-and-a-half years in the ground [coal mining], my dad had worked for the mining industry for twenty-five years, my grandfather worked for about twenty-something, thirty-something years in the mines. His father was killed in the mines. And to know that they gave their all—*everything* they had, they put into that work. . . .

. . . [P]eople are suffering and it's not right for people in power to take advantage of everyday working, taxpaying, breathing citizens. They're taking away from us and trying to make people believe that they're *giving* to us. They have made people believe that for a hundred years, or more—even from the beginning of time. People in power have *always* abused their power. (emphasis in original; Bell, 2013, pp. 78–79)

Flooding, coal dust air pollution, and coal slurry contamination are just a few of the injustices that residents living in Central Appalachian coal-mining communities must face. What is often difficult for people from outside the region to understand is why "just moving" is not an option for most. First of all, as in the case of Pauline Canterberry and Mary Miller, many residents cannot afford to move elsewhere because the coal industry's destruction and pollution have depleted their property values so much that they simply cannot afford to move elsewhere. But beyond the financial reasons is the incredible sense of attachment that many of these residents feel to their communities. Many Appalachian families have been living on the same land and in the same hollows for generations. Family cemeteries, favorite fishing holes, networks of friends and family, and a lifetime's worth of memories tie individuals to their "home-place." These connections are not easily left behind.

In this final excerpt, Lorelei Scarboro describes this connection to her home and how she feels when outsiders suggest that she simply move.

Everywhere we go, [people] say, "Why don't you just move?" I went all the way to Reno, [Nevada] for a training session. . . . As they listened, [the president of the company] just keep sitting there looking at me, and he said, "The easiest thing in the world to do would be to move." But it wouldn't. That would be the *hardest* thing to do, because that's the house I raised my kids in, that's the house my husband built. He's buried next door. The land that he loved has been in his family for generations, and I can't imagine driving out of the driveway for the last time and leaving him in the cemetery and everything else there. That would be the *hardest* thing to do. It's easier to fight and to try to, to try to save all that, because if I walk away from it, it's certainly destroyed. It's certainly blown apart and destroyed. So it's a whole lot easier to stay there and fight.

It's difficult to explain the attachment, the sense of place that Appalachians have. It's a connectedness to the land, to your surroundings. It's not the value of the house, it's not the price of the ten acres. It's the memories. It's what you have there. It's the life you share with the people you love. There's a whole range of emotions that go through me when people say, "Why don't you just move?" I mean it's everything from anger to sadness. . . . There are some times that it's all you could do just not to want to take people and shake them and try to make them understand, because it *wouldn't* be the easiest thing to do. It would be very, very difficult to walk away and allow it to be totally destroyed. (emphasis in original; Bell, 2013, p. 124).

Conclusion

Central Appalachia has been set aside as one of the United States' energy sacrifice zones. As it is exploited for its rich coal resources, the people and land of this region are treated as the expendable casualties of our nation's addiction to cheap electricity. As noted at the beginning of this chapter, Central Appalachia is not the only region that serves as a sacrifice zone for energy, however. The Gulf Coast serves as another devastating example of a region and people treated as expendable, as was overwhelmingly apparent during Hurricane Katrina in 2005 and then the BP oil spill of 2010.

Haney (2012) argues that the primarily black and poor residents of Louisiana's Gulf Coast are unjustly made to suffer the tremendous ecological and social costs of oil extraction and refining so that the rest of us living in North America can enjoy the benefits of cheap gasoline, without having to experience many of the actual environmental costs. While in 2007 the cost of gasoline at the pump was approximately $3 per gallon, the true cost of gasoline, accounting for all of the indirect and ecological costs of oil extraction, refining, and transportation, was actually around $15 per gallon (Lester R. Brown cited in Haney [2012]). The remaining $12 per gallon not paid by consumers is externalized onto the people living in oil-producing energy sacrifice zones like the

Gulf Coast. As Haney (2012) asserts, the individuals living in these regions pay this $12 difference in the form of technological disasters, pollution, acute and chronic health conditions, and the "military costs involved in protecting supply lines from the Middle East and North Africa" (p. 112). Similarly, the people of Central Appalachia are also forced to pay the difference between the price consumers see on their electric bills and the true costs of coal, which include air pollution, water contamination, losses in biodiversity, lost income, psychological trauma, destruction of homes, and the loss of a treasured landscape and way of life.

Haney (2012) argues that "because of our dependence on oil and the failure of corporations and the government to protect the region, we owe the people of Louisiana and of the Gulf Coast an economic and ecological debt" (p. 107). I concur. I believe, however, that we also owe the people of Central Appalachia (and people living in other sacrifice zones, such as tribal lands in the American southwest) an economic and ecological debt. This debt is one owed by each and every one of us who benefits from only paying a fraction of the true cost of electricity, gasoline, or other goods. How can we repay this debt to those living in energy sacrifice zones? Truthfully, our debt is so enormous that repayment will not be a simple or easy task. A good first step, however, is joining the fight for environmental justice in these communities. We need to educate ourselves about where our electricity or gasoline (or food or electronics) come from and learn who is paying the true cost of extraction and production. Then we need to educate our friends and family members about what we've learned. We need to get involved by finding organizations working to address these injustices and learn from their websites what we can do to help. We need to call or write our representatives to demand that the energy industry be held accountable for the pollution and destruction it is bringing to certain communities. And one of the most necessary things that absolutely has to happen is we need to reduce our consumption, and we need to greatly increase our willingness to pay more for the energy we do use.

References

Ahern, M. M., Hendryx, M., Conley, J., Fedorko, E., Ducatman, A., & Zullig, K. J. (2011). The association between mountaintop mining and birth defects among live births in Central Appalachia, 1996–2003. *Environmental Research, 111*(6), 838–846.

Ahern, M. M., & Hendryx, M. (2008). Health disparities and environmental competence: A case study of Appalachian coal mining. *Environmental Justice, 1*(2), 81–86.

Appalachian Voices. (2007). What are the economic consequences of mountaintop removal in Appalachia? Retrieved from http://www.appvoices.org/index.php?/mtr/economics/

Bell, S. E. (2009). "There ain't no bond in town like there used to be": The destruction of social capital in the West Virginia coalfields. *Sociological Forum, 24*(3), 631–657.

Bell, S. E. (2010). *Fighting king coal: The barriers to grassroots environmental justice movement participation in Central Appalachia.* (Unpublished Doctoral dissertation.) University of Oregon, Eugene.

Bell, S. E. (2013). *Our roots run deep as ironweed: Appalachian women and the fight for environmental justice.* Urbana and Chicago: University of Illinois Press.

Bell, S. E., & Braun, Y. A. (2010). Coal, identity, and the gendering of environmental justice movement participation in Central Appalachia. *Gender & Society, 24*(6), 794–813.

Bell, S. E., & York, R. (2010). Community economic identity: The coal industry and ideology construction in West Virginia. *Rural Sociology, 75*(1), 111–143.

Brown, L. R. (2008). *Plan B 3.0: Mobilizing to save civilization.* New York, NY: W. W. Norton.

Brulle, R. J., & Pellow, D. N. (2006). Environmental justice: Human health and environmental inequalities. *Annual Review of Public Health, 27*, 3.1–3.22.

Bullard, R. D. (1990). *Dumping in Dixie: Race, class, and environmental quality.* Boulder, CO: Westview Press.

Bullard, R. D., Mohai, P., Saha, R., & Wright, B. 2007. *Toxic wastes and race at twenty: 1987–2007: A report prepared for the United Church of Christ Justice & Witness Ministries.* Cleveland, OH: United Church of Christ.

Čapek, S. (1993). The "environmental justice" frame: A conceptual discussion and an application. *Social Problems, 40*(1), 5–24.

Dunn, L. (Producer & Director). (2000). *Green.* [Motion picture]. United States: Two Birds Film.

Eades, R. (2000). *Brushy Fork Slurry Impoundment: A preliminary report.* Retrieved from http://www.ohvec.org/issues/slurry_impoundments/articles/brushy_fork.pdf

Erikson, K. T. (1976). *Everything in its path: Destruction of community in the Buffalo Creek Flood.* New York, NY: Simon & Schuster.

Faber, D. (2008). *Capitalizing on environmental injustice: The polluter-industrial complex in the age of globalization.* New York, NY: Rowman & Littlefield.

Faber, D. (2009). The unfair trade-off: Globalization and the export of ecological hazards. In L. King & D. McCarthy (Eds.), *Environmental sociology: From analysis to action* (2nd ed.). New York, NY: Rowman & Littlefield.

Flood Advisory Technical Taskforce. (2002). *Runoff analyses of Seng, Scrabble, and Sycamore Creeks, Part I.* Division of Mining and Reclamation, Department of Environmental Protection. Retrieved from http://www.epa.gov/region3/mtntop/pdf/appendices/h/wvflooding/Flooding_Study__Part_01.pdf

Fox, J. (1999). Mountaintop removal in West Virginia: An environmental sacrifice zone. *Organization & Environment, 12*(2), 163–183.

Gaventa, J. (1978). Property, coal, and theft. In H. M. Lewis, L. Johnson, & D. Askins (Eds.), *Colonialism in modern America: The Appalachian case* (pp. 141–159). Boone, NC: Appalachian Consortium Press.

Haney, T. J. (2012). The Gulf Oil spill, ecological debt, and environmental justice in Louisiana: Lessons from sociology. In L. A. Eargle & A. M. Esmail (Eds.), *Black beaches and bayous: The BP Deepwater Horizon oil spill disaster*. Lanham, MD: University Press of America.

Hendryx, M. (2008). Mortality rates in Appalachian coal mining counties: 24 years behind the nation. *Environmental Justice, 1*(1), 5–11.

Hendryx, M., & Ahern, M. M. (2008). Relations between health indicators and residential proximity to coalmining in West Virginia. *American Journal of Public Health, 98*, 669–671.

Hendryx, M., Ahern, M. M., & Nurkiewicz, T. R. (2007). Hospitalization patterns associated with Appalachian coal mining. *Journal of Toxicology and Environmental Health, 70*, 2064–2070.

Hendryx, M., Wolfe, L., Luo, J., & Webb, B. (2012). Self-reported cancer rates in two rural areas of West Virginia with and without mountaintop coal mining. *Journal of Community Health, 37*(2), 320–327.

Kuletz, V. L. (1998). *The tainted desert: Environmental and social ruin in the American west*. New York, NY: Routledge.

Lerner, S. (2005). *Diamond: A struggle for environmental justice in Louisiana's Chemical Corridor*. Cambridge, MA: MIT Press.

Lewis, H. M., & Knipe, E. E. (1978). The colonialism model: The Appalachian case. In H. M. Lewis, L. Johnson, & D. Askins (Eds.), *Colonialism in modern America: The Appalachian case* (pp. 9–31). Boone, NC: Appalachian Consortium Press.

Lewis, R. L. (1987). *Black coal miners in America: Race, class, and community conflict, 1780–1980*. Lexington: University Press of Kentucky.

Lewis, R. L. (1999). Beyond isolation and homogeneity: Diversity and the history of Appalachia. In D. B. Billings, N. Gurney, & K. Ledford (Eds.), *Back talk from Appalachia: Confronting stereotypes*. (pp. 21–43). Lexington: University Press of Kentucky.

Loeb, P. (2003). *The floods of 2001. The coalfield communities of southern West Virginia*. Retrieved from www.wvcoalfield.com

Masterson-Allen S., & Brown, P. (1990). Public reaction to toxic waste contamination: Analysis of a social movement. *International Journal of Health Services, 20*(3), 485–500.

Orem, W. H. (2006, November 15). Coal slurry: Geochemistry and impacts on human health and environmental quality. U.S. Geological Survey, Eastern Energy Resources Team. PowerPoint Presentation to the Coal Slurry Legislative Subcommittee of the Senate Judiciary Committee, West Virginia Legislature.

Palmer, M. A., Bernhardt, E. S., Schlesinger, W. H., Eshleman, K. N., Foufoula-Georgiou, E., Hendryx, M. S., Lemly, A. D., Likens, G. E., Loucks, O. L., Power, M. E., White, P. S., & Wilcock, P. R. (2010). Mountaintop mining consequences. *Science, 327*, 148–149.

Pellow, D. N. (2004). *Garbage wars: The struggle for environmental justice in Chicago*. Cambridge, MA: MIT Press.

Pellow, D. N. (2007). *Resisting global toxics: Transnational movements for environmental justice*. Cambridge, MA: MIT Press.

Schnaiberg, Allan. (1980). *The environment: From surplus to scarcity*. New York, NY: Oxford University Press.

Scott, R. K. (2010). *Removing mountains: Extracting nature and identity in the Appalachian coalfields*. Minneapolis: University of Minnesota Press.

Scott, S. L., McSpirit, S., Hardesty, S., & Welch, R. (2005). Post disaster interviews with Martin County citizens: "Gray clouds" of blame and distrust. *Journal of Appalachian Studies, 11*(1 & 2), 7–29.

Sever, M. (2003). Settlement reached on coal slurry spill. *Geotimes*. Retrieved from http://www.geotimes.org/oct03/WebExtra101703.html

Turner, W. H., & Cabbell, E. J. (Eds.). (1985). *Blacks in Appalachia*. Lexington: University Press of Kentucky.

United Church of Christ Commission for Racial Justice. (1987). *Toxic wastes and race in the United States: A national report on the racial and socioeconomic characteristics of communities with hazardous waste sites*. New York, NY: United Church of Christ.

U.S. Census Bureau. (2010a). Table 1: 2009 Poverty and median income estimates—Counties. Small Area Estimates Branch. Retrieved from http://www.census.gov/did/www/saipe/data/statecounty/data/2009.html

U.S. Census Bureau. (2010b). 2005–2009 American Community Survey 5-Year Estimate. American Fact Finder fact sheet: Pike, Perry, Harlan, Letcher, Knott, Leslie, Martin, and Floyd Counties, Kentucky and McDowell County, West Virginia. Retrieved from http://factfinder.census.gov/ http://factfinder2.census.gov/faces/nav/jsf/pages/index.xhtml

U.S. Energy Information Administration. (2008). Table H.4co2: World Carbon Dioxide Emissions from the Consumption of Coal, 1980–2006. *International energy annual 2006.* http://www.eia.doe.gov/emeu/international/carbondioxide.html

U.S. Energy Information Administration. (2010). Figure ES 1. U.S. Electric Power Industry Net Generation, 2009. *Electric power annual with data for 2009.* Retrieved from http://www.eia.gov/cneaf/electricity/epa/figes1.html

U.S. Energy Information Administration. (2011). Figure ES 1. U.S. Electric Power Industry Net Generation, 2009. *Electric power annual 2009.* Retrieved from http://www.eia.gov/cneaf/electricity/epa/epa_sum.html

U.S. Environmental Protection Agency. (2005). *Mountaintop mining/valley fills in Appalachia: Final programmatic environmental impact statement.* Retrieved from http://www.epa.gov/region03/mtntop/p.4

Wells, L. A. (2006, August 13). Lawsuits muddy water project. *Appalachian News-Express.* Retrieved from http://www.newsexpresssky.com/articles/2006/07/30/top_story/01water.txt

West Virginia Office of Miners' Health, Safety and Training. (2003). *West Virginia coal resources by county 2003.* Retrieved from http://www.wvminesafety.org/PDFs/RESERVES2003.pdf

INDEX